George Ball: Behind the Scenes in U.S. Foreign Policy

George Ball:
Behind the
Scenes in
U.S. Foreign
Policy

❖·❖·❖

James A. Bill

Yale University Press   New Haven and London

Designed by James J. Johnson and set in Electra types by Tseng Information Systems, Durham, North Carolina.

Printed in the United States of America by Book Crafters, Inc., Chelsea, Michigan.

Library of Congress Cataloging-in-Publication Data

Bill, James A.

George Ball : behind the scenes in U.S. foreign policy / James A. Bill.

p.   cm.

Includes bibliographical references (p.   ) and index.

ISBN 0-300-06969-3 (cloth : alk. paper)

1. Ball, George W.   2. Statesmen—United States—Biography.   3. United Nations—Biography.
4. United States. Dept. of State—Biography.   5. United States—Foreign relations—1945–1989.
I. Title.

E840.8.B32B54   1997

973.92′092—dc20

[B]   96-33991

A catalogue record for this book is available from the British Library.

10   9   8   7   6   5   4   3   2   1

As I began to write this book in 1991, I received an unfriendly visit from an unpleasant aggressor known as Parkinson's disease. This debilitating, degenerative neurological disease attacks and eats away at the totality of a person. In scientific terms, Parkinson's disease results from the death of dopamine-producing cells in the substantia nigra, an area of the brain that controls muscle functions. My wife, Ann, son Tim, and daughter Rebecca moved to my side quickly, and we have stood together against the Parkinson's assailant. With the help of medication, physicians, and friends, we have held the invader at bay while I have researched and written this book.

I salute the one and a half million Americans who struggle courageously and desperately with Parkinson's disease. I dedicate this book, however, to the caregivers, those dedicated people who have helped persons afflicted with Parkinson's disease cope and survive. The caregivers give the most; they help the most; and they, too, suffer greatly.

Contents

Acknowledgments   ix
Introduction   xiii
Prologue   1

PART I. PRAGMATIC IDEALIST FROM THE MIDWEST

1. Personal Roots and Rites of Passage   19
2. Political Practitioner and Intellectual Gladiator   56

PART II. GLOBAL POLICYMAKER

3. The Politics of European Integration   101
4. Rebellion and War in Africa and Asia:
   The Congo and Vietnam   136
5. Public Policy and Private Dissent:
   Cuba, Cyprus, and the Middle East   176

PART III. STATECRAFT FOR THE TWENTY-FIRST CENTURY

6. The Essence of Statesmanship: George Ball and Prudence   203

Notes   233
Select Bibliography   261
Index   265

Acknowledgments

In writing this book, I am especially indebted to two individuals for their generous assistance. Rebecca Ann Bill, my daughter, researched and drafted the chapter on Ball, Monnet, and the European Community. She also acted as an exacting editor and decorated my drafts with the multicolored inks she used to make her comments and corrections. Rebecca also questioned many of my interpretations and conclusions; our vigorous debates not only rattled the dishes but unsettled my wife, Ann, and son Tim as well. Tim, meanwhile, punctuated his medical school education by providing me with valuable ideas and unwavering support.

Dr. Douglas Ball, a gentleman with a prodigious memory and an eagerness to help, assisted me throughout the eight-year period I worked on this book. Doug enthusiastically shoveled information at me until I nearly suffocated in Ballorabilia. Although the son of the subject of the book, Douglas Ball provided observations that were extraordinary in their candor.

George Ball's niece, Marion Tramel, the daughter of George's older brother Stuart, patiently explained the Ball family history to me. Like her late father, Marion is fascinated by genealogy, and as family historian she graciously shared family trees, albums, photographs, and anecdotes.

I spent more than twenty-three hours interviewing George and Ruth Ball before they passed away. John Ball, the oldest son, also met with me and poignantly shared his recollections about his father. Karen Vasudeva, George Ball's personal secretary, helped locate documents and interpret personal Ball idiosyncracies.

Several individuals read and critiqued chapters of this book. David DiLeo, the author of an excellent volume on George Ball and Vietnam, read the section on Vietnam. DiLeo provided insights into Ball and generously shared rare documents with me. Diplomatic historian Edward Crapol also carefully read the section on Vietnam. His critical and penetrating comments provoked lively debate and caused me to rethink a number of my interpretations. David Gibbs and Lewis Hoffacker commented on the section on the Congo, while John Tuthill and Helen Milbank critiqued the chapter on the European Community. Richard Norton assisted with the sections on Cyprus and the Middle East. My colleague Larry Becker, a talented philosopher-humanist, and John Washburn, an old friend and wise diplomat-scholar, evaluated the final chapter. Cyrus Ghani, a perceptive observer of human and political affairs who knew Ball well, read the first two chapters. He encouraged me throughout the project.

Michael T. Clark, my colleague at William and Mary, contributed significantly to this book. An original thinker, he stimulated ideas and provoked discussion that greatly improved the quality of this study. Michael Clark's intellectual assistance was especially valuable as I developed the conceptual framework for the final chapter.

Others who helped nourish my intellect and encouraged me throughout this project include James Akins, Gabriel Almond, Kai Bird, Conrad Blakey, Bruce Buchanan, William J. Butler, Tom Ferguson, Larry Hatfield, Georgia Hesse, Herbert Hirsch, Hartwell Hylton, Steven Jacques, Charles A. Kelly, Mohammad Koochekzadeh, Julius Mastro, Maury Maverick Jr., Monte Palmer, Hoyt Purvis, R. K. Ramazani, Walter Sullivan, Richard Ware, Donald Weadon, and Amir Zinatbaksh.

The following individuals graciously consented to personal interviews: Lucius Battle, W. Michael Blumenthal, McGeorge Bundy, William Bundy, J. William Fulbright, J. Kenneth Galbraith, Cyrus Ghani, Arthur Hartman, Roger Hilsman, Jerome E. Hyman, G. Griffith Johnson, James G. Johnson Jr., Nicholas Katzenbach, Donald Lamm, Lewis Lapham, John R. MacArthur, George McGhee, Helen Milbank, Paul Nitze, Peter Peterson, David Rockefeller, Eric Roll, Walt W. Rostow, Dean Rusk, Robert Schaetzel, Arthur Schlesinger Jr., James Schlesinger, George Springsteen, Roger L. Stevens, Philip H. Trezise, John Wills Tuthill, Helen Vahey, Cyrus Vance, and Allen Whiting. I also had telephone interviews with Pierre Gousseland, Lewis Hoffacker, Robert McNamara, Kenneth Thompson, and Raymond Vernon.

I wish to thank the Earhart Foundation, the Parten Foundation, the Lyndon B. Johnson Foundation, and the College of William and Mary for grants that enabled me to carry out this study. Antony Sullivan at the Earhart Foundation has been a strong source of encouragement and support over the years. So also was the late populist-philanthropist, the legendary Texan, J. R. Parten.

Dr. David Humphrey, formerly at the Lyndon Johnson Library, provided critical archival assistance, and Ben Primer, university archivist at the Seeley Mudd Manuscript Library at Princeton University, where the George Ball papers are housed, has also been exceptionally helpful.

At William and Mary, I owe special thanks to educators Paul Verkuil, Melvyn Schiavelli, and Edward Allenby, and, more recently, to President Timothy Sullivan and Provost Gillian Cell. Other William and Mary faculty members who assisted in various ways include Craig N. Canning, T. J. Cheng, David Dessler, Brewer Eddy, Robert Fritts, Ken Kambis, James Lee, Victor Liguori, John McGlennon, Leonard Schifrin, Joel Schwartz, Dennis Slon, Rod Smolla, Jack Van Horn, and John Williams. I also wish to thank the talented staff at the Reves Center for International Studies. I thank Mary McCabe and Ruthina Reagan at the Center, but I especially wish to recognize the outstanding professional assistance of Diane Gallagher, who helped me put the manuscript in final form. John Greenwood and Arslan Malik served as academic detectives, ferreting out sources and documents that resisted discovery. Melissa Johnson did a superb job of transcribing more than two thousand pages of interview notes. Nancy Marshall and her competent staff at Swem Library provided important bibliographic assistance.

Frank and Jarka Shatz of Williamsburg, Virginia, and Lake Placid, New York, carefully monitored the progress of the book and encouraged me throughout. Frank, an accomplished journalist of vast international experience, made many substantive comments throughout the project.

I am grateful to two delightful iconoclastic octogenarians, Wendy Reves and Jack Borgenicht, whose wisdom and support have helped stretch my mind and broaden my education.

At Yale University Press, Chuck Grench led an extraordinary team of talented believers whose enthusiasm and support made the author-publisher relationship a rare and real pleasure. My manuscript editor, Dan Heaton, has done a superb job in helping me improve the text of this book. All readers are sure to benefit from his professional assistance.

In the end, the love of my wife, Ann Bachhuber Bill, was the single most important factor enabling me to complete this book. Ann's unwavering faith, gentle encouragement, and infinite tolerance sustained me through this enterprise. This beautiful person's support rests behind every word and every page that follows.

Introduction

This volume is not a conventional biography. Instead, I have attempted to use the career and ideas of George Ball to uncover the essence of the American foreign policymaking system and to develop a model of statecraft for the twenty-first century. Because this study is more than the life story of one man, I have not sought to describe all the political and personal issues that concerned George Ball. Rather, I have selectively chosen to cover those events that most profoundly affected Ball and the world that he helped shaped.

After a Prologue that describes one particularly important day in the lives of George Ball and the America of the 1960s, the book takes shape as three interrelated sections. In the first two chapters, I describe and analyze the family roots and the personality of George Ball. While Chapter 1 emphasizes the personal over the professional, Chapter 2 focuses more upon the professional than upon the personal. This progression is logical and leads directly into the second part of the book, three chapters that present a number of foreign policy case studies.

The final section of the book consists of general lessons that can be learned from the George Ball story. In this concluding chapter, I develop a new model of statecraft by comparing the intellectual and professional approaches of George Ball and Henry Kissinger.

This book is not only about specific judgments and policies that shaped the world of the last half century. It is about a manner of thinking and a method of analyzing the political process. Like Ball himself, this study is concerned with the future, not the past. Few statesmen in living memory can compare with Ball as an exemplar in the formulation of wise and prudent policies in a turbulent world.

Politics involves the struggle for power and authority. Because the informal dynamics of politics are at least as important as the formal, official dimension, much that is vital in the political process resists direct observation and inspection. Less visible individuals operating in personal networks that transcend ideological, professional, and national borders often shape the agendas and determine key political decisions. George Ball represented one of the principal nodes in the American policymaking network that developed before World War II and that continued to influence policy into the last decade of the twentieth century. By observing Ball at work, we have an unusual opportunity to take a penetrating look into the U.S. foreign policymaking system.

As a result of his keen political insight, Ball provides a particularly powerful beam of light into the political process. Besides insight, however, Ball had foresight, a power of prescience that was legendary. In 1989, Oxford University Chancellor Roy Jenkins described George Ball as "the man who has been more nearly right on every major foreign policy issue of the past forty-five years than anyone else I know." Earlier, in a personal communication to Ball, General Matthew B. Ridgway wrote that he knew few individuals, living or dead, "involved in so many intractable foreign policy problems," who had been "more uniformly right in their judgments—made at the time and ever since confirmed . . . than you have."

George Ball's prescience intersected with his sense of humor. During the Adlai Stevenson campaign of 1956, for example, he witnessed the early effect of television on political campaigning. If this television influence should continue, he warned a New York audience, then it is entirely possible that the day could come when the American people would elect a Hollywood actor to the presidency!

Ball's capacity for powerful and prescient analysis of politics and society was made possible not only by his intellectual brilliance but also by a total commitment to his political calling and to his work as a lawyer and investment banker. Ball drove himself mercilessly. He dashed around the world constantly—lecturing, researching, consulting, networking, and negotiating. During his adult life, he made approximately five hundred trips overseas. Ball's family relationships suffered enormously from this frenetic career, and he sought, with limited success, to address the resulting problems on the run. In the end, Ball placed public service and profession above family harmony.

For sixty years, George Wildman Ball exerted influence in national and international affairs. As under secretary of state for five years, he had direct access to Presidents John Kennedy and Lyndon Johnson. Yet even at the zenith of his influence, he shaped policy from the second tier, a subcabinet power stratum where individuals quietly serve as links connecting policymakers with those who actually implement policy. Second-tier figures such as Ball are not subject to the same public scrutiny as cabinet secretaries and many White House officials. This lack of accountability broadens their freedom of political movement and enables them to take risks and promote policies with less inhibition than those who inhabit the highest official ranks of government.

Operating out of the second tier, George Ball was an integral part of the U.S. policymaking system during many of the most serious international crises of the second half of the twentieth century. He played a major role in the extended struggle for European integration and personally directed the transformation of U.S. trade policy in the early 1960s. Ball served as Kennedy's "commander in chief" during the Congo crisis and then played his most controversial role when he persistently challenged U.S. policy in Vietnam from the inside. He participated in the Cuban missile crisis deliberations as part of John F. Kennedy's inner circle and, during Lyndon Johnson's presidency, he took charge of U.S. policy concerning Cyprus, serving as special presidential envoy. In that capacity he traveled to London, Greece, Turkey, and Cyprus to negotiate with the various parties to the dispute.

Over the years, Ball interacted closely with such international political figures as Charles de Gaulle, Harold Macmillan, Edward Heath, Harold Wilson, Konrad Adenauer, Ludwig Erhard, Helmut Schmidt, Archbishop Makarios, Abba Eban, Moshe Dayan, Antonio Salazar, Ayub Khan, the Shah of Iran, King Hussein, Ismet Inönü, and Lee Kuan Yew.

During the last twenty-five years of his life, George Ball retained access to the highest policymaking levels in Washington. He answered calls for assistance and advice from Presidents Nixon and Carter and their secretaries of state and defense. As a respected village elder of U.S. foreign policy, he also exerted considerable influence through his writing, lecturing, and television appearances. Ball's special interests in the 1980s and 1990s included the continuing drive for European integration and the Middle East conflict, where he once again challenged conventional thinking and ongoing policy.

Besides his national connections and influence, George Ball enjoyed an international credibility and a far-flung constituency through his membership in the little-known Bilderberg group. Born in Europe, the Bilderberg group was an informal assemblage of some of the most influential European and American figures of the day. Members met every year to discuss privately major political and economic issues. George Ball was a founding member of the Bilderberg group, which held its first meeting in 1954 at the Bilderberg Hotel in Oosterbeek, Holland. Although the Bilderberg group had no permanent members, George Ball missed only one meeting in forty years. It was at Bilderberg that Ball established the personal international contacts that provided him with information and support throughout his career, whether he was in or out of government service.

A confidant and protégé of Jean Monnet, Adlai Stevenson, and Dean Acheson, Ball was a close friend of John Kenneth Galbraith, Arthur Schlesinger Jr., Dean Rusk, Walter Lippmann, James Reston, and John Chancellor. He also maintained warm relationships with David Rockefeller, Cyrus Vance, James Schlesinger, and J. William Fulbright. Ball himself served as mentor and role model to such individuals as Michael Blumenthal, Peter Peterson, Lucius Battle, Arthur Hartman, Phillips Talbot, John Tuthill, and dozens of others. It was George Ball who discovered Warren Christopher and gave him his first assignment in public service.

Ball's admirers included individuals of widely varied personality and political perspective. In 1979 Senator Fulbright called George Ball "the living American who had been most effective in changing things for the better"; James Schlesinger described him as a man of unusual "reflective intelligence," a courageous "intellectual gladiator"; W. Michael Blumenthal considered Ball one of the two or three greatest men he had ever met; Arthur Schlesinger Jr. praised Ball as a man of tolerance, humor, and resourcefulness who, despite the pressure of the situation, was never "rattled"; Kenneth Galbraith, a friend for fifty years, dedicated one of his books to George Ball; David Rockefeller praised Ball's "tremendous sense of integrity" and his deep commitment to moral and political principles. According to William Bundy, there was "nobody I ever worked with, ever seen in action that I more admire than George as a totally dedicated, selfless patriot who has raised more tough issues than anybody now on the public stage."

Ball, of course, had his detractors. They included individuals disgruntled by his blunt and stubborn commentary on such sensitive issues as Vietnam and the Middle East. Furthermore, Ball's sharp and ad hominem public criticism of such high-level politicians as Richard Nixon, Spiro Agnew, Henry Kissinger, and Ronald Reagan ricocheted back at him.

Ideologically, individuals on the left criticized Ball for his commitment to the primacy of multinational corporations, his belief in aggressive international interventionism, and his lifelong Eurocentrism. In their view, Ball was an imperialist who savored the comforts and privileges that accompanied high position in a Great Power. Ball, according to this perspective, disputed only the methods and tactics of Great Power diplomacy, not the philosophy. On the right, Ball's detractors reproached him for his commitment to internationalism and regional economic and political integration, his reluctance to resort to force in the resolution of political disputes, and his frontal attacks on political icons like Nixon and Reagan. To many conservatives, Ball was insufficiently nationalist: he was an internationalist and a dove.

In spite of George Ball's blemishes, his career stands on balance as an enduring model of excellence in statesmanship. He practiced a special prudence that enabled him to make the link between ideals and realities within a moral context. Ball was sensitive to the need to choose appropriate means to accomplish moral ends. He was a man of passionate beliefs whose political repertoire included great personal skills.

Although he sometimes succumbed to the manifold opportunities for manipulation and occasionally yielded to the seductive temptations of personal ambition, Ball managed to maintain an acute sense of proportion, objectivity, and balance. His midwestern roots contributed much to his direct, candid manner, and rich sense of humor. These characteristics in turn enabled Ball, a man of large ego, to resist the excesses of vanity. His self-interest was tempered by a commitment to the public good. In the terminology of the Greek philosophers, George Ball was a *phronemos*, a man of practical wisdom.

Upon the dawn of the twenty-first century, humankind stands witness to a world caught in the midst of transformation, a world where political, economic, and ethnic crises bubble up poisonously across the globe. As technology continues to shrink the world, these bubbles of crisis increasingly break into one another, deepening and spreading the toxins of ethnic hatred, economic inequity, societal crime, and political violence. In a world of such incoherence, no country, including the current American superpower, is immune from these diseases. The times cry out for sensitive, courageous, prescient, and prudent leadership. George Ball provides a rare model of such leadership. By focusing upon his life and career, I seek to help define the essence of statesmanship while at the same time deepening our understanding of the turbulent political world of the last half of the twentieth century.

George Ball was an uncommonly sensitive and sensible public official. Former Secretary of State Dean Acheson, two weeks before his death in 1971, sent a note to Ball in which he wryly wrote: "Keep on making sense; you have the field to yourself." George Ball may not have had the field entirely to himself, but he was one of relatively few who made a great deal of sense of the complex politics of our time. In this book, I endeavor to share this uncommon sense with the reader.

George Ball: Behind the Scenes in U.S. Foreign Policy

Prologue

Shortly after midnight on Wednesday, July 21, 1965, the under secretary of state awoke, switched on the bedside lamp, reached for the pencil and the yellow pad on the night table, and scratched out some ideas that he wanted to use during the critical meetings scheduled for the White House later that day. He then tried to get back to sleep.[1]

After dozing fitfully, fifty-four-year-old George Ball rose at 7 A.M., shaved quickly, put on his Anderson and Shepard tailored blue suit and red striped tie, gulped a quick liquid breakfast of Metrecal, stuffed a sheaf of papers (including the nocturnal notes) into his briefcase, gruffly said good-bye to his wife, Ruth, and hurried out of the red brick house on the corner of 35th Street and Woodley Road in Washington, D.C.

The chauffeur, Archie Steele, was waiting outside; he opened the rear door of the black Cadillac limousine and helped his six-foot-two-inch passenger into the right back seat. On the four-mile ride to the State Department, Ball calmly attempted to anticipate the events that he knew were scheduled to take place in the Cabinet Room of the White House beginning at 10:40 A.M.

George Wildman Ball was worried. The situation in Vietnam was deteriorating rapidly. President Lyndon Johnson's closest military and political advisers had been turning up the volume of their arguments in favor of a sharp increase in the U.S. military presence in South Vietnam. Secretary of Defense Robert McNamara had returned the day before from his sixth fact-finding trip to Vietnam. He had prepared a top secret report that would form the basis for the day's debate. Ball was certain that this report would recommend a major escalation in America's military presence in Vietnam. Furthermore, Ball knew that McNamara had strong support from U.S. military and political leaders who had on-the-ground experience in Vietnam, individuals like General William Westmoreland, Ambassador Maxwell Taylor, General Earle Wheeler, and Ambassador Henry Cabot Lodge. Wheeler and Lodge would be present at the meetings.

As if this was not enough, Ball wryly thought to himself that President Johnson's powerful and bright Washington inner circle members also seemed ready to up the ante. Besides McNamara, these included such formidable personalities as National Security Adviser McGeorge Bundy and Secretary of State Dean Rusk.

As Archie turned off of 34th Street and onto Massachusetts Avenue, Ball sat back and rested his head against the seat of the car. He was very tired. Two weeks earlier he had flown to Paris, where he had attended a series of NATO meetings. On his flight back on July 14, he received word that his old friend Adlai Stevenson had died of a heart attack in London. Upon arriving in Washington, Ball, at President Johnson's request, headed a delegation that flew to London to bring back the body. McNamara was in Saigon at the time, gathering information for his proposal to escalate the war.

Meanwhile, Under Secretary Ball was preoccupied with a number of other important policy issues. In recent days, President Johnson had become testy about criticism of his handling of the Dominican Republic crisis. Just two months earlier, he had sent more than twenty-two thousand U.S. troops to that Caribbean country. Now even members of his own administration had quietly begun to raise questions. In fact, three weeks earlier the president had called Ball to ask him to investigate disturbing reports about Richard Goodwin, the White House special assistant. Goodwin, it was rumored, had been arguing that the communist challenge had been overstated and that the United States had flooded the small country with far more troops than was necessary. Johnson was furious. Dean Rusk was also upset. Outside criticism was bad enough, but mutterings from within would not be tolerated. Johnson had ordered Ball to see that there was no dissent in the State Department. Ball recalled that the president had spoken coldly of reservations "about the boys over there not always agreeing with our policy."

Meanwhile, President Johnson was pressuring Ball to keep "Half Bright" (Johnson's name for Senator William Fulbright) in line and supportive of the administration's Vietnam policy. He also insisted that Ball work to neutralize the criticism of such journalists as Walter Lippmann, Mary McGrory, and Joseph Kraft—"your friends," the president called them. This situation put the under secretary in an unpleasant double bind and jeopardized his relations both with the president and with his old friends.

Most important to Ball, the negotiations in Europe focusing upon strengthening the European Economic Community (EEC) had not been faring well. In his trip to Europe earlier that month, he was exasperated to hear that French obstructionism had resulted in a halt to the discussions. Ever since he had worked closely with the French visionary Jean Monnet in the 1940s, George Ball had believed strongly in the dream of a united Europe. He considered European unity to be the most important issue of the day. Ball foresaw the time when some form of serious European union would add stability and strength to the world community. Today, however, he was upset by the situation in Europe. In particular, he blamed French President Charles de Gaulle for the halt in progress toward European consensus. Ball agreed with his friend Walter Hallstein, president of the EEC's executive committee, that a threat to the existence of the Common Market would be "the greatest destructive act in the history of Europe since the days of Hitler."

These problems, all whirling around Ball at the same time, were nibbling at his time and efficiency. Some of the most exasperating issues were the ones that seemed most inconsequential. He recalled the Firestone case, for example. In 1964, the United States had issued export licenses encouraging U.S. companies to do business in Eastern Europe. The Firestone Company had negotiated to build and equip two synthetic rubber plants in Romania. Now, under pressure from extremist groups in the United States as well as from competitors, Firestone had broken off negotiations. A fervent believer in free trade, Ball disapproved of such lobbying pressures. He also knew that the president and Senator Fulbright, chairman of the Senate Foreign Relations Committee, would be demanding explanations.

As the limousine approached Virginia Avenue, George Ball wondered how he could keep his sights focused on so many different and constantly moving targets. Lyndon Johnson relied heavily on him and used him as his political trouble-shooter at the Department of State. Certainly, this year had brought plenty of trouble to shoot. Ball thought to himself, "this goddamned Vietnam thing; it has the makings of a major catastrophe. The creeping escalation is about to burst wide open. But can it be stopped?"

George Ball knew that he was in a political battle. In his own mind, the only hope to arrest what he considered the mindless and costly escalation rested with the president himself. For the past nine months, Ball had been working late preparing memos for the president, analyzing the dangerous situation in Vietnam. Although the memos all seemed to blur together in his mind, he knew that they involved eight major efforts between October 1964 and July 1965.

In his memoranda, Ball had made a special effort to present his arguments as forcefully and convincingly as possible. In so doing, he put his considerable literary talents to work. He wanted the prose to be powerful but not extreme, colorful but not too dramatic. He sought to be skeptical but not cynical. The introduction of his June 18 memo to the president captured the essence of his approach: "Ralph Waldo Emerson once wrote: 'Things are in the saddle, and ride mankind.'" He went on to argue that the president had to prevent "things" from getting into the saddle in Vietnam. Today, he planned to make a similar argument.

When the limousine arrived at the State Department, Archie guided the ve-

hicle into the underground garage, and the under secretary took his private elevator to his office on the seventh floor. There he met with George Springsteen, his
chef de cabinet. Springsteen, a blunt, conscientious, no-nonsense administrator,
had been working overtime in coordinating efforts to provide Ball with data and
charts to back his arguments warning against increasing involvement in Vietnam.
The under secretary knew he needed such data to counter the flood of facts and
statistics that would flow from the lips of the always-prepared Bob McNamara.

After a half hour of consultations with Springsteen, Ball sat back and quietly
considered the forthcoming meetings. He thought about the major actors who
would confront him in the cabinet room. He would have to stand against a true
triangle of power, McNamara, Bundy, and Rusk. The three were sharply different personalities, but they were all uncommonly bright, all unquestionably loyal
to the president, and all committed to the view that their country could prevail
in Vietnam if more manpower and firepower were applied.

Ball knew that McNamara would be the point man. The secretary of defense
had reacted to Ball's October 1964 memorandum as if it were a "wounded snake."
McNamara's entire approach disturbed Ball. Using a vast arsenal of numbers and
statistics, the secretary of defense had a habit of slashing into Ball's arguments,
making them appear soft and spongy, arguments that seemed to lack the hard,
concise, convincing certainty that surrounds carefully presented data. In today's
meetings, McNamara would be particularly dangerous because he had just returned from Vietnam and would undoubtedly carry a briefcase overflowing with
new numbers.

National Security Adviser Mac Bundy represented a different kind of challenge. Ten years younger than Ball, Bundy had a brilliant mind and an impressive
capacity to debate. Although Ball respected Bundy's intellect, he had enormous
confidence in his own mental abilities; unlike many others in Washington, he
was never in awe of Bundy. Ball realized that Mac had effectively worked to
counter and neutralize his critical arguments about the United States' Vietnam
policy. Furthermore, over the past several months Bundy had developed growing
rapport with the president, who had begun to listen closely to his national security adviser's suggestions.

Nor in this situation would his close friend and immediate superior, Dean
Rusk, be of assistance. The secretary of state, described by Jack Valenti as a tall,
"grey bald stone mountain, impervious to the crunch and heavy breathing of in-
quisitive climbers," was, in Ball's view, an intelligent and distinguished figure. In
spite of many conversations over scotch during the quiet early evenings on the
seventh floor of the State Department, Rusk and Ball sharply disagreed over Vietnam policy. Rusk viewed it as a matter of political persistence, national will, and
military might. The United States had to do whatever it took to contain the com-

munist challenge. Ball knew that Rusk would speak sparingly at the meetings, but he could be counted on to raise penetrating questions and ultimately to side with the military "escalators." In the end, however, Ball thought, he was not worried about Dean. He knew Dean's position, and he knew Dean would play fair. But, good grief, it would be so much easier if he were somehow able to get Dean to think sensibly on this one.

George Ball understood that the president would be the key to the outcome. Over the past twenty months, Ball had worked hard to develop and maintain a close relationship with Lyndon Johnson. That was not easy, given the president's tortuously complex personality. It was especially difficult to hold the president's trust while at the same time managing to preserve one's own personal autonomy and self-respect. Johnson expected his subordinates to operate as emanations of his own presidential personality. Ball found such expectations unacceptable. Yet he needed to survive and to retain the president's confidence. Somehow he had managed to gain the confidence of the president. Lyndon Johnson listened to George Ball.

The under secretary enjoyed certain advantages in this complex game of power, politics, and personalities. Although he had never held elected office, Ball was, like Johnson, a shrewd, effective politician. The president knew that Ball understood American electoral politics because Ball had been deeply involved in the 1952 and 1956 presidential campaigns of Adlai Stevenson. Ball knew how to bargain, how to compromise, how to raise money, how to maneuver, and how to survive. Furthermore, both Ball and Johnson appreciated good humor, and the under secretary remembered many incidents of easy familiarity that had occurred between the two of them. He knew he had a special personal relationship with Lyndon Johnson, and he promoted and protected it. Just five days earlier, Ball had broken into tears at the memorial service at the Washington Cathedral for Adlai Stevenson. Lyndon Johnson, putting a comforting hand on Ball's shoulder, said, "George, I never trust a man who can't cry for a friend." Ball was touched by the president's gesture.

In spite of the rapport, the under secretary had a sinking feeling that Lyndon Johnson may already have made up his mind and that he was planning to increase U.S. ground forces in Vietnam. There were rumors that LBJ had signaled his inclination to accept the Pentagon's recommendations. Nonetheless, Ball knew that Johnson would listen and that he could be swayed by debate. In a few hours, the outcome of the forthcoming meetings would be—in every sense—history.

At 10:20 A.M., George Ball left his State Department desk, walked across the wide reception area to Dean Rusk's office, and waited as the secretary of state finished signing a stack of letters. At 10:26 A.M., Ball and Rusk left together for the White House. Chatting quietly about the importance of the meetings at hand,

Ball and Rusk entered the cabinet room in the west wing. As Ball nodded to several of his colleagues who were already seated at the huge boat-shaped table, he noted that the green draperies were drawn.

The under secretary took his seat immediately to the right of Rusk. Seated on Ball's right was Assistant Secretary of State William Bundy. Rusk's seat was immediately to the right of the president's high-backed black leather chair. Secretary of Defense McNamara was already at his seat, just to the left of the president. Deputy Secretary of Defense Cyrus Vance sat to the left of McNamara, with General Earle Wheeler next to Vance. By 10:40 A.M., Ball was seated along with fourteen of President Johnson's closest and most trusted advisers. It was time to proceed with the business at hand.

The Preliminary Presentation

As George Ball looked around the table, he saw what he liked to term "the usual suspects." Besides McNamara, McGeorge Bundy, and Rusk, the conferees included Henry Cabot Lodge, U.S. ambassador to Vietnam; General Earle Wheeler, chairman of the Joint Chiefs of Staff; Admiral William "Red" Raborn, director of the CIA; Cyrus Vance, deputy secretary of defense; John McNaughton, assistant secretary of defense for international security affairs; Richard Helms, deputy director of the CIA; William Bundy, assistant secretary of state for Far Eastern affairs; Leonard Unger, assistant to Bundy; Carl Rowan, head of the U.S. Information Agency; and two special assistants to the president, Bill Moyers and Jack Valenti. The president's chair was empty.

George Ball watched as Bob McNamara briskly passed a top secret paper around the room, one copy to each participant. After reading the memorandum, each individual somberly returned his copy to McNamara. Although Ball was not surprised at the thrust of the report, which proposed increased U.S. military involvement in Vietnam, he raised his eyebrows at the extent of the recommendation. Among several proposals, the Pentagon highlighted two in particular: First, the deployment of U.S. ground troops in Vietnam would be more than doubled. The report recommended that Allied troop strength be increased to forty-four battalions (thirty-four American and, if possible, ten Korean). This would increase the number of U.S. personnel in Vietnam from 72,000 to between 175,000 and 200,000. Second, the administration was requested to authorize the call-up of approximately 235,000 men from the reserves and National Guard. The memorandum justified this massive escalation by frankly stating that the situation in South Vietnam was worse than it had been a year before and that it was steadily deteriorating. Without more outside assistance, the government of South Vietnam seemed headed for certain defeat.

With the president absent, McNamara confidently initiated the discussion. In a flat, businesslike tone, he told the group that the memorandum represented his own view of the situation. He indicated, however, that the report's recommendations to escalate were supported by Generals William Westmoreland, Harold Johnson, and Maxwell Taylor, by Admiral Ulysses S. Grant Sharp, and by Ambassador Lodge. Ball noticed that McNamara then nodded to Lodge, who began the discussion.

Henry Cabot Lodge smoothly told the group that he was all for a diplomatic move if he thought there was any chance that diplomacy would be successful. Unfortunately, in his judgment, the timing was bad. Diplomatic efforts would only harden the enemy's resolve. Ball considered Lodge "an affable fellow" who had been called to his second stint as ambassador to South Vietnam. The president wanted to have a conservative Republican aboard in order to mute criticism from the right. During his first stint in Vietnam, Lodge had left the embassy in a horrid administrative tangle. Ball knew that Lodge seldom questioned the military establishment, nor did he ever frontally challenge U.S. policy assumptions in Vietnam. A man of modest intelligence, he was a New England patrician Republican who was more of a facilitator than a policymaker. In Ball's view, Cabot's opinion carried little weight with Johnson.

Secretary of Defense McNamara said that the recommended buildup of troops must not lead Hanoi, Moscow, and Beijing to believe that the United States was contemplating an invasion into North Vietnam. National Security Adviser Bundy responded that this could be handled by public announcements. He returned to Lodge's point by arguing that during the military buildup third parties could work on diplomatic initiatives. Lodge responded that "the president has done a remarkable job of forming public opinion so far. Very skillful."

Ball noted to himself that these introductory comments by Lodge, McNamara, and Bundy had effectively declared that escalation need not risk Soviet or Chinese intervention, that diplomatic overtures could continue, and that the president's name had been approvingly quoted in support of the new policy. He then saw the discussion quickly shift to military logistics and field capabilities.

Mac Bundy asked whether U.S. and South Vietnamese troops would be deployed in similar capacities in the field. McNamara, inserting another word of caution, pointed out that the government of South Vietnam had originally wanted the United States to send troops to the highlands. "This," said the defense secretary, "is unacceptable to us."

Dean Rusk lit a cigarette and asked: "Bob, what is the capability of GVN [Government of (South) Vietnam] to mobilize their own forces?" McNamara answered that the South Vietnamese hoped to increase their troops by ten thousand per month. He said the U.S. decision makers thought this was possible. McNamara, however, argued that he personally was not optimistic. He pointed out that the desertion rate was high, frankly declared that the GVN was a "nongovern-

ment," and suggested that the South Vietnamese were unable to push forward
on their own.

In contrast, the secretary of defense confidently stated that the morale of the
U.S. troops was "of the highest order. I am proud of their dedication and devotion. It reflects the belief that they are doing something worthwhile." General
Earle Wheeler, seated next to McNamara, emphatically nodded his assent. "I
agree," he stated, and he went on to analyze the state of the South Vietnamese
troops. Ball's mind wandered as Rusk asked a few more operational questions. He
then observed the discussion shift predictably to a third level, how best to sell the
troop-increase decision to the U.S. Congress and to the American people.

Secretary of State Rusk pointed out that if the McNamara report were accepted, it would be important to determine the best way to inform the public.
Timing would be important, he said. McNamara responded that the president
should inform Congress during the week of July 26, followed by a statement to
the public. Bundy suggested that the congressional presentation should be a Defense Department responsibility, while Rusk and the Department of State should
then do a presentation to the general public. Rusk argued that "we ought to get
civilians in the congressional testimony to disabuse the feeling that the military
is making the decisions." Bundy agreed and suggested that Rusk follow up the
president's speech with a statement of "total unanimity."

George Ball saw that his colleagues were on a roll. In less than forty-five minutes—in the absence of the president—they had approved McNamara's report
and had quickly decided how to present its recommendations to the nation. A
decision to move the United States full speed forward into the Vietnam jungles
had been made without a word of objection or even caution. Facing a fait accompli, Ball sharply stated: "It is one thing to ready the country for this decision. It is
another to face the realities of the decision. We can't allow the country to wake
up one morning and find heavy casualties. We need to be damn serious with the
American public. It is necessary to paint a somber picture and dispel any idea
that the postmonsoon season will see us over the hump." As President Johnson
entered the room, McNamara captured the initiative: it should be made clear to
the public, he said, that U.S. troops were already in combat.

The Middle Session

Like all the others in the Cabinet Room, George Ball stood up when the president entered. As he sat down, Ball noted that it was exactly 11:30 A.M. President
Johnson wore a gray suit and a blue tie. As he looked around the room at his advisers, it was clear that he was in a somber mood. After forcefully stressing the
need for great care to avoid any leaks concerning the discussion at hand, Johnson

nodded at McNamara, who again summarized his recommendations—200,000 troops in Vietnam by the end of the year and a reserve call-up of 235,000 men.

Ball noted that the president did not appear pleased. In response to McNamara's recommendation, Johnson fired off a volley of questions and concerns: "What will be the consequences of such a call-up of reserves? Have we wrung every single soldier we can out of involved third countries? Who else can help? Are we the sole defenders of freedom in the world? What other alternatives are available to us? We can always tell GVN that we are coming back home. Should we pull out? If we do, what are the consequences? Would we have to call up more troops and suffer more casualties later in the game? We have attempted to pursue negotiations. Doesn't this already make us look weak, like we're running around with a cup in our hands? What are our other options?"

The president's outburst left the room silent. McNamara predictably broke the silence by discussing the deteriorating situation in Vietnam. He estimated that the Vietcong controlled 25 percent of the population and argued that this control was increasing each day. He pointed to a map that showed the VC-controlled areas in red. Johnson asked whether it were not dangerous and foolhardy for the United States to put troops in these red areas. Shouldn't we limit our military mission?

General Earle Wheeler responded that the United States should initiate offensive operations that would seek out and confront the main VC force units. "They will have to come out and fight." Unable to contain himself any longer, George Ball asked: "Why does anyone think that the Vietcong will be so considerate as to confront us directly? They certainly didn't do that for the French?" Ball listened skeptically as Wheeler responded that it would be possible to harass the Vietcong until they would be forced to stop and fight.

In an attempt to reinforce Wheeler's response, McNamara argued that when faced with 175,000 U.S. troops, the Vietcong would probably use their troops in larger concentrations. In any case, he continued, the United States had the capacity to deal with guerrilla forces as well as with major military concentrations.

In Ball's mind, McNamara's attempt to rescue Wheeler only made their position more tenuous. The president seemed to sense the same thing, for he suddenly shifted the discussion by asking: "Is there anyone here who thinks we should not do what Bob McNamara's memorandum recommends? If so, I would like to hear from them now." There was silence in the room. Johnson leaned over and looked around Rusk and at Ball.

Long before the meeting George Ball had decided that he would oppose the escalation. He would stake out his position as strongly and convincingly as possible. If the consensus ran against him and if the president agreed, he too would accept the policy of the memorandum. But perhaps he could carry the day by bringing Lyndon Johnson over to his position. The president had now provided Ball with an opening and an opportunity. Ball chose his words carefully.

"We are engaged in a very perilous voyage, a very dangerous voyage. I have very grave apprehensions about our ability to defeat the VC because of the nature of the terrain, because of the softness of the political situation in South Vietnam, and because of other factors as well. Let me be clear, however: if the final decision is to go ahead, I will go along with the McNamara report." Looking directly at Ball, the president curtly responded: "I'm well aware of the dangers, George, but what other courses are open to us?"

Raising his voice slightly, the under secretary replied: "There is no course that will enable us to cut our losses easily. We should, however, weigh the costs of cutting our losses now as opposed to later. The pressures to create a larger war are going to be almost irresistible. I base my arguments not on any 'moral' position, but rather on cold-blooded calculation. We're simply going to have to take the risk that Southeast Asia might embrace communism. Whatever our losses, however, I believe that if we cut them now they will be short-term in nature."

The president looked at Ball and calmly asked: "What other road can I go?" The under secretary responded: "Take our losses now. Let the South Vietnamese government do what seems to come natural to it: let it fall apart. Begin serious negotiations. Frankly, there will probably be a takeover by the communists, and I know this is disagreeable, but . . ." Johnson interrupted, "Can we really make a case for this? Let's discuss it fully." Ball pointed out: "Mr. President, we have discussed it. I have had my day in court."

Johnson disagreed. "I don't think we have made a full commitment. George, you have pointed out the dangers, but you have not yet succeeded in providing workable alternatives. We have not always been right in this thing. We have no mortgage on victory."

Ball noted to himself that the president seemed uncomfortable with the course of events in Vietnam and that he wished to find a way out of the quagmire. Or was he only trying to justify to himself a decision he had already made to escalate? Johnson continued: "I want another meeting before we take further action. We have to look at all other courses of action carefully."

During his exchange with the president, Ball realized that the others in the room disapproved of his arguments. McNamara stared gloomily at the papers before him. Others shifted in their chairs. No one spoke in support of Ball's position.

Dean Rusk then cleared his throat, flicked some ashes from his cigarette into the ashtray before him, and slowly stated: "Look, it is fine to explore alternative options. On the other hand, if we had in 1961 responded firmly by sending 50,000 men out there, Hanoi might never have proceeded against the South. There is a lesson here." Ball knew that Rusk's words carried great weight. In three brief sentences, he had made the case for escalation. Ball had been thrown back on the defensive.

After brief statements by Carl Rowan and Henry Cabot Lodge on the nature of the South Vietnamese government, Johnson came back at Ball: "George, do you think that we have another course?" Slightly unsettled by Rusk's sharp intervention, Ball shot back: "I would not recommend that you follow McNamara's course!"

The president picked up one of the three pencils before him on the table and began doodling on a yellow pad. He hunched over in his chair and looked at Ball again. "Can you outline your doubts and offer another course of action? I think it best that we hear you out so that we can determine if your suggestions are sound and ready to be followed."

Ball confidently responded: "Yes. I think I can present to you the least bad of two courses. I'd present a course that is costly, but that cost would be short term in nature."

Johnson leaned back and said, "Fine. Then let's meet at 2:30 this afternoon to discuss George's proposals. Now let Bob tell us why we need to risk all those American lives."

As McNamara, backed by Wheeler and CIA head "Red" Raborn, developed the military option, Ball's mind wandered. The president had provided him with the opportunity he needed. But given the drift of the discussions this morning, he realized that his chances of turning this thing around were slim at best. He would have to spend the lunch hour carefully working up his presentation. A few moments later, at 1 P.M., he heard the president adjourn the meeting. After exchanging a few friendly words with Dean Rusk, he left the White House and hurried back to the State Department. He had work to do.

George Ball's Last Stand

Just after 2:30 P.M., the group of fifteen met again in the Cabinet Room. This time the president was in his chair as the session began at 2:40. Shuffling some papers before him, Johnson said, "OK, George, we're ready to hear what you have to say."

Ball had spent a hectic hour in his conference room preparing his presentation. He had drafted, organized, redrafted, reorganized. He knew that his comments had to be concise, hard-hitting, and persuasive. He had to get to Johnson. Bob, Dean, and Mac were already dug in too deeply. He knew the president's mind-set and intentionally sought to appeal to these prejudices. The emphasis had to be placed upon the realities of power and the exigencies of politics. Ball planned a three-pronged attack.

George Ball looked around the room, then at the president, and began his presentation with a short, clipped sentence: "Gentlemen, we cannot win a war in Vietnam. This conflict is going to be long and protracted. The best we can get out of this is a very messy conclusion. Furthermore, there always remains the possibility of armed intervention by the Chinese communists."

After pausing to let these thoughts sink in, Ball cleared his throat and continued: "There are a number of unpleasant consequences for us if we are caught in a long war in Asia.

"First, look at the galling experience of Korea. As our casualties increased, public support for the war decreased." At this point, Ball placed a chart in front of the president. Entitled "Correlation of U.S. Casualties in Korea with Public Attitudes Towards U.S. Involvement," the carefully drafted document showed that as American casualties increased from eleven thousand to forty thousand, public support of the war dropped some 20 percentage points. Ball's message was obvious. If the president chose to increase the number of U.S. troops on the ground in Vietnam, casualties would inevitably rise, and the already decreasing public support for the war would almost certainly plummet further. In making this argument, Ball knew that Lyndon Johnson was extremely sensitive about domestic criticism of his Vietnam policy.

After addressing the problem of public opinion on the important domestic front, George Ball next pointed to the tenuous situation of world public opinion. "If we could win this thing in a year's time, then we can hold on to much of our international support. On the other hand, it is my considered opinion that it will take at least two more years to begin to turn the tides of the conflict in our direction. The fact that we have put in so much manpower with no early definitive results will hurt us badly in the eyes of the world. It will, in fact, be a sign of U.S. weakness—a Great Power is unable to beat a bunch of guerrillas."

Ball then sought to buttress his thesis by stressing the likely protracted nature of the conflict. "From the beginning, we have underestimated the seriousness of the problem. We are still underestimating the seriousness of the problem. It is like giving cobalt treatment to a terminal cancer case."

At this point, the under secretary suggested a specific proposal. "We must work to cut our losses now. Every great captain in history is not afraid to make a tactical withdrawal if conditions are not favorable to him. We can't even find the enemy in Vietnam. We can't see him and we can't find him. He is indigenous to the country. The least harmful way to cut our losses is to let the South Vietnamese government decide it doesn't want us."

Looking around Rusk and directly at the president, George Ball concluded his introductory remarks tersely: "I have grave doubts that any Western army can successfully fight Orientals in an Asian jungle."

Ball knew that this kind of argument would affect President Johnson. And so it did. As if on cue, the president responded with concern in his voice: "This is important. Can westerners, lacking adequate intelligence as we do, successfully fight Orientals in jungles and rice paddies? I want McNamara and Wheeler to seriously ponder this question."

Johnson continued: "I agree that the situation is serious. I'm sorry we're embroiled in Vietnam, but dammit, we *are* there. If we were to pull out, wouldn't the other countries think Uncle Sam is a paper tiger? Wouldn't we lose credibility if we broke the word of three presidents? Wouldn't it be an irreparable blow?"

Ball responded: "A worse blow would be if the mightiest power in the world should be unable to defeat guerrillas."

Johnson shot back: "Then you are not basically troubled by what the world might say if we were to pull out?"

Ball answered: "Look, if we were actively helping a country with a stable, viable government, it would be a vastly different story. The Western Europeans, for example, look at us as if we have acted most imprudently."

The president responded with a small smile: "But I believe that these people [the South Vietnamese] are really trying to fight. They're like Republicans who try to stay in power, but don't stay there for long." Looking across the table at Lodge, Johnson said, "Excuse me, Cabot." As light laughter rippled around the table, Ball noted that the president's comment had defused the developing tenseness of the dialogue.

The under secretary recaptured the floor by alluding to a prediction by South Vietnam's president: "Nguyen Van Thieu spoke the other day and said the Communists would win the election."

"I don't believe that," snapped the president. "Does anyone here believe that?" Ball watched quietly as McNamara, Lodge, Bill Bundy, and Leonard Unger all indicated agreement with the president.

At this point, McNamara interrupted the Ball-Johnson dialogue by pointing out the fundamental weakness of the present government of Prime Minister Nugyen Cao Ky. He also stressed the absence of any democratic tradition in Vietnam. General Wheeler agreed that Ky was weak but said he was impressed by Thieu.

Obviously still concerned by George Ball's earlier arguments, the president, fiddling with his tie, said, "There are two basic points troubling me. Can westerners fight and win in Asia? And how can we effectively fight a war under the direction of a people whose government changes every month?" Nodding at Ball, he said, "All right, George, go ahead. Make your other points."

"Our Western European allies do not see what we are doing in Vietnam to be relevant to their own situations," Ball pointed out. "They are concerned about their own security. To them, troops in Berlin have real meaning; troops in Vietnam do not."

After a brief exchange between Ball and Johnson, McGeorge Bundy entered the debate. Ball had noted Bundy's silence until now and knew that Bundy had waited until the main points had been put on the table. As Bundy began to speak with quiet confidence, he looked from the president to Ball and back at the president.

"I would like to raise two questions. First, I wish it known that I agree with the main thrust of Bob McNamara's proposal. It is, however, the function of my staff to argue both sides. Concerning George Ball's argument: the difficulty in adopting it is that it would represent a radical switch from current policy, with little evidence that this switch would work. It runs in the face of all we have said and done."

Ball watched as Bundy's measured argument sank into the receptive minds of the men gathered around the table. A few of the participants nodded quietly in assent. Bundy continued: "I don't buy George's cancer analogy. There is immaturity and weakness present in our Vietnamese allies. But this is not cancer. Ball's entire analytical argument gives no weight to the losses suffered by the other side. It is, of course, true that a great many elements in George's argument are correct. We do need to make clear that this is a somber matter, that no single action will bring a quick victory. I think it is clear, however, that we are not going to be thrown out."

Ball sharply interrupted Bundy: "My argument is not that we get thrown out, but that we will get bogged down and will not be able to win. We'll double our bet and get lost in the rice paddies."

Bundy glanced impatiently at the under secretary and answered: "Please let me summarize my argument. The world, our country, and South Vietnam would be deeply alarmed if we just pulled out. Any major shift in our policy would be disastrous. In fact, we are better off to waffle through than to withdraw."

Dean Rusk moved in to buttress Bundy's argument. "If the communist world finds out we will not pursue our commitments to the end, I don't know where they will stay their hand. I am more optimistic than some of my colleagues. I simply don't believe that the Vietcong has made large advances among the Vietnamese people. We can't worry about massive casualties when we say we can't find the enemy. I don't see heavy casualties unless the Chinese should decide to get involved."

Glancing at his papers before him on the table, Ball was about to respond when McNamara spoke up. "I believe that George has vastly understated the cost of cutting our losses. I agree with Dean. The international effects of withdrawal would be catastrophic. Incidentally, I also think that George overstates the costs of my proposal."

George Ball listened as General Wheeler, Ambassador Lodge, and Leonard Unger all spoke in support of Bundy, Rusk, and McNamara. He knew his arguments had failed to sway the thinking of his colleagues. He watched glumly as the president suddenly changed the topic and mentioned the need to get more favorable press coverage behind U.S. policy. At 5:30 P.M., Johnson stood up and declared the meeting adjourned.

As George Ball gathered up his papers, he knew that his attempt to forestall the sharp escalation of U.S. involvement in Vietnam had failed. His friend, Dean Rusk, put out his last cigarette, leaned over to Ball, and offered a few words of comfort. The other individuals at the meeting stood in small groups quietly talking among themselves. As the under secretary walked out of the White House, he told himself that he had given it his best shot. He had indeed had his day in court. Now, he must hurry back to his office where he faced a half dozen world crises. None of them involved Southeast Asia.

At noon on Thursday, July 22, 1965, President Lyndon Johnson met with Secretary of Defense Robert McNamara and the country's military leaders. This group strongly supported the McNamara report and discussed how to best implement the military escalation. No one from the Department of State was present at this meeting. Later that day, Ball joined the president and thirteen others in the Cabinet Room to discuss the change in policy. Much of the session focused on how to best sell the escalation decision to the American people. Ball said little at this meeting.

Nor did the under secretary contribute much during two meetings on Monday, July 26, when the decision was made to attack two North Vietnamese missile sites. He observed as the U.S. ambassador to the United Nations, Arthur Goldberg, opposed the bombing, while such individuals as Special Adviser Clark Clifford and Vice President Hubert Humphrey spoke in support of the bombing decision.

On Tuesday, July 27, Ball attended a formal forty-minute National Security Council meeting in which President Johnson discussed the logistics of the escalation. The president also used the meeting to obtain NSC legitimacy for his action.

At noon on Wednesday, July 28, exactly one week after the fateful July 21 session, President Lyndon Johnson held a televised press conference and announced the momentous decision to escalate the U.S. presence in Vietnam. The president pointed out that American power "is a very vital shield. If we are driven from the field in Vietnam, then no nation can ever again have the same confidence in American promises, or in American protection." He went on to state that "we did not choose to be guardians at the gate, but there is no one else." He declared that he had ordered the 1st Air Cavalry Division, with supporting forces, to leave for Vietnam that very day, raising the total U.S. forces there from 75,000 to 125,000. More would be needed later. The president dramatically stated: "We will stand in Vietnam."

George Ball watched the Johnson speech in his office and thought back to the July 21 meetings. A few of his colleagues had sought to comfort him by pointing out that the president had actually decided to escalate the U.S. effort even before the meetings. Ball had discovered that Johnson had indeed authorized Deputy Secretary of Defense Cyrus Vance to cable McNamara in Vietnam on July 17 that Johnson's "current intention" was to escalate. But Ball knew of many times that Johnson's "current intentions" were later altered—the president often changed his mind. Furthermore, Ball had enormous confidence in his own persuasive powers and in his special relationship with Lyndon Johnson. In spite of the odds, he believed that he had had a reasonable chance to bring the president over to his position.

Ball then thought for a moment about the tactical approach he had taken on July 21, at a juncture that Clark Clifford later likened to Lyndon Johnson's Rubicon. Ball wondered whether he done everything he could to prevent the president and the country from crossing the Rubicon into what he felt was sure to be disaster. Perhaps he should have argued the domestic political implications more strenuously . . . Or he should have done more lobbying privately among the other participants . . . But Ball understood that such thinking was now irrelevant. The decision had been made. The course was set. He would stay aboard. Perhaps he could still make a difference. There would be numerous other difficult political crossroads to be negotiated. He needed to be there to help chart the turns. In so doing, he might lighten the costs, whether they be political, economic, or, most importantly, human.

President Johnson speaks at the July 21, 1965, White House meeting on Vietnam policy.

George Ball, left, and Dean Rusk listen intently during the July 21 meeting.

George Ball, arguing around skeptical Dean Rusk, makes his case directly to President Johnson.

An anguished Dean Rusk reacts to George Ball's arguments opposing dramatic increase in U.S. troops in Vietnam.

Lyndon Johnson examines Ball's statistics documenting decline in American public support for Korean War as U.S. casualties increased. Dean Rusk listens glumly.

I

PRAGMATIC IDEALIST FROM THE MIDWEST

1

❖·❖·❖

Personal Roots and
Rites of Passage

On Tuesday, November 7, 1961, Under Secretary of State George Wildman Ball, sensing that momentum was building for increasing U.S. military personnel in Vietnam, bluntly broached the subject with President John F. Kennedy. "Mr. President," Ball said, "to commit American forces to South Vietnam would, in my opinion, be a tragic error. Within five years we'll have three hundred thousand men in the paddies and jungles, and we'll never find them again."

President Kennedy glared at his tall, opinionated under secretary and caustically responded, "George, you're just crazier than hell. That just isn't going to happen."

Six years later, on November 2, 1967, when the United States had 485,600 combat troops in Vietnam, George Ball attended a meeting called by President Lyndon Johnson in the White House. Although Ball had resigned from his State Department position a year before, he joined a group of twenty "wise men" convened by the president to reassess U.S. policy in Vietnam. At this meeting, Ball argued forcefully that the United States extricate itself from Vietnam as soon as possible. Ball's pleas fell on the usual deaf ears as this senior advisory contingent urged the president to continue to pursue the war with vigor.

As the meeting broke up, Ball, frustrated and angry, confronted a small group that included Dean Acheson and Arthur Dean and blurted, "I've been watching across the table. You're like a flock of old buzzards sitting on a fence, sending the young men off to be killed. You ought to be ashamed of yourselves." Ball's old associates were stunned at the outburst and looked at him as if he were indeed "crazier than hell." [1]

George Ball was from the beginning an iconoclast. But his was an iconoclasm deeply rooted in the soil of midwestern common sense. Although his ideas were often rejected as "crazy" and impractical or unrealistic and impossible, Ball himself was taken very seriously. He may have been, as he once referred to himself, "a champion of lost causes," but his intelligence, style, and personal credibility enabled him to present unorthodox points of view to audiences that included the most powerful political figures of the twentieth century.

George Ball was a complex bundle of contradictions. Politically, he was realist and idealist, liberal and conservative, partisan and bipartisan, populist and elitist, parochial and global, isolationist and interventionist. Personally, he was intellectual and anti-intellectual, formal and relaxed, ambitious and nonchalant, tolerant and impatient. In matters of family and finance, he was both a modest success and a spectacular failure.

In his capacity to embrace contradiction in a constructive and effective nexus, Ball was not unlike the Midwest from which he sprang. States like Iowa, Illinois, and Wisconsin represented a slice of America where the climate could be both harsh and accommodating and where the people could be rock-hard conservative Republican and liberal populist Democrat. Iowa was a state that produced both revivalist Billy Sunday and presidential first lady Mamie Eisenhower; Henry Wallace and John Wayne. Illinois's native sons included Adlai Stevenson and Richard Daley; Wisconsin was the birthplace of Joseph McCarthy and Robert LaFollette.

George Ball's personality and ideas were to a large extent molded by the force of family and the culture that surrounded him during the first twenty-four years of his life. His father, Amos Ball Jr., and the Iowan environment left deep lifelong impressions on George. Americans often view Iowa as the state that anchors the United States, and they consider Iowans to be among the most genuine and reliable of citizens. This is "America's middle earth," "top choice America, America cut thick and prime."[2] Observers of American regional culture like to stress the hard-working, friendly, family-oriented nature of Iowans. Most importantly, Iowans are stereotypically considered to be people of vision who also possess great common sense. The flat expanse of their state encourages Iowans to look beyond, while the subtle diversity of Iowans (Germans, Swedes, English, Native Americans, Quakers, Mormons, Catholics, Methodists, Presbyterians, Conservatives, Progressives) engenders a certain down-home grounded tolerance.

Although stubbornly independent and individualistic, midwesterners are also highly social and they enjoy meeting in clusters—at church socials, around the stove at the country store, in quilting bees, on patriotic holidays, during threshing and barn-raising occasions, for softball and horseshoe contests, and at a myriad of family functions. On Saturday nights, for example, people would gather in different homes for supper and dancing, and upstairs "all the beds would be covered with coats and babies."[3]

Scholars have described the "central Midwest" as an area where "business and business success are most openly extolled as a proper purpose in life."[4] Midwesterners take a "no-nonsense attitude toward the world" and often express an impatience with indecision with such phrases as: "if we've got a job to do, do it"; "if we are going to fight a war, fight it"; "if a policy doesn't work, drop it."[5] In spite of this blunt approach to life, midwesterners also often have exhibited a witty, ironic sense of humor.

All of these regional characteristics were present in the Ball family. Indeed, they mixed and percolated most obviously through the personalities of Amos Ball Jr. and his youngest son George. Although George Ball departed the Midwest following his education and in some ways rebelled against that background, he never forgot his roots and often referred to them in his letters and political discourse.[6]

The Family

When Ruth Murdoch from Pittsburgh married George Wildman Ball on September 16, 1932, she soon found herself a somewhat unwilling appendage of what she bitingly called "The Family." The Family consisted of Amos Ball Jr., George's talented and ambitious father, Edna Wildman Ball, the quietly influential mother, and George's two brothers, Stuart and Ralph. Born in 1904 and 1907, respectively, Stuart and Ralph were both older than George, who was born on December 21, 1909.[7]

Two Amos Balls

Amos Ball Jr. was the dominant figure in The Family. Born in the village of Shaldon in Devon, England, on May 3, 1877, Amos emigrated to the United States with his mother, baby brother, and two sisters in 1882. His father had failed badly in the bakery business and, at the urging of his wife, Selina Scoble, had set out for America in order to survey the opportunities there. Selina's sister and brother-in-law had earlier emigrated to the United States and had settled in Toledo, Iowa, a tiny town in the middle of a state in the middle of America. From here, they wrote their family back in England, singing the praises of Iowa and America.

Amos Ball Sr., the son of a gardener, was a selfish, opinionated, feckless man whose self-righteousness found an outlet in his service as a local preacher of the Wesleyan persuasion in England, the Methodist religion in America. George Ball thoroughly disliked his grandfather, whose life seemed marked by "a shrewd sense of self survival," "a canny stratagem for avoiding work," and "a penchant for bad planning."[8]

This capacity for failure and bad planning is clear from the story of Amos's beckoning his wife, Selina, to bring the children and join him in America. After receiving her husband's letter, the enterprising mother lost little time in gathering her brood and setting sail. Meanwhile, Amos Sr. impetuously boarded a ship and left for England to help with the move. Somewhere on the Atlantic, the two ships passed one another. As Selina and the four small children reached North America, Amos was arriving in England.

Once Amos Sr. returned and the family was reunited, they made the long trip to Toledo. Unfortunately, they ended up in Toledo, Ohio rather than in Toledo, Iowa. They were five hundred miles short of their destination. When they finally found their way to Iowa, they were nearly penniless and their relatives were in no position to be of help. Amos eventually found the means to purchase a general store in Toledo, but Amos Jr., the eldest son, actually ran the store while his father "conducted a nonstop seminar in theology for cronies sprawled in perpetual session around the wood stove and spittoon."[9]

The Ball country store became the town's social and political center, where a wide cross section of the community met daily to discuss personal, economic, and political issues. Known as "the regular congregation," this group included individuals who had participated in the California gold rush, two former seamen who had visited ports across the world, an eccentric Scotsman, an old British soldier, and two grizzled veterans of the Civil War. Amos Jr. received much of his early education by listening quietly on the fringes of this fascinating congregation.

As a boy who observed his grandfather as only children can do, George Ball felt uneasy and confused by what he saw. He wondered about the cynicism of the old man and worried about the way Amos Sr. used people, including many of those closest to him. George was particularly disturbed by his grandfather's proclivity to promote his narrow version of organized religion, which included his constant denunciation of the evils of tobacco. But tobacco was Amos's best cash commodity, and the display cases in his general store were filled with boxes of cigars, packages of smoking tobacco, jars containing bars of plug tobacco, and a large assortment of pipes.

Although George found little to admire in his grandfather, he felt quite differently about his father. In fact, no other individual exerted more influence on George than his father, Amos Jr. Amos worked fourteen-hour days in his father's general store and lacked even a high school education. An ambitious young man with an unquenchable intellectual curiosity, he read incessantly, taught himself typing and shorthand, and watched for an opportunity to seek his fortune elsewhere.

On Monday, January 3, 1897, a cold snowy day, young Amos Ball caught the 7 A.M. streetcar to Tama. At Tama, he boarded a train for the twenty-minute ride to Marshalltown. He escaped Toledo to seek his fortune with the help of his strong mother and despite the objections of his father. Selina, the family backbone, financed Amos's departure with money she had carefully saved over the years and kept in a cookie jar. Once in Marshalltown, Amos Jr. found menial work at the offices of Standard Oil of Indiana (Amoco).

Amos Ball began at Standard Oil sweeping floors, running errands, and driving tank wagons. He was polite, hardworking, and reliable. When his stenographic skills caught the attention of his superiors, he was promoted to position of clerk. He never looked back and slowly and steadily moved up the hierarchy of Standard Oil until he became a vice president and director. His various promotions took him from Marshalltown to Des Moines in 1903 and from Des Moines to the head offices in Chicago on Thanksgiving Day, 1921. The following year he moved his wife and children to Evanston, Illinois.

Although well-read and bright, Amos was deeply self-conscious about his lack of formal schooling. This sense of insecurity caused him to drive himself even harder, and he earned a reputation in the company as a relentless achiever and competitor. His addiction to hard work was not restricted to the office, either; after the move to Des Moines he spent hours digging the basement for a home he was building for his family.

Amos Ball worked for Standard of Indiana for forty-seven years. He retired in 1944 as vice president of sales and as a director. Over the years he became a powerful spokesman and defender of his company. In August 1931, for example, when the company was under intense pressure over pricing and for importing foreign oil, Amos Ball traveled to Wichita, Kansas, where he delivered a major policy speech before a large and hostile audience. A general manager at the time, he effectively confronted the critics of the company. In the words of a *Wichita Eagle* editorial, "Altogether Mr. Ball was well received in Wichita, as befitted a man of his high standing, and his statements to last night's audience go far to help bring about a better understanding by all concerned."[10]

In his Wichita speech, Amos Ball revealed his business philosophy. After assuring the audience that Standard Oil would like to live by the golden rule, he argued that it was unfortunately impossible to do so "unless our competitors do likewise. Competition is much like war. If your competitor won't fight according to the rules, you have to fight as he does . . . or you lose out."[11] Between 1937 and 1938, Amos was caught up in a major government suit in which the government charged a number of oil companies with violating the Sherman Antitrust Act for colluding on jobber contracts. Ball pleaded no contest and was fined $15,000. Standard Oil paid the fine for him.[12]

In the 1920s, Standard Oil of Indiana had the reputation of a company on the move. The president and chief executive officer was a colorful, swashbuckling giant of a man named Robert W. Stewart. "Colonel Bob," as he was known, had ridden with Teddy Roosevelt's Rough Riders and was the kind of leader who demanded the total loyalty of his subordinates. Amos Ball was one of Stewart's protégés. When Colonel Stewart was shockingly implicated in the Teapot Dome scandal, John D. Rockefeller Jr., who owned the largest block of Amoco stock, confronted the Colonel and asked him to resign. This set the stage for a huge public power struggle. Stewart, combative but vulnerable, roared, "If the Rockefellers want to fight, I'll show them how to fight."[13] But Stewart's bluster and energetic defense failed; the Rockefellers carefully orchestrated a winning campaign among the shareholders and secured the dismissal of Colonel Stewart.[14]

When the Colonel went under, a number of his close associates sank with him. Amos Ball was not among them. He had carefully assessed the situation and had decided to swim free from the floundering Colonel. At the same time, however, he chose not to condemn his old patron. He resisted throwing complete support to Rockefeller, whom he also knew personally. Amos astutely survived a shattering company shake-up, but according to Ball family lore, if he had joined the Rockefeller camp, he would almost certainly have risen one day to the presidency of Standard of Indiana.

Amos Jr. had six brothers and sisters: Blanche, Elsie, George, Evelyn, Gladys, and John. Like Amos, Blanche and Elsie were unusually bright. Through marriage, three of the sisters were related to celebrities. Blanche married John Fisher Corbett, a brother of the boxer "Gentleman" Jim Corbett. Evelyn's husband was John Ernest Woodhead, and the U.S. national swimming champion Cynthia Woodhead is her granddaughter. Gladys married Ernest B. Hanks. The film star Tom Hanks is her grandson.

Of all the brothers and sisters, however, Amos accomplished the most. He was the reliable rock of the family. Indeed, his sisters Blanche and Elsie were disappointed and envious when Amos married. Because he was the oldest son, the other siblings expected him to provide for them. On many occasions, Amos did provide financial assistance to his father, brothers, and sisters. He helped his brother George find work with Standard Oil and assisted John to survive several financial misadventures. During the Depression, Edna and Amos sent numerous packages of used clothing to Gladys Hanks, who gratefully divided them among her four children. Gladys's daughter Hilda described her Uncle Amos as "our rich relative."[15]

In spite of his grim determination to succeed and his extraordinary ambition, Amos Ball had an engaging sense of humor. When George Ball's wife later described her husband's "roguish" side, she was using a word that also captured the nature of her father-in-law. The Ball humor was witty and outrageous. The grandchildren relate an incident in Cocoa Beach, Florida, where on one Christmas Eve in the 1940s Amos feigned an intense dislike for Santa Claus. Having arranged for someone to make some loud noises on the roof, Amos grabbed a loaded double-barreled shotgun and, running outside, he fired both barrels over the house. Growling in satisfaction, he came back into the house and quietly told the stunned family, "I got the old sonuvabitch that time."[16]

When Amos Ball Jr. died on Christmas of 1954, he left a family trust fund and estate valued at over one million dollars. In five decades of hard work, he had managed to convert the few dollars from his mother's cookie jar into an impressive fortune.

The Wildmans

While in Marshalltown, Amos Ball met a five-foot schoolteacher named Jessie Edna Wildman. After graduating from high school, Edna taught for a time in rural one-room schools north of Marshalltown. The Wildman family was rooted in Marshalltown and represented the essence of midwestern conventionality. On June 25, 1902, a year after Amos had been promoted to Standard Oil's divisional office in Des Moines, Amos and Edna Wildman were married. At the time, Amos's salary was $65 per month. On his county marriage registration form, Amos listed his occupation as "stenographer."

Edna Wildman was one of five children in a closely knit family. Both her father, John E. Wildman, and her mother, Phoebe Eleanor Kimberley Connors, were native Iowans, born in Jefferson County when Iowa was still a territory. John Wildman, who had served in the Civil War, had worked as a farmer, deputy sheriff, and state oil inspector before his death in 1916. A Mason and Methodist, he lived in the Marshalltown area for forty years. A courtly, unhurried, nonconfrontational gentleman, he was proclaimed an "old resident" in his obituary in the May 13, 1916, Marshalltown *Times-Republican*.

Edna Wildman grew up pampered and spoiled by her mother and her two older sisters. The center of her universe was Marshalltown, Iowa, and she felt content deeply embroidered into the fabric of the Wildman family. Family activities focused upon discussion and gossip about the community, the crops, and the weather. The Wildmans spent little time reading books, discussing ideas, or debating politics. They found it both more comfortable and more worthwhile to expend their energy reinforcing and caring for the fragilities of the relationships that bind family and friends. "No cross word was ever spoken among them and they were entirely happy just to be together."[17]

In family matters, the Wildmans, like the Balls, experienced a number of thorny problems. Edna's two brothers, Will (William Braden Wildman) and Ralph (John Wesley Ralph Wildman), had difficult personal lives and professional careers. Both were at one time employed by the local newspaper. Will, the more talented of the two, had purchased a newspaper in another part of the state. He had a nervous breakdown trying to run it and returned to Marshalltown to work for the *Times-Republican*. Ralph, meanwhile, encountered legal problems. He worked on the business side of the newspaper and was charged with diverting funds into his own pocket.

The union of the Ball and Wildman families was in many ways a marriage of opposites. The Ball side of the equation contained a cosmopolitan flair, a certain eccentricity, and an emphasis upon the cerebral and the intellectual. Amos Ball Jr. carried within himself an intense drive to succeed, to travel, to explore, to impress. He was a man who made every effort to improve his station. Although the Balls could be deadly serious, they also had a sharp, teasing sense of humor.

The Wildmans' nature belied their name. These were grounded, conventional people whose existence focused more on family than fame, more on farm than form. They valued the depth of their midwestern roots and were proud to be known as "old residents" of Iowa. They were a sedentary, stolid people who felt most comfortable discussing kin, baseball, local events, and the weather. Although not humorless, they lacked a sense of the absurd; their overriding preoccupation was with security and stability. Edna Ball embodied these principles. Although she reluctantly moved with her husband to Des Moines and Evanston, she spent the summers in Marshalltown with the children and the Wildman family. She had a "homing pigeon instinct for Marshalltown." In the twilight of her life, when hospitalized for senility, Edna always "imagined herself in a train going back to her beloved Marshalltown."[18]

There were, however, notable similarities between the Balls and Wildmans. Both families were religiously Methodist, politically Republican, and socially conservative. Each had its share of personal scandal, stress, and travail. Both closed ranks against outsiders and reified the concept *family*. Both were grounded in the Midwest.

Yet the Balls and the Wildmans sensed that they were very different. Each family discussed the other's shortcomings. The Wildmans considered the Balls to be arrogant, ambitious, and pretentious. The Balls thought the Wildmans pedestrian, boring, and parochial. In the words of one observer on the Ball side: "The Wildmans weren't much on intellectual conversation. . . . They had no intellectual interests. . . . They spent their time discussing the weather. If they were farmers, they discussed the crops and what they had eaten for breakfast or lunch or dinner."[19]

Although preeminently a Ball influenced by his extraordinary father, George Ball also carried within himself the midwestern flavor of the Wildmans. Along with his two older brothers, he grew up in a local Iowan environment in which his mother, Edna, and his grandmother Eleanor Kimberley Wildman provided a protective and controlled cover. As the youngest of three, George was particularly cuddled and coddled.

George Ball in Des Moines

As a baby and young child, George Wildman Ball's physical appearance was dominated by his head. It seemed disproportionately large, noticeably so: Edna was embarrassed to take the baby out into public. Family members quietly joked that this signified brilliance, that George needed a large cranium as a receptacle for what was sure to be an exceptional brain. As time passed and the growth of George's body caught up with his head, it became clear that these early casual comments carried considerable truth. Both parents, especially Amos, stressed intellectual pursuits. George began reading at age four. He penned impressive letters to Santa Claus, kept a personal diary at age eleven, served as sports editor of his grade school newspaper, and published a short story in the Des Moines *Evening Tribune* when he was in the fifth grade.

In early December 1917, young George wrote Santa Claus to the following effect: "I am sending you in what I want for Christmas. I'd like to have a tool chest and a few other things I think you can judge for yourself." In his letter a year later, he wrote: "I have been wishing for a vice [*sic*] for quite a while. I would like one like this illustration may show you." Enclosed was a picture of a "woodworkers' vise" that sold for $2.10. George signed his Santa requests, "Your friend, George Wildman Ball."

Typical entries in young George's personal diary reveal a vocabulary and style well beyond the average eleven-year-old's. *Sunday, December 26, 1920:* "Rose about 11:00. I didn't go to church for various reasons. One, too late. Had chicken for dinner. Retired 'bout nine." *Wednesday, January 19, 1921:* "Woke up with the expectancy of passing in a few days. Having lots of tests. Pulled through." *Friday, February 11, 1921:* "Pulled through and encountered some trials and tribulations." *Sunday, February 13, 1921:* "Reverend McDade preached the best sermon I have ever heard." *Tuesday, February 15, 1921:* "Received nothing, gave nothing."

Besides attending church on Sundays, the Amos Ball family engaged in one other family ritual. Every Saturday after lunch, the five Balls would leave their home at 1329 East Walnut and walk the ten blocks to the Des Moines Public Library. The imposing structure of sandstone and marble was George Ball's favorite home away from home. Here, the Balls would spend the afternoon reading and checking books in and out. In the evening, the Ball family procession would make its way back up Walnut Street. Each member of the family carried a satchel containing reading material for the next week. As George Ball recalled sixty years later, this "was a weekly adventure to which we all looked forward." [20]

At home, the Balls enjoyed reading aloud to one another. According to the oldest son, Stuart, the family began doing this "in order to get mother to read more." [21] In the evenings before bedtime, the boys would take turns reading aloud.

Reading aloud in the family setting was a pastime that George Ball promoted all his life.

George Ball grew up in an atmosphere of discussion and debate. Led by Amos, who was engaged in his own campaign of self-education, the family supper table was the scene of robust and outspoken intellectual interaction. Stuart, who harbored a fascination with history and genealogy, was an active participant in the ongoing family seminar, as was young George. Representative of the Wildman tradition that stressed harmony and friendly small talk, Edna and second son Ralph usually sat by as uncomfortable onlookers. When George carried the Ball style of intellectual combat to school and engaged his fourth-grade teacher in debate, the instructor resented the challenge. The feud that developed between teacher and student ended only when Edna marched into the school and had her son transferred to another class.

Amos and Stuart were worthy and mature intellectual opponents, and George often found himself intellectually outmaneuvered. When this occurred, he developed a tactic at a very early age that was to be of use throughout his career. Finding himself in an untenable position in which his arguments had failed to carry the day, the boy would slowly and deliberately fold up his napkin and softly but clearly pronounce: "Thank you very much. I'm through. Please excuse me." And he would leave the room. In making this orderly retreat, he learned to accept the inevitable and rarely carried personal grudges. The next day he would appear at the family table fresh and enthusiastically prepared to debate other topics.[22]

Amos Ball taught his sons to be observant and aware. During family walks, for example, he would suddenly stop and ask the children to describe the message found on a sign that they had just passed. He deliberately taught them to be alert and to develop their peripheral vision. Amos also thought it essential that the boys learn to speak with ease and confidence. To help develop this talent, he would have them stand on a chair to read and recite. In the words of Stuart, "I think it really did help to give self-possession. Just by the act of standing up on a chair, you knew the eyes of the family were all on you. You learned to feel the sense of eyes looking at you and not letting it bother you."[23]

The family move from Des Moines to Evanston in 1922 was traumatic only for Edna, who found herself even farther removed from her Marshalltown family nest. She compensated for this by taking her sons there to spend the summers. George, who savored the life of larger cities, deeply resented these periods back in the small town. In high school now, he became restless and easily bored; he strove to avoid the long Wildman family discussions, which he viewed as interminable and inane chattering. He found solace in reading, exploring, and joining Stuart in playing practical jokes on Ralph or his Wildman cousins.

Northwestern University and the Road to Law

There was never any doubt in the mind of Amos Ball that his sons would attend college. There was never any doubt in the mind of Edna Wildman that her sons would attend college as close to home as possible. Fortunately for Edna, Evanston was the seat of a fine university, Northwestern. All three sons earned their B.A. degrees at Northwestern; all three graduated from Northwestern Law School. In their imaginations, Amos and Edna foresaw a law firm named Ball, Ball and Ball.

His Northwestern years provided an enormously liberating experience for George Ball. He majored in English literature and refined his writing skills, skills that had already reflected great potential when he was a young boy. As an undergraduate at Northwestern, George attached himself intellectually to a brilliant, argumentative, and arrogant young teacher named Bernard DeVoto. DeVoto, who also influenced the thinking of Arthur Schlesinger Jr. and who later worked as editor for *Harper's* magazine, had graduated from Harvard in 1918 and taught English literature at Northwestern between 1922 and 1927. Ball became part of a cerebral group of students who were devoted followers of Benny DeVoto. In Ball's own words, DeVoto managed to transform a self-conscious, somewhat awkward young man into "an obnoxious little intellectual snob."[24] In the process, George Ball became an educated man, widely read in literature, history, and philosophy.

George Ball enrolled in honors courses in literature during both his junior and senior years. He read and especially enjoyed the works of Eliot, Joyce, Lawrence, Chesterton, Fitzgerald, and Hemingway. Among the philosophers, he much preferred Voltaire over Rousseau; he was attracted to the wittiness of Voltaire in contrast to the "cheerless" Rousseau. Years later, when Ball looked back on his education in the 1920s, he criticized his lack of course work in the physical sciences and modestly wrote: "I was too narrowly concerned with the arts of expression to know how little I had to express."[25]

More significantly, Ball decried the narrow, parochial perspective that seemed to pervade America in the 1920s. "We cared little for the world around us," he said; it was "a time of mindless complacency."[26] George Ball began to resist the strong pull of his family's conservative political and social values. He disagreed with the philosophy of the Harding-Coolidge era and questioned the intellectual underpinnings of the Republican Party. In this, he stood alone against the other four members of the Ball family unit. Stuart and Ralph, like their parents, were lifelong Republicans and chose to anchor themselves deeply in the soil of the Midwest. George found himself in a minority of one in the heated political discussions that took place around the Ball dinner table. He became an iconoclast within his own family.

Although George Ball had briefly toyed with the idea of pursuing a Ph.D. in English literature, he chose to enter Northwestern Law School. Here he did well, graduating near the top of his class. He found the study of law interesting, but later he admitted that the law degree provided a more important commodity: a passport that enabled him "to move easily back and forth across that prickly border between the public and private sectors."[27]

When Ball graduated from law school in the spring of 1933, he acquired a degree that was to serve him well for the rest of his life. In the process, he also found a lifelong partner. On September 16, 1932, he married Ruth Murdoch, and the two formed a union that was to last for more than sixty years.

Ruth Murdoch from Pittsburgh

During the summer of 1929, when George Ball was between his junior and senior years of college and his brothers Ralph and Stuart were enrolled in Northwestern Law School, mother Edna encouraged the three boys to make a trip to Europe. This uncharacteristic act by a protective mother is made comprehensible by the fact that her oldest son was engaged to be married, and Edna hoped that the trip abroad would cool a relationship she considered premature. Her plan backfired badly when Stuart was married a year later; furthermore, her youngest son George developed a relationship in Europe that was to lead to marriage as well.

Ruth Murdoch, a young woman from a well-to-do Pittsburgh family, was touring Europe in the summer of 1929. A graduate of Wooster College, Ruth had enrolled in the Department of Painting and Decoration at the Carnegie Institute of Technology and was traveling with her college roommate and a chaperone. In Paris, the Pittsburgh girls met the three Ball brothers, the two groups melded into one, and the young people experienced the excitement of Paris together. Later they managed to rendezvous in Nice, Rome, and London. At a time when the stock market was crashing in Prohibition America, this group of students danced and partied their way across Europe. At George's instigation, the Balls changed their return voyage plans and booked passage aboard the *Caronia*, enabling George to spend more time with Ruth.

The excitement, romance, and fascination of Europe was heady stuff for George Ball in this, his first trip abroad. He and Ruth Murdoch were immediately drawn to one another. Both were well educated and well read. They began reading aloud to one another aboard the *Caronia*, a pastime that they were to pursue for more than sixty years. Engaged at the time, Ruth Murdoch found that attachment "deflected by George," who won her heart and her promise to marry him. For the next three years, the couple maintained contact by mail, occasionally visiting one another. From time to time, George would visit Ruth in Pittsburgh, but it was not until September 1930, at the time of Stuart's wedding to Marion

Watrous, that Ruth traveled to Evanston. In Ruth's words, "I had been invited repeatedly to Evanston but my stuffy family thought it was more suitable to have George do the calling."[28]

Ruth, who "suffered agonies of shyness" when she met Amos and Edna, was both impressed and unimpressed with the Ball-Wildman clan, whom she observed in their element in Marshalltown, Iowa, after the wedding. She was "startled" by the Wildman house, which she described as "a small, frame house, hot and badly designed." She wondered to herself, "Where had all the Wildmans slept?" In interacting with the Balls and Wildmans, she at first worried about what to say. Fortunately, she soon discovered that this was no problem because "the Ball Family liked to have the floor."[29]

Ruth Murdoch's excursion into the central Midwest left her with mixed feelings: "The people and the land were new to me. I didn't like the land. It was flat except for a few little hills in Iowa. But the people have stamina. . . . I grew to admire them."[30]

Born on June 4, 1905, Ruth Sneathen Murdoch was the daughter of a Scot-Irish father and a mother of Dutch origin. Her father, James Bleakley Murdoch, was a horticulturist who raised flowers and had a lifelong addiction to travel. He raised his family, Ruth and her older sister Virginia, in Canonsburg, Pennsylvania, before moving to nearby Pittsburgh. Ruth's mother, Sarah Sneathen, was a deeply religious woman who read widely, enjoyed writing, and was also enamored of international travel. On both sides, therefore, Ruth was part of a family "restless to see the world." Ruth first traveled to Europe when she was five and spent numerous summers afterward traveling abroad with her parents. "Our summer explorations had a range of three continents, and we used any available means of transportation, including Western pack horses, Mexican burros, and Egyptian camels."[31]

The James Murdoch family witnessed its share of trials and tribulations. Besides suffering a stillbirth, Sarah lost two children in their infancy. Ruth suffered two consecutive summers with severe attacks of typhoid fever, a disease that killed her mother.

Ruth Murdoch was an extremely attractive woman. Standing 5 feet 6 inches, with high, aristocratic cheekbones, she reflected a quiet elegance. She was a strong woman who placed a very high value on personal privacy. As such, she was a product of her father's clan. "The Murdochs were steady Scots and taciturn. They did not voice their reminiscences."[32] She had a stubborn resilience and a willingness to seek the new and the different.

Ruth Murdoch also had a deep social conscience. The year before she was married, she returned from a trip to South America, put away her paintbrushes, and took a position as social worker in Pittsburgh. Plunged in the depths of the Depression, Pittsburgh was the scene of great unemployment and poverty. Ruth

Murdoch spent much of 1931 and 1932 looking after three hundred poor families in the slums of her hometown. Like her fiancé, she was a lonely Democrat in a staunchly Republican family.

With her marriage to George Ball, Ruth Murdoch took on the role of solid, loyal, and admiring wife who spent her life backing, supporting, and praising her husband. In her personal diary, she once wrote: "My greatest achievement in life was not to have had a painting placed in the Metropolitan Museum but to have snagged George, a higher form of art and in my view more rewarding."[33]

Ruth Ball was a well-educated and self-confident individual in her own right. Intellectually, she was knowledgeable about history, archaeology, art, and architecture. It was not unusual for her to read fifty or sixty books a year, and she wrote constantly, leaving approximately ten shelf feet of unpublished manuscripts in which she described in great detail family history and travel. She not only solved crossword puzzles but composed them. One was published as the *New York Times* Sunday puzzle.

In spite of her own intellect and talent, Ruth Murdoch chose consciously to build her entire existence around her husband. In the words of her youngest son: "Like her biblical namesake, she believed that it was her job to promote her husband's career, not her own interests. Thus, wherever he went, she went also." She was there whenever George needed her. "I keep myself available for hunting lost papers, clippings, books, stationery materials and the like—an eager Spaniel, waiting to retrieve." According to one close family friend, if George were to rush home and say to Ruth that they were leaving in the morning for the Arctic to live for five years, Ruth would simply begin packing the bags.[34]

Ruth was a fanatically loyal spouse who bristled furiously whenever anyone even hinted at criticism of George. In the graphic words of her older son: "She identified her role in life as standing at the foot of the pedestal and making sure that the pedestal was always clean and never got disturbed. And don't ever criticize the person standing on the pedestal or you got yourself into serious trouble."[35]

Ruth Ball's diaries are filled with paeans of praise for her husband, whom she defended fiercely. In 1970 and 1971, when George Ball was consulted by the Nixon administration, Ruth proudly referred to him as "my indispensable spouse," who was "chummily" called "George" by such politicos as Melvin Laird, Henry Kissinger, and William Rogers. When her husband received an honorary doctorate of law from Harvard in 1973, Ruth wrote that she was extremely proud of "Georgie," who was now "fully equipped to impose wise restraints that will ensure our freedom" during the dark days of Watergate. In 1980 she wrote: "George just keeps struggling as the majority of humankind play golf or stupidly view the boob tube."[36]

On September 16, 1932, George Ball married Ruth Murdoch in a small Presbyterian chapel in Pittsburgh. Because Ruth's father had recently died of a stroke, the ceremony was a small, quiet family affair. Although George had another year of law school left, Amos and Edna approved the wedding and agreed to pay rent of sixty dollars a month for the newlyweds' apartment in Evanston. Because the Ball family did not approve of drinking, champagne was not served at the dinner. After dinner, the couple took a train to New York. They spent the evening there, then took a boat to Bermuda, where they spent two weeks on an idyllic honeymoon.

It was not long into their marriage before Ruth found herself engulfed by and absorbed into the Ball clan. Among other things, Edna handed her a list of nineteen Ball and Wildman names—relatives who were to receive Christmas gifts, including an uncle who would like a box of Havana cigars and an aunt who should receive silk slips. Although she quietly resented such intrusions, Ruth slowly and quietly gave way before the force of The Family. Ruth did not feel the full impact of this kinship, however, until George had completed law school in 1933.

Upon graduation, George received an invitation to work in the Farm Credit Administration in Washington. A Columbia University lawyer and professor named Herman Oliphant was gathering young, bright, energetic graduates to participate in the New Deal. The dean of Northwestern's law school recommended George Ball as his candidate. George and Ruth were elated. An evening with The Family was planned. Expecting a congratulatory celebration, Ruth prepared a tray of cookies and an assortment of soft drinks for the auspicious occasion. Her description of the evening is revealing. To Ruth's "utter astonishment," the gathering was not a celebration "but a sort of board meeting to decide whether George should accept the job or not. They were all present. Some had misty eyes, as though George had been condemned to a leper colony for the remainder of his life." Ruth's outrage deepened when she discovered that her opinion was not to be considered.

"For two hours the matter was discussed, and never once was I asked my view. For a year I assumed that I was a member of The Family. . . . This experience taught me that I was still an outsider and that neither George nor I had The Family's respect as mature adults. We were merely children to be supervised."

Because of George's determination and persuasive skills, The Family, with a sad shaking of its collective head, reluctantly agreed to the Washington adventure. Ruth's reaction: "I was quite scornful of the whole proceeding. My in-laws lost stature in my estimation. What had happened to the courage of immigrants and frontiersman, that their vision was so limited? I said nothing to them or to George about my indignation. We had won our chance for the future." [37]

The Three Ball Brothers

The saga of George and Ruth Ball, their two sons, George's brothers, and all the in-laws is one that intertwines division with solidarity, anguish with contentment. Every twig and branch of the Ball family tree contains some sap of sorrow. Entangled in his professional career, George Ball was a driven man. His ambition and self-imposed standards of excellence forced him into the role of absentee husband and father. He was never able to turn his full attention upon family matters but struggled to deal with them on the run. When a family crisis developed, George would drop everything and rush to the occasion. His professional ambitions, however, never permitted him to attend to the everyday responsibilities essential to the careful nurturing of family health. These responsibilities fell by default upon the shoulders of Ruth.

George Ball's brothers, Stuart and Ralph, remained in the Midwest all their lives. Over the years, George developed a warm relationship with the oldest brother, Stuart, an intellectual in his own right. Stuart was a true gentleman and a lawyer's lawyer, who rose to the presidency of Montgomery Ward. He was fired in September 1952 by the autocratic chairman of the board, Sewell L. Avery, a man described in the Chicago newspapers as "impetuous and imperialistic." Stuart Ball departed his post in dignity and refused to attack Avery personally. In his farewell speech before the Junior Association of Commerce and Industry, Ball simply warned against hero worship and stated that the individual "must never surrender the right and ability to form independent judgment."[38] Stuart went on to practice law successfully; he was a superb trial lawyer who argued several cases before the United States Supreme Court.

Stuart Ball was a family man who left a modest estate, having spent much of his earnings on his home, travel, and the expensive needs of his three wives (he was twice widowed). He was extremely proud of his youngest brother, and throughout George's career Stuart regularly arranged speeches for George in the Chicago area. George, in turn, respected his brother's intellect but sometimes felt that Stu was a bit too professorial and lacked the fiery ambition of their father, Amos.

The second brother was a tragic figure, whose life eerily paralleled that of his namesake uncle, Ralph Wildman. Of the three Ball boys, Ralph Kimberley Ball, the middle brother, was increasingly the odd man out. When asked why Ralph is mentioned only once in passing in his autobiography, George Ball curtly explained: "Actually, we didn't have much in common."[39] Ralph, a railroad buff, did not share his brothers' fondness for ideas or high-powered intellectual debate. On May 18, 1977, Ralph Kimberley Ball was killed after falling under a railroad train in San Diego. Like his Wildman uncle, he had been involved in certain financial indiscretions and had made several ill-advised investments. Among other things, he borrowed large sums of money from the Amos Ball Trust without the authority of his brothers and trustees. He then invested this money in unproductive ventures.

On the other hand, Ralph was an extremely warm and friendly individual, who looked after his parents in their old age when Stuart and George tended to shrug off the responsibility. He was a low-key, personable figure whose legal specialty was trusts and probate. Stuart's oldest daughter counted Ralph as her favorite uncle despite his financial indiscretions; he was, in her words, "a very gentle heart."[40]

In response to Ralph's difficulties, The Family closed ranks to protect itself and its reputation. Over the years and despite his heavy professional schedule, George slowly took over more of The Family's responsibilities. He was only partly successful in this role, a role he accepted grudgingly and reluctantly. His most serious problems developed from within his own family unit, a unit carefully shaped and nurtured by Ruth and somewhat incidentally and sporadically influenced by George himself.

The Nuclear Family at War and Peace

Unable to have children of their own, George and Ruth Ball adopted two baby boys. John Ball "arrived" in 1936, while second son Douglas joined the Balls in 1939. George and Ruth were living in Evanston at the time. George had returned from his first stint in Washington, where, beginning in 1933, he had worked with the Farm Credit Administration, then transferred to the Treasury Department. In Washington he inhaled the intoxicating vapors of the New Deal and became an ardent admirer of Franklin Roosevelt. "The times were ebullient and yeast was in the air."[41] During these first two years in Washington, Ball began establishing contacts that were to help him for years to come. Although he worked closely with Henry Morgenthau Jr., his most important new acquaintance was a thirty-eight-year-old lawyer he met on the handball court. His playing partner was named Dean Acheson.

In April 1935, Ball returned to Evanston, where he took a position as a tax lawyer in a local law firm. He was extremely unhappy with this assignment. Not only did he find the work tedious, but he discovered that his ideas were quite incompatible with those of his colleagues. George found himself "quarreling with everyone who attacked the New Deal—and everyone did." Furthermore, he was annoyed that his partners did not appreciate his talent and experience. As Ruth recalled, the firm had dared to "put *him* to doing footwork; George Ball, whose first legal drafting in Washington involved a contract for $37,000,000. . . . George was very cast down." In 1939 he accepted a job with the prestigious firm of Sidley, McPherson, Austin, and Harper.[42]

At the new law firm, Ball became well acquainted with a junior partner and kindred spirit named Adlai E. Stevenson. As two lonely Democrats in the Sidley firm, they bonded quickly, and Ball joined Stevenson at the Chicago Council of Foreign Relations, an influential organization that Adlai chaired and promoted.

Together, Ball and Stevenson spent hours discussing domestic and international political issues. They were to remain personal friends and political compadres until Stevenson's death twenty-five years later.

With Adlai Stevenson's intervention on his behalf, Ball returned to Washington in 1942 to take a position as associate general counsel for the Lend-Lease program. Here, too, he fashioned new personal ties and lasting contacts, working with and befriending such individuals as John Kenneth Galbraith, Oscar Cox, Philip Graham, Eugene Rostow, Lloyd Cutler, and Daniel Boorstin.

When George and Ruth moved back to Washington, their sons John and Doug were six and three years old, respectively. Taking residence in Arlington, Virginia, the Balls began a style of family life that was to prevail for many years to come. George threw himself into his work with a vengeance and spent less and less time at home. He increasingly became an absentee father. This pattern hardened when, after a stint with the Foreign Economic Administration, he left for London to help direct the U.S. Strategic Bombing Survey. Ball was awarded a Medal of Freedom for his contributions to the USSBS. In the process, he came into contact with many individuals who were to be lifelong friends.

Working closely with John Kenneth Galbraith and Paul Nitze, Ball brought Adlai Stevenson over to work as his deputy. His experience with the Strategic Bombing Survey convinced Ball that wars could not be won from the air alone, no matter how many tons of bombs were dropped on a nation. Galbraith shared Ball's conclusions and, despite air force pressures, they produced a sophisticated statistical report that cast doubt on the effectiveness of air raids. This report noted "the astonishing ability to absorb air attacks displayed by the German civilian population" and concluded that "air raids prior to 1944 had relatively little effect on the output of weapons and ammunition."[43] Ball agreed with Galbraith's view that "strategic bombing was a disappointment" and that it "did not appreciably shorten the war."[44]

Along with Nitze and Galbraith, Ball spent a week in May 1945 debriefing Albert Speer, Hitler's minister of economics and Nazi Germany's production czar. In Galbraith's words, the interrogation "was brilliantly led by George Ball. Few men in our time have George's gift for improvisation. A mere suggestion as to a line of questioning and he would take it up in the manner of a man who had been thinking of nothing else for weeks."[45] Speer confirmed Ball's conclusion that the Allied bombing campaign made little critical difference in the outcome of the war. Speer pointed out, for example, that by bombing many small businesses, the Allies unwittingly freed up German labor for more productive war use. George Ball spent nearly a year abroad in 1944–45, and Ruth was left to raise the boys.

These war years were a particularly trying time for Ruth, who underwent two difficult surgeries while George was away, including a traumatic hysterectomy. George rushed home to be with Ruth for ten days after her first surgery and then returned a few months later when she had a kidney removed. Although he recognized that he was needed far more seriously on the home front and had no obligation to return to Europe, his ambition got the best of him. In his words, he acted "in inexcusable self-indulgence" and returned to England. "I do not regard that as my finest hour."[46]

These events proved to be an important if unfortunate watershed in the personal dynamics of the George Ball family unit. In Ruth's revealing words, "nothing was very reassuring as it had been in the ordered days of the Evanston years. I wanted to be back there in much the same way as Edna had longed for her Iowa parents' home. The war had not brought us tragedy and hardship as it had done to most of the world. But I knew it had changed me in a way that I did not like and that a sense of this would stay with me."[47] When George returned, the couple began to quarrel frequently and the relationship never quite seemed to be the same again.

From the beginning, the sons were a problem, especially John, a sensitive young man who felt uprooted by the move East and by the absence of his father. He was tormented throughout much of his life with poor health and bad luck. As a boy, he endured a series of ear infections; as a teenager he developed a stomach ulcer; later, he endured a bad back; and in 1982 he underwent quadruple bypass surgery. John, a charming and candid gentleman of considerable musical talent, earned his undergraduate degree from Swarthmore. After a year's study at the University of London, he earned a master's in Arabic studies from the American University in Beirut. Professionally, he became a financial analyst specializing in special situations research. Over the years, he worked for several different investment firms. His personal life was also unsettled; he married twice before finding a compatible, talented, and solid partner, Linda Ottandant. His second marriage produced a daughter and a son who were doted on by George and especially Ruth. The news of the second divorce was a terrible blow to Ruth and a major disappointment to George.

With George either away or completely absorbed by his work, John developed an antagonistic relationship with Ruth. Nor did he feel any deep affection for his father. Later in life, he frankly admitted his feelings for his parents. When asked, "Do you feel your father loved you?" John replied, "I have no idea. I think mother did but I never cared much for her. Her strict Scottish upbringing and my cavalier attitude toward life were 180 degrees apart." John frankly admits that he had a violent temper and that he and Ruth had some "hellacious fights."[48]

It is instructive to note that John Ball had a special love and admiration for his grandparents, Amos and Edna. He describes his feelings for Amos in the following words: "I loved that man. He was a superb human being. Now there was a father." He describes his grandmother Edna as "sweet" and "absolutely wonderful." When once reminded that George, Ruth, and Douglas described Edna and the Wildmans as boring, John scathingly responded, "They were boring. But they were something else. They were real. You could reach out and touch them and you felt flesh, not godly marble."[49]

Part of the reason for John's strong feelings and for the general climate of family tension is found in the character and personality of the second son, Douglas. Douglas was brilliant from the beginning. Widely read and possessing an extraordinary memory, he had the kind of intellect that impressed his grandfather and his father. Furthermore, he shared his Uncle Stuart's interests in genealogy and history. As the younger son, he was coddled and favored by Ruth, who was also in awe of her son's brilliance. As a child, Douglas was incorrigible and mischievous. The family annals are filled with examples of Doug's antics. Although he had a dry wit and unconventional sense of humor, he could also be very naive. Ruth recalled when the family dog, Ruggie, died before his time by ingesting lime he had discovered in the basement. Soon afterward, Ruth served Douglas a glass of limeade. Doug was horrified and refused to touch the drink. He suspected that his mother was trying to poison him and that he would go the way of Ruggie.

In social discourse, Douglas tended to dominate discussion, even in the presence of his father. His encyclopedic knowledge was such that, even as a child, he spoke with great authority on a myriad of issues. He spoke not in sentences, but in paragraphs and pages, and his conversation tended to take the form of strings of confident pronouncements and proclamations. As a result, he never really fit into any conventional educational setting. Furthermore, as with many individuals of uncommon brilliance, he lacked social graces.

In spite of his many idiosyncracies, Douglas Ball graduated from Wooster College and went on to earn an M.A. in history from Yale and a Ph.D. in economics from the London School of Economics. In 1991, he published a book on the financial basis for the defeat of the Confederacy. Throughout his life, however, he was unable to find a satisfactory academic position. This was true despite considerable assistance from both Ruth and George. At one point, Doug sent out nine hundred résumés with little response. In her diaries, Ruth often discussed the frustrations involved in Doug's job search. Always loyal to her family, she took it personally. After the history department at Erie in 1974 recommended him for a position, the dean demurred. As Ruth put it: "This miserable clot had to come down with a virus for ten days and could not be disturbed. While he was busily charting his temperature, some imbecile with tenure turned up and got the job because of his teaching experience."[50] George himself used all his connections and contacts in a huge effort to find his son an academic position—to no avail.

In the end, Doug, a good-hearted individual with a somewhat gruff demeanor, became a professional numismatist with a special expertise in the field of Confederate banknotes. He encountered difficulties in this career that required his father's interventionary assistance on more than one occasion. Once, for example, an ill-chosen business partner bilked him of a considerable sum of money. George simply picked up the tab for the misadventure.

Although Douglas Ball was never altogether comfortable with his parents (he described relations between father and sons as "peculiar"), he remained close to them.[51] Living and working in New York, he commuted to Princeton regularly, visited and gardened with his mother, played tennis and worked as a research assistant for George, and in the end cowrote his father's last book. John, on the other hand, was seldom close at hand. Psychologically and geographically, he remained remote from the family. Because Doug was the favored one, the intellectual, the young genius, the chosen one, John always felt himself somewhat of an unappreciated appendage—in his words, the prodigal son.

The George Ball family unit was in many ways dysfunctional. As time passed and his political career brightened, the pattern of professional precedence over family considerations that had been established in 1944–45 became institutionalized. Often, this absenteeism involved extended trips overseas. Although Ruth accompanied him abroad from time to time, most of the trips left Ruth behind with the boys. Furthermore, George loved the night life, the dinners, the dancing, the drinking, the parties, and the occasional flirtation. His was a bon vivant existence. Over the years, Ruth came to resent this, although she was careful to keep her feelings to herself.

Ruth called on George for assistance whenever a serious problem arose in the family. When this occurred, he would drop whatever he was doing and rush to the scene of the crisis. He was always available with the necessary financial aid. He never deserted his family in time of emergency. In this sense, he was not unlike his father, Amos. He was constantly bailing his sons and others out of trouble. In the words of his elder son, "He was always there with the money."[52]

In spite of the financial assistance, George Ball's sons did not consider him to be a loving father. He was not demonstrative of his feelings, and most of his life was preoccupied with professional and political issues. The older son, John, felt unloved, while Douglas, who was often trapped in the middle of confrontations between George and Ruth or between John and Ruth, found himself under enormous stress. Beginning in 1957, he began two years of professional counseling.

Behind this sad scenario, though, both Ruth and George, in their own ways, tried to make the family work. On rare occasions, George would express his feelings in writing. In a moving letter to Douglas in April 1986, for example, he advised his son to publish a book in order to find a place in academia. After praising Douglas for having given "your mother and me great happiness over the past 47 years," "for your demonstrated brilliant talents in a variety of fields," and for making "ordinary occasions special by your presence," George concluded that his suggestions "are born of love for you. We want to see you fulfill your very remarkable talents and thus achieve the tranquil state of mind which makes that possible."[53]

Birthdays and holidays were special events and were celebrated elaborately. The one anchoring event that did much to hold the family together was an annual Christmas visit to Cocoa Beach, Florida, where Amos Ball had purchased a house in a lovely beach setting. Here, beginning in 1945, The Family built a tradition of spending the Christmas holidays as a working, playing, relaxing, celebrating normal unit. For thirty-five years, between 1945 and 1980, The Ball family (and, on occasion, close friends and other relatives) spent their Christmases at Cocoa Beach.

The Building of European and Washington Communities

George Ball spent the decade of the 1940s preoccupied with European affairs. He developed a close association with the French thinker and activist Jean Monnet, and in 1946 he helped found a law firm that was to become one of the most distinguished in America: Cleary, Gottlieb, Friendly and Cox, later known as Cleary, Gottlieb, Steen and Hamilton.

No single individual, with the possible exception of his father, had more influence on the thinking and political methodology of George Wildman Ball than Jean Monnet. Monnet was a short, quiet French visionary who dedicated his life to the establishment of a European community. Like Amos Ball, Monnet was a self-educated and self-made man. George had first met Monnet during his employment at Lend-Lease, and in 1946 Monnet approached Ball to represent the interests of the French Supply Council.

Ball spent the second half of the 1940s and much of the 1950s working closely with Monnet. Like so many others, George was caught up in Monnet's web of dreams for a better world, for an integrated and united Europe. At Monnet's side, Ball watched a master politician at work. He admired Monnet's sense of the future and his understanding of a transforming world. He described Monnet as "preeminently a modern man," a man who perceived "the nature of the great tidal forces" at work in the world.

While sharing Monnet's commitment to ideals and a sense of the future, Ball also learned much about Monnet, the tough, dedicated, manipulative politician. He respected what he termed the "peasant shrewdness" of Monnet, "who had the capacity for gathering around himself the most impressive intellectuals, picking their brains, and inspiring them to work in almost a kamikaze devotion."[54]

Ball noted how Monnet avoided public positions while at the same time building strong personal ties with individuals in the bureaucracy who actually made the key decisions and who shaped policy behind the scenes. Monnet stressed careful communication and insisted on attention to detail in framing letters and documents. Ball was particularly impressed by the way Monnet captured victory from defeat, progress from setback, and success from disappointment. George Ball often commented on the unusual capacity of Monnet to convert crises into opportunities.

Having spent these early formative years of grassroots politics at the side of Monnet, Ball was a dedicated Europeanist and a committed proponent of European integration throughout his life. He remained in close touch with Jean Monnet until the man known as Mr. Europe died in March 1979.

When Jean Monnet first approached Ball, he did so through the newly formed law firm of Cleary, Gottlieb. With a Washington acquaintance from the early 1940s, Fowler Hamilton, and Hamilton's friend Hugh Cox, George Ball joined George Cleary, Leo Gottlieb, Henry Friendly, and Melvin Steen in the formation of the new law firm. According to his wife Ruth, what George wanted at this point was "status, financial opportunity, and freedom of action."[55]

At Cleary, Gottlieb, Ball fashioned a French connection: the first client he brought to the firm was the French government, a "real coup" on his part.[56] Ball pioneered the opening of Cleary, Gottlieb offices in Paris in 1949 and Brussels in 1960, advised the major French industrial federation known as the French Patronat, and designed a monthly newsletter entitled *France Actuelle* that provided U.S. industry with information about French commercial trends.

George Ball internationalized Cleary, Gottlieb and developed a very special relation with the firm. He was termed a "founding father" and remained a hero even after he left the firm as an active partner to join the Kennedy administration in 1961. After his government service, he continued his association as honorary counsel. Ball cherished his relationship with Cleary, Gottlieb throughout his life. Several of the founding fathers of the firm were, like Ball, natives of the Midwest. George Cleary himself was born in Wisconsin; Fowler Hamilton was born and raised in Missouri; Hugh Cox was born in Iowa and raised in Nebraska; Melvin Steen was from Minnesota. These were kindred spirits as well as friends and colleagues. In the twilight of his life in January 1990, George Ball wrote Jerome Hyman, an old friend at Cleary, Gottlieb. His concluding sentence summarized his feelings: "I value my association with Cleary, Gottlieb above all other events in my life." Younger colleagues like Ned Stiles spoke of Ball as "a giant among men." Stiles pointed out that "despite his relatively short tenure as a partner, no one had a greater influence in shaping the future of Cleary, Gottlieb."[57]

The late 1940s represented a time when George Ball, working from a new foundation of institutional support (Cleary, Gottlieb) and along with an extraordinary French thinker (Monnet), refined many of his ideas on international economic relations and regional integration. Europe and U.S.-European relations provided the laboratory for his experiments and the testing grounds for his theories. Like Monnet, Ball threw himself completely into his work and found himself constantly in transit across the Atlantic. Ruth estimated that between the end of the war and the mid-1950s, George made more than one hundred trips to Europe. In fact, he shuttled to Paris every month for a decade.

Aside from a family cruise to Europe in the summer of 1948, George's trips abroad during this period were strictly business treks. Ruth recorded unhappily in her diary that George was away "almost half the time." Nonetheless, she pointedly wrote, "I did not complain." According to Ruth, "The genius of Jean Monnet so mesmerized the intellectuals about him that other matters could wait." The two rambunctious sons, John and Douglas, who had "their ups and downs," tested Ruth's patience. Other personal family issues presented further challenges.[58]

In February 1947, George had a cancerous kidney removed. He now joined Ruth as members of the single-kidney club. In 1949, the Balls moved into a new home at 35th and Woodley near the Washington Cathedral. Here they were to reside for two decades.

That December, a small event occurred that reveals much about George Ball and the dynamics of his family. Before the drive to Cocoa Beach for the annual Ball Christmas celebration, the family hurriedly packed the car, loading it with suitcases, briefcases, typewriters, bird cages, tennis rackets, golf clubs, Christmas presents, lunch boxes, cartons of scotch and bourbon, and a telescope. Packing the car in the garage, they attached a luggage rack to the top of the automobile and laboriously crammed it to the brim. Early the next morning, they awoke early, and George, anxious to get on the road for the mad dash to Florida, herded everyone into the car. Outside, a steady, icy rain was falling. George started to back out of the garage but encountered a snag. The garage door lacked clearance for a loaded luggage rack.

Amidst considerable cursing and shouting, "George threw himself into frenzied exertions of untying the tarpaulin, unloading the bags, unscrewing the rack and driving out into the rain. There, in the deluge, the car's elaborate superstructure had to be set up again."[59] Once it was repacked, the family settled in for a twenty-hour ride directly from Washington, D.C., to Cocoa Beach, Florida. Once in an automobile, George would hunker down behind the wheel and drive single-mindedly for his destination. He would allow no stops for food; sandwiches and drinks were carried in the car. The driver of the Ballmobile stopped only for fuel and to collect speeding citations. The record time for the annual December race from Washington to Florida was seventeen hours. George Ball was truly a driven man.

Political Ideals and Practical Realities: Stevenson and Bilderberg

The atmosphere of the early 1950s in America was contaminated by the stench of McCarthyism, which carried fear and distrust into the highest echelons of government. Although many political figures tiptoed for cover, a few refused to be intimidated and stood up in defense of the principles of the U.S. Constitution. Because George Ball was a discriminating joiner, he was never associated with any groups that could be labeled as communist fronts. Nonetheless, he worked with such colleagues as Leon Lipson and Adam Yarmolinsky at Cleary, Gottlieb to defend many of those who were falsely accused by McCarthyite organizations. Ball despised McCarthyism and its climate of fear.

In the fall of 1951, Ball received a call from Joseph Alsop. The conservative, tough journalist reported that Henry Wallace had been summoned to appear before the McCarran subcommittee, which was busy investigating alleged communist sympathizers in the U.S. government. Wallace, a former vice president, secretary of agriculture, and secretary of commerce in the administrations of Franklin Roosevelt and Harry Truman, was a liberal idealist with Iowan roots. Ball, like Alsop, considered Wallace to be a somewhat muddled if well-meaning political innocent. Nonetheless, they both felt that Wallace deserved the right to defense and counsel. Alsop told Ball that he had been turned down by every competent lawyer in town and asked whether George would defend Wallace before the McCarran committee. Ball courageously agreed to help. He found Wallace to be "modest, compassionate, and gentle, but the obstinacy of his idealism so impelled him to reject all troubling realities that he seemed quite incapable of comprehending his own predicament."[60]

With Ball's coaching and assistance, Wallace survived the "fanatical McCarthyites, principally old women exuding venom and muttering virulent curses." On October 24, 1951, Alsop, whose political views were usually opposed to those of Ball, wrote George "to express my gratitude to you for your courageous and self-denying contribution to the common effort to make truth and decency prevail over the McCarran subcommittee. You were superb—superb to take on without cavil a task noone [sic] else had the guts to take; and superb also in your handling of a very difficult assignment. I owe you a debt which I cannot repay." Ball's personal papers contain other letters from those grateful for his representation during the difficult days when the fear of McCarthyism hung over the land.[61]

In a long letter published in the *Washington Post* on May 5, 1953, George Ball sharply criticized an Eisenhower loyalty-security order that was written to protect the federal service from subversion. In this system, security officers could level charges against government employees without disclosing the details of evidence behind such charges. Careers were easily snuffed out in this atmosphere of silent and incomplete accusation. In his hard-hitting critique, Ball argued that "an employee faced with unfounded charges can be intimidated into resigning, rather than stake his reputation in a game where the cards are stacked against him. Those employees who remain in the service will be dull where they ought to be daring, subservient where they ought to be critical. . . . What kind of recruits can our Government attract, and how effectively will it guard our national security, if it puts a premium on rigidity of thought and flexibility of principle?"[62]

It was in the 1950s that George Ball found himself involved in what a politician of the time called the real "combat of politics."[63] Besides doing battle with the dark ideological forces of McCarthyism, Ball found himself at the vortex of national presidential politics. In 1952, he strode enthusiastically into the inner circle of an old midwestern friend, the two-time Democratic presidential candidate Adlai Stevenson.

Stevenson, Nixon, and the 1952 and 1956 Presidential Campaigns

George Ball was a central player in Adlai Stevenson's inspired but impossible run for the presidency in 1952. Although he had only four years of political experience as governor of Illinois, Stevenson became the Democratic Party's candidate because of his impressive reformist record as governor and his quietly charismatic persona. The governor immediately found himself embroiled in an uphill struggle against a popular if inarticulate military hero, Dwight David Eisenhower.

Stevenson gathered around himself an impressive coterie of supporters and strategists, including Wilson Wyatt, Willard Wirtz, Bill Blair, and Carl McGowan. His speechwriters and idea men constituted perhaps the most talented group of writers ever assembled for a presidential campaign. They included Arthur Schlesinger Jr., John Kenneth Galbraith, David Bell, Bernard DeVoto, John Fischer, and Herbert Agar, among others. One other individual who was an integral part of Stevenson's inner circle and one of his leading strategists was George Ball. Ball was forty-three years old at the time, nine years younger than Governor Stevenson.

At first glance, Ball and Stevenson were sharply different personalities. Stevenson, the midwestern patrician-aristocrat, was short, dumpy, and forever rumpled. Ball, son of an Iowan Horatio Alger, was tall, neatly attired, and commanding in appearance. Although they were very different personalities, Ball and Stevenson shared a friendship that endured for more than twenty years. To be sure, the two men had much in common. Both were midwestern liberals, intellectual in approach, and internationalist in perspective. Both were lawyers, and both were highly literate and refreshingly witty. Both were, in different ways, ambitious; both sought political power.

President Harry Truman himself approached Adlai and lobbied him to be the Democratic candidate. It was George Ball, from his offices in Washington, who helped arrange the meetings between Truman and Stevenson. When in Washington, Stevenson stayed at the Ball's home, where he and George debated the pros and cons of his candidacy. Adlai insisted repeatedly that he did not want to run for the presidency, while Ball pleaded that he keep an open mind on the matter.

Stevenson's meetings with Truman were disastrous. Truman, blunt and brusque, was annoyed by Adlai's evasive and unenthusiastic attitude toward the proffered candidacy. After their first meeting in January 1952, Stevenson reported to Ball that he had "made a hash" of the session. The president, in true Truman-esque manner, had argued: "Adlai, if a knucklehead like me can be president and not do too badly, think what a really educated smart guy like you could do in the job." [64] Adlai's coyness and his later tactless and counterproductive criticisms of the Truman administration alienated the president, who, although he campaigned for Stevenson against Eisenhower in 1952 and 1956, was privately deeply disappointed in the Democratic candidate. In a letter he never mailed to the Illinois governor, Truman wrote: "I'm telling you to take your crackpots, your high socialites with their noses in the air, run your campaign and win if you can. Cowfever [Estes Kefauver, Stevenson's 1956 running mate] could not have treated me any more shabbily than you have." [65]

There were, of course, many reasons why Stevenson was reluctant to run in 1952, but Ball understood that one fundamental consideration transcended all the others. Adlai understood that no Democrat could defeat Eisenhower in 1952. Although he would not admit it, Stevenson did not relish a hard, stressful campaign in which he would play the role of political sacrificial lamb. Yet, when the Democratic Party genuinely drafted him at the convention in Chicago, Stevenson proudly accepted the nomination. In spite of his protestations, Stevenson had been careful not to take himself completely and finally out of the running.

The Democratic convention in Chicago in August of 1952 was an exhilarating and unforgettable experience for the Ball family. George arranged for Ruth, John, and Douglas to join him at the convention hotel, the Conrad Hilton on Michigan Avenue. Here, all four Balls joined in the pandemonium of the convention process. Sixteen-year-old John managed to acquire a press badge and spent long hours on the convention floor interviewing delegates. Doug was on the telephone with his father while Ruth moved back and forth between the convention arena and the television set in the hotel room. During this exciting event, George Ball brought his family into the process in a way they would never forget.

George Ball played a major role in encouraging his old friend from Illinois to remain in the race. Stevenson himself admitted George's influence in a letter he wrote to Ruth Ball: "George's interest and confidence in me is one of the most compelling reasons why I have not taken myself out of this situation conclusively and long before this." [66] But Ball did much more than nurse Adlai's ego. He set up a Stevenson information center in his Washington law office, recruited his old teacher Bernard DeVoto to put his writing talents at the disposal of the Stevenson campaign, and, along with two others, he established a Volunteers for Stevenson network across the country.

It was George Ball who introduced Adlai Stevenson both to Arthur Schlesinger Jr. and to John Kenneth Galbraith. When Ball learned that Schlesinger was going to be on the same train to Chicago as Stevenson, he asked for Schlesinger's berth and seat numbers. Ball passed this information on to Adlai, who, once aboard the train, approached Schlesinger and introduced himself. The two spent most of the trip in conversation and found that they shared many ideas and philosophies. Their friendship dated from this journey, a meeting quietly arranged by George Ball. Likewise, it was Ball who telephoned Galbraith and convinced him to come immediately to Illinois to join Stevenson's speech-writing team just after Stevenson won the Democratic nomination for the presidency.[67]

The energetic George Ball also recruited a powerful and effective finance chairman when he convinced Roger L. Stevens to join the Stevenson camp. Although relatively unknown in the early 1950s, Stevens, a talented theatrical producer who had recently purchased the Empire State Building, was an unconventional millionaire with an active social conscience. Stevens had lunch with Ball in New York and agreed to help raise money. He had not yet met Adlai Stevenson but decided to assist because he found Ball persuasive and because he had long wanted to observe the inner workings of the American political system. A Democrat himself, Stevens knew many Republican businessmen who quietly agreed to contribute to the Stevenson cause. Stevens remained a lifelong friend of George Ball.[68]

Throughout the 1952 campaign, Ball stood behind Adlai Stevenson, providing constant support and advice. Refusing to play by the traditional political rules, Adlai often took positions based not on how many votes he would garner but rather on his judgment of the merits of the cases at hand. Ball watched nervously as his candidate alienated labor, the oil industry, Catholics, the Israel lobby, and especially the right wings of both parties. Stevenson bluntly told the oil lobbyists that he opposed their attempts to gain expanded offshore rights for the states. When he refused even to take a neutral stand on the issue, his advisers told him that without the support of Texas and other oil states, he simply could not win the election. To this warning, Stevenson coldly responded, "But I don't have to win."[69] John F. Kennedy, who had mixed feelings about Stevenson, later stated: "One reason I admire him is that he is not a political whore like most of the others. Too many politicians say anything when they think it will bring them votes or money."[70]

Most importantly, Adlai Stevenson stood solidly and fearlessly against the rising tide of McCarthyism that was then washing across the land. In this political battle, he found himself taking on both Senator Joseph McCarthy and Eisenhower's thirty-nine-year-old running mate, Richard M. Nixon. Stevenson loathed Nixon and over time lost all respect for Dwight Eisenhower as well. His distaste for Eisenhower was based upon the general's refusal to defend his old friend and mentor, General George Marshall, against McCarthy's vicious personal attacks,

attacks that preposterously impugned Marshall's loyalty and patriotism. Instead, Eisenhower constantly sidestepped the issue, even going so far as to pretend that he could not hear questions from the audiences when they raised the Marshall case. These were not Ike's greatest moments.

Eisenhower used Richard Nixon as his hatchet man during the campaign. He turned the other way when Nixon, brimming with self-righteousness and political ambition, slashed away at the character and reputation of his political opponents. Nixon embraced the hatchet analogy. In September 1952 he stated: "If the dry rot of corruption and communism which has eaten deep into our body politic during the past seven years can only be chopped out with a hatchet—then let's call for a hatchet."[71]

Standing at Stevenson's side, George Ball watched incredulously as Nixon went on the attack. Besides calling Stevenson and President Truman "traitors to the high principles in which many of the nation's Democrats believe," Nixon charged that "Stevenson holds a Ph.D. degree from Acheson's College of Cowardly Communist Containment," and that "the word of Truman and Acheson, as well as that of Acheson's former assistant, Adlai Stevenson, gives the American people no hope for safety at home from the sinister threat of Communism."[72]

Although George Ball urged Adlai to strike back at Nixon, Stevenson thought it best to try to remain above the fray and to ignore the personal attacks. On a rare occasion, he would use humor in response. He once said that Nixon "was the kind of politician who would cut down a redwood tree, and then mount the stump and make a speech for conservation." He later called Nixon "McCarthy in a white collar."[73]

George Ball found nothing amusing about Nixon. For the next forty years, he opposed Nixon and his cronies whenever and wherever he could. He considered Nixon to be a serious threat to the very principles upon which the American political system was based. The Watergate revelations did not surprise Ball; in fact, he had earlier predicted that some such scandal would destroy Nixon. Richard Nixon died just one month before George Ball passed away in the spring of 1994. During the last days of his own life, Ball watched in astonishment as American leaders, including President Bill Clinton, rushed to pay homage to the disgraced former president. When Clinton declared the day of Nixon's funeral a national day of mourning, Ball, shedding his usual graciousness, did not mince words. "This is the most obscene orgy of revisionism that I've seen in this country. Why should they rehabilitate this son of a bitch? People who should know better are being carried away in emetic ecstasy."[74]

Dwight David Eisenhower easily defeated Adlai Stevenson in the 1952 elections. Although Stevenson received over 27 million popular votes (compared with Eisenhower's 34 million), he carried only nine states and lost the electoral college vote 442–89. In spite of the loss at the polls, many of Stevenson's ideas were adopted and emphasized in the 1956 campaign and several of his programs were translated into reality during the Kennedy and Johnson administrations. Although his candidate had lost, George Ball considered the 1952 campaign one of the most exhilarating political experiences of his life. In his view, this had been Adlai Stevenson's finest moment.

After the 1952 campaign, the 1956 election results were predictable and anticlimactic. Stevenson was again solidly defeated by Eisenhower. George Ball fought another losing battle at Stevenson's side. In 1956, however, a number of unpleasant turf struggles developed among those gathered around Adlai. In spite of his close personal association with Stevenson, Ball found himself elbowed out of Adlai's inner circle in Illinois by "professionals" like Willard Wirtz and Barbara Ward. Nonetheless, Ball played a critical role in Stevenson's winning the nomination over Tennessee Senator Estes Kefauver.

After losing to Kefauver in the Minnesota primary, Stevenson found himself in a must-win situation in Florida. George Ball took charge of Adlai's Florida campaign and Stevenson won a hard-fought race by a mere 12,000 votes. This crucial victory slowed the Kefauver momentum and pointed the way to a Stevenson victory in California.

Adlai Stevenson intensely disliked the brutal low-level politicking that occurred in political primaries. By the time of the Democratic convention, Stevenson was exhausted and distracted. Both he and his campaign had lost what Ball called "ebullience." On election eve, George Ball flew with Stevenson from Boston to Chicago, where he was at Adlai's side at the Sheraton Blackstone Hotel when the disappointing results were announced. Eisenhower had won with 457 electoral votes to Stevenson's 73.

George Ball learned some important political lessons from the campaigns of the 1950s. Stevenson had chosen to take principled positions and used the campaign experience as an opportunity to introduce new and different ideas. In 1956, he surprised the country when he called for a moratorium on the testing of nuclear weapons. In fact, he suggested that the United States unilaterally cease testing. Stevenson also argued that the United States should abandon the military draft and develop a volunteer army. Although Ball saw merit in these proposals, he was shocked both by the counterproductive nature of their presentation and by the fact that neither recommendation had been seriously analyzed. In March and again in May of 1956, he contacted Stevenson with suggestions concerning the moratorium issue.

From this experience, Ball concluded that new ideas, no matter how important and innovative, must be introduced in a manner and at a time when there is some reasonable hope that they will be received and implemented. His experiences with Jean Monnet had taught him that such ideas must be carefully presented in all their ramifications. If they are not, they cannot be rationally and successfully defended. Stevenson made Ball uncomfortable because Adlai felt a need "to take the high road," "to educate people on cosmic questions," and to focus strongly on "the great generalities of foreign policy."[75] In Ball's view, by insisting always on the high road and on occupying the high ground, one risks sitting frozen in splendid isolation, leaving others to build the indispensable foundations of political institutions far below the summit.

Although George Ball had a special affection and genuine respect for Adlai Stevenson, he disagreed with many of his friend's ideas. He often considered them fuzzy and unfinished. Late in his life, Ball revealingly concluded: "I was very close to Adlai. He affected my life not so much in the realm of ideas as in the fact that he was moving into a world of big affairs and took me along and paved the way for me."[76]

Ball found in Adlai too much of the patrician and the prima donna. He privately considered Stevenson lazy and was distressed by the fact that the governor did little reading. He became frustrated by Adlai's coy reticence to take positions and, in such situations, to resort to what Ball called "the dusty answer."[77] Ball noted that Stevenson did not relish the bargaining and haggling integral to the political process, nor did he enjoy performing before the mass media. The governor disliked speaking extemporaneously, and he avoided television appearances.

With the dawn of television, George Ball realized that the American political process was in a state of transformation. Political success would now increasingly depend upon the candidate's charm and acting skills. Makeup artists, speech coaches, and public relations firms would become central to the electoral process. Candidates would be packaged and marketed like cola, corn flakes, and dog food. Although Ball decried this situation, he recognized the power of the media and worked hard to develop his own communication skills. In a speech in New York in 1956, he made a statement that was far more prescient than even he could imagine at the time. With the advent of television, Ball warned his audience of the day when some Hollywood actor might become president of the United States. The audience was terribly amused by such a preposterous idea.

Tunnels, Travels, Family, and Finances

Even as he was being baptized into the realities of presidential politics in the 1950s, George Ball remained busy at Cleary, Gottlieb, where he represented Venezuelan oil interests, Cuban sugar businesses, and French economic enterprises. He regularly attended Common Market meetings and commuted to Paris and London. Beginning in 1956, Ball, a man ahead of his time, lobbied strenuously for the construction of a tunnel beneath the English Channel. This project fit nicely into his deep commitment to the establishment of a European Community. In discussing the "chunnel" project, as it was already being called, Ball presciently stated, "Although many people now believe that the tunnel has become obsolete, I am confident that it will, sooner or later, be built, simply because the logic is so compelling."[78]

On the personal and family side, the 1950s were years of travel, adventure, sadness, and financial failure. In 1953, George and Ruth visited the north African countries of Morocco, Algeria, and Tunisia. In July and August of 1954, they took Amos and his companion, Mildred Froehlich, and niece Sally Kean on an extended trip through Europe. This was a special journey for Amos, who, with George's help, wrote a small, privately produced book describing the trip.[79] In 1955, Ruth and George traveled to Greece; in 1957, they visited England, France, Belgium, and Germany; and in 1958, they took Douglas, John, and John's first wife, Peggy Noel, on a six-week automobile trip across Europe, visiting France, Switzerland, Austria, Yugoslavia, and Italy. Finally, in the fall of 1959, George, Ruth, John, and Douglas took a monthlong excursion to the Middle East.

The 1950s were difficult years of adolescence for sons John and Douglas. Although Ruth bore most of the responsibility for raising the boys, George intervened during periods of crisis. After a number of unpleasant school experiences, both John and Doug ended up enrolling at Millbrook, a private boys' school in upper New York. John graduated from Millbrook in 1954 and went on to Swarthmore. Douglas finished Milbrook in 1957, attended George Washington University, and then graduated from Wooster College.

On Christmas Eve of 1954, Amos Ball suffered a severe heart attack, and he died of a second attack on Christmas Day in Cocoa Beach. The sudden death of the old patriarch shook the foundations of the Ball family. Fortunately, Amos's book, describing his European trip earlier that year, had arrived just before his death. He spent his last two days proudly reading the book with the family and re-living the trip abroad. Edna, suffering from senility, was living in a nursing home in Wisconsin when her husband died. She passed away the following year.

In April 1957, George Ball and three friends who had fought shoulder to shoulder in the Stevenson campaigns purchased a newspaper, the *Northern Virginia Sun*, with offices in Arlington, Virginia. Ball's fellow investors included Clayton Fritchey, who served as publisher; Philip M. Stern, editor; and Arnold Sagalyn, assistant publisher. Although he had little to do with the day-to-day operation of the *Sun*, Ball was listed on the masthead as general counsel. The investment proved to be a disastrous mistake from the beginning. Ball and his three colleagues extended their losing streak from politics into the world of business.

Although there is no mention of the *Sun* in Ball's autobiography, the family never forgot the enormity of the failure. Thirty years later, George would wince when the newspaper was mentioned. It was estimated that this white elephant cost George Ball half a million dollars. In order to survive this huge loss, George had to borrow heavily from the Amos Ball Trust, and "it all just went down a great rat hole."[80]

Besides being plagued by three printing strikes and continual equipment failure, the newspaper sought to deliver a liberal message in an extremely conservative area. According to Ruth, "The notion was that by the next Democratic convention, we would all be millionaires, contributing generously to the Party in checks and with rousing editorials."[81] George Ball himself wrote many of these editorials and watched the advertising revenues shrink. Faced with bankruptcy, the partners deserted the enterprise. By March 1961, when all four partners had severed their relations with the paper, the *Sun* was losing $100,000 each quarter.

The *Northern Virginia Sun* episode seemed to set the pattern for a series of ill-fated financial investments made by George Ball over the years. In his words, "Once in a while, I would foolishly decide that there was an opportunity to make a killing somewhere, and I'd put my money in, and I was the one who got killed."[82]

The Beginnings of Bilderberg

George Ball was extremely sensitive to the importance of personal networks. Ruth described this principle succinctly when she wrote in her diary that "to succeed in this world, one must be well introduced."[83] By the end of the 1950s, Ball had built an impressive network of personal and political contacts. This network consisted of four overlapping segments. The oldest segment consisted of influential individuals encountered in the 1930s and early 1940s during Ball's first experiences in Washington and in Europe as part of the Strategic Bombing Survey. These personalities included such men as Dean Acheson, Fowler Hamilton, Eugene Rostow, Adlai Stevenson, Arthur Schlesinger Jr., John Kenneth Galbraith, Paul Nitze, and Helmut Schmidt. With the exception of a few individuals like Schmidt, this earliest section of the network was largely national in character.

The second segment consisted of individuals associated with Jean Monnet and Cleary, Gottlieb. Ball's association with Monnet established the foundation of his European web of contacts, which included Robert Marjolin, Pierre Uri, and Walter Hallstein, as well as such influential Americans as John J. McCloy, David Bruce, Robert Bowie, and Robert Lovett. It was during this period also that Ball came to know Walter Lippmann, who was to become one of his closest friends and most severe critics.

Ball spun the third section of his network during his involvement with the Stevenson campaigns. Here, he became well acquainted with the Democratic Party's entire establishment, including wealthy financial backers like William

Benton and Mrs. Herbert Lehman. As public relations coordinator and "idea man" for Stevenson, Ball became closely acquainted with the leading journalists of the day. By February 1956, when he held a small stag party at his home for René Mayer, the president of the European Coal and Steel Community, Ball was on a first-name basis with such guests as Philip Graham and Ferdinand Kuhn of the *Washington Post*, Walter Kerr of the *New York Herald Tribune*, and columnists Joseph Alsop, Marquis Childs, and Eric Sevareid.

Ball further exercised his burgeoning influence, telephoning David Rockefeller and asking him to sponsor a small dinner party for Mayer. He followed up with a letter to Rockefeller, suggesting several names for an invitation list.[84] Ball's connection to Rockefeller had been established and strengthened two years before when the two men attended a private meeting of select European and U.S. leaders in the Netherlands. This preeminently international assembly became the fourth and most important segment of Ball's extensive network of influence.

On May 29, 1954, seventy-four Western political and financial leaders gathered for a three-day conference at the Bilderberg Hotel in Oosterbeek, Holland. Their goal was to establish a high-powered forum to promote and protect European and U.S. relations. A feeling of malaise concerning intra-European and U.S.-European relations was building. The concepts of a United Europe and a European defense force were under fire. The Marshall Plan had recently completed its ministrations. European leaders were concerned about the future and felt the need to assess and improve the situation.

The idea for the Bilderberg group originated in the mind of a flamboyant Pole and international adventurer named Joseph Retinger. One friend described Retinger as "a sort of *Eminence Grise* of Europe, a Talleyrand without portfolio."[85] Among many other exploits, at age fifty-seven and with no training in the fields of intelligence and war, Retinger had parachuted into Poland, where he joined the underground in 1944. While engaged in dangerous guerrilla activities, he suffered a degenerative neurological disease and lost the use of his hands and feet. After escaping Poland, he decided to establish an informal organization of dignitaries to improve U.S.-European relations.

In 1952 Retinger approached Prince Bernhard of the Netherlands and asked him to serve as honorary head of the organization. The forty-one-year-old German-born Bernhard had married Crown Princess Juliana in 1937 and had been a military leader and inspiration in Holland's struggle against the Nazis. As such, he was a genuine war hero and a respected international figure.

After establishing a small European committee, Retinger and Bernhard turned their attention to the United States. Bernhard's closest contact there was General Walter Bedell Smith, then under secretary of state for Eisenhower. Bernhard had known Smith during the war, and the two were fishing friends as well. Smith, who never became involved in Bilderberg himself, contacted C. D. Jackson, another White House aide, who in turn approached John Coleman and George Ball, two key leaders in the Committee for a National Trade Policy.

From the very beginning, George Ball was the leading American "Bilderberger." Although there were no permanent members of the group, Ball made himself indispensable to the organization. Between 1954 and his death in 1994, he attended every meeting of the Bilderberg group but one. By 1994, he and David Rockefeller were the only original founders still in regular attendance. In addition to their regular meetings, the Bilderberg group had a steering committee that usually met twice a year to plan programs and to discuss the participant list. George Ball sat on the steering committee for twenty-five years. In this position, he played a critical role in shaping the direction and discussion of the organization.

Because Bilderberg has no permanent membership list, the group is highly fluid and ever-changing in composition. Steering committee leaders have carefully sought to recruit individuals in three overlapping categories. First, the Bilderberg leaders have emphasized the need for their members to exercise considerable power and influence. They have consciously attempted to recruit individuals referred to by Joseph E. Johnson as "big shots" and "movers and shakers."[86]

Second, the organizers have been on the lookout for younger personalities who are on their way up the ladder of power. In the words of Johnson, "We have tried, and quite deliberately, to bring in younger people who looked as if they might have a future."[87] The steering committee selected Denis Healey, for example, when he was but an opposition Labor Party member. Bill Moyers was recruited just after leaving the White House. Moyers served on the steering committee for several years before resigning, to the great disappointment of Ball and other old-time Bilderbergers.

Finally, the steering committee decision makers have emphasized the need for diversity. They have made a point of inviting individuals who represent different points of view. One of the consistent rivalries that resulted from this policy was that between George Ball and Denis Healey. Both were bright founding members of Bilderberg, but they disagreed strongly on such basic issues as European integration—and they irritated one another personally as well. Bilderberg also brought together a wide variety of personalities drawn from business, government, academia, and banking. On occasion, the steering committee issued invitations to captains of the mass media and leading journalists.

The Bilderberg ground rules are severe. All sessions are closed and off the record. Although there is an agenda, there are no resolutions passed or votes taken. Conference participants usually number between 70 and 120 and, with one partial exception, wives have not been invited. The conference location is rotated, with no country hosting the event in consecutive years. The Bilderberg meetings have been financed primarily from private sources and on occasion from such organizations as the Ford, Exxon, and Rockefeller Foundations, along with the Carnegie Endowment for International Peace.

The participants at the first Bilderberg meeting in 1954 included seventeen influential Americans and fifty-seven Europeans drawn from ten countries. The European representatives included eleven Britons, nine French, nine Dutch, seven Germans, and seven Italians, as well as representatives from Belgium, Denmark, Greece, Sweden, and Norway. Besides Ball, the Americans present at the first Bilderberg meeting included David Rockefeller, Paul Nitze, George McGhee, and Harry Heinz. The distinguished Europeans included Denis Healey, Oliver Franks, and Hugh Gaitskell of Great Britain, and Guy Mollet and Antoine Pinay of France. Four issues dominated that first meeting: communism and the Soviet Union, peoples of the underdeveloped world, economic policies, and European integration.

The Bilderberg group was a very special organization in George Ball's life. In his own words: "It has been a remarkably useful organization. In fact, of all the organizations I have ever joined or belonged to, Bilderberg has been the most useful." Not typically a joiner, Ball resisted membership in many other organizations, including the Trilateral Commission. Bilderberg was enough. According to Ball, Bilderberg was "enormously effective, especially in providing a forum where people could talk perfectly freely, and where acquaintances can be made." In his view, the formal sessions were less valuable than "people hav[ing] private conversations over dinner in the evenings, taking walks in the woods, doing all kinds of things. They get to know one another. These are people who have influence on affairs, either directly as members of governments or members of opposition coming into governments."[88]

David Rockefeller, whose long association with Ball was based on their common membership in the Bilderberg group, has echoed Ball's judgment. Rockefeller described Bilderberg as "one of the most interesting organizations that I belong to" and admitted that "it gave me an opportunity at a relatively early age to become acquainted with some of the leaders in Europe and the United States on a very informal basis, where one got to know them on a first-name basis."[89] Rockefeller was only thirty-eight years old when he attended the first Bilderberg meeting. He and Ball, who was forty-five at the time, were among the youngest participants.

From May 1954 until May 1960, George Ball attended nine Bilderberg conferences. When he joined the Department of State as part of the Kennedy administration in 1961, therefore, he already knew most of the leaders of the Western world. They had, after all, been Bilderbergers together.

By the beginning of the 1960s, George Ball, already a seasoned and scarred political veteran, had become difficult to overlook by those who would put together the next Democratic administration. Ball had a deep vested interest, therefore, in the outcome of the 1960 presidential campaign. Although he was ready to do combat against Richard Nixon, at the same time he had to make a number of delicate decisions concerning his position with respect to the Democratic Party candidates who were scrambling for the presidency. George Ball was prepared to make those decisions.

2

❖·❖·❖

Political Practitioner and
Intellectual Gladiator

George Ball approached the 1960 presidential sweepstakes with some trepidation. He personally favored Democratic Party candidates Hubert Humphrey and Adlai Stevenson, but he realized from the beginning that Senator John F. Kennedy was a formidable force. In spite of his reservations about Adlai's losing streak and his annoyance with the governor's reticence once again to commit himself as a candidate, Ball supported Stevenson—but in a subdued and quiet manner. As in the past, Stevenson consulted Ball about the campaign. They spent a week together in July 1959 on William Benton's yacht in the Mediterranean brainstorming the issue.

Ball watched the well-organized, well-financed, and intimidating Kennedy machine defeat Humphrey in the Wisconsin primary in April and crush him in West Virginia in May. Many of his closest friends who had been strong Stevenson supporters were now joining the Kennedy political bandwagon. Among others, John Kenneth Galbraith and Arthur Schlesinger Jr., frustrated by Stevenson's unwillingness to declare his candidacy, threw their support to Kennedy.[1]

George Ball understood well the powerful nature of the Kennedy political machine. Once Ball received a call from Adlai Stevenson just after Kennedy had met with the governor at his home in Libertyville, Illinois. At this meeting, which took place the day after the Oregon primary, Kennedy asked for Stevenson's support and invited him to deliver his nominating speech at the Democratic convention. As usual, Stevenson demurred and refused to make any promises. Stevenson told Ball that Kennedy briefly lost his composure and grimly warned: "Look, I have the votes for the nomination and if you don't give me your support, I'll have to shit all over you. I don't want to do that but I can, and I will if I have to." Stevenson was outraged and bitterly told Ball that "I should have told the son

of a bitch off but, frankly, I was shocked and confused by that Irish gutter talk."
George Ball never forgot that telephone call and drew two conclusions as a result. First, the Kennedys would do whatever was necessary to win and would most likely defeat Stevenson and all other contestants. Second, the John Kennedy–Adlai Stevenson relationship would be forever marked by tension and distrust.[2]

With Robert Kennedy as point man, the Kennedys methodically elicited the support of city bosses across the country. In Connecticut, for example, party kingpin John Bailey had a heart-to-heart talk with former Senator William Benton, a wealthy friend of both Stevenson and Ball who had been helping finance the Humphrey campaign. Bailey told Benton that if he continued to provide Humphrey with funds, he would never hold another elective or appointive job in Connecticut. John Kennedy had Governor Abraham Ribicoff warn all Stevenson supporters that if they continued to finance Humphrey's campaign, Adlai Stevenson would not even be considered for secretary of state.[3]

George Ball watched the Kennedy juggernaut with fascination and some alarm. He considered Robert Kennedy to be the ruthless force behind such tactics, and he never really liked or trusted Bobby. According to Ball, "My relations with Bobby were never very good; he had been very snotty about Stevenson." Later, Ball developed more respect for Robert Kennedy because of his position during the Cuban missile crisis. When asked whether perhaps Bobby had matured a bit over the years, Ball responded, "Perhaps a little bit, but it's a matter of degree. I think it would take a hell of a lot of maturing."[4]

Although he was not as actively engaged in the campaign as in the past, Ball did work with John Sharon, Oklahoma Senator Michael Monroney, and Monroney's assistant Tom Finney in support of Stevenson. Sharon, a thirty-three-year-old assistant to Ball at Cleary, Gottlieb who worked out of Ball's law office in Washington, took the lead in promoting Adlai's cause in 1960. In spite of his wavering confidence in Adlai and his growing sense that Kennedy would win the nomination, George Ball remained loyal to Stevenson. He did, however, adopt a much lower profile. Moreover, he maintained links with the Kennedy camp through his strong personal connections with people like Galbraith and Schlesinger.

In many ways, George Ball's position in the 1960 campaign paralleled the one that his father, Amos, had taken twenty-five years earlier, when he was trapped between Colonel Stewart and John D. Rockefeller. Amos had formally remained loyal to his old patron the colonel, but he avoided unnecessary entanglements with Stewart while adopting a very low profile. George Ball formally remained loyal to Stevenson, but he did cut back on his partisan activities. He let Sharon, Monroney, and Finney take the lead. Ruth Ball recalled, "George, after working hard in the two presidential campaigns for Adlai Stevenson, did not participate, except financially and with occasional speeches, in the 1960 campaign."[5]

Both Stevenson and Ball campaigned hard for Kennedy once the Massachusetts senator had won the Democratic nomination. Stevenson gave more than
eighty speeches on Kennedy's behalf, and Ball made appearances and prepared
op-ed pieces for the candidate. In a hard-hitting October 1960 letter to the *New
York Times*, for example, Ball wrote that Nixon's "boast that he 'knows Khrushchev' is no more than name-dropping. The relevant question is whether he
comprehends the major trends and forces of the day and possesses the intellectual and moral capacity with which to deal with them. To this question Senator
Kennedy has given a powerful affirmative answer in his perceptive statements on
our foreign policy now gathered together in 'The Strategy of Peace.'"[6] Kennedy,
ever alert to the issue of loyalty and personal support, was aware and appreciative
of the Stevenson and Ball activities.

The Stevenson/Ball Task Force Report

John F. Kennedy commissioned a series of overlapping task force reports that
would serve as discussion pieces critical to the formation of his domestic and foreign policy. Kennedy set up twenty-nine different study groups that submitted
reports to him. Ball advised Adlai to approach Kennedy about "the possibility of
your setting up an *ad hoc* group to formulate a specific foreign policy program
for execution during the first months of next year."[7] Ball argued that such a contribution would maximize Adlai's chances to be appointed secretary of state.

Having developed similar reports during his association with Jean Monnet,
Ball understood the value of serious strategic planning. He was equally aware of
the political value of such an initiative and saw it as a way for Stevenson's support-
ers to gain entrée to the Kennedy administration. Ruth Ball put into writing what
was obviously on George's mind: "When John Fitzgerald Kennedy was elected,
George, who always thinks ahead, had prepared briefing material for the new
President. To do this, he had formed a task force of assistants." Ruth continued:
"George had made the analysis, with suggestions about procedures. President
Kennedy was properly impressed by the document and by George's ability and
foresightedness. It is not surprising, therefore, that when staff appointments were
made, George became the Under Secretary of State for Economic Affairs."[8]

Although Ruth somewhat exaggerates the role of her husband in the report
process and overstates the importance of this report in George's political appointment, Ball was in fact the major force producing what became known as the
Stevenson Report. Theodore White has referred to this document as "Stevenson's
most important contribution to the Kennedy campaign."[9] In reality, the task force
report was George Ball's contribution. It was Ball who recruited the researchers
and experts and who in fact wrote most of the draft. Ball knew from the begin-

ning that he "would have to take the laboring oar of drafting the report—at least until we had produced a next-to-final draft that he [Stevenson] could polish." [10]

Ball's task force report for Kennedy was a masterpiece. The report consisted of two parts and two support papers. The first section focused on decisions and actions to be taken before January 20, while part two emphasized events after January 20, with an outline for a new foreign policy. The two support papers provided a restatement of U.S. foreign economic policy and an argument for partnership between a united Europe and the United States. [11]

The Stevenson/Ball report was far-reaching. It proposed the creation of a NATO strategic nuclear deterrent. It also addressed ongoing international crises in Algeria, Berlin, and Cuba, while at the same time presciently warning that "explosions may break out" in Laos, the Congo, the Dominican Republic, and Iran. The report lamented the dilution of the authority of the secretary of state, arguing for the preeminence of the state department in foreign policymaking. The document also recommended a fundamental reassessment of U.S. commercial policy, with an emphasis upon breaking down trade barriers wherever possible. Furthermore, it argued for a united Europe in cooperation with America, stressing the principle that "regionalism is the key to strength and control," and it proposed rapprochement with China, developmental aid to sub-Saharan Africa, and a new enlightened policy toward Latin America. The report recognized a "world in revolution" and warned that the "revolutionary age confronts us with a potential shift in the world power balance of a magnitude hitherto unknown. Two-thirds of the world's peoples are emerging from centuries of domination by a handful of power centers."

Although the report was prepared by a team, Ball recruited the players, and his fingerprints are all over the document. With his own expertise on trade policy and European affairs and his sensitivity to Stevenson's belief in the importance of the Third World, Ball provided a report that reflected a neat synthesis. It produced policy recommendations for an integrated world, a world in which politics and economics were systemically related and the problems of America, Europe, and the Third World were inextricably intertwined.

Neither Stevenson nor Ball presented the task force report to Kennedy. Instead, John Sharon, Ball's assistant and "legman," delivered it to Kennedy in Palm Beach, Florida. [12] Kennedy was delighted with the report and mistakenly assumed that Sharon had written it. It was some time before he realized the author's true identity.

George Ball further bolstered his image in John Kennedy's mind by preparing a second significant task force document. He spent the final six weeks of 1960 organizing this study, entitled "Report to the Honorable John F. Kennedy by the Task Force on Foreign Economic Policy (FEP)." This report consisted of an analysis of the principal economic problems confronting the United States and a long discussion of commercial policy, foreign aid needs, and national and international organizations necessary for the implementation of new economic policies. The study emphasized Ball's favorite ideas, trade liberalization, tariff cutting, and the reorganization of the foreign aid program. FEP placed special emphasis upon the European Economic Community, where "beyond economic unity lies the long-term prospect of political union on the continent."[13]

In preparing the FEP report, Ball solicited the expertise of such individuals as Richard Gardner, Raymond Vernon, Robert Bowie, Harlan Cleveland, Kenneth Galbraith, Lincoln Gordon, and W. W. Rostow. There could be no doubt this time, however, about the identity of the author of the report. Centered at the top of the inside title page was written, "George W. Ball, Chairman." Below, Ball listed two other names, Myer Rashish ("Secretary-Commercial Policy") and George S. Springsteen ("Secretary-Foreign Aid"). Other contributors were listed simply as "consultants."

Ball's role in drafting both the Stevenson and FEP reports for Kennedy undoubtedly enhanced his credibility in the eyes of the president-elect. Furthermore, many of the recommendations in these reports became policy during the Kennedy and Johnson presidencies.

Ball Enters the New Frontier

When John Kennedy offered Adlai Stevenson the UN ambassadorship instead of the secretary of state's office, George Ball argued long and hard for Stevenson to accept the opportunity. At the same time, Ball had political ambitions of his own and was disappointed when he learned that the position he had hoped for, under secretary of state for economic affairs, was to be offered to Republican William C. Foster.

At this point, George Ball's network of friends moved into action. When John Sharon informed Stevenson that Kennedy planned to appoint Foster, Adlai telephoned Senator William Fulbright, who was vacationing in Florida. Stevenson suggested to Fulbright that he visit the president-elect, who was staying at the Kennedy home in Palm Beach. In Ball's words, "Fulbright, who was one of the laziest men I knew, actually got up early and drove across the state to see Kennedy and tell him that this was terrible, that he was getting too many Republicans in his administration, and in any event, that I was preeminently the fellow for the job."[14]

Shortly after Fulbright's mission, John Kenneth Galbraith met with Kennedy and weighed in personally for Ball. As a result of this intensive lobbying effort, Ball won the appointment. George Wildman Ball, with the help of his friends, had elbowed his way into the New Frontier.

The inauguration of John F. Kennedy as thirty-fifth president of the United

States on January 20, 1961, was one of the most exhilarating events in the life of George and Ruth Ball. At this, "one of the most glorious of inaugurals," the Balls, like President Kennedy himself, "savored every moment."[15]

George's oldest brother, Stuart, and his wife, Marion, traveled from Chicago to be present at the ceremonies. Stu was enormously proud of his youngest brother, and both George and Ruth basked happily in this family recognition. Ken Galbraith, who had been nominated as Kennedy's ambassador to India, and his wife, Kitty, also stayed at the Ball's residence during the inauguration. George and Ruth loved the social whirl of parties, the political attention, and the contagious enthusiasm that permeated the milieu of the New Frontier.

Among those with whom the Balls celebrated at the ceremonies were George's boss, newly appointed Secretary of State Dean Rusk, and his wife, Virginia. Ball had first become acquainted with Dean Rusk during the Stevenson campaigns but had developed a stronger bond with the Georgian during the Bilderberg meetings. Although Rusk had not been present at the inaugural meeting in 1954, David Rockefeller and Ball saw to it that he was invited to the meetings in 1955. From that time on, Rusk joined Ball as one of the central forces within the Bilderberg establishment. The Balls and Rusks were to become close lifelong friends.

The Kennedy administration was filled with old acquaintances and colleagues of George Ball. Many were fellow Stevensonians; some were Bilderbergers. Still others were individuals whom Ball had known in Washington in the decades prior to 1961. Besides the Rusk, Stevenson, and Galbraith appointments, Kennedy named Arthur Schlesinger as special assistant in the White House, Paul Nitze as assistant secretary for international security affairs, George McGhee as under secretary for political affairs, Robert J. Manning as assistant secretary for public affairs, and Fowler Hamilton as head of the Agency for International Development. Two Illinois natives and former Stevenson supporters, Arthur Goldberg and Willard Wirtz, were named secretary and under secretary of labor, respectively.

John Kennedy made several other key appointments that were to intersect significantly with the career path of George Ball in the years ahead. These appointments included Robert McNamara as secretary of defense, Douglas Dillon as secretary of the treasury, and McGeorge Bundy as special assistant for national security affairs. At a subsecretarial level, the new personnel included Cyrus Vance and William Bundy in the Department of Defense and Averell Harriman, Roger Hilsman, Alexis Johnson, Phillips Talbot, Lucius Battle, and Harlan Cleveland in the State Department. In Ball's political universe, there was one further critical appointment. Kennedy named Chester Bowles as under secretary of state. Bowles, second in rank in the Department of State, was George Ball's immediate superior.

Bowles and Ball

In the fall of 1959, Chester Bowles became the first prominent liberal to endorse John F. Kennedy's candidacy for the presidency. Throughout the campaign and for a short time thereafter, he provided Kennedy with foreign policy advice and served as chairman of the Democratic Party's platform committee. Kennedy felt indebted to Bowles and paid that debt with the appointment to the State Department.

Born in 1901, Bowles, a Connecticut Yankee and graduate of Choate School and Yale University, was sixteen years older than John F. Kennedy. Bowles, along with William Benton, formed an advertising firm in 1929 that prevailed in spite of the Depression, becoming an enormous success and source of great wealth. In 1948, Bowles won a surprise victory in the Connecticut gubernatorial race.[16] After Bowles lost his bid for reelection in 1950, President Truman named him ambassador to India, where he served until March of 1953. After failing to secure his party's nomination for the Senate, he was elected to a congressional seat in Connecticut in 1958.

During the 1950s, Chester Bowles established his credentials as a bona fide liberal. He supported disarmament, urged the opening of communication with Communist China, and believed fervently in the importance of the Third World. He was sympathetic to African, Asian, and Latin American demands for neutralism and nonalignment, and he argued for major infusions of foreign aid to these countries.

In many ways, Bowles resembled Adlai Stevenson. Only fourteen months apart in age, both were from well-to-do families, and they had been schoolmates at Choate; both were highly intellectual and verbosely articulate; both were impatient with administrative detail; both were crusaders who liked to view themselves as somehow above politics; and both were supreme internationalists who emphasized the special significance of the Third World. It is not surprising, therefore, that these kindred spirits, Chester Bowles and Adlai Stevenson, became friends who supported one another whenever possible.

The Kennedy clan, however, entertained severe reservations about Bowles, despite his crucial early political support for John Kennedy. They noted his sympathy for both Humphrey and Stevenson; they distrusted his high-mindedness and floating idealism; they quietly criticized his high-profile prolixity. At times, they even doubted his personal and professional loyalty. These doubts, which increased with time, were shared by Secretary of State Dean Rusk.

Bowles had played a major role in Kennedy's recruitment of a new generation of talented foreign policymakers. This group included individuals of the stature of Edward R. Murrow, Edwin Reischauer, and Roger Hilsman. By championing such new talent, Bowles made many enemies in the old establishment.

He lengthened his list of enemies when he promoted a plan to reform U.S. foreign missions abroad by putting all personnel and agencies in the field under the coordinating control of the ambassador.

Kennedy had actually inserted Bowles in the State Department to shake things up and to reform an organization that he considered a quagmire. Bowles took this role seriously. In the process, he alienated many individuals, including the ever-cautious, stony Dean Rusk. The secretary was uncomfortable with energetic visionaries who rushed about calling for rapid reform. In the words of George Ball, "Dean thought Chet was not in this world. He considered him fuzzy." [17]

If he made Rusk uneasy, Bowles made Robert Kennedy outright angry. When the information leaked that Bowles had opposed the Bay of Pigs invasion and when he sharply questioned U.S. intervention in the Dominican Republic, Bobby, who viewed Bowles as an idealistic gadfly, questioned his political loyalty as well.

George Ball considered Chester Bowles a thoroughly decent human being but had mixed feelings about him nonetheless. Although the two had known one another since the Stevenson campaigns, they had never been close friends. Furthermore, Ball was well aware that Bowles had in fact recommended a Republican friend, William C. Foster, for the State Department position that Ball had ultimately obtained.

Ball considered Chet Bowles to be a naive version of Adlai Stevenson. In his autobiography he referred to the under secretary simply as "the Idealist." He did not share Bowles's preoccupation with the Afro-Asian world and mischievously described Bowles's romanticized briefings to the mass media as "Up and Down the Mekong River with Chet Bowles and Gun and Camera." [18]

Throughout 1961, Ball worked more closely with Dean Rusk than with Bowles and, as the year wore on, Rusk began shifting Bowles's responsibilities to Ball's desk. Ball later explained that "Dean was quite frank that Chester Bowles was rather driving him up a tree and asked if I would take over more and more of the political stuff, which I did, though I had no business doing it." [19]

According to Bowles himself, he and Rusk had "little opportunity" to meet regularly. Meanwhile, Ball and Bowles kept "promising one another to have a long talk," but they had "few useful exchanges." [20] Instead, Rusk and Ball worked closely together and Bowles found himself increasingly frozen out of State Department decision making. While Rusk and Ball were Bilderberg brothers, Chester Bowles never attended a Bilderberg meeting.

In some ways, Chet Bowles and George Ball were different sides of the same coin. Both were Stevensonian Democrats who advocated U.S. involvement in a rapidly changing world. While Ball stressed the preeminence of Europe, Bowles focused his attention on the Afro-Asian/Latin American world. Ball's emphasis was primarily upon economic problems, while Bowles accented political issues.

As a political actor, George Ball moved quietly and cautiously, always weaving influential individuals into his expanding web of personal connections. Bowles, on the other hand, moved publicly in great bursts of enthusiasm, tearing his way through personal and bureaucratic networks in his impressive campaign to reform the American foreign policy system. Bowles was a visionary with little political savvy; Ball was a visionary with great political sense. Little surprise, then, that George Ball walked the corridors of political power much longer than Chester Bowles.

By midsummer 1961, serious rumors circulated that Kennedy was about to fire Bowles. The under secretary's friends, including Adlai Stevenson, rallied to his cause. But it was only a matter of time. On November 26, 1961, in a move that became known in Washington as the "Thanksgiving Day Massacre," Dean Rusk handed Chet Bowles a press statement announcing a series of administrative changes. Bowles was to become a roving ambassador to replace Averell Harriman, who was named assistant secretary for Far Eastern affairs. George Ball took Bowles's place as under secretary, while George McGhee moved into Ball's position as junior under secretary.

Chester Bowles was, in his own words, "angry," "shocked," and "saddened" by his dismissal.[21] His appointment as the president's special representative on Asian, African, and Latin American affairs somewhat soothed his feelings. But he resigned a year later, convinced that the Kennedy administration was neglecting the Third World. He then accepted a second stint as ambassador to India, a post he held until April 1969.

George Ball was not in Washington for the Thanksgiving Day Massacre. While he was attending a high-level meeting regarding GATT (General Agreement on Tariffs and Trade) in Geneva, Ball received a call from Rusk on the evening of November 25, informing him of his promotion and new responsibilities. Ball was not surprised. Earlier, Rusk had bluntly told him that he wanted Ball to take over more of the political responsibilities at the State Department because "Chet isn't up to it."[22] Thus, George Ball began his career as the influential under secretary of state that was to last for fifty-eight months, a tenure in the position second only to that of Sumner Welles in Franklin D. Roosevelt's administration.

Kennedy and Ball

Although the Kennedys entertained some of the same reservations about George Ball that they held about Chester Bowles, they considered Ball a team player who approached politics with a degree of pragmatism and realism that they valued. Working well with Dean Rusk and John Kennedy throughout 1961, Ball had managed to overcome his Stevenson associations. According to Rusk, who has said that he supported Ball for the position: "I had a little trouble with Bobby Kennedy because Bobby was very keen on appointing true, blue Kennedy people to the top jobs, and George Ball had not been a Kennedy person. He was an Adlai Stevenson person. But I managed to prevail over his objections."[23]

Rusk was not the only one pushing for Ball. Special White House adviser Arthur Schlesinger Jr., who had known Ball since 1945 when they met in Europe, argued Ball's case to the president. He told Kennedy that "Ball could be depended on as the president's man in the department. He is loyal to you and believes in your policies. It would be a great error . . . to replace Bowles [with] someone who is neutral or Republican. . . . Ball is imaginative, practical and able."[24]

Although stationed on the periphery of John Kennedy's inner circle, George Ball gained credibility with the president as time passed. Ball was a much more effective administrator than Bowles. Rusk and State Department Executive Secretary Lucius Battle praised Ball's efficiency. Bowles had allowed letters and papers to pile up on his desk where they lay for weeks. Ball kept the paper train moving. In the words of Luke Battle, "Compared to Chet Bowles, Ball was the essence of order. Working with him was an absolute joy for me. He was very bright, very gutsy, very funny."[25]

Since Dean Rusk was little interested in economics, trade, and the situation in Europe, Ball took control over these matters. Even before he was named under secretary, Ball discussed these issues personally with the president. He saw Kennedy four to five times a week in various meetings and periodically received telephone calls from the chief executive. Because Kennedy was personally interested in European affairs and trade issues and because Ball was the highest ranking figure at the State Department tracking these matters, Kennedy turned to Ball whenever he had questions concerning these issues.

The Kennedy administration hit the ground running in 1961. Crises broke out in Cuba, Berlin, the Dominican Republic, Laos, and the Congo. The administration also found itself confronting thorny problems concerning the European Community, commercial and foreign aid issues, defense and space policy, and nuclear testing and disarmament initiatives. Furthermore, during that same year, the Kennedy government sought to organize the Peace Corps, the Alliance for Progress in Latin America, an Arms Control and Disarmament Agency, and a National Advisory Council for the Arts.

During this first year on the chaotic New Frontier, George Ball focused his attention on three major issues: European integration, trade and tariffs, and the Congo. He spent two weeks in London during March, focusing on trade and the European Community, while June and July were devoted to the textile trade problem. Ball traveled to Hong Kong and Japan during the first three weeks of July on a delicate mission to address the textile quota issue. With the tragic death of UN Secretary-General Dag Hammarskjöld on September 13, 1961, Ball took charge of U.S. policy toward a tangled and entangling situation in the Congo, where a Katangan secession movement intensified a regional conflict that carried severe international consequences.

Ball worked hard to encourage British membership in the Common Market. In March, he spoke with Edward "Ted" Heath, the lord privy seal, who supported Ball's position. Prime Minister Harold Macmillan, however, presented a problem for Ball. While speaking favorably about European integration, Macmillan defined the community in extremely limited terms. In his view, Britain was far from ready to accept Ball's idea of a European union that was to evolve into a political community. Although Ball encountered effective resistance in Britain and in several other European countries, he succeeded in converting John Kennedy to the cause of European integration. Meanwhile, he patiently prepared for a long struggle.

Ball had greater success with the issues of free trade and textile quotas. In his drive to win votes in the presidential election, Kennedy had promised to protect the powerful U.S. textile industry by means of import quotas. Such policy was anathema to George Ball, who believed that competition and free trade were critical to the economic well-being of the United States. He considered the textile interests to be selfish and short-sighted. Unfortunately, upon entering the Kennedy administration, he discovered that he was a minority of one. Such key players as White House Deputy Counsel Myer Feldman and Secretary of Commerce Luther Hodges were strong supporters of mandatory quotas.[26] Nonetheless, Kennedy put Ball in charge of the textile problem, a problem that would occasion the under secretary "more personal anguish than any other task I undertook during my total of twelve years in different branches of the government."[27] Among those who worked with Ball to counter the forces of protectionism were a thirty-six-year-old Los Angeles lawyer named Warren Christopher and Carl Kaysen, a forty-one-year-old economist who served as deputy special assistant to the president.

Through an inspired series of political maneuvers, Ball managed to hold the line against quotas. He outflanked the textile magnates by dividing the industry into parts and negotiating separately with cotton, silk, and wool interests. During meetings with the leaders of the industry, he pointedly wore a suit made in Britain, shoes manufactured in Hong Kong, and a silk tie made in France. As he left one session with the industry representatives, Ball overhead one participant say, "That's the slyest bastard I've seen in years. We certainly have to watch him." Ball found such grudging respect "heartwarming."[28]

Ball also informed the American textile leaders that he was about to put together an international textile agreement that would satisfy all parties. After talking textiles and trade in Hong Kong and Japan in July of 1961, Ball flew to

Geneva to conclude an international textile agreement that flexibly limited both exports and quotas. Ball proudly considered this effort "a major tour de force" and "a landmark business." [29] His effort led directly to the Trade Expansion Act of 1962.

In the last months of 1961, George Ball found himself embroiled in the Katangan secessionist crisis in the Congo. In the Department of State, the contentious issue pitted the European Bureau against the African Bureau, with the Bureau of International Organization Affairs holding a middle position. Meanwhile, the Belgian mining interests, the American religious Right, southern congressmen, and politicians like Richard Nixon and Senator Thomas Dodd all combined to complicate the issue and to impede its resolution. George Ball even found himself at loggerheads with his old friend Adlai Stevenson on this issue. Throughout this African crisis, George Ball was the only U.S. official to present a comprehensive public statement of policy, in an address in Los Angeles on December 19, 1961. Although Ball and his colleagues managed to contain the problem, they did not solve it; in 1964, during the Johnson administration, it came back to haunt U.S. leaders.

During the last two years of the Kennedy presidency, George Ball played an important role in a wide variety of economic and political affairs. In January and October 1962, he traveled to Panama; in August and September of 1963, he visited the dictator Antonio Salazar in Portugal and President Muhammad Ayub Khan in Pakistan. He also increasingly found himself involved in a growing crisis in Vietnam. There were two issues, however, one economic and the other political, on which he had an especially significant impact. In early 1962, he guided a far-reaching trade bill through Congress, and the Trade Expansion Act was signed by the president in October. During that same month, Ball was one of a dozen major players in the Cuban missile crisis—and one of the few who argued for a political rather than a military solution.

John F. Kennedy and George Ball enjoyed a relationship of considerable mutual respect. During his abbreviated presidency, Kennedy came to rely more and more on Ball, a man he viewed as intellectually tough, bureaucratically astute, and personally loyal. Because Kennedy lacked understanding of international economics and because Rusk considered economics a dull and dismal science, Ball became the president's expert on international finance and monetary policy. Ball, on the other hand, found Kennedy smart and quick, but not terribly profound. Ball's witticisms and dry humor, which he habitually used to build rapport, were lost on JFK. This unresponsiveness troubled Ball, who never came to consider the president a close friend.

In George Ball's judgment, John Kennedy resisted all impulses to think strategically. He was a politician of the moment. Ball considered Kennedy "intensely pragmatic" and found it "very hard to keep discussion going within the framework of any large policy."[30] Yet Ball admired Kennedy's political instincts, his personal charisma, and his imagination in proclaiming the New Frontier.

Just as he had learned much from his experiences with his father, with Jean Monnet, and with Adlai Stevenson, George Ball learned from John Kennedy. Ball remembered one piece of advice in particular. Kennedy warned him about the political dangers of appearing to be too smart. People do not like to feel inferior, the president said; a man who seems to have all the answers and to know too much will find others coalescing against him. Kennedy pointed out that this mind-set was especially prevalent in the U.S. Congress. JFK once told Ball: "Just a suggestion, George; don't give the committees the impression you're too well-prepared. A Senator told me the other day that some of his colleagues thought you had too many answers. They don't like a witness that seems to know more than they do."[31]

The Ball Boys

From the very beginning, George Ball carefully gathered a group of talented, dedicated professionals to assist him in his responsibilities at the State Department. He had witnessed firsthand the masterful recruitment techniques of Jean Monnet in the 1940s and 1950s. Indeed, he himself had been one of the most important political satellites that circled around Monnet, advising, reporting, debating, challenging, writing, and always supporting. Ball's modus operandi was to find good people, sprinkle them strategically throughout the bureaucracy, and grant them the autonomy necessary to do their jobs.

Ball's inner circle consisted of a small group of extremely competent and loyal staff members. These men headed his secretariat. The most important were Robert Schaetzel, George Springsteen, and Arthur Hartman. Ball had recruited Schaetzel, Springsteen, and Hartman to assist him when he was coordinating the task force reports for Kennedy. Schaetzel acted as Ball's first chief special assistant for a short period of time before taking a position in the European Bureau as deputy assistant secretary for Atlantic affairs. He went on to become ambassador to the European Community and a statesman in his own right, spending his life promoting European integration and U.S.-European relations.

George Springsteen replaced Schaetzel as special assistant and ran Ball's office until 1966, when Ball resigned as under secretary. Springsteen, who was extremely protective of Ball, ran the office with an iron fist. Ball considered Springsteen "even more valuable than Schaetzel" because he was "an absolute rock head," who would "never accept anything that he thought I would disapprove of."[32] Although never a very popular personality, Springsteen complemented Ball well because the under secretary needed a bureaucratic hatchet man.

Arthur Hartman's tenure overlapped both Schaetzel's and Springsteen's. Hartman had begun his government service with the Marshall Plan and first met George Ball when the two men worked in different capacities for Jean Monnet. Hartman left Ball's office in 1963 to direct the economic section at the U.S. embassy in London and ultimately became ambassador to France and to the Soviet Union. He was a man of great substance and insight. His place was in turn taken by Robert Anderson, who was later replaced by Jack Myerson.

All of these special assistants shared George Ball's vision and interests. Bob Schaetzel recalled, "What bound us all together was that we very much believed in the same things that George believed in."[33] Throughout their careers, these "special Ball assistants" considered themselves near and dear friends of George Ball. Springsteen continued to work in a wide variety of organizational and research capacities for Ball into the 1990s.

Beyond the secretariat, two dozen Ball boys were involved in substantive policymaking. This all-star list included such experts in economics and trade as Michael Blumenthal and the lesser-known Griffith Johnson and Philip Trezise in the Bureau of Economic Affairs. Their expertise was supplemented by the talent of Robert Roosa, Carl Kaysen, Raymond Vernon, and Richard Gardner. Within the State Department hierarchy, Ball relied heavily upon Lucius Battle, Phillips Talbot, Harlan Cleveland, John Tuthill, Edwin Martin, Frederick Dutton, and Abram Chayes. Ball worked closely with Bill Bundy and John McNaughton of the Department of Defense and Robert Bowie, a Harvard professor who had been in and out of government for years. Robert Manning and James Greenfield held the two key posts in the State Department's Bureau of Public Affairs. Ball's old friend Foster Hamilton served as Head of AID for fourteen months. These individuals were internationalists who supported Ball's worldview of European integration and free trade.

Many of the Ball boys had midwestern roots, but most had either studied or taught at Harvard. Edwin Martin had studied at Northwestern at the same time as Ball. Philip Trezise and Robert Roosa were born and raised in Michigan's Upper Peninsula and studied at the University of Michigan. John McNaughton was born in a small town in Indiana, and Abram Chayes hailed from Chicago. Tony Solomon earned his B.A. at the University of Chicago. Other members of the George Ball network had more exotic roots. Michael Blumenthal, for example, who was one of George Ball's most successful and loyal proteges, was born in Berlin and raised in Shanghai.

Harvard affiliates surrounded Ball. Richard Gardner, James Greenfield, Arthur Hartman, and Griffith Johnson all earned undergraduate degrees at Harvard. Johnson also earned an M.A. and Ph.D. there, while Solomon held a Harvard M.P.A. Bob Bowie and Abram Chayes had Harvard law degrees, while John McNaughton, Robert Roosa, Tony Solomon, and Ray Vernon all taught in one capacity or another at Harvard. Robert Manning was a Harvard Nieman Fellow.

Among the many brilliant and less-known protégés of George Ball was John F. Campbell, who graduated with honors from Harvard in 1961. Campbell, who worked for Ball in the State Department and who later helped him research *The Discipline of Power*, enjoyed Ball's deepest admiration and respect.[34]

In addition to this cadre of Ball boys, several others in the State Department worked closely and cooperatively with Ball, among them U. Alexis Johnson, deputy under secretary of state for political affairs; W. Averell Harriman, assistant secretary of state for Far Eastern affairs; and Charles Bohlen, special assistant to the secretary of state. Two other important actors were George C. McGhee, under secretary for political affairs, and Roger Hilsman, director of intelligence and research and later under secretary. McGhee, a gentleman with modest organizational skills, was sometimes ignored by Ball, while Hilsman, a bright but outspoken analyst, was forced to resign in February 1964 by Johnson and Rusk with Ball's concurrence.

On Wednesday night, November 20, 1963, at 9:20 P.M., George Ball telephoned President Kennedy to report his observations concerning an Organization for Economic Cooperation and Development meeting he had just attended in Paris. The under secretary focused his remarks on the problems facing the European Common Market. Kennedy suggested that Ball meet with him after his presidential visit to Texas. George Ball never spoke with John F. Kennedy again. The president was assassinated in Dallas two days later.

In the chaos of the moment, Ball played a crucial transitional role. Because Secretary of State Dean Rusk had departed for Japan and was in the air flying west from Hawaii at the time of the assassination, Ball served as acting secretary of state for a short but critical period. Among other things, he prepared an agenda of action and supervised the drafting of proclamations and messages for the new president. He put together a memorandum of action for Lyndon Johnson and was waiting at Andrews Air Force Base when Johnson and the body of John Kennedy arrived. Along with a handful of others, he consulted closely with the new president and helped make the complex arrangements involved in receiving foreign guests and dignitaries. Although Ball had known Lyndon Johnson casually, he was unsure of the future. He understood that Johnson had resented Kennedy's eastern establishment brain trust and that relations between LBJ and the late president's inner circle had been tense.

The Johnson Years

From November 23, 1963, until his resignation on September 30, 1966, George Ball worked closely with President Lyndon Johnson. During these years, Ball's political influence was pervasive. His dissenting role in American foreign policy during the escalating Vietnam conflict is generally known. What is less known is the wide range of responsibilities that the under secretary undertook during the frenetic days of the mid-1960s.

Ball was involved in intensive and extensive lobbying activities with the U.S. Congress on behalf of administration goals concerning coffee and sugar quotas. During the fall of 1963, he worked closely with President Johnson, Vice President Humphrey, Under Secretary of State for Political Affairs Averell Harriman, and AID Director David Bell in enlisting the support of numerous key congressmen for the administration's beleaguered foreign aid bill. He was a major policy actor in the Cyprus conflict and in the continuing upheaval in the Congo. Ball was consulted concerning crises in the Dominican Republic, Brazil, Indonesia, the Middle East, and Czechoslovakia. He played an important role in pursuing his favorite cause of European integration and helped shape American policy toward NATO while supporting the controversial Multilateral Force (MLF). Furthermore, he influenced the presidential appointments of ambassadors and other political and diplomatic personnel.

George Ball worked in tandem with Secretary of State Dean Rusk. His influence can be seen in his attendance at National Security Council meetings held during the Johnson administration. Between August of 1964 and September of 1968, Johnson called forty-five meetings of the NSC. George Ball attended thirty-six of these meetings, more than anyone else in the Department of State, including Secretary Rusk himself, who was present at thirty-three. In two dozen of these meetings, Ball joined Rusk in attendance, indicating the confidence that both Johnson and Rusk had in Ball's judgment. Even when he was ambassador to the United Nations for a few short months in 1968, Ball was called to Washington to participate in key NSC deliberations on the crises in Czechoslovakia and Vietnam.

Ball's influence, however, transcended the formal NSC meetings. He was also invited to participate in the small Tuesday luncheons where many important policy debates were aired during the Johnson presidency. From 1964 through 1966, Under Secretary Ball was present at fourteen of these luncheons. He was called back three times from his ambassadorship to the United Nations to attend Tuesday luncheons in 1968.

Besides his role in the NSC and Tuesday meetings, George Ball also worked directly with President Johnson in a host of other small, personal contexts. These included ad hoc, free-floating meetings in the Cabinet Room, the Oval Office, the outer office, the second floor of the mansion, and at the ranch in Texas. Furthermore, Ball had direct telephone access to the president, and the two called one another often. They spoke on the telephone approximately two hundred times in the three years that Ball was under secretary. By encouraging and supporting Ball's presidential access, Secretary of State Rusk did much to increase the power and influence of his deputy.[35]

The Johnson-Rusk-Ball triangle was an extraordinary political constellation. The three sides of this triangle—Ball-Rusk, Ball-Johnson, Johnson-Rusk—were equally strong. Although Lyndon Johnson often attacked, belittled, and humiliated his advisers and subordinates, he seldom used these techniques on either Rusk or Ball. LBJ trusted his two top lieutenants in the Department of State. When the three men, all over six feet tall, stood together, they usually towered over other White House advisers and could look one another in the eye.

Lyndon Johnson and Dean Rusk came from similar origins in the American South. Both had pulled themselves up by their rural bootstraps. Johnson was born in a three-room farmhouse in Stonewall, Texas, in August 1908. Six months later Rusk was born in Cherokee County in Georgia, the son of a poor Presbyterian minister and postman. Rusk was so poor as a child that his mother made his shorts out of discarded flour sacks. Rusk and Johnson often joked about their humble origins and discussed the comparative advantages of outhouses and indoor plumbing. In spite of these difficult origins, however, Rusk attended Davidson College, won a Rhodes Scholarship, and in 1952 became president of the Rockefeller Foundation. Most importantly, Rusk, who once described his appearance as that of a bartender, never threatened Lyndon Johnson. Thoroughly professional and completely loyal, he was content to stand quietly in Johnson's shadow. Rusk knew Lyndon Johnson as well as anybody outside the Johnson family and in Johnson's words was "loyal as a beagle." He protected Johnson and served to smooth out some of the Texan's many rough edges.[36]

Many of those who worked in the State Department considered Dean Rusk to be a gentleman whose dignity compelled them to refer to him as Mr. Rusk. He was Dean to very few people. Even President Kennedy had referred to him as Secretary Rusk or Mr. Rusk. Rusk operated within a protective wall of reserve. He was an extremely wary individual who seldom spoke out in meetings. He preferred to confer with the president before or after the formal sessions. In every way, he was a cautious, faithful supporter of the status quo.

Rusk and Ball

Dean Rusk was deeply influenced by General George C. Marshall, with whom he worked closely in the State Department during the late 1940s. Rusk idolized Marshall, who was stern, unpretentious, aloof, and thoroughly professional. Marshall refused to show his emotions. According to one story, Marshall, when asked about his undemonstrative nature, responded that he had few emotions and the ones he did have were reserved for Mrs. Marshall. Balding and Buddhalike, Dean Rusk, too, showed few emotions. George Ball was the only individual outside Rusk's immediate family with whom the secretary displayed his feelings.

By his own admission, George Ball loved Dean Rusk. And the feeling was reciprocated. The two friends together ran the State Department, dividing the labor. When one had to travel abroad, the other was sure to remain in Washington to look after the department. In their five years of working together, only once were they out of the country at the same time.[37] Rusk's confidence in his colleague was so great that he turned many political and economic matters completely over to Ball. Rusk felt secure enough both in his position and in himself that he never felt threatened by Ball, no matter how close the under secretary became to the president. In Rusk's words, "I had several people working under me who wanted my job. I knew it. They knew it. They knew that I knew it. But I never got the impression that George was waiting for me to get out of the way, and he was thoroughly qualified to be secretary of state."[38]

At various meetings concerning Vietnam policy, an issue about which Ball and Rusk sharply disagreed, Rusk allowed Ball to argue his position directly to the president. Rusk, seated between Ball and the president, would sit, quietly smoking and listening carefully to Ball's arguments. At appropriate moments, Rusk would quietly and succinctly argue his own position.

In the end, George Ball and Dean Rusk agreed on most substantive policy matters. Furthermore, they institutionalized a bonding social routine that involved an informal meeting over drinks every evening on the seventh floor of the State Department. At the end of the day, one or the other would walk over to the other's office. Usually, Ball would make his way to Rusk's office, where the secretary had access to duty-free liquor through embassies abroad. Scotch was the preferred drink, and Rusk taught Ball to drink Scotch neat. Both men drank heavily. In these evening sessions, the two statesmen compared notes on the events of the day and made decisions on policy and personnel matters. Sporadically, other important State Department officials would be invited to join the two, but it was basically a Rusk-Ball ritual. Ball was, in Rusk's own words "my alter ego."[39]

Ball complemented Rusk. Rusk feared the press and considered journalists to be the enemy. He was uncomfortable when the mass media were present and would drink a couple of scotches to calm his nerves before his press conferences. Ball told Rusk that he should learn to use the press to his own advantage: "Dean, you're making a big mistake. You ought to be in the position of having a certain number of close friends in the press who you can use when you want to get stories out the way you want to get them out."[40]

In contrast to Rusk, Ball relished working with members of the press and enjoyed sparring with them intellectually. He viewed the attention of the mass media as an opportunity and enjoyed using leading journalists to present and promote the administration's policies. Moreover, Ball maintained special personal relations with such influential opinion makers as Walter Lippmann and James Reston. Over the years, he had constructed back channels to such individuals.

During his years in government, these channels were in constant use. Whenever possible, Dean Rusk dodged behind Ball, letting his trusted assistant handle the delicate business of public relations.

Lyndon and George

George Ball preferred Lyndon Johnson to John F. Kennedy. In his words, "I knew many John Kennedys, but I knew only one Lyndon Johnson." [41] Ball viewed Johnson as a more complex, unpredictable, and interesting personality than Kennedy. Although there was much in Johnson that piqued and upset Ball, there was also much he admired in the Texan. Ball marveled at the way LBJ had developed his personalistic mode of politics into a fine art. He watched the Texan pressure, wheedle, intimidate, beg, or threaten in order to achieve his goals. To Johnson, bargaining was the very essence of politics. Ball, who had watched Jean Monnet's successful use of similar if less flamboyant techniques and who had witnessed Adlai Stevenson and Chester Bowles rely more on ideological, unbending, institutional methods unsuccessfully, learned from Johnson.

Ball, in fact, had already developed great skill of his own in the area of informal, highly personal politics. Ever since he came to know Dean Acheson on the handball court in Washington in 1934, Adlai Stevenson in the law offices of Sidney, Austin in Chicago in 1938, John Kenneth Galbraith in Lend-Lease and the Strategic Bombing Survey in the early 1940s, and David Rockefeller at Bilderberg in 1954, Ball worked to build and reinforce important personal relationships. Ball and LBJ sensed this human aspect of personal politics in one another.

Ball and Johnson strengthened their relationship over time. Humor was an important arrow in their quivers of personalistic politics. They used humor when communicating with one another as well as with others. Although LBJ's sense of humor was rather more crude and profane, while Ball's was more witty and intellectual, both men enjoyed this form of communication. Whatever the strengths of the rest of Johnson's inner circle may have been, humor was not one of them. People like McGeorge Bundy, Robert McNamara, and Walt Rostow were tense and intense individuals who had little time for jokes or personal anecdotes. George Ball provided LBJ with welcome relief from such grim solemnity.

One of Ball's favorite anecdotes provides an insight into his relationship with Johnson. German Chancellor Ludwig Erhard was visiting the Johnson ranch in December 1963. Erhard was professorial in bearing, and LBJ wanted to impress him. During breakfast, Johnson began boasting about his chief advisers. Dean Rusk was a Rhodes Scholar and former head of the Rockefeller Foundation. Bob McNamara had been an instructor at Harvard Business School and had run the Ford Motor Company. Mac Bundy had been a Dean at Harvard. Then, noticing Ball sitting across the table, Johnson said, "And, Mr. Chancellor, George Ball there, he's an intellectual, too." Later, as they were leaving the breakfast area, Ball grabbed the president's arm and quietly whispered, "Mr. President, you just called me an intellectual. Where I come from those are fightin' words." Johnson looked at Ball and said, "Don't worry, George, I know that you ain't no half-ass egghead."[42]

After several months of soul searching, George Ball submitted his resignation as under secretary in September 1966. He resigned quietly and refused to use the occasion as an opportunity to critique his former colleagues or their policies. Ball resigned for both professional and personal reasons. In spite of his easy relationship with the president, he had come to realize that his influence on policymaking had waned considerably over the past year. He was especially disillusioned about Johnson's refusal to reconsider the United States' deepening involvement in Vietnam, a policy that Ball had strenuously challenged since 1964.

Furthermore, family problems had become suffocating. His personal financial situation had deteriorated to such a degree that he found himself unable to make ends meet. He was, in son Douglas's words, "busted."[43] His annual government salary of less than $25,000 was but one-fifth of what he had been making at Cleary, Gottlieb. Moreover, during the year before he resigned, his son John struggled to find suitable employment, Ruth's sister went through a difficult divorce, brother Stuart's wife, Marion, had been diagnosed with a serious illness, and Ruth broke both ankles and heels in a painful fall that hospitalized her for weeks and debilitated her for months. George Ball needed rest and time to recuperate personally, financially, and professionally.

In a letter dated September 21, 1966, Lyndon Johnson accepted Ball's resignation "with deep personal as well as official regrets." The president, however, did not want Ball to be totally removed from the political playing field: "Although you have earned the right to private life, after these five and a half years in the line of fire, I would like to think that I shall be able to call on you from time to time in the days ahead."[44]

Lehman Brothers, the United Nations, and Hubert Humphrey

Upon his resignation, George Ball had a spectrum of employment opportunities. His options included a full-time job with his beloved law firm, Cleary, Gottlieb, a position with oil mogul Armand Hammer, and an offer from an investment banking firm, Lehman Brothers. Because of his need for money and his respect for Robert Lehman, the courtly head of Lehman Brothers, George Ball joined the firm as a senior partner in their New York office effective January 2, 1967.

George Ball's oldest son, John, landed a position with Lehman Brothers before his father, in early September 1966. The family was delighted at John's good fortune and George described it as "a case of nepotism in reverse." He joked, "Do you think John will let me in his bank? John is learning the business from the bottom up and I am going to learn it from the top down. At some time, we ought to meet in the middle."[45]

Bobby Lehman's firm was torn by factionalism and cutthroat competition. Lehman foresaw that the end of the family firm was coming and was trying to attract a stellar group of very able people because he recognized that a lot of the people he had there shared only one thing, "a common thirst for loot."[46] After Bobby Lehman died in 1969, Ball was thrust into a maelstrom of boardroom politics that was more vicious than anything he had witnessed in the high circles of the U.S. government. But before the Lehman firm exploded, Ball received an important telephone call from Washington, D.C. It was April 1968, and Arthur Goldberg had just indicated his intention to resign as U.S. ambassador to the United Nations. Lyndon Johnson called to ask Ball to take Goldberg's place.

George Ball wanted nothing to do with the United Nations. He had been out of government for only eighteen months and had just settled into a new and lucrative career. In 1967, he had led a high-powered group of American industrialists to Korea, made three business-related trips to Europe, and, with Ruth, traveled to Iran for the spectacular coronation of the shah. Meanwhile, Ball retained political influence in Washington and worked industriously on his first book, *The Discipline of Power*.

On November 1, 1967, and again on March 25, 1968, Ball attended "wise man" senior advisory group meetings at the White House to review the Vietnam situation. In January 1968, he chaired a committee to investigate the USS *Pueblo* incident, an embarrassing U.S. faux pas in which the North Koreans had seized an intelligence-gathering ship. George Ball found himself enjoying the best of both the private and public worlds.

On the home front, January and February 1968 saw the Balls move from their Washington home of twenty years to New York City, where they took up residence in an elegant apartment on the thirty-seventh and thirty-eighth floors of the western tower at 860 UN Plaza. In spite of his many professional responsibilities, Ball insisted on helping with the move. He loaded several cases of wine and liquor and a number of the heaviest items, such as the safe and filing cabinets, into a rented truck. He then drove the overloaded vehicle to New York, where, with the help of friends, he unloaded it and carried the items up to the new apartment. In this display of what Ruth Ball termed "madness," George also personally helped carry in 250 cartons of books. The next day he flew to Washington for a meeting with Rusk and a television interview concerning the *Pueblo* incident. After two days at the White House, he flew to San Francisco, then returned to New York a day later for the closing on the apartment.[47]

Lyndon Johnson dismissed Ball's reluctance to take the UN position. He had Rusk telephone Ball, and at the same time he contacted Lehman Brothers personally and "really wrung necks and twisted arms." [48] As a result, Ball's colleagues at Lehman's urged him to take the position. Echoing Johnson's words, they argued that he owed it to the president and the country. Realizing that LBJ had him "surrounded," Ball reluctantly accepted the ambassadorship. He did not actually assume his duties at the United Nations until June 25, 1968, when Goldberg vacated the post. Many of his UN colleagues rushed out to purchase Ball's book, *The Discipline of Power*, which had been published on April 1. In this book, written when Ball was a private citizen, Ball minces no words in describing his political ideas on a wide variety of issues.

In July, Ball made an official trip to the Middle and Far East, and in August he represented the United States at the United Nations during the Soviet intervention in Czechoslovakia. Ball locked horns with Soviet Ambassador Jacob Malik, who justified the invasion in terms of the need for "fraternal solicitude." Ball responded that the "fraternal solicitude" that the Soviets were showing Czechoslovakia was precisely "the kind Cain showed Abel." [49] Other than the Czech crisis, Ball found the United Nations post extremely boring. While there, he used to great advantage a skill that he had developed over the years: sleeping with eyes open, "an exercise requiring a posture of meditation with the hand just shading the eyes." [50]

In fact, in 1968 Ball's attention was monopolized by the domestic political scene in America. He watched with increasing agitation as his old bête noire, Richard Nixon, built up momentum against Democratic candidate Hubert Humphrey in the presidential sweepstakes. At the same time, Ball was greatly disturbed by the antiwar violence that had erupted across the country. On March 31, Lyndon Johnson had announced that he would not run for president. In April, Martin Luther King had been assassinated. Given the violent incoherence that bubbled throughout the country and the increasing possibility that Richard Nixon might become the next president, George Ball decided after only three months on the job to leave the United Nations and join Humphrey's presidential campaign. In Ball's frank words, "I hated Nixon. I despised the fellow." [51] George Ball would never forgive himself if he did not do what he could to keep Nixon from winning the presidency.

Besides his animus toward Nixon, Ball had to consider the political possibilities that awaited him in the slim chance that Humphrey should win. Although Ball officially stated that he did not seek any post in a Humphrey administration, it was common knowledge that he stood an excellent chance of becoming Humphrey's secretary of state.

Ball had become weary of Johnson's inflexible Vietnam policy. He complained bitterly to close friends about "Johnson's stiffening on the question of an unconditional bombing halt." He was "convinced that this stiffening gravely compromised the U.S. negotiating team in Paris." [52] Although he castigated U Thant for supporting an unconditional bombing halt, Ball himself entertained a position very close to that of the UN secretary general.

In the early fall of 1968, George Ball telephoned Lyndon Johnson at his Texas ranch and told the president that he was resigning his position at the United Nations effective September 26. Ball determinedly said, "Mr. President, I have always asked you before I have made any major decisions. This time I'm not asking you but I am telling you what I have decided to do." Ball went on to explain his antipathy to Nixon and his need to help Hubert Humphrey, who was trailing by seventeen points in the polls. Johnson, realizing that Ball's mind was made up, did not seriously attempt to dissuade him. He only asked Ball to refrain from announcing his decision until the White House could find a suitable replacement. Otherwise, as Johnson put it, the administration would look "jerky."[53]

Ball's sudden resignation from the UN position was hasty and clumsy. He stepped down one week before he was scheduled to deliver the major U.S. address at the opening of the General Assembly.[54] At the same time, he imprudently and publicly attacked Secretary General U Thant's call for a cessation of the bombing of Vietnam. After only three months actively on the job, Ball alienated many officials in the United Nations by his abrupt resignation.

The Humphrey Campaign of 1968

At the time of his resignation, Ball telephoned Hubert Humphrey who had been unaware of the Ambassador's plans. Humphrey was delighted to have Ball join him and named him as his chief foreign policy adviser. Ball told Humphrey that the only way to reverse the Nixon momentum was to take the offensive and to separate the Humphrey position on Vietnam from that of the Johnson administration. Ball volunteered to be point man in this effort. In a number of press conferences and media appearances, Ball launched a series of vehement attacks on Nixon. These attacks began with his resignation statement where he wrote that he sought to devote all his energy "to help assure the election of Hubert Humphrey and the defeat of Richard Nixon." He went on to pointedly note that "it is essential that the President of the United States be a man with settled principles and clear vision."[55]

In a free-swinging press conference the day after he announced his resignation, Ball summarized his views on Nixon: "It's important that people not forget that he was called 'Tricky Dick.' I have known him for twenty years and I remember why he got that name. The very cynicism with which he selected his running mate is a grave indication of his narrow principles. He was willing to choose a fourth-rate politician and a hack [Spiro Agnew] to a position which could be only a heartbeat from the presidency. This demonstrated shocking callousness."[56]

Ball's favorite phrases when describing Nixon were "no settled principles" and "no real convictions." [57]

Ball's attacks stirred up the campaign as indignant Republicans went on the counterattack, labeling Ball as Humphrey's new hatchet man. Even the evangelist Billy Graham jumped into the fray—to Ball's delight. Graham charged that Ball had hit Nixon "below the belt" and declared that he had "known Richard Nixon intimately for twenty years. I can testify that he is a man of high moral principle." [58] Graham hastened to add that he did not intend to get involved in politics.

George Ball also played a key role in helping draft a hard-hitting speech that Humphrey delivered in Salt Lake City on September 30. In an account of the maneuvering that surrounded the preparation of this speech, one source describes Ball as "a big, burly fellow with a large nose, rather unruly gray hair, and surprisingly often a look of suppressed frivolity on his face, as though he had just thought of an improper joke. . . . Ball is a good man to have around when you are reassessing." [59] In the Salt Lake speech, Humphrey called for a halt to U.S. bombing and thereby began to distance himself from Johnson on the Vietnam issue. In the words of Theodore White, the Salt Lake speech was "critical" in Humphrey's "recapture of initiative." [60]

Ball did much to blunt the Nixon drive and helped turn Humphrey's campaign around. After Ball joined the Humphrey team, the Minnesotan Democrat seemed to find new spirit. By election eve, Nixon's seventeen-point lead in the polls had been whittled to only two percentage points in both the Harris and Gallup polls. Although Nixon received 301 electoral votes to Humphrey's 191 (George Wallace received 46), the popular vote was very close indeed: 31,785,480 Americans voted for Richard Nixon, while 31,275,166 people cast their ballots for Humbert Humphrey. George Ball had fought hard in one more losing cause. [61]

Lyndon Johnson and his inner circle were privately upset by Ball's resignation and decision to join the Humphrey campaign. In an extraordinary forty-minute meeting on September 25, Johnson discussed the situation with Clark Clifford, Dean Rusk, and Walt Rostow. [62] Clifford gave an account of a telephone conversation in which he had tried to talk Ball out of leaving. According to Clifford, Ball had stated: "I cannot permit myself to remain quiet any longer about Nixon. This is my country."

Ball's old friend Dean Rusk nodded at Clifford's report: "He said the same thing to me. He is misestimating [*sic*] the political situation. It would be interpreted as a break with the administration." Clifford demurred: "He said he does not intend to break with the administration." Rusk: "Ball quits two months after he takes office!" Clifford: "He has an excellent statement."

After listening to this discussion with increasing annoyance, Lyndon Johnson stated, "The time when he should have decided this was when he agreed to serve." The president later said, "Ball's going to Humphrey is part of a movement to the 'dove' side. . . . [Antiwar Democratic candidate Eugene] McCarthy is an admirer of Ball's." Clifford concluded that "this may be a desperation move" by Humphrey.[63]

George Ball believed that Lyndon Johnson himself was a major reason for Humphrey's defeat in 1968. Ball liked Humphrey, the happy warrior who chattered ceaselessly and optimistically. He enjoyed pointing out that Hubert never had an unexpressed idea. Johnson, on the other hand, considered Humphrey to be an annoying idealist who lacked common sense. In Ball's judgment, Johnson was jealous of Humphrey's popularity and his easy manner with people. LBJ once complained to Dean Acheson that "after all I've had done for the country, you'd think the American people would love me." Acheson responded, "Mr. President, it's simple. You're not a very lovable person."[64]

Johnson knew Humphrey's serious reservations about Vietnam policy. After Humphrey cautiously voiced some objections at a high-level meeting, he found himself frozen out of Johnson's important foreign policy councils and Tuesday luncheons. He became a lonely figure in the White House. At a Tuesday luncheon on September 12, 1968, Humphrey was the subject of critical discussion. Johnson and his inner circle felt that the vice president was getting out of hand. Clark Clifford argued that Humphrey "need[ed] a man . . . we trust and respect to give him correct guidance."[65]

Although Lyndon Johnson told his own advisers that he wanted Humphrey to win, his actions said otherwise. He angrily refused to allow any of his cabinet members to endorse Humphrey. Ball knew that the president was having telephone conversations with Richard Nixon and concluded that Johnson might have cut a deal with Nixon, a man the president was known to despise. Actually, Johnson's preferred candidate for president was Republican Nelson Rockefeller, whom LBJ had secretly urged to run.[66]

By helping sink Humphrey in 1968, LBJ also helped sink Ball, who hoped to become secretary of state in a Humphrey cabinet. As Ball told Joseph Kraft: "Nobody who has done what I have done, who has spent his whole adult life in the world of international affairs, could possibly say he wouldn't want to be Secretary of State. I'd love it."[67]

In spite of their differences, Lyndon Johnson and George Ball remained friends and respected one another to the end. At a January 16, 1969, farewell ceremony honoring Dean Rusk, Johnson took the opportunity to praise George Ball: "I can't let this occasion go by without paying my tribute to George Ball. He is one of the ablest, most loyal and most courageous men that I have known in public life." In his autobiography, Ball describes how he "gained fuller appreciation—to the point of admiration—for [Johnson's] capacities and qualities. . . . He was a remarkably effective man with extraordinary shrewdness, phenomenal driving force, and an implacable will. . . . He was always kind to me, and in time we developed an affectionate rapport." Ball was well aware of Johnson's foibles, his crudeness, his ego, and his personal manipulativeness. He managed to look beyond these failings, however, and saw a man of idealism, a Texas populist, a man who had a vision of an America free of poverty, discrimination, and inequity. George Ball saw a man who was willing to pay the price to do what was necessary to achieve these ideals. In Ball's view, Lyndon Johnson was a great man, and great men are not without great blemishes.[68]

On January 20, 1969, Richard Nixon was inaugurated as the thirty-seventh president of the United States. George Ball, who had opposed Nixon politically for a decade and a half, was deeply troubled about the future of the country. Ruth Ball said of that January 20: "It was the inauguration of this Republican president and we feared the worst."[69]

The 1970s: *Private Public Power*

George Ball's partisan attacks on Nixon during the campaign carried costs. Because some of his elderly, outraged Republican partners at Lehman Brothers needed a cooling off period and because Ball needed a rest himself, he and Ruth took an extended trip to France and Spain after the elections. Meanwhile, Ball had become something of a pariah on Wall Street, and he lost his position on the boards of directors of such major companies as Standard Oil of California, Singer, and Upjohn. When Ball rejoined Lehman Brothers in mid-January of 1969, he did so with a vengeance.

For George Ball, 1969 represented a key transitional year. It was the year of his 60th birthday and a time when, using Lehman Brothers as the springboard, he vaulted aboard a rapidly moving professional track that took him across the United States and across the world. During that year alone, he made fourteen international trips, including an extensive tour around the world. Meanwhile, Ball gave speeches in a dozen different U.S. cities in 1969, including Houston, Philadelphia, Detroit, New York, Buffalo, Albuquerque, and San Francisco.

During the 1970s, Ball worked hard to strengthen and extend his international contacts and to maintain his national image and influence. In the decade, he delivered 114 speeches and wrote 84 articles that appeared in such influential publications as *Foreign Affairs, Harper's, Life, Fortune*, the *Washington Post*, and the *New York Times*. He also wrote a regular column for *Newsweek*. In April of 1974, Harvard University presented Ball with its prestigious award as "the year's outstanding statesman-businessman."

George Ball enjoyed testing his ideas on college campuses. During this period, he spoke at thirty-four universities. He delivered commencement addresses or received honorary degrees at Brandeis, the New School, Harvard, Carnegie-Mellon,

Williams, Michigan State, Denison, Bates College, and American University. By 1973, he had been awarded fifteen honorary degrees. In addition, Ball testified nineteen times before congressional committees in Washington in the 1970s. He was a regular guest on such television interview programs as CBS's "Face the Nation," ABC's "Issue and Answers," and PBS's "MacNeil-Lehrer Report."[70]

Besides these intellectual ventures, Ball wrote a second book, entitled *Diplomacy for a Crowded World*.[71] Published in 1976, this substantial study of international relations appeared just as the presidential campaign was gathering momentum. Having completed this widely and favorably reviewed book, Ball immediately began preparations to write his autobiography.

Ever an internationalist, George Ball continued to attend Bilderberg meetings. In spite of his crushing political responsibilities in the 1960s, he insisted on attending every Bilderberg meeting during that period. In the 1970s, the meetings convened in Switzerland; Woodstock, New York; Belgium; Sweden; France; Turkey; England; Princeton, New Jersey; and Austria. Within Bilderberg, Ball continued to wield enormous influence, and he played a steadying role when the secretive organization was shaken to the core by a scandal that surrounded Bilderberg's cofounder and figurehead, Prince Bernhard of the Netherlands.

In February 1976, Bernhard, known internationally as a war hero, international conservationist, goodwill ambassador, and "the flying Dutchman of industry," was accused of accepting a $1.1 million secret payment from the Lockheed Corporation to promote the sale of that company's aircraft to the Royal Netherlands Air Force. The accusations continued throughout the year, and a group of Bilderberg regulars sought to prepare a petition in support of the beleaguered prince. When the group approached George Ball, he refused to sign the petition, pointing out that such an act was both uninformed and premature. He considered the reputation and well-being of the Bilderberg group to be the most important consideration under the circumstances and warned of the consequences if Bernhard were found guilty. In early September 1976, a special investigatory commission issued a devastating report that blackened the name of the Prince. The Dutch prime minister read a statement from Bernhard, who said, "I accept full responsibility for this and thus accept the disapproval expressed by the commission in the report."[72] In 1976, no Bilderberg conference was held.

Ball, Kissinger, and the Nixon Presidency

In spite of Ball's Nixonian allergies and his past attacks on the Republicans, he found himself periodically consulted by the Nixon administration during the early 1970s. As an experienced member of the establishment, his influence transcended administrations. Ruth Ball was only slightly exaggerating when she observed in 1970 that "George is rapidly becoming an underground presidential adviser."[73]

Nixon had not even taken the oath of office when his national security adviser, Henry Kissinger, invited Ball to Washington for a January 12 meeting in the White House. In late April, Secretary of Defense Melvin Laird summoned Ball to Washington to consult with him on defense issues. These contacts continued sporadically throughout the early years of the Nixon administration. After a March 1972 trip to Japan, for example, Ball shared his impressions with Henry Kissinger in Washington. In March 1973 and again in September, he met with Kissinger to discuss the deteriorating state of the administration. As late as March of 1975, during the Ford administration, Kissinger consulted with Ball on issues of foreign policy.

Although Richard Nixon deeply resented Ball's ad hominem attacks in 1968, he was not above soliciting Ball's political assistance when it was needed. In May 1971, Nixon asked Ball to help the administration defeat Senator Mike Mansfield's proposal to withdraw U.S. forces from Europe. Ball, who shared the administration's alarm about such an act, turned lobbyist for Nixon. Quietly working out of the vice president's office near the Senate chamber, Ball spent a busy week in Washington meeting with senators from both parties and urging them to oppose the Mansfield plan. Ball's political credibility and his persuasive argumentation were among the major reasons that the Mansfield plan was defeated. During the episode, both Kissinger and Nixon consulted closely with the Democrat. After the legislative battle was won, Nixon called Ball and expressed his gratitude. Ball took the opportunity to warn the president about the need for the White House to improve its poor relations with Congress. He never spoke with Nixon again.

Although George Ball cooperated politically with Nixon and Kissinger, he held neither man in high regard. During the very time he was in contact with them, he was preparing a book in which he sharply criticized their styles and goals. In *Diplomacy*, Ball describes Kissinger as one who considered himself the "Master Player," "the lonely cowboy," for whom "secrecy is essential." Ball colorfully compares the United States to a juggler who must keep many balls in the air at the same time. But Kissinger, "the virtuoso, always center-stage under the spotlight, has specialized in trying to throw two balls at a time to record heights, while letting the rest ricochet aimlessly around the stage."[74] For Ball, Kissinger's primary and overriding preoccupation was with Henry Kissinger. Kissinger was narcissistic in the extreme.

Coups and Conflict at Lehman Brothers

With the death of Bobby Lehman in 1969, the investment banking firm of Lehman Brothers fell into a state of malaise. Internal tensions and nasty personal competition broke to the surface, and the firm's morale disintegrated. Several powerful senior partners withdrew their capital and walked away from the firm, and a crusty, authoritarian personality named Frederick L. Ehrman took control as chairman. Ehrman was a disaster. He sought to rule the venerable firm by fear. Ehrman succeeded only in uniting a disparate group of Lehman employees in a common cause: Ehrman's ouster.

With business sharply declining and costs increasing, the firm found itself losing unprecedented sums of money in the early 1970s. The historically successful commercial paper division of the company, headed by a loud, aggressive trader named Lewis L. Glucksman, had suffered severe losses in 1973. Glucksman's position was in jeopardy, and George Ball provided important support for Glucksman and others at Lehman who had established commendable records over time.

Ball was the only senior member of the firm who had the credibility and courage to lead a coup against Ehrman. Working out of his New York apartment, which served as the center of coup operations, he managed to convince the board to dismiss Ehrman. On July 25, 1973, he rushed home from a business trip to Algiers, and that weekend, when Ehrman's two strongest supporters were out of the city, Ball called the board meeting that resulted in the dismissal of the chairman. George Ball did not exaggerate when he told a writer, "I organized a palace revolution."[75]

In her diaries, Ruth Ball graphically describes the 1973 coup: George "singlehandedly created a *coup d'etat* in the firm. It was his idea to oust the chairman and bring in a new one, Peter Peterson. . . . Within two days George had lined up a majority of votes on the board and his maneuver was a *fait accompli* before people knew what had happened to them. I keep being informed that Wall Street banking is a 'dog eat dog' enterprise and have concluded that George does not intend to be gnawed. He was quite prepared to resign if the reorganization had not been feasible and return to the Cleary law firm."[76]

Although Ball was the logical successor to Ehrman, he refused the opportunity. Instead, he did the next best thing: he played a key role in selecting the new chairman, a forty-seven-year-old Republican named Peter G. Peterson. Peterson had been with the firm for less than two months and was not a natural choice for the position. George Ball, playing the role of kingmaker, smoothly maneuvered Peterson into the chairmanship. Soon after the coup, Ball began taking Peterson on international missions, where he introduced the new chairman of Lehman Brothers to industrial and political leaders throughout Europe. Like Michael Blumenthal and so many other impressive figures before him, Pete Peterson became a loyal and committed Ball boy.

Peter Peterson grew up in Nebraska, the son of a poor Greek immigrant. He attended Kearney State Teachers College and MIT before transferring to Northwestern, where he graduated summa cum laude in 1947. After earning an M.B.A.

from the University of Chicago, he pursued a career in advertising. He developed a friendship with a tennis partner and wealthy neighbor, Charles Percy, the president of Bell & Howell. In 1961 Peterson became president of Bell & Howell, and when Percy became a U.S. senator in 1966, Peterson took his place as Chief Executive Officer.

In 1971, President Richard Nixon appointed Peterson presidential assistant for international economic affairs, and in 1972 Nixon named him secretary of commerce. After a rocky period in this position, Peterson served as a roving trade ambassador for Nixon. Peterson and his vivacious wife, Sally, became popular celebrities on the Washington social circuit, where they hobnobbed with the elite. This sparkling lifestyle did little to endear Peterson to Nixon and his inner circle. Although Peterson and Henry Kissinger developed a close friendship, Peterson found himself locked in a debilitating rivalry with Secretary of Treasury John Connally. Nixon backed Connally and humiliated Peterson. In Kissinger's words, Connally "simply ran over Pete Peterson on international economic policy. . . . He had reduced Peterson to the role of spectator even before Nixon ended Peterson's agony by appointing him Secretary of Commerce, a position he filled with great distinction."[77]

After this unpleasant interval in the Nixon White House, Peterson looked back to the world of private enterprise and was offered positions both at Salomon Brothers and at Lehman. Although Ehrman took the lead in the recruitment process, George Ball was a major reason why Peterson decided to join Lehman Brothers. Peterson, who knew Ball primarily by his continuing and almost legendary reputation for international economic wisdom, was enormously impressed by the man. "In June of 1973, I joined Lehman Brothers, most importantly because of George's persuasive powers. I loved George."[78]

As chairman of Lehman, Peterson took an office directly next to the one occupied by George Ball. The two executives became close friends, and Peterson seldom made any important decision without consulting the experienced gentleman in the office next door. With George Ball at his side, Pete Peterson turned Lehman Brothers around. By 1975, the firm was earning profits of $25–30 million per year. Sensing the changing nature of the world and the need to transform the traditional role of investment banking, Peterson introduced a number of significant organizational changes. He emphasized strategic planning and the rationalization of the business, oversaw important mergers with Abraham and Company in 1974 and Kuhn Loeb in 1977, and dramatically changed the membership of the board of directors in 1976. He cut the number of employees and the number of partners in half.

At the time Peterson assumed the chairmanship, the firm faced a critical shortage of capital. George Ball offered a timely and unexpected solution. He introduced an old friend, Enrico Braggiotti, the president of Banca Commerciale

Italiana, to Peterson and Lehman Brothers. After considerable negotiation involving Ball, Peterson, Braggiotti, and others, BCI invested $7 million in Lehman in exchange for 12 percent of Lehman stock. Braggiotti bought into Lehman Brothers because of his high regard for Ball and Peterson.

Although George Ball was not an investment banker and understood little of the technical details of the business, he played a critically important role as a negotiator, mediator, and facilitator. Pete Peterson credited Ball with extraordinary "convening power."[79]

Ball's skills were tested one more time at Lehman Brothers. Lewis Glucksman, who had made a comeback with Peterson's accession, turned against Peterson and, in a bizarre and brutal grab for power, sought to replace him as head of the firm. Peterson, who had naively supported Glucksman and made him co–chief executive officer, was stunned and horrified when the trader bluntly told him in an extraordinary five-hour meeting in July 1983 that he intended to take Peterson's job.

The Glucksman-Peterson clash shook Lehman to the core. The gulf between the two men developed out of the difference between traders and bankers. In this case, however, the personalities of the individuals exacerbated the tension and made the conflict inevitable. Although both men were sons of immigrants and both were highly ambitious personally, they shared little else. Peterson was smooth, civil, and somewhat haughty, an integral member of the American establishment. When he dropped names like David Rockefeller and Henry Kissinger, he did not exaggerate his relationships with them. Peterson was a connoisseur of the arts who led the lifestyle of the rich and the famous.

Lew Glucksman resented the Peterson persona. Rumpled, arrogant, insecure, often crude and profane, he could be brutally frank. Talented and well educated, he was not afraid to work in the trenches. Descriptions of Glucksman have not been kind to the feisty little trader. He has been described as a "jungle fighter." Reportedly, one fellow board member observed that "Glucksman's flaw was that there was an angry pig inside the man. He wasn't after money. He was after power, complete control." Glucksman once shocked his colleagues when at a meeting with the smooth, patrician grand old man of the firm, Bobbie Lehman, Glucksman registered his disagreement by bellowing, "I don't give a rat's ass."[80]

As the Peterson-Glucksman clash threatened to tear Lehman Brothers apart, George Ball stepped into the breach. Once again, only Ball had the credibility and courage to mediate. After an exhausting series of meetings with both parties during a two-week period in July, Ball negotiated a deal. Peterson agreed to step down as chairman of Lehman Brothers in return for a lucrative financial package. The severance agreement allowed Peterson to immediately withdraw his $7 million in equity in the firm, to continue to receive one percent of Lehman's profits over the next five and a half years, and to receive a retirement payment of

$300,000 annually over that same period. Furthermore, Lehman Brothers agreed to invest $5 million in a new venture capital firm established by Peterson.

Although Peterson did not have the stomach to fight Glucksman, with George Ball's help he departed Lehman with a fortune and went on to other highly successful business ventures. Glucksman had attained his goal as well; he took charge of Lehman as sole CEO. Lehman quickly went into a financial tailspin, although it was not entirely Glucksman's fault. Old feuds resurfaced, and in 1984, the proud old company was purchased by Shearson/American Express.

Even George Ball's critical interventions and valuable mediating skills could not save Lehman Brothers. He did, however, help extend its health and reputation for a decade and, in the process, assisted many individuals in the firm. Ball's own financial interests, however, were not particularly well served by his tenure at Lehman Brothers. Although his annual salary was respectable, it fluctuated considerably, and the cash bonuses he received in the earlier years were relatively modest. The largest fortunes were made in the sale of the firm. By the time of the Shearson buyout, Ball was virtually retired and lacked any shares in the company.[81]

George Ball retired as a partner of Lehman Brothers in October 1982. Although he made several close friends at Lehman and received retainers from the company through 1988, he harbored a profound dislike for investment banking. Since the days of Adlai Stevenson, he considered bankers selfish and obsessed with money. Ball liked to quote Stevenson's description of bankers after Adlai had finished some delicate negotiations in Omaha in the late 1930s: "I've just spent a magnificent morning with the bankers. The greed ran down their faces like sweat."[82]

His experiences at Lehman Brothers had not endeared Wall Street banking to Ball. The intrigue, greed, vicious competition, and backbiting disgusted him. Because the profession had paid his bills for many years, Ball seldom criticized investment banking publicly. Privately, however, his remarks were scathing. He described investment banking as "a rotten business" and vehemently stated that "investment bankers are the lowest quality characters outside of vaudeville performers." In Ball's judgment, traders were particularly "miserable people."[83]

Personal Trial and Travail

For George Ball, the 1970s were painfully bracketed by the presidencies of Richard Nixon and Jimmy Carter. His political disappointment, moreover, was overlaid by considerable personal travail. As Ruth and George worked to make a home of the house they bought in Princeton, New Jersey, in 1976, their sons' struggles continued. Although Ball refused to complain or even to discuss these difficulties, they are graphically related in Ruth Ball's diaries. John's home in New Rochelle, New York, sustained major damage when frozen radiators burst. John struggled valiantly with illness and, lacking steady employment, piled up considerable debts. Douglas spent much of the time seeking a teaching position.

The nadir of the decade occurred in 1974. The family faced enormous financial problems. After Peter Peterson took control of Lehman Brothers, he cut the partners' 1974 salaries back to $75,000 per year. George Ball felt the pinch more than most. According to Ruth, George had to pay a "considerable number of John's accumulated debts and is supporting seven of us." To meet these financial demands, George and Ruth mortgaged their apartment and other possessions. Ruth dug into her own savings in order to help pay for the "heavy outlay of clinic expenses." [84] George spent the Fourth of July that year in Columbia, Maryland, editing someone else's book in order to make some badly needed extra money.

To capture the depressing flavor of the time, it is worth quoting Ruth Ball at some length: "It has been a temptation to me to withhold this bleak passage in my family history. But to do so would give an incomplete account of our lives. And it would deny to any reader a sense of the courage, devotion, skill and dogged determination that George has applied in facing his many responsibilities. He is within one year of retirement age and might expect to have a five-day rather than seven-day work week. His efforts to make financial provision for our old age and the security of our descendants have been greatly curtailed by these unexpected contingencies. . . . I see George's shoulders sag and I miss the exhilaration his voice has always had about ideas and plans. There can be no plans until our bills are paid, our sons self-sufficient, our family visits restored." [85]

The year of Watergate and the forced resignation of Richard Nixon was a year of profound unpleasantness for George Ball and his family as well. Tribulations large and small piled up around them. During his unsuccessful quest for employment, John had his pocket picked in New York City in August. He and his wife, Gail, were divorced that fall. The absence of Gail and the two grandchildren made the annual family Christmas in Cocoa Beach, Florida, a depressing and glum affair. George and Ruth were heartbroken. Shortly after the Balls left their home in Florida, burglars broke into the house, ransacked the place, and stole everything of value. George Ball summed it up well: "This year nothing works." [86]

George Ball and Jimmy Carter

George Ball realized that the 1976 presidential election provided him with an excellent opportunity to be appointed secretary of state. In the words of one pundit, "Ball pops up, like a cork, every election year." [87] Although sixty-seven years old, Ball had remained active in political affairs and had maintained a huge reputation in the Democratic Party. Furthermore, in the summer of 1976, he had published a hard-hitting and thoughtful book, *Diplomacy for a Crowded World*. This study represented a frontal attack on the foreign policy of Republican presidents Richard Nixon and Gerald Ford. It particularly criticized the political style and policies of Henry Kissinger. The timing of the book could not have been better.

Because of an old promise, Ball began by backing the candidacy of Hubert Humphrey. As Georgia's Governor Jimmy Carter moved to the fore, however, George Ball shifted his support to Carter. But Ball and Carter never established sound personal rapport. Ball's early impressions of Carter were negative, and Carter, in turn, maintained nagging doubts about Ball's loyalty and commitment.

George Ball first met Jimmy Carter at a luncheon at Lehman Brothers in October 1975. Ball came away from the session singularly unimpressed. Carter appeared naive, overconfident, and absorbed by the minutiae of electoral politics. He seemed to avoid the substantive issues of politics and, in Ball's judgment, he lacked vision.[88] Furthermore, Ball was never convinced that Jimmy Carter was seriously interested in his ideas.

The relationship between the two men also suffered from a misunderstanding early in Carter's presidential campaign. When asked for the names of his foreign policy advisers, Carter listed George Ball as one of several. Journalist Rowland Evans quizzed Ball about his position as one of Carter's leading foreign policy advisers. Ball denied it, saying he had met Carter only once and had not been in touch with him since. When Evans wrote a column highlighting the discrepancy, Carter was embarrassed.

Actually, Ball's personal files reveal that he had been in direct touch with Jimmy Carter beginning in May of 1976. In a personal note dated May 30, 1976, Carter wrote: "I read your letter, memorandum and your book this weekend and will be a better candidate because of it." Ball responded on June 9, offering Carter a campaign slogan: "A government of all the talents." Carter never adopted this slogan and backed away from Ball somewhat. Nonetheless, Ball persisted. In a long letter of August 10, 1976, after returning from an extended trip to Europe and Australia, he offered his services to Carter, requesting a meeting with the governor.

In the four-page letter, Ball reminded Carter of his preparation of the 1960 Stevenson Report for Kennedy. Ball pointed out that this report and the various task forces enabled Kennedy "to get off the mark with a flying start," and he offered, "If you thought it useful, I would be glad to work along the same lines quietly." Ball also volunteered to make speeches and to write them for Carter. He stressed his own agreement with Carter's foreign policy ideas: "I can explain and defend your foreign policy position with conviction since I find myself in complete agreement with the views you have expressed; in fact, the foreign policy lines I have developed and advocated in my recent book parallel your own expressed views with remarkable fidelity." Ball enclosed a nine-page document entitled "Why American Foreign Policy Needs Jimmy Carter." [89]

Carter never accepted Ball's offer. Ball addressed his next communication, a September 1976 policy paper on Western Europe, to second-level Carter advisers. The political competition for secretary of state had begun. Others in the running for the top foreign policymaking positions included Cyrus Vance, Paul Warnke, Henry Owen, and Zbigniew Brzezinski. By the time Ball began sending materials to Carter, Brzezinski had already been supplying the Georgian with foreign policy position papers for more than a year. He had also begun clogging the access channels to Carter.

Ball was an early casualty in the cabinet competition, in part because of his highly independent demeanor and forceful personality. He further undermined his candidacy by criticizing Israeli policy in the Middle East. He bluntly urged the implementation of UN Resolution 242, which called for Israel's withdrawal from all the territories occupied during the 1967 war. In exchange, the Arabs would recognize Israel's right to exist. Ball's recommendations produced a storm of protest from Israel's many supporters in the United States, who let Carter know that George Ball was an unacceptable choice for secretary of state.

Brzezinski summarized the reasons for Ball's rejection when he told Jimmy Carter that George Ball would be "an assertive individual but probably somewhat handicapped by his controversial position on the Middle East." [90] Carter already had Brzezinski, and he did not need another "assertive" foreign policy figure, especially one who carried heavy political baggage. Brzezinski argued against Ball's nomination. During the competition for cabinet positions, Ball had been asked about reports that he might be Jimmy Carter's secretary of state. Ball tartly responded, "I'm sure the Democratic Party could do a lot worse, and I'm sure they will." [91] In the end, Carter felt more comfortable with Cyrus Vance, a loyal, less threatening individual. In any case, Carter intended from the beginning to act as his own secretary of state.

When George and Ruth Ball cast their votes for the Democratic ticket in the 1976 presidential election, they did so with little enthusiasm. In Ruth's words: "Our voting for Mr. Carter was without conviction. He won and we hoped this would not be one more on the list of unfortunate presidents." [92]

Although Jimmy Carter offered George Ball the ambassadorship to either London or Paris, Ball politely refused the opportunities. From time to time during his presidency, Carter or his advisers would call for advice from Ball. Nonetheless, Ball did not become significantly involved until the time of the Iranian revolution in late 1978.

Relying heavily on National Security Adviser Brzezinski and preoccupied with the Camp David Accords, Carter completely misread and misunderstood the explosive situation in Iran. On the advice of Treasury Secretary Michael Blu-menthal, Carter called in George Ball for an independent assessment. Ball, who had a long acquaintance with Iran and had visited the country a half dozen times, set up office in the White House on November 30, 1978. Skeptical of the gov-ernment information on Iran, Ball consulted with outside experts. After nearly two weeks of study, he prepared a paper that included an analysis and policy rec-ommendations. After presenting his report to a cabinet-level group that included Brzezinski, Ball met with President Carter to discuss his conclusions.

In an eighteen-page memorandum entitled "Issues and Implications of the Iranian Crisis," Ball argued that the shah was finished as an absolute monarch. He pointed out that military repression was doomed to failure and that it risked turning Iran into another Lebanon. He recommended that the shah transfer full power to a government responsive to the people. He suggested a "council of notables" composed of responsible opposition figures known for their personal and professional integrity.

Although Ball's proposal was mild, given the lateness of the date, Brzezinski opposed it strenuously. The national security adviser, working with a profound ignorance of Iran and relying on distorted information provided him by the shah's ambassador to the United States, Ardeshir Zahedi, had taken charge of Iran policy. Brzezinski believed the shah could be salvaged and that a military government could maintain control. Like Zahedi, Brzezinski imagined a restoration similar to the one of 1953, when covert U.S. action helped the shah return to power after a nationalist insurrection.[93]

When Ball went in to present his report to Carter, to his surprise, "there was Zbig sitting there."[94] Carter told Ball that he appreciated the report but he would not accept its recommendations since he would not presume to tell another head of state what to do. Ball argued that Carter, in suggesting that the shah step down, would only be responding to a friend's desperate plea for advice. Under the influ-ence of Brzezinski, the president put aside Ball's report.

According to George Ball, the only positive result of his consultantship to Carter was his argument that the president not send Brzezinski to Tehran. Appar-ently, Brzezinski felt that his presence in Iran would in some way help the shah. Ball listened to Brzezinski's plan and sharply told Carter, "With all due respect, [this] is the worst idea I have ever heard."[95] Knowing that Ball had heard many bad ideas over his long career, the president was impressed. He vetoed the idea of a Brzezinski Tehran trek.

After Ball left the White House, he watched in disgust as Carter and Brze-zinski bumbled and stumbled their way through disastrously conceived policies concerning Iran. Such policy involved sending an ill-prepared military general to Iran as a political mediator, the ill-advised admission of the shah into the United

States, thus precipitating the hostage crisis, and the ill-fated hostage rescue attempt in April 1980. One result was the honorable resignation of Secretary of State Cyrus Vance and his replacement by Edmund Muskie.

Ball, now locked out of the corridors of influence by Brzezinski, did what he could to suggest alternative policies, writing and speaking publicly on the issue whenever he had the opportunity. He thoroughly approved when Carter finally turned Iran policy over to Muskie, who favored a low-key diplomatic approach as opposed to Brzezinski's confrontational military emphasis. In referring to this shift, Ball stated that the policies were "two Poles apart." [96]

The Last Years: The 1980s and 1990s

During the last decade and half of his life, George Ball lacked his accustomed access to the highest political echelons in Washington. He found himself badly out of step with the ideas and policies of the Reagan and Bush administrations. When Democrat Bill Clinton took the presidency in 1992, the situation did not improve for Ball. Nonetheless, he stayed active and continued his career as a political commentator. During these last fifteen years, he wrote three books, delivered an estimated three hundred lectures, made more than eighty overseas trips, and participated in nonstop meetings in Washington and New York. He failed to heed Whitman's advice and spent little time "loafing by the foot path."

Politically, George Ball remained active at Bilderberg meetings and did not miss a session over the last decades of his life. He organized his own discussion group of experienced Democrats that met several times annually at the Century Club in New York. In spite of his distaste for Reagan and Bush, he pursued his old policy of exerting influence whenever possible, regardless of whether Democrats or Republicans were in power. Although he enjoyed limited access to the Republican leadership of the 1980s, he maintained his ties with such individuals as David Rockefeller, while establishing new links with bright Republicans like James Schlesinger. On occasion, he even managed to present his provocative ideas to conservative Republican politicians in Washington. In April 1984, for example, he spoke to "the Wednesday group," a clique of conservative House members, providing them with a tough critique of U.S. policy errors in the Middle East and Latin America.

When Ball traveled to Washington or New York, he scheduled back-to-back appointments that stretched from early morning into the evening. Typical was a visit to New York on Wednesday, May 8, 1985. The seventy-six-year-old commentator left his home in Princeton on the early morning train to New York. In New York, he began with a session at the offices of *Harper's* magazine and from there went to a meeting with McGeorge Bundy. After the Bundy appointment, he made an appearance at the Council on Foreign Relations and then met with a writer. Ball next appeared on the MacNeil-Lehrer report in a high-pressured live discussion of the "Star Wars" initiative. He finished the day at a black-tie dinner at the American-Austrian Foundation, where he delivered an address in honor of Ambassador Gruber. He arrived home in Princeton at midnight.

Besides his position on several corporate boards of directors, Ball took leadership positions in educational and charitable organizations. He served on the board of trustees of the Woodrow Wilson School at Princeton and accepted the presidency of the Asia Society when John D. Rockefeller died in an automobile accident. Earlier, he had chaired the U.S. fund-raising committee for the expensive restoration of Canterbury Cathedral. By 1989, Ball had resigned from many of his memberships and boards. He did not, however, resign from political combat. Besides his mediating role in the internal conflict for control at Lehman Brothers in the early 1980s, Ball also quietly joined an underdog group that sought to rescue and reform *Harper's* magazine.

The Rescue of Harper's *Magazine*

Lewis Lapham, editor of *Harper's*, first met George Ball in the early 1970s at a social gathering in New York. In 1980, *Harper's* collapsed financially and was acquired by the MacArthur Foundation through the good offices of John "Rick" MacArthur, whose father, Roderick, was the most influential member of the foundation. The foundation then appointed a Board of Directors of the *Harper's* Magazine Foundation to oversee the magazine. The board members represented an extremely cautious and conservative point of view, which immediately put them in conflict with Lapham, the outspoken, iconoclastic editor. In Lapham's view, the foundation directors were a covey of "pious," "illiterate" individuals who "represented the very worst aspects of the establishment" and "who had no sense of humor whatsoever." [97]

In some desperation, Lapham looked for someone of experience and wisdom who might also be persuaded to join the board and to provide some quality and balance. After considerable reflection, Lapham was able to identify one such person—George Ball. Ball was Lapham's only kindred spirit who also had the reputation and eminence to be acceptable to the board. Shortly before the first directors' meeting, Lapham telephoned Ball and asked him to consider joining the board. Although he had many other commitments, Ball agreed to help. According to Lapham, "Ball shuffled into the January 1981 inaugural meeting with his mischievous grin, offered his greetings, and everyone was enormously impressed. He was obviously the most eminent and impressive person in the room."

In spite of Ball's presence, the board, horrified by some of Lapham's sardonic columns critiquing U.S. culture and politics, dismissed the editor from the magazine. The immediate cause was a March 1981 article in the *Washington Post* in which Lapham bitingly declared the United States to be a wasteland for the arts. He wrote that no matter how much money was thrown at the arts, "one couldn't change a cornfield into an Italian garden. Americans have a talent for brilliant interpretation and performance, but they haven't got the knack for making works of art."[98]

Retribution was swift. In a letter to three members of the Harper's board, MacArthur executive J. A. Diana wrote that the Lapham piece had occasioned "considerable discussion and concern" at the foundation. "If there had been a motion on the table to close Harper's last Friday, I believe it would have passed without any difficulty. Lewis [Lapham] at this point has a margin of error of about zero in my estimation."[99]

Rick MacArthur, a bright young journalist who dedicated much of his time to fighting the ogre of censorship and who had originally rescued the magazine, was dismayed but could do nothing.[100] The board hired another editor, Michael Kinsley, who was unable to stem the magazine's financial hemorrhaging and who also managed to alienate powerful board members. In the meantime, Rick Mac-Arthur joined the board as president and then publisher. When Kinsley departed, MacArthur saw an opening to rescue the magazine from its mediocrity and financial distress. He was also sensitive to the fact that, in George Ball, he had an ally and kindred spirit at the table. George Ball, like Lewis Lapham and MacArthur himself, was a "maverick."[101]

MacArthur asked Ball to meet him at the Perigord, Ball's favorite New York restaurant. Here, they agreed to be coconspirators and settled upon a strategy to rescue Harper's. When the beleaguered Kinsley resigned, MacArthur and Ball worked to bring the talented Lapham back as editor. Lapham presented a proposal for a new format for Harper's, and, with George Ball's support, MacArthur carried it to the other board members. Ball wrote a few letters and made follow-up telephone calls. In a June 1983 communication to the only other member of the board with national stature, Ball urged Walter Cronkite to support the Lapham appointment. In Ball's low-key words: "Lapham is ready and eager to come back as editor if his ideas meet with the sympathy of the Board. I have known Lapham for many years. I like him and would be willing to try it."[102] Cronkite agreed to support the MacArthur-Ball position.

Several of the board members were nonetheless horrified. Not only did they find Lapham and his ideas repulsive, they felt it would be humiliating to rehire someone they had just fired. MacArthur responded: "Well, George is for it, and I'm for it, and others seem sympathetic." Ball's persona commanded such respect and his reputation was so strong that a few of the board members began to waver. After their lobbying, MacArthur and Ball calculated the votes and concluded that the outcome would likely be a deadlock. According to MacArthur, "I was determined to win. George was, of course, a player; he too wanted to win." Together MacArthur and Ball decided they would win this one.

MacArthur carefully planned the date of the meeting in order to assure the attendance of those who would favor the proposal to appoint Lapham editor. The resolution passed, and, to the chagrin of several of the board members, Lewis Lapham returned as editor.

Working closely with MacArthur, Lapham built *Harper's* into a great success. In 1988 and again in 1989, it won the National Magazine Award for essays and criticism. In 1994, it won three major awards, and in 1995 Lewis Lapham himself was honored by winning the National Magazine Award for his essays and criticism. Financially, *Harper's* had gone from more than a million dollars in debt to a break-even point in 1995, when its paid circulation climbed to 220,000. George Ball's efforts had been vindicated. From 1983 until September 1988, when he resigned from the board, he continued to play a supportive role and helped recruit advertisers for the magazine.

The editors and staff of *Harper's* were grateful to George Ball for rescuing their magazine. He had done so quietly and almost single-handedly. In the words of publisher Rick MacArthur, "George Ball was a great man. I was only twenty-six years old; he didn't know me from Adam. He didn't give a damn that I was the grandson of the founder of the MacArthur Foundation . . . and yet he was willing to take a chance and risk a little bit of his reputation supporting me. . . . He is the only establishment person I know who is really admirable. . . . My hero, really, from Vietnam days and I doing the maverick thing together—and winning!"[103]

Outside of the people at *Harper's*, few others knew of the role that Ball played in the resurrection of the magazine. Even his sons and closest confidants were unaware of this episode. Like his quiet representation of Henry Wallace thirty years earlier, Ball moved into a situation and did what he thought best, regardless of the time and risk and lack of recognition or reward.

Arabs, Israelis, and the Final Days

While quietly mediating conflict in places like Lehman Brothers and *Harper's*, George Ball moved into the center of the international public debate on the Arab-Israeli imbroglio. He dedicated the last fifteen years of his life to grappling with this problem. In the process, he found himself engaged in one of the most contentious and controversial political struggles of his career.

Ball approached the Arab-Israeli issue with customary candor and blunt commentary. He believed that the Israeli hard-line policy of Menachem Begin and the Likud Party was a recipe for disaster. He argued that by occupying Arab land and subjugating the Palestinian people, Israel was compromising its treasured moral assets, weakening its economic well-being, and endangering its long-term survival. Furthermore, he concluded that the United States was encouraging this behavior through its unquestioning support for Israeli policy.

His criticism of Israeli policy made Ball the target of the extremist partisans of Israel, whose blistering letters filled with threats and accusations crammed his file cabinets. Ball's reaction to these attacks was a somewhat astonished bemusement, and he responded by sharpening his pen and redoubling his efforts to present his point of view.

Ball first staked out a major public position in this explosive intellectual no-man's land in an article that appeared in *Foreign Affairs* in the mid-1970s, "How to Save Israel in Spite of Herself." [104] Besides producing numerous other articles and speeches, Ball wrote two books addressing this thorny issue. In 1984, in response to Israel's disastrous 1982 invasion of Lebanon, he produced a scathing short book entitled *Error and Betrayal in Lebanon*. Then, after six years of hard work and with the assistance of his son Douglas, in 1992 Ball published his major study on the Middle East crisis, *The Passionate Attachment: America's Involvement with Israel, 1947 to the Present*. This last book, a documented, withering attack on Israeli government policy and U.S. foreign policy toward Israel, received negative reviews in major American newspapers by partisans of Israel. At the end of his life, Ball lamented that the book had received neither the attention nor the even-handed reviews he thought it deserved.[105]

Ball's writings on the Middle East were unapologetically argumentative. Although he arrived at his position after careful research and consideration, he made little attempt to present all sides to the issue or to provide academic objectivity. Ball's focus was upon policy, and therefore he consciously played the role of advocate. Such an approach exposed him to intense criticism. Yet, this had long been George Ball's modus operandi. Once he had carefully staked out a position, he candidly and consistently argued that position regardless of the personal or political fallout. This was the case whether it involved Vietnam policy in the early 1960s or Middle East policy in the early 1990s.

George Ball's intellectual and political encounters in the 1980s and 1990s were in many ways a welcome relief from the debilitating parade of personal and family problems and tragedies that he faced during the last years of his life. Ball suffered two strokes in the late 1980s. In August 1990 his wife and lifelong companion, Ruth, fell at home and broke her hip. After difficult surgery, she began to have mental lapses and became increasingly disoriented. In the summer of 1991 she slipped into the terrifying world of Alzheimer's, and George watched helplessly as her condition deteriorated until her death on August 11, 1993.

Even as he sought to place Ruth in a nursing home in July 1993, another distressing problem bubbled to the surface. When he had retired in 1982, Ball appeared to have an ample estate and enough current revenue to live more than comfortably. Unfortunately, his earned income, directorships, speech and writing income, and consultantships diminished year by year. Taxes on his Lehman stock eroded his capital, as did generous gifts to family and employees. Falling interest rates lessened his income. He felt so much financial pressure that he put his Princeton home of sixteen years on the market only weeks before his death.

Ball dealt with such adversity to the best of his ability and refused to freeze in place. Now in his eighties and after two strokes, he continued to play tennis with Douglas. He traveled internationally, faithfully attending the annual Bilderberg meetings, and in December of 1993 and January of 1994 he participated in a cruise that took him from Singapore to Malaysia and Indonesia and back to Singapore. He intended to join Michael Blumenthal and others on a cruise up the Yangtze River in China in late spring, and then to fly to Helsinki to attend the 1994 Bilderberg meetings. He planned to visit a Wyoming dude ranch in August of 1994.

While he continued to be physically active, Ball also remained intellectually engaged. With the Middle East book finally completed, he immediately began work on another manuscript. This volume was to be a social and political critique of human society at the end of the twentieth century. Ball began his study of the fin de siècle by focusing his attention upon the impact of the computer revolution and the meaning of the information superhighway. He planned to analyze the pervasiveness of greed, the commercialization of education, and the financing of political campaigns. In sum, Ball intended to study the relation between continuity and change viewed through the lens of the tightening tension between technology and humanity.[106]

On January 23, 1990, Peter Peterson and Michael Blumenthal hosted an elegant eightieth birthday party for their old mentor at the River Club in New York. The sixty-six people in attendance included Adlai Stevenson, III, Arthur Schlesinger, David Rockefeller, John Chancellor, James Schlesinger, and Warren Christopher. After several moving and amusing tributes to Ball had been completed, the guest of honor took the dais. Instead of delivering a short talk laden with appreciative banalities, he took the occasion to give a substantive and provocative address, an address he had written especially for the occasion. In a powerful overview of eighty years of history, with a sharp look into the future, Ball never mentioned Vietnam or the Middle East. For Ball, these had been merely signposts that represented costly struggles along the road to a more important destination.

Instead, George Ball spoke of what the founders of the country had considered America's "exceptionalism." After highlighting the seriousness of demographic, environmental, and ethnic-tribal challenges across the globe, he criticized the U.S. proclivity to isolationism, unilateralism, and militarism. What, he asked, do we mean by American exceptionalism? Ball proclaimed: "There is little exceptionable about military strength or economic weight; other nations have also gone far in that direction. What is truly exceptional is moral leadership, which means a firm adherence to principles and the rejection of certain arrogant practices that have now become almost automatic in our political life."

George Ball concluded, "Let us earnestly try to set the tone for America in the new century and the new millennium by recognizing that we can achieve a stable and peaceful world only by developing the requisite political will. That means turning our back on much of the nonsense by which we have recently been living, adjusting policy to take account of the fact that the world is fast changing and acknowledging to ourselves that what may have seemed fanatic idealism before has now become realistic politics." [107]

George Wildman Ball entered New York Hospital on May 25, 1994 and was diagnosed as having advanced abdominal cancer. He died at 6:30 P.M. on Thursday, May 26, 1994. An exceptional man, George Ball led a life reflective of the "exceptionalism" that he saw in his country. In the simple, understated words of senior statesman Cyrus Vance, "George Ball was a man who made a difference." [108]

Amos Ball Jr. and
Edna Wildman Ball, 1928

George W. Ball, age four

Left to right, Ralph, George, and
Stuart Ball, circa 1916, above,
and circa 1929

George W. Ball, age twenty-one

Ruth Murdoch Ball,
circa age thirty-five

George W. Ball in his political prime

Ruth and George Ball with sons Douglas, left, and John and John's wife, Linda Ottenant Ball, 1981

George Ball in his study in Princeton, 1990

II

GLOBAL POLICYMAKER

3

The Politics of European Integration

Throughout his career, George Ball focused much of his energy on the formation of a European community. Both as a private citizen and as a public official, Ball remained committed to the idea of a working, thriving, growing European economic and political union. Ball was a Common Marketeer par excellence. His keen understanding of the U.S. political process enabled him to work effectively to promote a united Europe.

After World War II, Europe faced serious economic and political challenges. Economically, the Marshall Plan enabled the battered European countries to get back on their feet. In spite of U.S. assistance, however, strong nationalist sentiment threatened to undermine the tenuous postwar stability. In this highly unsettled situation, many believed that only European integration could alleviate the threat of renewed conflict. Among the advocates of a united Europe were Jean Monnet in France and George Ball in the United States. Recalling his discussions with Monnet, Ball wrote, "Though hacking our way through the trees by different paths, we usually came out at the same clearing in the forest, and on one point we were unanimous—that the logic of European integration was inescapable." [1]

In 1957, France, West Germany, Italy, Belgium, the Netherlands, and Luxembourg—dubbed the Six—signed the Treaty of Rome, calling for the formation of the European Economic Community. The groundwork for the EEC had already been painstakingly laid in 1950 when Monnet, Ball, and others had cooperated to establish the Schuman Plan (the European Coal and Steel Community, or ECSC). For both Ball and Monnet, the Schuman Plan was only the first step toward an economically and politically integrated Europe.

After the enactment of the Schuman Plan, Ball turned his attention to promoting British entry into the Community, a struggle that was to continue for two decades. When the French rejected British entry in 1961, Ball lobbied for the creation of a European army. His support for the Multilateral Force (MLF) had its roots in the 1950s, when he had sought to garner support for a European Defense Community (EDC). Ball saw British participation and a European army as two steps that would strengthen the political nature of the European union and reinforce ties among members.

The Roots of Ball's Support for European Integration

George Ball's background and worldview help to explain his devotion to the idea of an integrated Europe. He was a lifelong advocate of free trade, and in this context he espoused the principles of a European commercial union. Moreover, his early association with "Mr. Europe," Jean Monnet, influenced both his political mind-set and his political style. Furthermore, as a founding partner in Cleary, Gottlieb, Ball became part of a law firm that sought to break down the barriers to international trade. The firm had the foresight to recognize the inevitability of a globalized economy. Thus, the partners expanded operations to Europe long before most other U.S. law firms opened offices across the Atlantic.

When Ball inaugurated Cleary, Gottlieb's Paris office in 1949, he gained valuable exposure to Europe and built a network that served his firm well. Through his work as a lawyer, Ball began to fashion personal and professional ties to Europe years before he assumed his influential position in the U.S. government. As he became increasingly absorbed in European affairs, Ball made a total commitment to his work. In a letter to his financial adviser, he explained, "If I have not gotten rich it is my fault and not yours. I just returned from my fifth trip to Europe this year and my schedule is badly out of joint."[2]

Ball's legal career provided him with the opportunity to strengthen the foundations of his long association with Jean Monnet and to become more active in the struggle for European integration. He approached Monnet in January of 1953 and proposed that Cleary, Gottlieb represent the ECSC. He argued that his law firm would promote the ECSC's image in the United States and would lobby to secure World Bank support. After his meeting with Monnet, Ball reported to Leo Gottlieb that the firm would represent the ECSC "in conducting a public relations program in the United States and . . . in connection with financial negotiations looking to a World Bank loan of several hundred million dollars."[3]

Ball's astute work in Europe benefited Cleary, Gottlieb and promoted the general goal of European integration. His activities also caught the attention of the U.S. Senate. Robert Burr filed a statement with the Senate Finance Committee attacking Ball and Cleary, Gottlieb for acting in European rather than U.S. interests. The accusation, repeatedly levied against Ball throughout his career, included criticism of Ball's role in the creation of the Committee for a National Trade Policy (CNTP) in 1953.

Senator Mike Monroney of Oklahoma responded to Burr's invectives by placing in the record a statement prepared by Ball. The CNTP, Ball pointed out, "for the first time in history has joined important elements of American business and industry together, not to work for import subsidies or higher tariffs, but to assist in the development of a national trade policy." At a more personal level, Ball wrote: "In August 1953 my law firm was asked by Mr. [John] Coleman to act as counsel of the organizing group in supervising the legal steps necessary to create the Committee for a National Trade Policy. . . . When the committee was organized, my firm was retained as general counsel and I was elected secretary, with the task of keeping the minutes, and also a director." Ball stated that he and the firm resigned from the committee in October 1954.[4]

George Ball did, in fact, play a central role in organizing the committee. In a personal letter written in August 1953, he stated: "I have been trying for six months to get this Committee off the ground and I believe we have now succeeded." Ball also helped to define the committee's mission: "We are setting up a Committee to make an all-out offensive against the tariff next year. Perhaps if United States tariffs can be materially reduced and some continuity in our commercial policy assured, European business will feel more interest in the United States market."[5] By defining the CNTP's mission as reducing protectionist policies like the tariff, Ball assured that the committee would advance his free trade ideals.

As a free trader, Ball opposed protectionist policies that hindered the flow of commerce among nations. Late in his life, Ball articulated his views on international trade: "I believe in free trade. I feel strongly about it, and I once took the initiative to create something called the Committee for a National Trade Policy. . . . I read enough Adam Smith as a young man to believe that this was the way it ought to work. . . . The only efficiencies that you could get were by letting the market make the decisions for you."[6] Ball believed in Adam Smith's "invisible hand" as the most efficient organizing principle for global commerce.

Ball saw free trade as the locomotive force behind regional integration. According to Ball's vision:

> The only effective solution is to evolve beyond the concept where a single nation state defines a market or an economic area. . . . I can think of few things less desirable for the prosperity and peace of the world than a resurgence of protectionist sentiment in America. For should we begin to close our markets through special concessions to special groups, we may be sure that the doors of the outside world will to that degree be nudged shut in our face. . . . If, on the other hand, the world does move toward freer trade and if Europe and Latin America get on with the establishment of larger trading

units, then the multinational corporation has a bright future. Indeed, it could be the harbinger of a true world economy.[7]

George Ball used the CNTP to help loosen and liberalize U.S. trade policy. At the same time, in his work with Jean Monnet, he pursued a similar goal for Europe. Then John S. Coleman, president of the Burroughs Corporation and the first head of the CNTP, recommended Ball as a founding member of the Bilderberg group, which met for the first time in May 1954. Over the years at Bilderberg, Ball was able to present his ideas in support of free trade and European integration to one of the world's most influential audiences.

George Ball was the quiet linkage figure in the international chain of influence that championed European integration. He mobilized individuals and groups as disparate as Jean Monnet, Cleary, Gottlieb, CNTP, and Bilderberg. Neither Monnet nor the leaders of Ball's law firm, George Cleary and Leo Gottlieb, ever attended a Bilderberg meeting, but their presence was not necessary. George Ball was there.

Ball's vision of integration, however, extended beyond the economy. Regional groups like the European Community would exist as the seeds of something much greater—political cooperation and integration. Ball envisioned a world in which the flow of trade would weaken the borders dividing nation-states: "While the structure of the multinational corporation is a modern concept, designed to meet the requirements of a modern age, the nation state is a very old-fashioned idea and badly adapted to serve the needs of our present complex world."[8]

George Ball never wavered in his conviction that free trade should be one of the guiding principles of international politics. In his judgment, trade restrictions were economically stultifying and politically divisive. Ball believed that commerce and trade had become "so world-striding as to render national boundaries more formal than formidable."[9] Jean Monnet could not have agreed more.

Monnet and Ball: Political Kindred Spirits

Jean Monnet had an enormous impact upon the thinking of George Ball. The short, intrepid Frenchman generated a vision that influenced presidents and prime ministers. When asked who had the greatest impact on her husband's life, Ruth Ball responded, "Jean, Jean."[10] George Ball's relationship with the "Father of Europe" endured for thirty-four years, from 1945 until Monnet's death in 1979. The two shared a passion and belief in the goal of European integration, and they reinforced one another's thinking over the years.

Both Monnet and Ball were men of vision who thought strategically. They understood that a world in painful upheaval provided an opportunity to build fundamentally new and better institutions. Monnet summarized this important idea concisely and convincingly: "You can only create well in a certain amount of disorder." [11]

In 1945, Ball began to work for the French Supply Council, an organization designed to promote postwar recovery. Here, Ball served as Monnet's general counsel, "to help him reduce his ideas to coherent exposition and, in the process, help him think." From the beginning, Monnet relied heavily upon Ball, about whom he wrote: "His reactions and opinions on our plans were very useful and constructive. There was a constant exchange of ideas between George and us. And when we had doubts about the possible reaction of the U.S., we questioned him. The advice he gave us was not only inspired by our interest but by his knowledge of the U.S. and his keen feeling that understanding between France and the United States was essential." The two men shared a constructive and creative relationship in which ideas flowed freely. Monnet described his interaction with Ball as "a creative relationship, an exchange, a collaboration and if he learned from me I certainly did learn from him, a great deal." [12]

Ball acted as a sounding board for Monnet. Because of his trust in Ball and his respect for Ball's intellect, Monnet shared ideas with Ball long before he presented them to others. Arthur Hartman believed that Ball "was one of the few people who saw the 1950 Declaration [Schuman Plan] before it was made public." [13]

Between 1945 and 1954, Ball and Monnet maintained constant communication. Their professional relationship was reinforced by personal ties between their families. The wives, Sylvia Monnet and Ruth Ball, were an important component in the friendship. According to Monnet, "We know each other's families. When I was in Washington . . . I met his wife and saw her regularly." In her diaries, Ruth Ball constantly referred to Jean Monnet and the warm friendship that developed between the two families. In a 1967 letter, after a visit to the United States, Monnet thanked Ball for his hospitality: "You were very good to me and it was a great joy to find that you and I were at the same work as we were twenty years ago." At the end of a typed letter to Ball in 1969, Monnet added a handwritten note: "When do you intend to visit Paris? Don't forget me." [14]

The major pillar supporting the lifelong friendship between Ball and Monnet was their shared commitment to the goal of European integration. According to Ball, the failure to convince the British to join the European Economic Community from the onset was one of Monnet's greatest disappointments. Like Monnet, Ball measured success and failure in these terms, and he was disappointed that their joint plans for a unified Europe were so slow to be realized. Both visionaries, however, knew that they had helped plant the seeds of European economic integration, and perhaps ultimately, of political unification. Monnet once told Ball: "It'll go on. What we've started will continue. It has momentum." [15]

George Ball and Jean Monnet shared similar goals and employed similar political tactics in service of those goals. Congressman Hale Boggs of Louisiana recognized the importance of these similarities in his response to President John Kennedy's query: "Tell me, Hale, who is the Jean Monnet of this country?" Boggs answered, "We don't have a Jean Monnet, but there's one man in your administration who is closest in approach: George Ball."[16]

The Ball-Monnet similarities can be partially explained by their parallel backgrounds. Both men spent their formative years in bucolic settings—Monnet in Cognac, Ball in Iowa—where common sense, clarity, and candor were considered virtues. Both were the sons of fathers who had worked hard to achieve significant successes in their respective professions. Each pursued diverse careers and gained early exposure to a variety of life experiences. Ball believed that Monnet's broad background, including his employment in the family's brandy business, provided the Frenchman with special advantages. He was a salesman, a businessman, and an economist. Monnet used lessons learned in one context as springboards for success in another context. Ball, meanwhile, majored in English literature, earned a law degree, and held several positions in law and government.

Although both Ball and Monnet became involved in policymaking, neither man ever held elective office. Instead, they worked through those who had been elected. Both had the perspicacity to understand the importance of personal relations in politics. They made it a point to gain access to key decision makers. One observer attributed Monnet's success "not only to his special talent for hounding those he wished to persuade without giving offense, but to a shrewd cultivation of friends in high places, and a certain prescience in placing his own associates and disciples in strategic positions."[17] George Ball was also a master at building personal networks.

In seeking to build links to influential public officials, each man emphasized that he had never run for office or sought formal power. As a result, they were seldom viewed as political rivals or dangerous competitors to officeholders. For Monnet, the best profile was low profile: "Since I did not get in statesmen's way, I could count on their support. . . . In my line of work, kudos has to be forgotten. I have no particular taste for secrecy, despite what some people say; but if I can best expedite matters by self-effacement, then I prefer to work behind the scenes."[18]

Ball respected Monnet's ability to convey his ideas to powerful political leaders: "The essence of his charisma was that Jean sought nothing for himself. If he could get others to launch—and take credit for—his ideas, so much the better. Thus, anything but an intellectual, Monnet could attract and even captivate intellectuals." Monnet, on the other hand, tended to view Ball in similar terms. He repeatedly referred to Ball as a "man of good will" with a special "human quality," who "does not like to rule people" but "wants to convince people."[19] In his *Memoirs*, Monnet describes Ball in two crisp sentences: "Powerfully built, he exuded strength and level-headedness, like many Americans of his type, whose massive appearance matches their striking command of both physical and intellectual resources. His wisdom, his boldness in taking decisions, and his loyalty to his friends gave him great moral authority, even then."[20]

Although not as self-effacing as Monnet, Ball was willing to work outside the limelight in order to protect his access to influential decision makers. He once told Monnet that he sought to provide those in power with vision. He was less interested in authority associated with the formal trappings of government than he was in wielding power with those who counted. Thus, James Reston once described Ball as a man who acted "by being a connecting rod between people, by being obscure, patient, and obstinate, and never taking credit for what he did."[21]

Ball and Monnet pursued a political strategy in which they focused their attention upon the government's "second tier." They realized that not all public officials with the most influence occupy the highest echelon of government. Those who worked in the second tier, the step just below cabinet secretary or minister, were involved both in policymaking and policy implementation. According to Ball, Monnet "sought the acquaintance of the individual of lesser rank in his target's chain of command who actually prepared the initial drafts of documents that provided his boss with advice and new initiatives. He sometimes spent day after day with that lowly but tactically placed minion." John Tuthill has emphasized Monnet's "sense of who held the reins of power" and his ability to identify lower-profile individuals who understood and supported European integration.[22]

Ball took a similar approach. Hartman observed that Ball had friends buried in middle-level echelons of the bureaucracy, in places like government banks and treasury departments. Ball had a sixth sense that helped him recognize the officials who shaped government decisions relating to trade and economic integration. Tuthill has gone so far as to refer to this approach as a kind of Ball-Monnet "conspiracy" that enabled the integrationists to prevail in many political struggles.[23]

Both Ball and Monnet had analytic minds. Both carried a special passion and zeal for their work. Monnet was impressed by Ball's extraordinary analytic capacity. In fact, both men had an unusual capacity to break complex questions down to their bare essentials and to understand and explain these essentials. They fervently believed in what they were doing.

Ball and Monnet were men on a mission. Both were perfectionists with exacting work ethics. Monnet never hesitated to call Ball, day or night, whenever he needed Ball's advice. If necessary, Ball would drop everything and take the first available flight to France. Because both men understood the need to communicate their ideas clearly and convincingly, they paid special attention to their written presentations. Ball was a superb craftsman of word and phrase, and because he also understood Monnet's ideas, the Frenchman relied on him to articulate the benefits of a European community. According to Ball, his exchanges with Monnet were intense and demanding: "Monnet wanted a punching bag. He wanted somebody he could throw ideas against. . . . We would talk for forty-five minutes or an hour. . . . He'd then say, 'All right, give me a draft early this afternoon.' I would give him a draft; he'd read it, sort of scowl, frown and say, 'This is not it; we haven't got it yet. Revise it and let me have it at the end of the day.' So I would take it back and do another draft. This, too, would not be adequate. We would go round and round until we sometimes made the complete circle and would come back to something very close to the first draft. He was an absolute perfectionist."[24]

Although they shared many similarities and were close personal friends, Ball was clearly the junior member in the relationship. Twenty years older than Ball, Monnet was the master, Ball the apprentice. Personally Monnet and Ball were quite different. According to Eric Roll, an old friend who knew them both well, Ball was a "bon vivant"; he loved the "high life." Monnet, on the other hand, lived a much more modest, secluded life; his tastes were simpler, and he was not a joiner.[25]

Monnet could be hypnotic and enchanting and was able to recruit individuals to his cause through the sheer force of his personality. Besides his many disciples in Europe, Monnet had American supporters. They included such influential individuals as John J. McCloy, Robert Lovett, Dean Acheson, Felix Frankfurter, Walter Lippmann, and James Reston. Monnet liked to refer to this distinguished group as his "well-informed friends." But even within this group, George Ball was special. According to Roll, the relationship between Ball and Monnet was "very, very close"; it was "sui generis." Ball not only shared and helped articulate Monnet's vision, but he also worked intimately with Monnet over a long period of time in a major campaign to transform that vision into reality.[26]

Ball and the European Coal and Steel Community

In 1946, Jean Monnet approached the United States for financial assistance to help France meet the challenge of postwar reconstruction. Although he failed in his overtures, the Monnet Plan anticipated the Marshall Plan, also known as the European Recovery Program (ERP). One of the greatest economic reconstruction programs in history, the Marshall Plan provided over $13 billion in economic relief to a devastated Europe.

The economic motivation for the Marshall Plan involved more than financial assistance to Europe. Policymakers in Washington realized that without a European market, U.S. industries would suffer and unemployment would sharply increase, crippling the American economy. In the concluding paragraph of his long book, one leading scholar of the Marshall Plan describes it as "one of the most successful peacetime foreign policies launched by the United States in this century."[27]

Although it had a huge economic component, the ERP was primarily a political program. It was intended to serve as a catalyst for European cooperation and integration, and it was created as a western counterweight to the Soviet Union and the expanding international challenge of communism. The ubiquitous Jean Monnet helped shape the Marshall Plan from the European perspective. He regularly consulted George Ball, who was at the time assigned to look after French and European affairs for Cleary, Gottlieb. In the United States, Dean Acheson, George Kennan, Charles Bohlen, Will Clayton, David Bruce, Charles Kindleberger, John McCloy, Walter Lippmann, and William Fulbright were among those who helped develop and promote the Marshall Plan. The roles of Monnet and especially Ball in the formation of the Marshall Plan have been largely overlooked.

On July 15, 1947, sixteen European nations created the Committee for European Economic Cooperation (CEEC). Jean Monnet needed informed insights into American attitudes toward European recovery, so he asked George Ball to come to Paris to help the CEEC draft a report responding to the Marshall Plan's proposals. Working out of a tiny Parisian office, Ball secretly helped Monnet prepare the CEEC report. On September 3, 1947, Ball flew to Washington carrying what he later termed a "pirated copy" of the CEEC draft report.[28] Playing the role of mediator and human connecting rod, Ball discussed the draft with friends in the State Department, and on September 8 he flew back to Paris to help revise the final report that was submitted on September 22.

Under U.S. pressure, the European countries created a permanent organization to replace the CEEC. On April 15, 1948, the sixteen European states set up the Organization for European Economic Cooperation (OEEC). Working with another protégé of Monnet's, Robert Marjolin, Ball helped draft the plans establishing the OEEC, an organization designed to coordinate European reconstruction with the ERP.

From the beginning, the OEEC disappointed many U.S. officials, who had hoped that the new body would transcend narrow nationalist interests and form the basis for effective supranational action. The British, however, did not see the OEEC in the same way. Protective of their own special relation with the United States and reluctant to compromise their sovereignty in any way, British leaders undercut the power and credibility of the OEEC. Britain caused the organization to institute a veto mechanism that required all major decisions to be unanimous. In the words of one scholar: "The United Kingdom blocked all efforts to give the organization independent authority, and when the OEEC emerged, . . . it was little more than a vehicle for intergovernmental cooperation, and not, as the Americans had hoped, a supranational organization."[29]

In strictly economic terms, the OEEC successfully helped administer the Marshall Plan and reduced tariffs among European countries. The OEEC survived until 1960, when it was transformed into the Organization for Economic

Cooperation and Development (OECD). In spite of its economic achievements, the OEEC disappointed integrationists in the United States and Europe because of its lack of political content.

Once he realized that the OEEC lacked any effective political plan, Monnet lost interest in the organization, shifted his emphasis, and began to pursue European integration on a different track. Given British intransigence, he focused on establishing a cooperative pact between the two major continental powers, France and Germany. Although Ball, like Robert Marjolin, appreciated the strides taken by the OEEC to liberalize trade and promote the convertibility of currency, he strongly endorsed Monnet's political strategy.

On May 9, 1950, French Foreign Minister Robert Schuman announced the creation of the European Coal and Steel Community (ECSC). During the months before this declaration, Monnet and his associates had been carefully preparing the plan, and Monnet had personally sold the idea to Schuman and the French government.

With Britain standing aloof and France and Germany deeply suspicious of each other's ambitions, peace in Europe seemed tenuous. Furthermore, it was clear that any successful European economic recovery would be impossible without German participation. Thus, Monnet had conceived a plan to promote French-German cooperation around an important common interest. Because coal and steel were indispensable for both economic and military strength, the plan called for the two resources to be pooled. In Ball's words, this pooling "would render moot the issue of German industrial domination, since it would create the conditions for common expansion with competition but without domination." Furthermore, Ball, like Monnet, saw the ECSC as the real first step toward European unification.[30]

Ball considered the Schuman Plan—which was really Monnet's—to be the work of a "tactical genius." By focusing upon a narrow but critically important sector, Monnet and the integrationists were planting a seed pregnant with future possibilities. Once coal and steel were successfully pooled, other resources would also inevitably be pooled. Monnet's tactical political approach was analogous to the tank warfare once advocated by Charles de Gaulle: concentrate all power on a limited point, then spread out behind the lines.[31]

George Ball had limited influence on the drafting of the Schuman Plan. But after Schuman's May 1950 announcement, Monnet called on Ball, who flew to Paris in June. During the next year, the American lawyer worked to help overcome U.S. and German doubts about the plan. As was often the case throughout his career, Ball occupied a unique position in the negotiations. He was a private American working for the French government to secure a delicate cooperative agreement between two suspicious European countries.

In addressing U.S. concerns about cartelization and German fears regarding their own industrial sovereignty, Ball cooperated closely with such U.S. officials as the ambassador to France, David Bruce, and his energetic financial attaché, William M. Tomlinson. Ball also worked with the U.S. high commissioner for Germany, John J. McCloy, and McCloy's aide Robert Bowie. Working at Monnet's side, Ball kept "Mr. Europe" in constant communication with these important U.S. actors. According to David DiLeo, Ball's and Monnet's work on the Schuman Plan was "perhaps the most auspicious, and pregnant example of their work together."[32]

After months of difficult negotiation, representatives of the Six signed the ECSC Treaty of Paris on April 18, 1951. In August 1952, it was ratified by the six national parliaments. Jean Monnet became the first president of the Community's High Authority.

The Schuman Plan encountered enormous difficulties in implementation, as national sensitivities constantly collided. Its record was, at best, mixed. Politically, the organization achieved one major goal. By providing a supranational forum for the presentation of ideas and the resolution of conflict, it created an ambience and sense of "Europeness." In so doing, the ECSC ignited the spark of political integration and cleared the path to the establishment of the European Economic Community in 1957.

For George Ball, this kernel of economic and political integration represented a major achievement. His experiences with Monnet in the 1940s and early 1950s deepened Ball's belief in the importance of European integration. In the 1950s, therefore, Ball took every opportunity "to put in his oar" in favor of liberal trade policy and an integrated Europe. Whether he was working on the Adlai Stevenson campaigns, attending Bilderberg conferences, or traveling internationally on Cleary, Gottlieb business, Ball lobbied in favor of the vision that he and Jean Monnet had shared in the busy years of 1945–52. Meanwhile, Cleary, Gottlieb, continued to serve as legal counsel in the United States for the European Economic Community and as legal adviser to the High Authority of the ECSC.

In George Ball's judgment, the Treaty of Rome, which established the European Economic Community in 1957, represented a major historical landmark. He viewed the EEC or Common Market as the logical consequence of the Schuman Plan and agreed enthusiastically with West German integrationist Walter Hallstein, who stressed the political dimensions of the EEC: "We are not integrating economies, we are integrating politics. We are not just sharing our furniture, we are jointly building a new and bigger house."[33]

Ball spent a great deal of time in the 1960s enthusiastically explaining the construction of this "new and bigger house" to influential U.S. audiences.[34] Ball's message to each audience was the same. The creation of a European Common Market provided an extraordinary economic opportunity for the United States. Thus, he argued that U.S. leaders should work to achieve "a greater and greater freedom for trade while at the same time encouraging the nations of Europe to extend their commercial relationships into broader aspects of economic and political integration."[35] Ball reaffirmed his ideas in testimony before Congress: "The men who were responsible for the Treaty of Rome, which serves the Common Market both as a constitution and a code of laws, were inspired by the desire to make progress toward political integration, ultimately toward European federation. Economic integration for them was simply the means to a political end."[36]

The Collective Defense Approach to European Integration

In seeking political integration in Europe, George Ball supplemented the economic approach with a more controversial attempt to develop systems of collective defense. He invested both time and energy in promoting two ill-fated collective defense schemes for Europe, the European Defense Community (EDC) in the 1950s and the Multilateral Force (MLF) in the 1960s. Ball believed that if the European states could find a way to pool their military forces, they would take a giant step in the direction of political integration. A country's defense capability is basic to survival and central to the principle of national sovereignty. By integrating defense forces, nation-states would move away from narrow nationalism and toward the ideal of supranational organizations. In the words of British Labor party leader Denis Healey, Ball "saw the MLF as the grit in the oyster, round which the pearl of European unity would form."[37]

The instability and uncertainty of the post–World War II era gave rise to the concept of a European army. Supporters of the collective defense idea saw the EDC as the means to achieve prudent German rearmament within a controlled and cooperative environment. According to John Tuthill, the first modern attempts to create a European army were the results of a "small group in Europe supported by another small group in the U.S. urging European unity."[38] Jean Monnet in France and George Ball in the United States were leading members of these small groups. The military integrationists sought to establish the EDC as a parallel organization to the ECSC.

In October 1950, the French Assembly approved a proposal written by Jean Monnet that outlined the plans for a European army. The Pleven Plan, named after French Premier René Pleven, became the basis for the EDC Treaty that was signed by the Six in May 1952. The next step would be ratification by the European parliaments.

The idea of a European defense force ignited a debate that raged across continental Europe and into Britain and the United States. Britain rejected the idea outright, and the United States initially responded with considerable skepticism. Monnet in France and his associates in the United States mounted a massive lobbying campaign in support of the EDC. Europeanists like John J. McCloy,

David Bruce, George Ball, and—after some early misgivings—Dean Acheson, all supported the EDC.

In June 1951, Monnet met with President Eisenhower in Paris and convinced the president of the value of a European army. Monnet told Eisenhower, "Without unity, everyone will go on seeking power for himself. . . . The strength of the West does not depend on how many divisions it has, but on its unity and common will. . . . To rush into raising a few German divisions on a national basis, at the cost of reviving enmity between our peoples, would be catastrophic for the very security of Europe." Eisenhower responded: "To sum it up, what you are proposing is that the French and the Germans should wear the same uniform. That's more a human problem than a military one." The president understood Monnet's position and concluded: "What Monnet's proposing is to organize relations between people, and I'm all for it."[39]

Ironically, while Monnet was lobbying U.S. leaders, George Ball was working to influence French public opinion. Employed at the time by Cleary, Gottlieb, Ball had only recently established the firm's office in Paris. Having worked for the French government for several years, he occupied a strong strategic position from which to exert influence. Like Monnet, Ball remained deeply committed to the EDC. He was delighted when four of the six signatory nations ratified the plan. Although he knew that the vote would be close in the French Assembly, he counted on Premier Pierre Mendes-France to produce the support needed for ratification.

The French were unenthusiastic about the EDC and nervous about German rearmament. Moreover, the integrationist forces in the French Assembly had lost influence, and the country was in no mood to surrender any of its military leverage. Ball recognized this and did what he could to rally French support. In one instance, for example, he boldly attempted to bring bipartisan U.S. pressure to bear on the French government.

Ball solicited the help of Democrat and friend, Adlai Stevenson, and convinced Stevenson to write a letter recommending the EDC to Mendes-France. In a private memorandum to John Ferguson, a colleague in Cleary's Paris office, Ball wrote: "I connived to get Adlai to write a personal letter to Mendes-France telling him in effect that the American position on the EDC was not a partisan matter but a matter in which all Americans believed."[40]

On August 25, 1954, Stevenson released a statement in which he admitted writing a personal letter "to my friend, Mendes-France" indicating that he "was alarmed by developments with respect to the EDC." Stevenson declared his support for the EDC as both a Democrat and private citizen and concluded: "I earnestly hope that the events of the next few days will give a new vitality to the EDC. As a step toward European unification, it can greatly assist in building a strong, free and peaceful world."[41]

Five days later, Mendes-France presented the EDC treaty to the French Assembly. With the French surrender at Dien Bien Phu, continuing tension in Tunisia and Algeria, and the economy in turmoil, Mendes-France chose not to do battle over the EDC. He submitted the treaty without government endorsement. The Assembly voted not to discuss the issue, thereby killing any chance for French ratification. In the words of one analyst: "This procedural tactic was the burial ceremony of the EDC, and a setback for both the plans for a more effective Western defence system and the hopes and ambitions for a more united Europe."[42]

Monnet and Ball realized the serious implications of the French rejection, and both were deeply disappointed. The Stevenson ploy had failed; the letter had been leaked to the French press. In his memo to Ferguson, Ball had warned that the rejection of the EDC would invite the rearmament of Germany through NATO. Sardonically, he wrote: "And what will the froggies do then poor things? Hide their heads under their wings, poor things?"[43]

On August 31, the day after the French Assembly killed the EDC, Ball wrote a long letter to French industrial leaders in which he argued that the French decision had severely alienated the U.S. government. He warned that American leaders had begun to question the political wisdom of Mendes-France. Ball concluded, "The shock in Washington today results, therefore, not merely from the disappointment at the failure of the treaty, but also from surprise at the discovery that Mendes-France opposed it in principle."[44]

A month later, Ball penned a "personal and confidential" letter to Jean Monnet. Referring to his August memorandum to French leaders, Ball confided, "As I knew that many French industrialists had opposed the EDC, I thought it useful to try to impress on them the catastrophic implications of their own folly." Ball urged Monnet to look ahead and declared that two opinions dominated American thinking about Europe: first, in the long run, the only hope for a strong and stable Europe lay in integration; and second, a German military contribution is necessary for the defense of Western Europe.[45]

Although Monnet was badly shaken by the rejection of the EDC proposal, he viewed it as a tactical setback and prepared for the next opportunity to plant institutional seeds of European unity. The Western European Union (WEU), established by Britain and Germany in 1954 to facilitate military cooperation, was a weak organization made redundant by NATO. The integrationists did not find another opportunity to promote a serious and substantial European defense force until the end of the decade.

Like its precursor, the EDC, the Multilateral Force (MLF) represented a plan to pool European military forces. As the perceived danger of nuclear war increased, MLF advocates sought a way to limit the threat by a multilateral effort that included the participation of the United States. The idea for this multinational nuclear fleet had been first systematically presented in a report prepared by Robert Bowie for Eisenhower's Secretary of State Christian Herter. Bowie, who possessed a gifted and creative mind, was a kindred spirit and a friend to Ball and Monnet.

The MLF, however, had many other strong advocates in the United States, the same individuals who consistently supported European unity, including Deputy Assistant Secretary of State for Atlantic Affairs Robert Schaetzel, Henry Owen of the State Department's Policy Planning Staff, Assistant Secretary of State for European Affairs Foy Kohler, Assistant Secretary of State for Policy Planning Gerard Smith, U.S. Ambassador to the OECD John Tuthill, and U.S. Ambassador to NATO Thomas Finletter.[46]

George Ball was the leader of this group. In the words of John Tuthill: "The head Bishop of this movement was George Ball. In the role sort of like a parish priest I was a member of this 'Happy Band.' And because the rest of the U.S. government was basically indifferent we pretty much had our way."[47]

Ball lobbied for the MLF with both Robert McNamara and Dean Rusk and with Presidents Kennedy and Johnson. The under secretary viewed the multinational military pact as a serious means of controlling nuclear proliferation. Most importantly, however, he believed that the MLF would stand as the central building block for the edifice of Western political integration. According to Arthur Schlesinger, the idea "appealed to the advocates of strategic interdependence as a means of preserving the unity of the deterrent and at the same time of giving NATO allies a nuclear role. . . . It brought new and urgent pressure on the European governments to move toward federation."[48]

The MLF was a difficult idea to sell. As Richard Barnet wrote: "The macabre surface vessels, with their lethal cargoes, their crews chattering away in languages incomprehensible to one another, and the ships' stores stocked with everything from stout to ouzo, made perfect targets for bureaucratic sniping." The French flatly opposed the idea; Germany only grudgingly accepted it; and Britain, which had originally supported the plan in the context of Macmillan's bargain at Nassau, tried to retreat from its commitment. British Labor leader Denis Healey provided the most scathing criticism of the MLF, labeling it a "military monstrosity" that "offered no answer to the European demand for more influence on the American decision to use nuclear weapons. . . . Essentially an American recipe for 'artificial dissemination,' it was bound to create far more problems than it would solve."[49]

In the United States, the multilateralists carried political weight and enthusiasm far out of proportion to their number. Such was the "fervor" of these "indefatigable bureaucrats" that "with the prodigious efforts of weighty men like George Ball and Jean Monnet the MLF moved inexorably like an armored personnel carrier down the corridors of power."[50] As the MLF chugged along, it rolled over the opposition of the American military establishment and such adamant critics as Assistant Secretary of Defense Paul Nitze. Only when the MLF reached the center of the power corridors did it crash and burn.

Although John F. Kennedy cautiously accepted the MLF idea, he had serious reservations about its practicality. Lyndon Johnson shared these reservations, but like Kennedy, he was reluctant to oppose the considerable support that the MLF had generated both within his own administration and in certain circles in Europe. At the same time, however, he was uneasy about the deep opposition that the proposal had aroused. Within the Johnson White House, an internal struggle developed over the MLF. The principal protagonists were Under Secretary of State George Ball and National Security Adviser McGeorge Bundy.

Originally sympathetic to the MLF concept, Bundy had become increasingly skeptical as the idea picked up momentum in Washington. He recognized the strong opposition to the idea in both houses of Congress. In addition, Bundy concluded that the Western European countries were unlikely to accept the plan. Britain and France seemed unalterably opposed. In Germany, beyond Konrad Adenauer, support for the MLF was tenuous. Bundy concluded that without European support, it would not be prudent for the United States to continue promoting the idea.

After Lyndon Johnson became president, George Ball realized the necessity of gaining the chief executive's support for the MLF. On April 10, 1964, Ball, Thomas Finletter, and Gerard Smith briefed Johnson concerning the proposal. At this meeting, Ball, who had an excellent understanding of Johnson's mentality, focused his argument on Germany. He contended that the MLF was an effective way to control Germany. LBJ accepted Ball's argument and emphatically responded: "The Germans have gone off the reservation twice in our lifetime and we've got to be sure that this doesn't happen again, that they don't go berserk."[51] The president's decision to support the MLF represented a high point for its elated proponents.

With British Prime Minister Harold Wilson scheduled to visit Washington in December, the pro-MLF group in the Johnson administration began to organize a coordinated strategy. At this point, McGeorge Bundy decided to become more actively involved with the issue. On November 25, 1964, the very day that U.S. Ambassador David Bruce in London tried to convince Wilson of the MLF's importance, Bundy launched a frontal attack on the idea. In a memorandum to Rusk, McNamara, and Ball, he called attention to diminishing European support for the MLF and suggested that the United States let it "sink out of sight."[52]

Ball counterattacked by traveling to London, where he assured Wilson that the United States remained committed to the MLF. In his memoirs, Wilson recalls that Ball, "always friendly" and "very direct," informed the British that the

U.S. government expected Wilson to support the MLF. If he chose not to do so, then he would be well advised to cancel his visit.[53] In response to Ball's maneuver, Bundy went directly to the president.

On December 6, 1964, the day before Wilson's arrival in Washington, Bundy sent a memorandum to Lyndon Johnson containing "an alternative view" on the MLF. Bundy recalled that Kennedy had entertained reservations about the MLF because "if he could only get the MLF by major and intense U.S. pressure, it was not worth it." Bundy then warned Johnson that the proposal confronted formidable opposition. The most important of these opponents included Charles de Gaulle, the U.S. professional military establishment, commentators like Walter Lippmann and George Kennan, the Armed Services Committee, and the U.S. Senate, where, Bundy noted, "I know of not one hardened supporter, while there are many skeptics and many outright opponents."[54] Johnson used this secret memorandum to counter Ball's arguments in a December 8 meeting during the visit of Prime Minister Wilson.

Always attuned to the political winds, Johnson sensed the hardening opposition to the MLF in both Europe and Congress. He used Wilson's visit as cover under which to retreat from the proposal. Wilson had cleverly recommended that the idea of an MLF be jettisoned and replaced by the formation of the Atlantic Nuclear Force (ANF). This watered-down defense plan, in which Britain and the United States would commit an equal number of Polaris submarines to NATO, served as the mechanism that helped destroy the MLF. Denis Healey, Wilson's defense secretary, who had accompanied him to Washington, reported that the meeting went "smoothly enough," and called it "Ball's Last Stand." In Healey's colorful description, "In spite of George Ball's desperate pleading, Johnson agreed to drop the MLF in favour of the ANF. Within a year the ANF had also sunk without trace, because nobody wanted it. As Franz Josef Strauss put it, ANF was the only fleet in history which had not been created, yet torpedoed another fleet which had never sailed."[55]

Although the MLF was nearly dead, George Ball refused to give up. In early February 1965, he prepared a pro-MLF public speech as part of a campaign to resuscitate the proposal. Ball showed the speech to McGeorge Bundy, who immediately sent a confidential memorandum to the president urging Johnson to prohibit Ball from giving the speech: "I am sorry to say that I can imagine nothing less constructive than a long speech by a known American partisan arguing the case for the MLF in the first week of February." Bundy secretly argued to Johnson that this was not the time "for a sound of divided trumpets within the Administration."[56]

On February 3, 1965, Secretary of State Rusk called Ball to relay the president's demand that neither Rusk nor Ball give any speeches on the MLF at this time. When Rusk asked whether the president had seen Ball's speech, the under secretary said that he had shown it only to McGeorge Bundy. Ball assured Rusk that he no longer intended to give the speech. Rusk expressed doubt that Bundy had "pumped" Johnson about Ball's prospective speech.[57]

In fact, for the second time during the MLF bureaucratic infighting, Bundy had surreptitiously gone to the president without informing Ball. Ball angrily let Bundy know that he and the Department of State would not tolerate such devious behavior. From then on, despite their policy differences, the two men worked well together.

George Ball's intense campaigns in support of the EDC and MLF demonstrated his unwavering commitment to European integration. In his autobiography, Ball makes a curious statement concerning the MLF: "Though I have sometimes been spoken of as the principal advocate of the Multilateral Force, I never felt fervently about it, seeing it solely as a political instrument and fully recognizing that it was a clumsy if not unworkable military concept."[58] In a personal interview, Ball argued that he had recognized from the beginning that the MLF was "nonsensical" as a military instrument. In his judgment, "it was a purely political battle."[59] When measured against Ball's advocacy of the MLF, his later criticism seems strangely inconsistent. There are two explanations for the apparent contradiction.

First, Ball was never one of the so-called "theologians" or "missionaries" who sought the MLF as if it were the Holy Grail. He was more a political realist than were such individuals as Robert Schaetzel, Henry Owen, and Gerard Smith. Schaetzel has described Ball as standing somewhat separate from the other MLF proponents while providing "a kind of detached, somewhat bemused support."[60] According to one informed observer, Ball became convinced that the MLF project had fallen into the hands of "zealots" like Schaetzel and Owen, who pursued the idea to the point that they "scared off" the politicians; their tactics ran against Ball's realism.[61] In this context, Ball's advocacy lacked the fervency of many other multilateralists.

Second, the paradox of Ball's commitment is glossed by the phrase "political instrument." Unlike a number of his colleagues who fought the battle for collective European defense treaties, Ball viewed them neither as ends in themselves nor as instruments designed merely to domesticate the threat of nuclear power. He was well aware of their unwieldy and unrealistic nature. Nonetheless, he fought for their establishment because he considered them to represent important strides along the path to political integration. In Ball's judgment, the MLF "was conceived as an organic experiment in cooperation, not a mathematical solution of the problem."[62] Even if the EDC and the MLF failed to become realities, Ball viewed all the energy and activity devoted to their formation as positive and constructive. The politics surrounding these schemes of collective defense focused attention upon the drive for multilateral cooperation and integration rather than upon international conflict and division.

Ball, Kennedy, and the Trade Expansion Act

George Ball's long experience in the related fields of international trade and European integration provided him with the expertise that impressed John F. Kennedy when the Massachusetts senator assumed the presidency in January 1961. Kennedy was already conversant with these issues and was moderately receptive to the idea of European integration. He was somewhat less enthusiastic about free trade. Although many individuals lobbied Kennedy on the issues, George Ball took the lead in converting the president to both causes. According to Ball, "I was the one who effectively made American policy with regard to Europe and the Common Market." He found Kennedy to be "very susceptible" to "my coaching" in these matters.[63]

On December 31, 1960, Ball, who had chaired a group known as the Task Force on Foreign Economic Policy, presented the president-elect with a major study on foreign economic policy. The FEP report, a paper that contained many of the ideas Ball had proposed in establishing the Committee for a National Trade Policy six years earlier, impressed President Kennedy.

Emphasizing the importance of free trade, the FEP report stated: "The Task Force believes that foreign economic policy can be most effectively used to serve our foreign policy objective if it is directed at establishing an open and competitive Free World economy in which the forces of economic growth will have full play." The report continued: "Central to our relations with the other industrialized nations is the need to eliminate obstructions to the free flow of goods within the total industrial and agricultural economy."[64]

In its initial pages, the report also addressed the issue of European integration: "Another significant problem in our relations with the other industrialized countries of the Free World is the divisive effect of two competing trade blocs in Europe—the European Economic Community (the Common Market) and the European Free Trade Association." In the FEP study, Ball presented the vision that he had shared with Monnet of a future political union for Europe. The report explicitly criticized Britain and the EFTA because the latter was "purely and simply a free trade area" and had "no political objectives of a positive character." The report went on to stress the importance of the recently established Organization for Economic Cooperation and Development (OECD).[65]

Ball's campaign to gain President Kennedy's support for his economic and political philosophy involved more than the submission of a single document. The under secretary also carefully arranged for meetings between Kennedy and knowledgeable members of his extensive personal network. One important and influential friend who presented his ideas to Kennedy was Jean Monnet.

During the early stages of Kennedy's presidency, Ball continued to confer with Monnet. Just as Monnet had consulted earlier with Ball concerning his major proposals, now Ball solicited Monnet's assistance in the preparation of the FEP report. When Monnet traveled to Washington in March 1961, Ball took him on a busy circuit of meetings with key members of the new administration. Ball even arranged a meeting with the president, and Monnet and Kennedy liked and respected one another.

As Ball moved to implement his plans concerning free trade and European integration, he found himself with many natural allies in or near the Kennedy administration. His allies included such experienced and influential Europeanists as David Bruce, McGeorge Bundy, Walt Rostow, and Dean Acheson. At a working level, the under secretary consulted closely with a number of bright individuals who shared his ideas. Key among these "Ball boys" were Robert Schaetzel, Henry Owen, John Tuthill, Arthur Hartman, and John Leddy.[66] These individuals were personally acquainted with Monnet and were highly supportive of his ideas.

Ball and his Europeanist friends represented a formidable phalanx of believers in integration. They respected one another and possessed an esprit de corps that contributed to their effectiveness. At the center stood George Ball and Jean Monnet. The intellectual power and personal commitment of Ball and Monnet inspired the political activities of this group. The Ball-Monnet enthusiasm was infectious.

Ball's personal network, moreover, extended beyond Washington. The integrationists had their counterparts in Europe, where Robert Marjolin, Walter Hallstein, Etienne Hirsch, and Pierre Uri complemented Monnet. One analyst wrote that this Euro-American group "formed a network not only of colleagues but also of friends devoted to a common cause. These bonds of friendship increased the cohesiveness of the group and made it possible for a relatively small number of men to exert a strong influence within the Kennedy administration."[67]

The FEP report had represented the latest formulation of Ball's long campaign opposing protectionism and supporting European integration. Along with two other reports that Kennedy had commissioned (the Bowie and Acheson reports), Ball's study established the intellectual foundation for the reform of outdated U.S. trade practices. It also set the stage for what was to become the Trade Expansion Act of 1962.

Since 1934, the Reciprocal Trade Acts Agreement had determined tariff reductions through a process of item-by-item haggling. The act required congressional approval every two years and was to be considered for renewal in June 1962. To free traders such as Ball and his aide, Michael Blumenthal, the 1934 legislation did not go far enough in eliminating protectionism. Blumenthal has pointed out that the Reciprocal Trade Act provided the executive branch with the authority "to negotiate tariffs down on a reciprocal basis, item by item. Congress would then peril point many commodities and say you can't go below 'x.' It became increasingly difficult to accomplish anything as everything was peril pointed."[68] As a result, tariffs tended to remain high.

George Ball sought legislation that would eliminate the peril points. In fact, he hoped to create an entirely new U.S. trade policy. The proposed TEA would grant the president the unprecedented power to make across-the-board tariff cuts in exchange for trade concessions from other nations. Moreover, the president could totally abolish tariffs on manufactured goods traded primarily between the United States and the Common Market. The TEA proposed a major revision in U.S. commercial practices and a reduction in protectionist policies that had hindered trade with Western Europe. Throughout 1961, Ball and his colleagues planned a new system in which tariffs would be reduced by across the board percentage cuts.

George Ball developed the ideas in the TEA through the mechanism of brainstorming sessions, à la Monnet. Ball never hesitated to recruit the best and the brightest individuals for free-wheeling sessions in his office. For instance, Ball had earlier turned to Raymond Vernon, a Harvard professor and former State Department economist, who had headed a committee on trade policy during Stevenson's 1960 run for the Democratic presidential nomination. Vernon had been a consultant for the FEP and then took a six-month leave from Harvard to work with Ball in the Kennedy State Department. The work of Vernon and his committee produced much of the substance of what was to become the TEA. Vernon and his associates, for example, suggested that tariff cuts be made across the board rather than be negotiated product by product.[69]

In brief, the TEA authorized the president to make 50 percent across-the-board reductions for most products. It also enabled the chief executive to eliminate tariffs if the United States and Common Market countries together accounted for at least 80 percent of the world export value of all articles within the category in question.

Ball and the Kennedy administration sold the TEA to Congress and the American people by presenting it as a necessary response to the burgeoning European Common Market. With the U.S. economy in the doldrums and the Common Market growing stronger, Washington policymakers had grown increasingly concerned about discrimination against American exports. In the words of Secretary of Commerce Luther Hodges, "We need . . . a trade policy that will assure us access to this booming market [Europe]." Treasury Secretary Douglas Dillon asserted that the TEA's purpose was to help the United States "bargain down the outside tariff of the Common Market." During the campaign for the TEA, Kennedy told Congress that "the two great Atlantic markets will either grow together or they will grow apart. . . . That decision will either mark the beginning of a new chapter in the alliance of free nations—or a threat to the growth of Western unity."[70]

These arguments became the essence of the administration's lobbying campaign to push the TEA through Congress. Knowing that the trade act would encounter strong opposition, Kennedy organized a massive effort to promote the trade bill both in Congress and in the press. Believing that Luther Hodges would be more effective than Ball in lobbying before Congress, the president charged the secretary of commerce with ensuring passage of the legislation. Chairman of the House Ways and Means Committee Wilbur Mills had convinced the president that congressmen would be much more receptive to a businessman from the Department of Commerce than to a lawyer from the State Department. In Kennedy's effort on behalf of the TEA, he sent the largest delegation before Congress that he had ever sent to promote a bill.

With the courtly secretary of commerce from North Carolina out front, Ball worked behind the scenes in support of the bill. Ball, for example, helped arrange a meeting between House majority whip Hale Boggs and Jean Monnet in France during the summer of 1961. Initially Boggs, an influential Louisiana congressman, had been skeptical about the trade bill. His conversations with Monnet, however, convinced him that the TEA was crucial to the economic health of the United States and to the future of U.S.-European relations. Boggs became an important ally of the TEA in Congress.

At critical moments, Ball stood before congressional committees to testify in favor of the TEA. In August of 1962, for instance, he testified for seven hours before the Senate Finance Committee in an attempt to dissuade Congress from proposing a weaker version of the bill. He feared that the committee would try to amend the legislation by including a clause obliging the president to increase tariffs when another country restricted U.S. imports. In his testimony, Ball declared: "If we threaten to raise our tariffs, we invite counterthreats. Retaliation breeds retaliation." He warned that such threats could instigate "a chain reaction that would bring about the closing of markets against our exports all over the world."[71] Congress heeded Ball's words and resisted weakening the act's support for free trade.

Nevertheless, the TEA encountered fierce opposition from members of Congress. Prescott Bush, the Republican senator from Connecticut and father of George Bush, and Representative Tom Curtis of Missouri represented a group that charged that tariff reductions would accelerate imports at an even greater rate than the expected increase in U.S. exports, thus intensifying the already serious imbalance of payments problem. Ball countered by arguing that in the short run the United States had security needs for certain foreign products, but in the long run import restrictions would invite retaliation and trade conflict.

Ball worked with the mass media and influenced writers for such publications as *Fortune* and the *Saturday Evening Post* to produce articles in support of the TEA. He also addressed influential business groups across the country. In a November 1961 speech before the National Foreign Trade Convention in New York, Ball stated: "In a world where we must all unite or perish there is no place for an inward-looking economic nationalism. We can no more retire into an economic Fortress America than we can retire into a political Fortress America. In the economic struggle that lies ahead, it would not even preserve us from fallout, much less a direct attack." [72]

In October 1962, the Trade Expansion Act passed by a vote of 298–125 in the House and 78–8 in the Senate, and President Kennedy enthusiastically signed the bill into law. Representative Boggs described the act's passage as "the most significant event of this decade. It could be one of the most significant events of the century." *Newsweek* predicted that the TEA might "come to rank in importance with the Marshall plan." [73] Although such assessments may have been overstated, the TEA did, in fact, transform U.S. trade policy at a crucial historical moment. George Ball left his indelible imprint on the trade bill, a piece of legislation that he persuasively sold to the Kennedy administration and then helped guide through the thickets of Congess. In 1965 Ball recalled that one Sunday he had "blocked out the whole Trade Bill and brought it in one Monday morning. . . . It was substantially the bill in the form in which it was finally passed." He immodestly acknowledged, "I invented the Trade Bill." [74]

Ball and the British Challenge to European Integration

George Ball championed the Trade Expansion Act as a mechanism to strengthen the U.S. economy by breaking down trade barriers among nations. Furthermore, Ball admitted that the TEA was designed to encourage Great Britain to join the Common Market. The campaigns to promote British participation in the EEC and to support the Trade Expansion Act were intertwined. [75]

Throughout his public life, Ball argued that before the United States and Europe could hope to establish effective institutions for economic and political cooperation, the Europeans themselves must take meaningful strides toward unity. In his judgment, such strides included the participation of the major European powers, France, Germany, and Great Britain. A Common Market without Great Britain was incomplete. Moreover, Ball considered the European Free Trade Association, an organization in which Britain took the lead, to be a narrow, shoddy response to the EEC.

Great Britain had historically considered itself separate from continental Europe and had aggressively protected its sovereignty. Furthermore, Britain valued its own special relation with the United States and mistrusted any scheme that might involve traditional enemies like France and Germany in decision making that touched British national interests. These attitudes prevailed long after the special relation with the United States was no longer so special.

Ball considered British resistance to the EEC to be a major obstacle to economic and political integration. He often quoted Dean Acheson's 1961 speech: "Great Britain has lost an empire and has not yet found a role. The attempt to play a separate power role . . . is about played out."[76] For years, both privately and publicly, Ball struggled to bring about British entry into the European Community:

> Intimate British participation in the affairs of the Continent could provide the necessary element of strength and solidarity; it could moderate these latent instabilities and provide a permanent balance, securing democracy in Europe. . . .
>
> So long as Britain remains outside the European Community, she is a force for division rather than cohesion . . . a giant lodestone drawing with unequal degrees of force on each member state. But if Great Britain now decides to participate in the formidable efforts to unite Europe, she can, and I am sure she will, apply her unique political genius—in which we have great confidence—toward the creation of a unity that can transform the Western world. . . .
>
> We recognize this is a very big step for the British people . . . at the same time we feel that if the British people made the decision to join and if a mutually satisfactory agreement was worked out with the Six, it would represent a very great contribution to the cohesion and strength of the Western world.[77]

Ball knew many leaders of the British political establishment personally. He expanded and strengthened these contacts through his attendance at Bilderberg and his frequent trips to London. At Bilderberg conferences and in England, Ball strenuously argued that British membership in the EEC was in the deepest interests of both Great Britain and the Six.

The Ball campaign for British inclusion took place on many fronts. Besides attacking on the British front, he argued the case in Washington, Paris, and Bonn. In Washington he had many allies, including those with whom he had lobbied for the TEA. Also, both Secretary of State Dean Rusk and President Kennedy agreed with Ball and supported British inclusion. Although Ball had influential friends in France and Germany, Charles de Gaulle and Konrad Adenauer stood far above everyone else in determining the directions of their respective societies. Ball knew them both, but his influence with them was limited.

In early 1961, Ball received word that the British government planned to apply for Common Market membership. Britain hoped to modernize its industrial sector and to accelerate its trade with the Common Market countries. Moreover, the British had begun to feel frozen out of the European action and now sought to assume a greater leadership in the region. On March 30 in London, Ball met with Edward Heath and a group of senior civil servants, including an old friend, Joint Permanent Secretary of the Treasury Sir Frank Lee. Heath, lord privy seal in Prime Minister Harold Macmillan's cabinet, proved to be Ball's kindred spirit. Heath had argued unsuccessfully for British participation in the Schuman Plan in 1950 and later became known as the "Mr. Europe" of Britain.

At the March 1961 meeting, Heath and Lee indicated that Britain was seriously considering joining the EEC. When Sir Frank Lee directly asked Ball whether the United States would support a British move to join the Common Market, Ball said that support was contingent upon British acceptance of certain principles. In particular, he emphasized the idea that a united Europe must move in the direction of political integration. Ball told the British delegation that the EEC's institutions should not "become mere technocratic bodies; they should continue to develop politically. If Britain joined the EEC, it should be on the understanding that the present institutions did not form a completed edifice but would continue to evolve and that the Rome Treaty was not a 'frozen document' but a 'process.'"[78]

In committing the United States to this position, Ball was pushing the limits of his authority. Ball later admitted that the president "had given me no mandate to state American policy with such assurance. . . . Thus, in describing the American position, I was not sure whether I was making American policy or interpreting it."[79] In fact, this technique of proclaiming policy that was yet in the stage of formation was vintage George Ball. He took advantage of the opportunity to describe his preferred policy as U.S. policy. Because Ball's stated positions were accepted as official U.S. policy by the other negotiating parties, the under secretary presented the administration with policy faits accomplis.

Edward Heath shared Ball's vision of a European community evolving in the direction of a political union. Ball sensed, however, that Prime Minister Macmillan was unconvinced. In an April 1961 memorandum to President Kennedy, the under secretary warned that Macmillan, in his forthcoming trip to the United States, would try to use "traditional British-type compromise that would give the UK the best of both worlds—the full commercial advantages of a loose association with the Common Market without any economic or political involvement in the Continent."[80]

During Macmillan's April visit to Washington, he asked Kennedy how the United States would react to a British application to join the Community. When Kennedy directed the question to Ball, the under secretary took the opportunity to reiterate the position he had outlined to Heath in London: "America would welcome it if Britain should apply for full membership in the Community, explicitly recognizing that the Rome treaty was not merely a static document but a process leading toward political unification." Macmillan seemed to accept Ball's argument and later, at a social gathering, he personally confirmed his agreement to Ball.[81]

Once back in England, however, Macmillan took a different public position. He denounced any political ramifications of European integration. In July 1961, he told the *Financial Times* and the Parliament that "the EEC is an economic community, not a defense alliance or a foreign policy community, or a cultural community." Ball and Macmillan had a different vision of the Community and each criticized the other in his memoirs. Macmillan recalled: "President Kennedy himself was helpful and sympathetic throughout . . . [but] there was always Mr. George Ball of the State Department who seemed determined to thwart our policy in Europe and the Common Market negotiations." On his part, Ball crisply wrote that "Macmillan's private conversations, particularly with regard to such sensitive political issues as Europe, were often far more forthright than his public statements or official actions."[82]

Actually, Macmillan was using his public stance against political integration as a tactic designed to work Britain into the Common Market in a way that would allay the fears of the EFTA and Commonwealth countries. In addition, he had to respond to the influential forces within Britain who strongly opposed Community membership. He sought to bargain Britain's way into the EEC. Ball refused to bargain. As prime minister, Macmillan tried to provide cover for Edward Heath, who was determinedly struggling to bring the United Kingdom into position to apply for EEC membership. In the struggle for European integration "Heath found his life's cause"; indeed, it provided Heath with "a transforming vision which he could pursue with unexpected passion."[83]

In the admission campaign, Frank Lee and Eric Roll of the Ministry of Agriculture assisted Heath. Like Lee, Roll, "one of the most subtle [and] cosmopolitan minds in Whitehall,"[84] had known George Ball for years. They had met in Washington in 1941 during Roll's tenure with the British Food Mission and Ball's association with Lend-Lease. They worked together during the Marshall Plan period and were, in Roll's words, "very close friends."[85]

After several months of intricate negotiations, Heath formally presented Britain's application for admission to the EEC on October 10, 1961. Heath's announcement represented, in the words of one British statesman, "the reversal of a thousand years of English history."[86] Quietly cheering from the sidelines in Washington, George Ball watched expectantly as negotiations between Britain and the various EEC countries continued throughout 1962.

Then, in December 1962, Ball accompanied Kennedy to Nassau for an important bilateral conference with the British. The cancellation of the Skybolt, an air-to-surface missile system that was to be shared with Britain, had upset the British. Secretary of Defense Robert MacNamara had publicly and clumsily announced the program's cancellation during a visit to England in early December.

At the Nassau conference, Kennedy, feeling the pressure from Great Britain, promised the British access to U.S. Polaris missiles. Although Ball realized that Kennedy had already decided to accede to Macmillan's requests, he argued mildly but futilely that such a nuclear commitment would best be made within a multilateral context involving other European allies. The Nassau meetings, described by Ball as "probably the worst prepared summit meetings in modern times," set the stage for a dramatic announcement by French President Charles de Gaulle.[87] In a press conference on January 14, 1963, only three weeks after the Nassau meetings, de Gaulle delivered what Ball termed a "thunderbolt": France had rejected British application for membership in the Common Market.

De Gaulle's veto angered George Ball. Along with Monnet, Heath, and the other dedicated Common Marketeers in the United States and Europe, Ball bitterly blamed de Gaulle for the failure to enlarge the Community. In a more general context, Ball considered de Gaulle's decision a victory for narrow nationalism over the developing drive for supranational organization.

In June 1963, shortly before Kennedy traveled to Europe, George Ball wrote a paper for the president entitled "The Mess in Europe and the Meaning of Your Trip." The memo contained the essence of Ball's philosophy concerning Europe and the international order. Throughout the paper, Ball denounced the destructive force of nationalism and blamed de Gaulle for reviving it. After labeling de Gaulle's nationalist mind-set "a mischief and a danger," Ball wrote: "Nationalism can work in only one direction. It can push Europe back towards its old fragmentation, can reinstate old rivalries, revive old grievances. But it is a destructive force. It cannot build anything, since nationalism motivated by a desire for dominance or hegemony, no matter how deceptively decked out, is the negation of internationalism and supranationalism."[88]

In November 1967, de Gaulle again vetoed British membership. The French president stated that "Britain will enter the Common Market one day [but] no doubt I shall no longer be here."[89] De Gaulle served as president of the Fifth Republic until his resignation in 1969, at which time Monnet, Ball, and others immediately renewed a campaign that resulted in British membership in 1973. Since 1973, the Common Market, despite periodic setbacks, has gained momentum and members. Under its latest title of European Union, the Community had grown to fifteen member countries by 1996.

The Long Shadow of Charles de Gaulle

George Ball once said that every time some country extended the hand of friendship across the sea to France, General de Gaulle put a dead fish in it. Moreover, Ball informally poked fun at de Gaulle, referring to his vaunted *force de frappe* as a *force de crap*. Ball, who had engaged in negotiations personally with de

Gaulle on several occasions, found the great leader to be impossible. The different worldviews of the two Frenchmen, Monnet and de Gaulle, shed light upon
the difficulties in the Ball–de Gaulle relationship.

De Gaulle summarized his stance on European integration cogently and persuasively in a famous January 1963 press conference:

> England is, in effect, insular, maritime, linked through its trade, markets, and
> food supply to very diverse and often very distant countries. . . . In short, the
> nature, structure and economic context of England differ profoundly from
> those of the other states of the Continent. . . .
>
> It must be agreed that the entry first of Britain and then of those other
> states will completely change the series of adjustments, agreements, compen-
> sations and regulations already established among the Six. . . .
>
> Moreover, this Community, growing in that way, would be confronted
> with all the problems of its economic relations with a crowd of other states,
> and first of all the United States. It is foreseeable that the cohesion of all its
> members, who would be very numerous and very diverse, would not hold for
> long and that in the end there would appear a colossal Atlantic Community
> under American dependence and leadership, which would soon completely
> swallow up the European Community.[90]

De Gaulle took it upon himself to guarantee that the United States would not
"swallow up" France. The French president distrusted the special relations between the United States and Britain and feared that Britain would act as a Trojan
horse for U.S. interests in Europe. He was convinced of the need for France to
produce its own nuclear deterrent and doubted that the United States or Britain would risk nuclear war with the Soviet Union to protect France. The United
States' unilateral policy during the Cuban missile crisis of 1962 — risking nuclear
war without seriously consulting its closest allies in Europe — convinced de Gaulle
that France must take care of itself.

The Nassau conference confirmed de Gaulle's worst fears. At Nassau, de
Gaulle saw the United States and Great Britain cut a nuclear defense deal, again
without even consulting the other European allies. Nassau documented "Britain's incestuous ties to America." In the words of Arthur Hartman, the Nassau
agreement was "the straw that broke the camel's back as far as de Gaulle was
concerned."[91] Furthermore, de Gaulle considered British membership in the
Common Market to be a major threat to French power within the EEC. He also
worried that a British presence could upset the developing economic and political linkage that marked French-German relations.

Although George Ball did not agree with de Gaulle's arguments, he could
understand them. What he could not understand was de Gaulle's complete commitment to nationalism and his opposition to any kind of supranationalism. De

Gaulle feared "the progressive erosion of national sovereignty in a supranational polity that bureaucracies and governments would be unable to stop, reverse, or even slow down."[92]

In a perceptive analysis of de Gaulle's political philosophy, U.S. Ambassador to France Charles Bohlen wrote that his "central thought seems to be that the State (Etat) is the natural and indestructible unit in national [sic] affairs. Ideologies . . . are passing phenomena which change, but the State as an entity . . . is the infrangible permanent unit upon which I would say all of de Gaulle's policy is based. It follows from this conception that he would be very much against any form of integration—anything that would water down the authority of the fundamental unit."[93] Such a worldview stood diametrically opposed to the position of Ball and Monnet.

Coming from two opposing perspectives, George Ball and Charles de Gaulle found one another politically difficult and frustrating. Having encountered Ball at two earlier meetings, de Gaulle greeted him at a third: "Monsieur Ball. Not you again!" At a more personal level, however, each recognized a sense of humor in the other, and they communicated quite well. The two statesmen developed a routine; the general would speak in French and Ball in English. Ball, who never learned French and self-consciously referred to himself as a "linguistic idiot," nonetheless praised de Gaulle's clear and precise French.[94]

Ball concluded that, while Monnet was preeminently a modern man, de Gaulle would have been best born in the time of Louis XIV. Ball recognized that Monnet and de Gaulle respected one another, but he considered Monnet to be *of* the French people while de Gaulle thought himself to be *above* his people. The root of the difficulties in Ball–de Gaulle relations concerned vision. The French president stood astride the path that Ball and Monnet hoped to blaze for an integrated Europe. In blocking that path, de Gaulle antagonized integrationists like Ball and Monnet.

From de Gaulle's perspective, on the other hand, his actions involved a legitimate defense of French independence and dignity. For the French president, the challenge coming down the path consisted not only of Britain but also of the United States, surging along behind its English client. George Ball was not as sensitive to this perspective as he might have been and, as a result, in criticizing de Gaulle, he did little to build trust between France and the United States.

After de Gaulle announced his decision in February 1966 to pull French military forces out of NATO, Ball responded with a series of strongly worded public statements. In a March 20, 1966, interview with *Le Monde*, Ball warned that France's decision had saddened and worried the United States deeply, and that by attempting to go it alone militarily, France had "diminished" its own security. In early April, Ball asserted that France's noncooperation with NATO might force the West to use nuclear weapons "earlier than we might otherwise do." Finally, in a major State Department foreign policy briefing on April 29, the under secretary blasted "the decision of the government of one European nation state to separate itself from the others and to seek a special position of primacy in Western Europe."[95]

Lyndon Johnson, who had himself been complaining about de Gaulle, leaked the story that Ball had gone too far in his criticisms of the French President. LBJ called attention to a memorandum in which he reminded U.S. officials that "bad manners make bad diplomacy." For the historical record, Johnson later wrote that he had urged patience and restraint at the time. "When a man asks you to leave his house, you don't argue; you get your hat and go." As he reached for his hat and prepared to leave, Ball apparently decided to warn the neighborhood of the consequences of this departure.[96]

Although he professed disapproval of Ball's actions, Johnson looked the other way while Ball continued his commentary over a period of several weeks. In his reaction to de Gaulle, Ball bypassed his usual diplomatic tact and leveled uncharacteristic public criticisms. Like Monnet and other Europeanists who had seen their plans disrupted before by de Gaulle, Ball reacted in disappointed frustration. To Ball, de Gaulle represented the leader who championed the forces of a "self-centered nationalism" that obstructed "the great unfinished business of Europe."[97]

Ball's European Legacy: The Principles and the Methodology

George Ball was an internationalist, an interventionist, and an integrationist. He refused to accept the nation-state as a given and sought to break down the barriers that divided nations. Ball based much of his political philosophy upon the principles of free trade and European integration. He fought the imposition of quotas and tariffs and argued that multinational corporations operating in an environment of free trade provided the institutional seeds for economic integration and international cooperation. Ultimately, in Ball's judgment, such organizations would dilute nationalist sentiment and hasten the development of supranational institutions. These institutions, in turn, would one day lead the way to political union.

Ball presented his ideas concerning international trade and regional integration consistently but incompletely for many years; he did not pull together the strands of this theory until 1967. In a seminal speech Ball described a world caught in the midst of "pervasive" and "accelerating" change in which "the political boundaries of nation-states are too narrow and constricted to define the scope and activities of modern business." Ball predicted that "conflict will increase between the world corporation, which is a modern concept evolved to meet the requirements of the modern age, and the nation-state, which is still rooted in archaic concepts unsympathetic to the needs of our complex world."[98]

Ball suggested that rather than bring global organizations under the control of particular nation-states with their parochial perspectives, it would be better to "internationalize" or even "denationalize" the parent companies. Recognizing the utopian nature of this idea, Ball recommended the establishment by treaty of an international companies law to be administered by a supranational body composed of citizens from a wide variety of nation-states. This body would enforce antimonopoly laws but would also protect against uncompensated expropriation.

Ball's declaration of the obsolescence of the nation-state system encountered strong criticism by groups representing a wide array of political philosophies. On the right, patriotic citizens' organizations and proponents of protectionism attacked him for compromising his country's sovereignty. In the U.S. House of Representatives, one congressman accused him of seeking to establish a "cosmocorp" that would become a "cosmocop" to "cosmocon" sovereign nations.[99] On the left, scholars and political activists portrayed Ball as an apologist for exploitative and predatory multinational corporations.

George Ball defended his cosmocorp theory by using the empirical example of the European Economic Community. In fact, the EEC was the laboratory within which Ball worked to formulate his theory. In his presentation, Ball pointed out that "six countries of Western Europe have frontally attacked the stifling restrictions imposed on trade by shedding the ancient concept of nation-states. They have created a thriving common market."[100]

Working at the side of Jean Monnet, Ball attempted to convert his theories into realities in Europe, the region that he considered to be the global heartland. The two world wars, both of which exploded out of Europe, enormously affected Ball. Like many other statesmen of his generation, Ball sought a foolproof means to prevent a third world war: "We want to see an end to the corrosive rivalries among the European nation-states that, in two successive generations, led the West to the edge of suicide."[101]

Ball used every means at his disposal to promote economic integration and political unification in Europe. Between 1945 and 1960, he used his position in Cleary, Gottlieb to back the integrationist cause. He supported the creation of the ECSC (1950), the EDC (1952), the EEC (1956), and the OECD (1960). Once he moved into a position of influence in the Kennedy and Johnson administrations, Ball continued to pursue his agenda, sponsoring the Trade Expansion Act and promoting the Multilateral Force.

While working with Jean Monnet during the long campaigns for free trade and European integration, George Ball developed several tactics that were to serve him well in other political contexts. First, he carefully built wide-ranging personal networks. The nodes at the centers of these networks consisted of political kindred spirits who also became personal friends. Second, Ball believed that the achievement of the policy goal took precedence over public recognition and personal political advancement. Like Monnet, Ball understood that low-profile politics were usually the most effective politics.

Third, Ball believed that at some point the political administration had an obligation to present its policy principles effectively to the public. Ball emphasized that one's message must be communicated with clarity and conviction. Finally, Ball stressed persistence. He expected to encounter obstacles, opposition, and setbacks. He believed in perseverance, never losing sight of one's goals, and, whenever necessary, endeavoring to use obstacles as stepping stones to success.

George Ball developed an extraordinary personal network. Even before the Ball network came to include Presidents Kennedy and Johnson in the early 1960s, the under secretary's personal web already encompassed such influential Americans as Dean Acheson, Adlai Stevenson, John McCloy, Arthur Schlesinger Jr., David Rockefeller, John Kenneth Galbraith, Walter Lippmann, and James Reston. Through his work with Monnet, Ball was able to plug directly into the French visionary's extensive European network and to form lasting friendships with kindred spirits like Pierre Uri, Etienne Hirsch, Walter Hallstein, and Robert Marjolin.

Through the Bilderberg group, Ball expanded and strengthened his ties with influential Americans and Europeans. Ball's earliest Bilderberg contacts included British statesmen who opposed European integration. Laborite leaders Hugh Gaitskell and Denis Healey, for example, were both present at the inaugural session of Bilderberg. Although personal friends, Ball and Healey often engaged in sharp debate at Bilderberg sessions over the question of Europe. On the other hand, over time, Ball later helped pack Bilderberg with such pro-EEC figures as Edward Heath, Eric Roll, Walter Hallstein, Robert Marjolin, and Max Kohnstamm.

The strongest section of Ball's personal network with respect to European affairs consisted of lesser-known U.S. officials that John Tuthill referred to as "our happy band." An extremely talented and dedicated group, the "happy band" clustered around Ball and provided a committed core of support for European integration. Consisting of such individuals as Robert Schaetzel, Arthur Hartman, Gerard Smith, and Tuthill, this group worked at the middle levels of the State Department, where they served both as policymakers and policy executors. Deeply committed to European unification, these were precisely the kind of "second tier" officials whom both Ball and Monnet counted upon and courted. Having burrowed deeply into the core of the government bureaucracy, they were in an excellent position to be either policymakers or policy breakers. Furthermore, despite their modest status within the official hierarchy, Schaetzel, Hartman, Smith, and Tuthill all attended Bilderberg meetings at one time or another.

Just as Ball kept a low profile, working in the shadows of Dean Rusk, Robert McNamara, and McGeorge Bundy, the "happy band" worked in the shadows of Ball. In Europe, Jean Monnet, who provided much of the inspiration for European integration, steadfastly refused to seek any official position in the French government. He purposefully avoided taking credit for ideas that could advance the public political careers of others. This cabal was rare in that its members generally gave priority to policy goals over personal advancement. The names of Monnet, Ball, and their many integrationist followers, therefore, are relatively unfamiliar to the general public.

George Ball fervently believed in correct and effective communication, both oral and written. In order to provide such communication, Ball argued that it was essential that policy principles be formulated, debated, understood, accepted, and then articulated. He was, therefore, constantly writing policy speeches and preparing memoranda. In the political struggles surrounding European integration, Ball prepared dozens of major memoranda and policy statements. Before Kennedy even assumed the presidency, Ball had directed the preparation of two major task force studies. After completing the Stevenson Report, he submitted the Foreign Economic Policy Report on December 31, 1960. On the following day he sent a carefully organized memorandum to incoming Secretary of State Rusk and Under Secretary Chester Bowles. In this four-part document, Ball provided a twenty-one-point foreign economic policy agenda for the new administration. In both the FEP report and the January 1 memorandum, Ball laid out his vision for trade policy and European union. In order to implement these ideas, he emphasized the need for a comprehensive foreign economic policy bill.

George Ball believed that the effectiveness of any report was directly proportionate to the strength of its grammatical and syntactical presentation. Ball's insistence on clear exposition and logical organization meant that any report bearing his signature involved a multitude of drafts. Because Monnet shared this perfectionism, it was not unusual for their joint reports to involve as many as twenty different drafts. Both the FEP report and the January 1 memorandum stand as evidence of Ball's writing and organizational skills. Ball presented the material in the documents logically, lucidly, and persuasively.

Finally, George Ball was a persistent man. He seldom faltered in his fifty-year campaign for free trade and regional economic and political integration. Whether as a public official or as a private citizen, he promoted both causes whenever and wherever he had the opportunity. While under secretary, he used every means at his disposal to advance these goals. Ball carried the free trade/European community torch from the Kennedy administration to Lyndon Johnson. In the MLF struggle, he refused to admit defeat, and only the heavy hand of LBJ could pull him off the case. After he left government in 1967, Ball struggled to help keep the torch burning through six subsequent presidencies.

Over the years, Ball remained in close touch with both Jean Monnet and Robert Marjolin. In 1976 he had Thanksgiving dinner with Jean and Sylvia Monnet at their home in France; in 1978 he attended Monnet's ninetieth birthday party in Paris; and in 1979 he lunched with Robert Marjolin before the two of them attended Monnet's funeral. The Marjolin-Ball lunches took place on a regular basis in New York City throughout the 1970s and early 1980s. During the Reagan and Thatcher periods, Ball commiserated with Marjolin about the weakened health of the European Community. Ball noted the frustrating resilience of the nation-state system and the resistance of strong national leaders to the idea of a European union. Prime Minister Margaret Thatcher's frontal attacks on the European Community in the late 1980s particularly troubled Ball. In the early 1990s, Ball followed closely the struggle between what the *Financial Times* termed the "Euro-enthusiasts" and the "Euro-skeptics."

In spite of the many problems and setbacks, the European Community moved in the 1990s far beyond its structure of the 1960s. At the time of Ball's death in 1994, the Community had evolved into a huge interstate economic, social, and political organization that included the European Commission, the Council of Ministers, the European Parliament, and the Court of Justice. With fifteen members, and many more clamoring for admission, the European Community had moved ahead significantly in the creation of a true common market.

In 1987, the Commission ratified the Single European Act, which outlined the program for achieving a single market, an economic and monetary union, and a single currency. An EC summit in Maastricht, Netherlands, in 1991 provided a draft treaty and a timetable for moving the Community to full economic and monetary union. Furthermore, amendments were approved at Maastricht that pushed the Community in the direction of greater political integration. These amendments called for more unified defense and foreign policies and increased the Commission's authority in the areas of environment, health, education, and culture. The Maastricht treaties also proposed the establishment of a union citizenship.

Although the ratification of the Maastricht treaty stalled in the mid-1990s, the movement toward European integration has continued on all fronts. Jean Monnet once reminded George Ball that together they had helped create a new supranational community and had given that creation a relentless momentum from which there would be no retreat. In 1991, although admitting that labor pains would surely accompany the birth of any new unified European economy, Ball argued that "substantial progress" was continuing to be made and that now "younger Europeans" were helping to maintain the "remarkable momentum."[102]

In a massive attempt to analyze the events of the twentieth century, the Marxist intellectual Eric Hobsbawm asserts that the end of the century is a time of severe disconnection between the public and the politicians, between the people and the state. Hobsbawm's conclusion concerning this "democratic predicament" is eerily reminiscent of George Ball's "cosmocorp" thesis. Hobsbawm argues that the only effective global structures today are private business and supranational institutions like the European Union.[103]

With the collapse of the communist system and the appearance of a post–Cold War era marked by violence and disarray, Ball's warnings about the inadequacy of the nation-state system seem more relevant than ever. Ball's faith in the multinational corporation as the critical force for supranationalism and global peace, however, raises important questions. Ball recognized that the "cosmocorps" could run amok, and he recommended a new supranational legal system to balance the power of both the multinationals and the nation-states. But Ball underestimated how much the multinationals would widen the global gap between the haves and the have nots. Moreover, he did not address the fact that these huge businesses would oppose the revolutionary change necessary to uproot corrupt and oppressive traditional regimes.

In a provocative essay evaluating the relative merits of the multinational and nation-state models, Robert Heilbroner concluded that because we do not yet know how to organize large masses of people effectively, "we have to depend on the nation-state with its vicious force and shameful irrationality and the corporation with its bureaucratic hierarchies and its reliance on greed."[104] Heilbroner concluded that at this point in history both modes of social organization seem necessary. Ball disagreed. He believed that the activities of the multinationals would assist in the creation of regional economic and political groupings that would in turn sound the death knell of the obsolescent nation-state system.

The European Union experiment represents the major global test case for George Ball's thesis. Although the nation-state stubbornly resists, the process of European integration continues to develop along many fronts. A U.S. government publication analyzing the European Union concludes that "the possibility of a united Europe, once only an ideal, is now closer to reality than ever before."[105] George Ball played a significant role both in shaping the ideal and in bringing that ideal closer to reality.

4

❖·❖·❖

Rebellion and War in Africa and Asia:
The Congo and Vietnam

During his campaigns in the early 1960s for the transformation of U.S. trade policy and for the promotion of European integration, George Ball also found himself embroiled in other important political issues. This was a time of exploding international crises. In 1962 alone, there were coups or countercoups in the Dominican Republic, Burma, Argentina, Syria, Yemen, Laos, and Peru. Secretary of State Dean Rusk delegated to Ball the primary policymaking responsibility for the Congo crisis while also assigning the under secretary major roles in the Cuban missile crisis and the Cyprus problem. Meanwhile, Ball slowly insinuated himself into the debate over Vietnam policy.[1]

George Ball took over the responsibilities for Congo policy in the fall of 1961. On September 13, Ball sent a major policy memorandum concerning the Congo to President Kennedy. The September memo provided the basis for Ball's major policy speech in Los Angeles on December 19. George Ball became, in the words of National Security Adviser McGeorge Bundy, Washington's commander in chief of Congo affairs.

The Congo Crisis: Dilemmas and Policymaking

One of John F. Kennedy's earliest and most complex challenges developed in the heart of Africa. After gaining its independence from Belgium in June 1960, the Congo (later Zaire), an artificially constructed political unit of two hundred tribes and ethnic groups, exploded into violent upheaval along tribal and regional lines. When Belgian citizens still resident in the country became targets of attack, Belgium reintroduced troops into the Congo to provide protection. Anarchy and violence swept across the region.[2]

Less than two weeks after its independence day, the former Belgian Congo shattered into three major pieces: the central government in Leopoldville headed by President Joseph Kasavubu and Prime Minister Patrice Lumumba, a regional government in Stanleyville led by Antoine Gizenga, and the southern secessionist state of Katanga headed by Moise Tshombe in Elisabethville. Katanga, rich in copper, cobalt, and other minerals that provided more than half the Congo's foreign exchange and tax revenues, represented the strongest separatist movement.[3]

Belgium, Great Britain, and France, along with influential groups in the United States, supported Katangan secession. The powerful corporation Union Minière du Haut Katanga (UMHK), headquartered in Brussels, maintained offices in Katanga and brought its considerable influence to bear in favor of secession. The British invested heavily in the multinational parent company of the UMHK, the Société Générale de Belgique. Although in its final days the Eisenhower administration adopted a cautious attitude toward the Congo crisis, it sympathized with the Katangan/European position.

The United States, the Soviet Union, the United Nations, and the Congo

John Kennedy became president when much of the Afro-Asian world was torn by revolutionary change and was struggling to break free from the grip of colonialism. Charismatic leaders like Jawaharlal Nehru, Kwame Nkrumah, Fidel Castro, and Gamel Abdel Nasser captured the imagination of citizens of the developing world. The watchwords of international politics were *nationalism, neutralism,* and *nonalignment,* and old systems of "colonialism" and "imperialism" became the targets of condemnation across the globe.

Unlike the Eisenhower administration, the Kennedy government maintained a special sensitivity to the growing importance of the developing nations. While a senator, John Kennedy had developed a deep personal interest in African affairs. During his campaign for the presidency, he had criticized Eisenhower's policy and argued that the United States had "lost ground in Africa because we have neglected and ignored the needs and aspirations of the African people."[4]

The Congo crisis coincided with the intensifying Cold War competition between the United States and the Soviet Union. Increasingly, the two superpowers confronted one another in Africa, Asia, and Latin America. The Congo crisis overlapped with U.S.-Soviet conflict in Angola, Cuba, Laos, Vietnam, and Iran. Nationalist leaders in Cuba, Egypt, and India sought to protect their nations' autonomy by playing one superpower against the other.

Although the Soviet Union initially supported the UN Security Council resolution of July 14, 1960, giving the United Nations a mandate to intervene in the Congo, Moscow, alarmed about western support for the Katangan secession, soon reversed its position. After the radical Congolese leader Gizenga lost his position in Stanleyville and Lumumba was assassinated, the Soviets adamantly opposed U.S. and UN activities in the Congo.[5] The hardening Soviet position alarmed many congressional cold warriors who viewed all Congo developments through red-tinted glasses.

Patrice Lumumba, the prime minister in Leopoldville and the most charismatic of the Congolese leaders, was a mercurial nationalist of fiery and unpredictable disposition. Many citizens across the Third World considered Lumumba the Congolese equivalent of Cuba's Castro, Egypt's Nasser, or Ghana's Nkrumah. The western press, on the other hand, tended to portray Lumumba as a dangerous communist agent. In the words of UN official Brian Urquhart: "Nothing could have done more to misrepresent the reality of Lumumba. His first international act as prime minister was to appeal for American intervention in the Congo, hardly the act of a 'Soviet puppet.'" Urquhart described Lumumba as "a courageous, unstable, inexperienced, imaginative, quicksilver, and patriotic man who went disastrously wrong."[6]

After a falling out with Kasavubu, Lumumba took political control in Leopoldville and approached both the United States and the United Nations for assistance in suppressing the Katangan rebellion. When the Eisenhower administration refused to intervene and the United Nations hesitated to act, Lumumba turned to the Soviet Union for help. The tactic alarmed many U.S. policymakers, who began to consider Lumumba a crypto-communist. The Central Intelligence Agency established a heavy and intrusive presence in the Congo and drew up elaborate plans to "remove" Lumumba. Although the CIA reportedly did not directly implement these plans, the Agency was probably involved in a plot in which Tshombe sympathizers of Katanga assassinated Lumumba on January 17, 1961.[7]

With the death of Lumumba and the continuing intransigence of Tshombe, the United Nations hesitantly initiated a military campaign against the Katangan rebels. In the summer of 1961, a bland politician named Cyrille Adoula assumed control of a coalition government. At the United Nations, Secretary General Dag Hammarskjöld personally took charge of the Congo problem. A remarkable leader of balance and vision, Hammarskjöld flew to the Congo in July to negotiate an agreement between Leopoldville and Elisabethville. The secretary general understood the emotional and complex nature of the Congo imbroglio. He told colleagues that the United Nations' effort in the Congo was like giving first aid to a rattlesnake and compared the Congo situation to a political bordello with a number of foreign madames.[8] Shortly after Hammarskjöld made this statement, the rattlesnake struck and the foreign madames intensified their struggle for control.

On September 17, 1961, during another journey to Africa, Hammarskjöld was killed when his plane crashed before landing at Ndola in Northern Rhodesia, where he was scheduled to meet with Tshombe concerning a cease-fire plan. After Hammarskjöld's tragic death, UN Deputy Secretary General Ralph Bunche and

U.S. Ambassador to the Congo Edmund Gullion applied enormous pressure on the disputing parties to negotiate an agreement. On December 21, 1961, Adoula and Tshombe signed an accord in which Tshombe agreed to reconsider secession and to recognize the authority of the central government.

Moise Tshombe, described by one observer as "a master of procrastination and of the reinterpretation of agreements," had no intention of abiding by the accord; convincing Tshombe to honor pacts "was like trying to get an eel into a bottle." [9] He reneged on his promises and dragged out the crisis for another year. The Katangan leader hoped to buy enough time for Western sympathizers to rally the support necessary to force the Kennedy administration to accept Katangan independence.

In spite of Tshombe's tactics, the United Nations, now headed by Secretary General U Thant, kept the pressure on the Katangan leader. In September 1962, the Katangan rebels harassed and killed a number of UN officials and soldiers. In response, UN troops entered Katanga in December and occupied Elisabethville and other key cities. On January 15, 1963, Tshombe surrendered, thereby ending the Katangan secessionist movement. [10]

The thirty-month Congo crisis resulted in the preservation of the Congo as a nation-state. More generally, the outcome provided the United Nations with peacekeeping credibility and provided an early example of the politics of preventive diplomacy. But the Congo episode also demonstrated the enormous difficulties involved in seeking peace when the great powers hold opposing positions. Although the military struggle took place in Africa, much of the political battle was fought in New York, Washington, and the capitals of Europe.

The Washington Lineup

Decision makers in Washington were deeply divided concerning the Congo crisis. The major fault line separated the "Third Worlders" from the "Europeanists." Kennedy, unlike Eisenhower, had packed his administration with individuals who had special expertise concerning the developing countries of Asia, Africa, and Latin America. Many of these Third Worlders became involved in the Congo crisis, and one analyst referred to them as the "New Africa" group. [11] The Africanists included Adlai Stevenson at the United Nations; Chester Bowles, under secretary of state and roving ambassador; G. Mennen Williams, assistant secretary of state for African affairs; Harlan Cleveland, assistant secretary of state for international organization; and Edmund Gullion, U.S. ambassador to the Congo and former political counselor in Vietnam.

The Third Worlders condemned the Katangan separatist movement. They interpreted the movement as an attempt by old European colonial powers to protect their wealth and privilege at the expense of the fledgling Republic of the

Congo. The Africanists urged the United States and the United Nations to use whatever force necessary to put down the Katangan movement. They argued that the newly independent countries across the globe were watching to learn whether the United States would side with the old colonialist states of Europe or with the burgeoning independence movements.

The Europeanists, on the other hand, considered U.S. interests to be primarily intertwined with Europe. Such individuals included presidential adviser Dean Acheson, Under Secretaries of State Averell Harriman and George McGhee, Ambassador to Belgium Douglas MacArthur II, and the eminent retired foreign service officer Robert Murphy.

The Europeanists had spent most of their professional careers preoccupied with European issues. They believed that the United States had to protect its relations with countries like Britain, France, and Germany. The Europeanists judged the unity of NATO to be a major U.S. priority and did not want to risk division in the alliance over a disagreement in Africa. Although some Europeanists recognized the growing relevance of the Third World, others entertained curiously quaint and paternalistic ideas about the new states. The former secretary of state and Kennedy confidant Dean Acheson, for example, had little confidence in the new leadership in Africa. He described the native African leaders as a group for whom "the perverse stimulation of personal ambition operating in areas of almost total ignorance [contributes] to a full measure of confusion. A bright child at the controls of a car on a major thruway could produce comparable disaster." [12] Acheson and like-minded thinkers believed that the Africans could never establish effective nation-states.

The personal and philosophical animosity that marked relations between Dean Acheson and Adlai Stevenson highlights the differences between the Third Worlders and the Europeanists. Acheson, who considered Stevenson an indecisive idealist, referred to him as "the weak man from the Midwest" who presided over the UN "department of emotion." Acheson scornfully referred to Stevenson as "Fat Boy." Stevenson on the other hand, considered Acheson overbearing, outdated, and unprofessionally vindictive. [13]

Under Secretary George Ball was neither strictly a Third Worlder nor a Europeanist. Although his experience would seem to have placed him in the Europeanist camp, some analysts considered him a Third Worlder/Africanist. [14] Actually, members of both groups claimed Ball because the under secretary took a pragmatic, nonideological stance concerning the Congo crisis. He had strong ties to both camps and enjoyed close personal and professional relations with both Acheson and Stevenson.

The Cacophony of International Lobbying

The disagreements within the U.S. Department of State over the Katangan secession represented a microcosm of a much broader and more complex international conflict. The contours of the Congo crisis resisted definition by existing ideological models or theoretical frameworks. Just as U.S. government circles were divided concerning Congo policy, so too were business, religious, professional, regional, and political groupings in the United States and abroad.

Within the United States, an unlikely assortment of individuals and groups immersed themselves in the Congo controversy. The Europeanists in the government, for example, found themselves supported in the cause of Katangan independence by peculiar allies. In general, the partisans of Katanga included conservative political and religious groupings who interpreted the Congo crisis as a deadly battle of the West against communism. The Katangan lobby considered Tshombe to be a courageous freedom fighter who sought to rescue Katanga from the clutches of a communist-oriented central government led by Soviet stooge Patrice Lumumba. The pro-Tshombe forces included southern senators, Protestant religious leaders, the John Birch Society, and such public figures as Richard Nixon and former President Herbert Hoover. More surprisingly, both Averell Harriman and Douglas Dillon sympathized with Tshombe. Other supporters of Katanga included Bishop Fulton Sheen, Albert Schweitzer, and Connecticut Senator Thomas Dodd. Dodd, who campaigned incessantly for Katangan independence, was a Democrat with a history of supporting right-wing dictators.

Union Minière and its parent company, Société Générale de Belgique, lobbied intensively in the United States in favor of the secession. The primary interest group was the Katanga Information Services, and the overall effort was led by a persistent lobbyist named Michel Streulens. In his autobiography, George Ball emphasized the important role of "Belgian financial interests." [15]

Great Britain and France also supported Belgium and Katangan independence. Enormous financial interests and investments in Katanga drove British policy in the Congo. But in spite of Britain's powerful lobbying effort, the United States opposed the Katangan secession. The effectiveness of the Third Worlders in the Kennedy administration and the proclivities of John Kennedy himself combined to make the anti-Katangan position official U.S. policy. George Ball played a central coordinating role in this African drama and campaigned successfully for an end to secessionist movements in the Congo.

Ball wrestled intellectually with the Congo issue. He frankly admitted that he found the problem confused and confusing. On the one hand, he felt that Katanga possessed the resources, common history, and international credibility necessary for the establishment of a viable nation-state. Like Averell Harriman, Ball was personally impressed by Tshombe, whom he compared favorably with the other Congolese leaders of the time. Ball nonetheless opposed the process of Balkanization, the splintering of nation-states into different regional, religious, or ethnic units. Ball believed that if secession were allowed to occur in the Congo, the entire continent of Africa risked rebellion in the name of some local sovereignty or claim to autonomy. The under secretary also feared that support for Katangan independence would expose the United States to charges of colonialism and would leave Africa exposed to the blandishments of the Soviet Union.

Although Ball came down on the side of the Third Worlders, he never became ideologically and emotionally bound up in the anti-Katangan cause. In this respect, he differed from his old friend Adlai Stevenson, who vociferously argued for an end to the Katangan secession by any means necessary. From his seat as U.S. ambassador to the United Nations, Stevenson argued forcefully for military intervention to preserve the territorial integrity of the Congo. Known as "wool-heads" by the Europeanists, Stevenson and a State Department group that included Chester Bowles, Mennen Williams, African specialist Wayne Fredericks, and especially Edmund Gullion had great influence with President Kennedy. Kennedy, apparently surprised that a "wool-head" like Stevenson could be so tough, remarked to an associate: "Adlai's got an iron ass and, my God, in this job, the nerve of a burglar."[16]

Although he agreed in general with the "wool-heads" concerning Congo policy, Ball opposed the early application of military force and favored negotiations. He worried about the long-term repercussions of a policy that might bring further violence to the region and that could ultimately pave the way for corrupt and dictatorial leadership in the Congo. Ball and Stevenson had a serious falling-out over Congo policy. Ball found himself "conducting a running argument with Stevenson"; their disagreements "led to the most heated argument I ever had with Stevenson, and it was painful for both of us."[17]

Big Business and the Making of U.S. Congo Policy

Thirty years after the Congo crisis, meticulous research has uncovered a network of international business interests that played a role in the formulation of Congo policy. The political scientist David N. Gibbs presents a "business conflict model" to explain the policy dynamics of the Congo crisis. Gibbs states that the business conflict model "correctly predicts the political dominance of business interests, the existence of inter-business conflicts, and the direct ties between business and government."[18] He claims that the struggle in the Congo is better explained by the business conflict model than by any other theory.

Gibbs argues that the widely publicized role of the Belgian and British business interests that supported the Katangan secession represented only part of the story. The powerful and highly visible Union Minière (UMHK) found itself locked in competition with a number of other international corporations that sought access to the rich Katangan mineral fields. Gibbs declares that policy-makers like Adlai Stevenson and George Ball, among others, had close ties to the anti-Katangan corporations, and that these ties determined their policy positions.

The business conflict study impressively documents the personal and professional relations that undergirded the anti-Katangan coalition. Gibbs's study identifies two principal nodes of influence, a low-profile influential entrepreneur named Maurice Tempelsman and a Swedish conglomerate known as the Liberian-American Swedish Minerals Company (LAMCO).[19]

THE TEMPELSMAN CONNECTION

Maurice Tempelsman, owner of a diamond trading firm and supporter of the Democratic Party, has been described by one analyst as "a friend and supporter of Adlai Stevenson" who "had a liking for mixing conspiracy with commerce in his African trade."[20] The shadowy Tempelsman retained the services of Adlai Stevenson and Stevenson's law firm, Paul, Weiss, Rifkind, Wharton, and Garrison. Stevenson worked for Tempelsman throughout the 1950s and into the 1960s. He helped the diamond merchant gain access to nationalist groups in African states, including the Congo. According to Gibbs, when Stevenson became ambassador to the United Nations in 1961, he continued to assist Tempelsman.

Among many schemes, Tempelsman proposed a barter deal whereby the Kennedy administration would purchase industrial diamonds from the Congo in exchange for U.S. agricultural commodities. Gibbs writes that "Tempelsman apparently hoped to act as a middleman and make a substantial profit."[21] Although Stevenson admitted that his law firm represented Tempelsman, he denied that the firm had ever done any business with respect to the Congo. Nonetheless, according to Gibbs, documentary evidence indicates that Stevenson had indeed intervened on Tempelsman's behalf concerning business in the Congo. He approached George Ball, for example, about the Tempelsman barter deal. In a letter to Stevenson dated August 10, 1961, Tempelsman wrote: "I just want you to know that I appreciate your help with George Ball."[22]

THE LAMCO LINKAGE

While the UMHK economic interests supported the Katangan secession, other powerful multinational companies took an anticolonial, antisecessionist position. According to Gibbs, the most important of these was LAMCO, a predominately Swedish syndicate consisting of six mining companies. LAMCO reportedly sought to gain access to Katangan wealth. Furthermore, some observers believed that LAMCO hoped to shut down the mines in Katanga in order to raise copper prices at a time when there was a surplus on the world market.

The Gibbs study documents a complex web of personal and business relationships that connected LAMCO to several key Congo policymakers both in the United States and in the United Nations. Bo Gustav Hammarskjöld, for example, the brother of the UN secretary general, sat on the board of directors of Grangeburg, the largest of LAMCO's constituent companies. Furthermore, Dag Hammarskjöld selected Sture Linner, a managing director of LAMCO, to direct the United Nations' technical assistance program in the Congo. Gibbs concludes that Hammarskjöld family interests "appear to have influenced UN policy in the Congo, at least with regard to personnel selection."[23]

LAMCO also had U.S. linkages. George Ball's firm of Cleary, Gottlieb, Steen, and Hamilton, for example, served as legal counsel for LAMCO. Fowler Hamilton and Melvin Steen, both old friends and law partners of George Ball, held directorships in two different LAMCO affiliates. According to Gibbs, "The LAMCO group was thus well placed to influence both U.S. and UN policy."[24]

On September 12, 1962, Donald Bruce, a Republican congressman from Indiana, read on the floor of Congress a long report entitled "Is Katanga on the Auction Block?"[25] In his speech, Bruce asked: "Was it possible, indeed, that selfish financial interests might underlie the vicious United Nations and United States policy toward Katanga?" Relying heavily upon European sources, Bruce, a supporter of Tshombe and the Katangan secession, suggested an international plot by an "American-Swedish combine." Bruce raised further questions in his report: "Mr. Speaker, would it not be a a shocking revelation to learn . . . that a private combine had advance information of United Nations action against Katanga and allotted a giant sum of money for the purpose of getting control of the mineral concessions of Katanga?" The Indiana congressman went on to ask: "Was there such a plot? I do not know that there was. I do not know that there was not."

Bruce pointed out the Cleary, Gottlieb connection with LAMCO through the Hamilton and Steen directorships and then emphasized George Ball's connection with the firm: "Hence, the man who directly helped to establish our policy toward Katanga has been affiliated with the key figures already outlined in this little drama." Bruce had been calling for an investigation into U.S. Congo policy since the fall of 1961.

Gibbs, implying that Ball's Cleary, Gottlieb association shaped his policy recommendations in favor of the anticolonialist, pro-LAMCO position, notes that Ball "completely changed his perspective" in October 1962 and "briefly joined the pro-Katanga group." Ball's alleged change of heart stands as a serious challenge to the business conflict model and requires special explanation. Noting that Bruce gave his speech in September and that Ball reconsidered his Congo position in October, Gibbs concludes that Ball had been frightened by the accusations. "These right-wing attacks *may have* influenced policymaking in the Kennedy administration. *There is evidence* that the polemics intimidated George Ball, who had previously supported UN policy."[26]

The business conflict approach stands as a stimulating model for explaining U.S. foreign policy toward the Congo. One can assess the model by focusing upon the role played by George Ball, one of the key policymakers in the Congo crisis. What exactly was George Ball's position concerning Congo policy? What were his motivations? What were the basic principles upon which he acted? How did his network of personal friendships influence his thinking? Did he have vested interests in the outcome? If so, what were they?

Crisis and Conspiracy in the Congo

Shortly after George Ball took charge of Congo policy in September 1961, he prepared a special memorandum for President Kennedy. In the memo, Ball argued that "giving Katanga independence or effective autonomy would be a serious setback for US policy." He provided three reasons for this conclusion. First, Katangan secession would lead to bloody civil war. Second, an independent Katanga could not maintain itself as a viable political unit. It could survive for a while "only as a kind of enclave of colonialism, dominated and financed by white elements and particularly by big Belgian banking and mining interests." Third, Katangan independence would shatter Afro-Asian faith in the United Nations and the western world. Ball concluded: "With our support the UN can and must show that we mean what we say where colonial interests are involved."[27]

In the September memorandum, Ball suggested that the United States encourage negotiations to bring about the peaceful integration of Katanga into an independent Congo. He urged, however, that the United States not dictate terms for a settlement, pointing out that "what is wrong with the present constitution of the Congo is that it was written by white men and not negotiated among the Congolese themselves to reflect their own conception of their interests." In conclusion, Ball recommended that the United States assist the United Nations in building a military force strong enough to persuade Tshombe that negotiation was his only alternative.

Ball's September memorandum became the backbone of U.S. policy toward the Congo. Ball believed that any important policy must be rationally formulated, carefully articulated, and publicly presented. Throughout his political career, he emphasized the need for position papers that rigorously stated the basic assumptions and goals of policy along with recommendations for the implementation of these goals. On December 19, 1961, using the September memo as a guide, Ball delivered a public statement in Los Angeles articulating U.S. policy in the Congo.

In the Los Angeles speech, Ball stated that the U.S. objective in the Congo was a "free, stable noncommunist government for the Congo as a whole." He affirmed U.S. support for the UN intervention, which he described as "remarkably successful." In his view, if the United Nations had not been available to play this role, "we would have had to invent it." Finally, Ball condemned the Katangan secession and declared that the issue "is not self-determination. . . . There is no legal, political or moral basis for these secessionist efforts."[28]

In the address, Ball emphasized the communist threat. He warned the American public that secessionist movements meant chaos and civil war and that such political incoherence could "lead to the establishment of a communist base in the heart of Central Africa." The under secretary asked "all Americans" to "ponder" this fact.

When the State Department later published Ball's speech as a pamphlet, the text contained a number of revisions suggested by President Kennedy. The major change involved the insertion of an italicized paragraph highlighting Soviet obstructionism. The added reference to the Soviet Union stressed that *"the U.S.S.R . . . has consistently opposed the U.N. operation in the Congo."*[29]

In spite of Ball's policy statement, events during the summer of 1962 caused the Kennedy administration to reexamine its Congo policy. The president wavered in his antisecession stance and asked Ball to seek a compromise solution that might result in a Congolese confederation including both Adoula and Tshombe. While Tshombe stalled for time, the UN financial situation became desperate. Kennedy and his advisers clumsily attempted to assist the United Nations by forcing a $100 million bond bill through Congress. In Great Britain, the Macmillan government resisted U.S. pressure and continued to support Tshombe and Katangan independence. The Conservative Party sympathized with Tshombe: "He was prowhite, anticommunist, and dedicated to the preservation of European property"—in short, "not such a bad chap."[30] Back in Africa, Cyrille Adoula, America's choice to lead the Congo, faced mounting political difficulties. Meanwhile, in the United States, the highly visible pro-Katangan groups intensified their lobbying activities.

Furthermore, by fall of 1962 the Kennedy administration faced a series of international crises that included political fallout from coups in Peru, Argentina, and Yemen. In October 1962, Chinese troops invaded India, and during that same month the United States confronted the Soviet Union in the Cuban missile crisis. Under these volatile circumstances, Kennedy and Ball chose to search for a compromise that would enable the United States to disengage from a politically sticky and unpredictable situation in the Congo.

The reconsideration of Congo policy created a tense struggle among Kennedy's foreign policymakers. Ball faced off against the Third Worlder/Africanist camp led by Edmund Gullion and Adlai Stevenson. Ball felt that Gullion was acting "hysterically" and that his campaign against Katanga "had taken on the quality of a religious war, with Tshombe in the role of an anti-Christ."[31]

The under secretary found himself trapped between Kennedy and Stevenson. As Ball later explained, "I was always the fellow that the President put on the telephone to cool off Stevenson. I was in the rather unhappy position where Adlai would call me as an old friend whenever he was unhappy about a policy. And then I would have to defend what I thought was the President's or Rusk's views. . . . And it always put me in a very awkward position because I'm sure Stevenson thought that I had kind of sold out."[32] An accomplished bureaucratic infighter, Ball, although outnumbered, successfully implemented the Congo policy reassessment.

As part of this reassessment, Ball quietly brought Lewis Hoffacker, the U.S. consul in Elisabethville, to Washington. Hoffacker was a sensitive, courageous diplomat who had traveled throughout Katanga in his automobile flying a small American flag as he sought to stop the fighting and bloodshed. In his words, "I didn't like to see people shooting at one another. I was a peacemaker on the ramparts." Although some sources have labeled Hoffacker as pro-Katanga, he was in fact reporting what he saw in Katanga. Hoffacker has said, "I was never for secession. We were groping for peace."[33]

In bringing Hoffacker to Washington in early fall of 1962, Ball ignored formal State Department channels and set up a meeting between Hoffacker and President Kennedy. This technique, which Ball used several times in his career, helped provide the president with a better grasp of the situation in the conflict zone. With Kennedy's support, Hoffacker carried a letter back to Tshombe from Senator Dodd urging the Katangan leader to agree to negotiations. Although Tshombe agreed to negotiate, he really had no intention of doing so and, in Hoffacker's words, he "deceived us once again."

On December 9, 1962, with the support of President Kennedy, George Ball sought the opinion of a third party concerning Congo policy. Ball called on Roger Hilsman, director of the State Department's Bureau of Intelligence and Research (INR), and Hilsman's resident African specialist, Robert C. Good. Ball told Hilsman and Good that current U.S. policy was failing. He admitted that he was beginning to think that withdrawal might be the best policy. Ball asked for a fresh analysis of the situation and requested a list of policy alternatives and a final recommendation.[34]

The INR study concluded that the United States had only two alternatives, either to apply whatever pressure was necessary to defeat the Katangan secession or to disengage entirely. Both alternatives carried serious risks. The use of UN military forces could result in a bloodbath and might still fail. On the other hand, the Hilsman team felt that disengagement carried even greater risk. Pulling away from the problem could result in an extended civil war. Such a conflict would in turn provide opportunities for expanded Soviet intervention. Furthermore, the analysts argued that it was impossible to guarantee that any disengagement would be permanent. The United Nations and the United States might later be pulled back into the Congo maelstrom under even worse conditions.

Ball and Kennedy accepted the INR recommendation for continued engagement and, if necessary, the use of military force. According to Hilsman, "George Ball felt much the same—the notion of getting out was tempting, he said, but when you thought it all through the risk was just too great."[35] Shortly after the Hilsman report, Tshombe's troops initiated a series of attacks that included an assault on the U.S. Consulate in Elisabethville. In response, the United Nations began the final military offensive that resulted in the defeat of the Katangan rebellion.

In retrospect, Roger Hilsman, who Ball later fired from his State Department position, credited Ball with the Congo breakthrough: "It took a lot of guts on George's part to bypass everyone and to pick us over at INR to define our Congo policy." Hilsman admitted that Ball may not have agreed completely with the final recommendations, but he supported them completely. "Ball engineered the solution. He was really great. He gave us the ball and told us to run with it. He then backed us to the hilt once we did. His backing was critical."[36]

As a central player in the Congo crisis, George Ball's actions and decisions cannot be explained in terms of business conflict models or personal network analyses. Although it is possible to trace personal connections involving Ball-Stevenson, Stevenson-Tempelsman, Ball-Hamilton, Hamilton-LAMCO, there is no evidence that Ball made decisions based on these ties. In fact, the record demonstrates quite the opposite.

Although the Tempelsman intervention thesis may partly explain Adlai Stevenson's position on Congo policy, it does not account for Ball's decisions.[37] That Stevenson may have lobbied Ball does not prove Ball's acquiescence. Ball and Stevenson had their one major falling out over Congo policy. Furthermore, documentary evidence reveals that Ball consistently opposed Tempelsman's barter scheme.

In June and July 1964, several U.S. senators wrote Ball on behalf of Tempelsman and his business proposition. Ball responded to each senator with essentially the same letter denying the request. In a July 30, 1964, letter to his friend Senator William Fulbright, for example, Ball wrote, "I have reviewed *again* the proposal by Leon Tempelsman & Sons to barter American surplus agricultural products for industrial diamonds from the Republic of the Congo." After explaining why such a proposal would not benefit U.S. national interests, Ball rejected the idea: "I do not feel that we would be justified in determining that the foreign policy advantages of the present proposal would outweigh the potentially adverse economic consequences."[38]

After accurately noting the personal links among Cleary, Gottlieb partners Fowler Hamilton, Melvin Steen, and George Ball and documenting the LAMCO professional ties of Hamilton and Steen, Gibbs implies that these connections may explain Ball's anti-Katangan position. Ball knew that Fowler Hamilton had ties with LAMCO, but he denied ever discussing Congo policy with his Cleary, Gottlieb associate.[39] Although it is still plausible that Ball's position was influenced by the LAMCO connection to Cleary, Gottlieb, Gibbs fails to provide the evidence to back the assertion.[40]

Officials who worked closely with Ball on the Congo crisis have dismissed the hypothesis that Ball's position on the Congo may have been influenced by business considerations. Roger Hilsman called Gibbs's thesis "some kind of conspiratorial theory." In the words of Lewis Hoffacker: "Ball was looking for a peaceful solution to the problem. He had no conflict of interest. He was a patriot who was in it for Uncle Sam's interests. The U.S. government was lucky to have that guy up there."[41]

The contribution of the business conflict model is that it calls attention to the important impact of business interests upon the foreign policymaking process. In the case of the Congo, it calls attention to the quiet involvement of business figures like Maurice Tempelsman, who persistently exerted pressure on the U.S. foreign policymaking process. Although the model provides insights into the behavior of some actors, it is less successful in explaining the motivations of others. The close relationship between Maurice Tempelsman and Adlai Stevenson reinforced Stevenson's opposition to Katangan secession. Tempelsman used the Stevenson contact and others to seek government support for his economic ventures. On the other hand, although Ball had been approached by Tempelsman and Fulbright, the under secretary based his policy recommendations on other considerations.[42]

George Ball ultimately formulated his Congo policy decisions on the basis of his deep concern about the dangers of Balkanization. He feared that if the Congo were allowed to shatter into pieces, the process would spread across Africa and the developing world: "There was no logic in the division of states within Africa. The lines separating one nation-state from another had been haphazardly determined by one colonial army colliding with another. If the Congo were allowed to fragment, it could begin a process that could result in a totally Balkanized Africa."[43]

Ball also sensed the strength of the anticolonial revolution under way in the Third World, and in spite of his Eurocentric background, he thought it prudent that the United States support the forces of change that were sweeping across the globe. Unlike the Third Worlder idealists, however, Ball never became ideologically bound to the cause of political integration in the Congo. He wrestled with the question and in the end chose to seek the advice of a disinterested third team of State Department analysts. When the INR team proposed a strong antisecession approach, Ball supported the recommendation. He understood, however, that political problems would continue in the Congo.

In 1963–64, Ball's fears were realized when tribal rebellions broke out in the eastern sectors of the country. Prime Minister Tshombe and Joseph Mobutu, the head of the Congolese military, were unable to put down the rebellion. When the rebels took three thousand foreign hostages in November 1964, including American missionaries and government officials, Ball tried to persuade Lyndon Johnson to provide American C-130 aircraft to carry Belgian paratroopers on risky rescue missions. Johnson, worried by the deteriorating situation in Vietnam and exasperated by the chaos in the Congo, reacted angrily. After the first rescue attempt saved the lives of numerous hostages and the Belgians began lobbying for a second attempt, Johnson called Ball and declared that he did not "want to get tied in on the Congo and have another Korea, another Vietnam, just because of somebody wandering around searching for 'Jesus Christ.' We made a mistake first of all running the Belgians out and taking the position we did on Tshombe and then embracing him, wrapping the colonial flag around us and acting unilaterally, becoming labeled as aggressors."[44]

Nevertheless, Ball, with the assistance of Rusk, persuaded the president to approve the second mission. Although more than one hundred hostages died in the attempts, the missions resulted in the rescue of approximately two thousand foreigners. Ball often confided that his role in these rescue attempts caused him enormous emotional stress.

Increasingly preoccupied with the Vietnam imbroglio and weary of the Congo situation, the White House and foreign policy advisers like Ball and Rusk turned away from Africa, letting the CIA take charge of the field.[45] In November 1965, with the CIA's active support, General Mobutu took control of the Congolese political system. Mobutu, who Ball described as "shrewd, ruthless, and corrupt" and favored by "American business interests," imposed a harsh and venal dictatorship that has endured for more than thirty years.[46] Late in his life, George Ball wondered whether the Congo policy he had helped shape in 1962 had not been a case of both short-term success and long-term failure.

Clusters of Crises: From the Congo to Vietnam

During the Congo crisis of 1962, Ball participated in numerous policymaking decisions concerning other international emergencies. These crises tended to overlap through time. The pattern was repeated in 1965, when Ball became increasingly involved in Vietnam policy. Along with his continuing activities in support of the process of European integration and his responsibilities for overseeing the explosive situation in Cyprus, Ball participated in high-level policy discussions of uprisings in Kashmir, Indonesia, and the Dominican Republic.

Ball also made several trips abroad in 1965. He attended NATO meetings in Europe in April, May, and July and participated in the Bilderberg gathering that met at Villa d'Este in Tivoli, Italy, during the first week of April. In August and September, Ball traveled to Europe with Secretary of the Treasury Henry Fowler. Besides conferring with the finance ministers of Italy, West Germany,

Sweden, Belgium, the Netherlands, and Britain concerning international monetary reform, Ball met with President de Gaulle to discuss Vietnam and the future
of NATO. Finally Ball delivered seventeen speeches during 1965, on subjects
ranging from the management of nuclear weapons to the organization of the
State Department. He also testified before congressional committees and made
several television appearances.

Ball and Vietnam: The Politics of Dissent

With the benefit of hindsight, many policymakers have professed their early
understanding of the futility of the Vietnam war and their quiet opposition to
the Johnson administration's escalation of the conflict. In fact, however, George
Ball was the only high-level U.S. official who consistently opposed the war, beginning in the Kennedy administration. Ball's position did not become widely
known until the publication of the Pentagon Papers in June of 1971. In its lead
editorial the *New York Times* decried "the missing factor" in U.S. policy toward
Vietnam: lack of discussion of the war's raison d'être and the rationale for massive U.S. involvement in that war. According to the editorial, the premise behind
U.S. involvement "seems to have been accepted without question by virtually
everyone in the top ranks, except Under Secretary George Ball."[47]

The publication of the Pentagon Papers made Ball an instant celebrity. To
many Americans, traumatized by the human and economic costs of the war,
Ball's idiosyncratic warnings brought him into public view as a man of courage
and wisdom. In some circles he was viewed as an American hero. Somewhat uneasy about the sudden notoriety, George Ball sought to downplay his role in the
Vietnam drama, pointing out that "there are no devils and no villains in this situation." Although he supported the publication of the Pentagon Papers, he urged
readers to resist hasty conclusions based on dry, "clinical" official prose.[48]

In spite of Ball's cautious disclaimers, his insight and prescience concerning
the Vietnam war are a matter of record. According to David DiLeo, the author of
an excellent study of George Ball and Vietnam, the under secretary's predictions
concerning the Vietnam conflict were extraordinary in their accuracy: "Indeed,
after examining his dissenting memorandums one would suspect that they were
written after, and not before, the American agony in Southeast Asia."[49]

As the lone dissenter in the halls of White House power, Ball carried on a quiet
but persistent campaign to reform U.S. Vietnam policy. Clark Clifford, McNamara's successor at the Defense Department who tried to pick up the pieces of
a failed Vietnam policy, described Ball as "utterly fearless in expressing his own
opinions."[50] Outnumbered, outranked, and outstaffed, Ball doggedly presented
and defended his position in the slippery terrain of high-level bureaucratic politics. In a revealing recollection, William Bundy, the perceptive assistant secretary

of state for Far Eastern affairs (1964–69) and brother of National Security Adviser McGeorge Bundy, described George Ball in the following terms: "The memories flood back, too many to recount, including a fateful meeting in late June 1965 when [Ball] made clear that he would be writing to LBJ to say we should not go in deeper in Vietnam—he was as usual candid about the consequences, never pretending that they would be slight but insisting that in the wider sphere of policy they should be accepted. For a brief moment as we walked back to his office from a meeting next door, I thought of joining him, but then did not, urging instead an impractical middle course. He was more honest, and he was right in the only court that counts, that of history."[51]

The United States' involvement in Vietnam stands as an unpleasant reminder of the limits of American power. In a century of unprecedented national triumph, during which the United States emerged from two world wars as the most powerful nation-state on earth and later witnessed the disintegration of its only serious rival, the Soviet Union, the loss in Vietnam remains a deep wound on the American psyche. This wound refuses to close completely and continues to influence U.S. behavior in international affairs.

In the Vietnam war, the United States saw nearly 58,000 of its young men killed and another 304,000 wounded. The South Vietnamese military deaths totaled more than 224,000, and another 571,000 were wounded. North Vietnamese and Vietcong battle deaths reached more than 660,000. The number of military deaths in the Vietnam war approached one million. Over the years, the United States flooded Vietnam with more than six million troops, and support personnel and dropped more than six million tons of bombs in Southeast Asia. In spite of this massive effort, the United States, frustrated and bitter, ultimately withdrew from the conflict. The last U.S. soldiers departed on March 29, 1973. On April 29, 1975, a day before the communist troops captured Saigon, the last American citizens were evacuated from the city. The Vietnam war was over.[52]

The war divided the American people and tore the country apart. Massive antiwar demonstrations exploded in the streets, while political leaders and both political parties found themselves held hostage by the war. In the end, the costs of the Vietnam war went beyond the material, economic, and political; they were human and moral as well. In Washington, few political leaders understood the dangers of entering Vietnam. In Congress, only a few, like Senators William Fulbright and Mike Mansfield, understood; in the high levels of the executive branch of government, George Ball stood alone.

Ball Enters the Vietnam Arena: The Kennedy Presidency

Although he was preoccupied with such issues as free trade, European integration, and the Congo during the early months of the Kennedy administration,

George Ball was troubled about the situation in Southeast Asia.[53] During 1962 and 1963, Roger Hilsman, director of the State Department's Bureau of Intelligence and Research, who had worked closely with Ball during the Congo crisis, influenced the under secretary's thinking concerning Vietnam.

A prickly, pushy personality of great talent, Hilsman was a West Point graduate whose honest pugnacity and willingness to confront the military earned him the support of John Kennedy. Hilsman argued that the communist challenge in Vietnam was primarily political rather than military. He insisted that large-scale military operations would alienate the Vietnamese people and that only fundamental political and social reform could address the challenge in Vietnam. By the beginning of 1963, Hilsman questioned the U.S. approach to the Vietnam war and concluded that the Diem regime was hopelessly corrupt and destined for failure. Although uncomfortable with Hilsman's brash and freewheeling personal style, Ball listened carefully to Hilsman's forebodings and arranged for him to meet with the president in January 1962. Meanwhile, Ball himself occasionally briefed both Secretary Rusk and President Kennedy on the situation in Vietnam.

In April 1962, Ball sought to convince the administration that the United States should carefully develop and articulate a policy for Vietnam. Using his December 19, 1961, Congo address as a precedent, he argued the need for an analogous public statement on Southeast Asia. Ball presented the idea to National Security Adviser McGeorge Bundy, stating that the American public was hopelessly confused "because nobody has given an orderly statement as to why we are there and what we are doing." Although Bundy thought that making a policy statement was "a good thing to do" and Ball "was a brave man to do it," he urged caution because Kennedy wished to keep Vietnam a low-profile item. Kennedy would worry "that the speech will make the news, rather than the situation itself making the news."[54]

On April 28, 1962, Ball mentioned to Kennedy that he planned to give a speech on Vietnam. Two days later, in an address to the Economic Club in Detroit, he adopted a hard line, stressing the communist threat: "Any U.S. retreat in one area of struggle inevitably encourages Communist adventure in another. . . . We cannot continue to lead the free world unless we enjoy—and deserve—the confidence of those who think as we do." Ball predicted in Detroit that the United States would prevail in Vietnam. He warned, however, that "this is not a type of struggle congenial to the American temperament" but one that "represents a type of threat that we would be well advised not to underestimate."[55]

In the Detroit speech Ball established the approach that he was to use during Lyndon Johnson's presidency. He defended the administration's Vietnam policy publicly while questioning and criticizing it inside the White House. Ball's speech also did precisely what Bundy had feared: it made the news and initiated a lively discussion about Vietnam policy in the mass media. Journalists of varying political persuasions used the speech as the whetstone on which to grind their editorial axes. Kennedy was not amused, and McGeorge Bundy gingerly reprimanded Ball for not submitting a copy of the speech to either the president or himself. Ball asked Bundy to remind Kennedy that he had mentioned the speech beforehand and to convey to JFK that he was "sorry about it." Regardless of the personal fallout, George Ball had achieved his goal: he had brought the festering Vietnam question to the attention of the public and the president.[56]

George Ball and the Demise of Ngo Dinh Diem

Ball's influence on Vietnam policy during the Kennedy presidency was felt in another noteworthy incident, the controversial decision to jettison South Vietnamese President Ngo Dinh Diem. Ball had long questioned Diem's oppressive and corrupt leadership. He had noted the sinister influence of Diem's brother Ngo Dinh Nhu, the leader of the South Vietnam security forces, and Nhu's "vicious and vindictive" wife, the notorious Madame Nhu.[57] The Nhu clan represented an upper-class Catholic minority who lived in isolated and opulent splendor.

In May 1963, the Diem regime quelled a Buddhist demonstration, killing a number of unarmed monks or bonzes. The violence triggered a series of suicides; several bonzes set themselves afire in protest against the oppressive rule of Diem and the Nhus. Madame Nhu's crass reference to these "bonze barbecues" illustrated the state of the Vietnam leadership, a leadership allied with the United States.[58]

On August 21, 1963, Nhu's American-trained special forces went on a rampage, attacking a number of Buddhist pagodas and beating and arresting hundreds of monks. The attack occurred despite Diem's recent assurance to U.S. Ambassador Frederick Nolting that the Diem government would no longer persecute the Buddhists. The U.S. embassy in Saigon cabled Washington to warn of the explosive nature of the situation and to report that a number of Diem's generals were discussing a coup.

This wild attack by the Diem regime against the Buddhists proved enormously embarrassing to the United States. When visiting American journalists like David Halberstam of the New York Times began to file reports alleging U.S. complicity in the attacks, President Kennedy himself became alarmed.[59] With Dean Rusk away at Camp David, George Ball worked with Kennedy in an attempt to control the damage. Together, Ball and the president agreed to rush Henry Cabot Lodge directly to Saigon. Nhu had cut the telephone lines from the U.S. embassy, making it difficult for the United States to assess the situation and increasing Kennedy's exasperation and impatience with the Diem regime.

On August 24, 1963, Roger Hilsman and Averell Harriman, under secretary of state for political affairs, completed the draft of a critical cable addressed to

Lodge. The toughly worded message stated that Nhu's actions had become intolerable and that Diem must dismiss Nhu and his coterie. Otherwise, "We must face the possibility that Diem himself cannot be preserved." The cable concluded that Lodge and his team "should urgently examine all possible alternative leadership and make detailed plans as to how we might bring about Diem's replacement if this should become necessary." [60]

As circumstances would have it, the leading foreign policy decision makers— Kennedy, Rusk, McNamara, Bundy, and CIA head John McCone—were all away from Washington at the time, leaving Under Secretary George Ball in charge. In the late afternoon, as Ball was finishing nine holes of golf, Hilsman and Harriman approached him with the alarming news from Vietnam and the draft of a cable. The officials drove to Ball's home, where they discussed the situation. The under secretary thoroughly approved of the message and made only stylistic changes. As Ball later wrote, "We could not retain our self-respect as a nation so long as we supinely accepted the Nhus' noxious activities. Encouraging coups, of course, ran counter to the grain of America's principles but Diem's legitimacy was dubious at best; we had in effect created him in the first place." [61]

Ball called President Kennedy in Hyannisport, briefed him, and related the key passages of the cable. The president agreed to approve the message if Dean Rusk and Roswell Gilpatric, McNamara's deputy, endorsed it. Ball telephoned Rusk, who, believing that Kennedy had approved the telegram, cautiously concurred. Bundy's deputy at the national security council, Michael Forrestal, whose views on Diem coincided with those of Ball, Harriman, and Hilsman, obtained the approval of three other deputies, Gilpatric for McNamara, Richard Helms for John McCone at the CIA, and General Victor Krulak for General Maxwell Taylor, special military adviser to the president. Ball then sent the cable.

When the members of Kennedy's foreign policy first string returned to their offices the following week, they were distressed to discover that the cable had been sent. Maxwell Taylor and John McCone were especially upset; McNamara also disapproved. They argued that it was unwise to seek to remove a leader without a guarantee that the successor would be an improvement. In the words of McNamara, who attributes much of the Vietnam disaster to this particular incident: "Supporting a coup meant putting the future of South Vietnam—indeed, the future of all Southeast Asia—in the hands of someone whose identity and intentions remained unknown to us." [62]

Furthermore, Taylor, McCone, and McNamara decried the manner in which the decision had been made, pointing out that once Ball received tentative approval from the president, he used Kennedy's position to bring Rusk aboard. With the imprimatur of Kennedy and Rusk, it was an easy matter to gain the support of the second string. Taylor later described the Hilsman-Ball group as "a small group of anti-Diem activists" who acted to "perpetuate an egregious end run." [63]

In spite of the debate in Washington, the August 24 cable did not result in Diem's removal from power. In Ball's words, the effort "proved a damp squid."[64] Although Ball, Harriman, and Hilsman continued to oppose Diem, Kennedy's other advisers urged caution. When the South Vietnamese generals hesitated to move against Diem, the situation continued to smolder.

Meanwhile, President Kennedy himself criticized Diem during a television interview on September 2, 1963. In late September, the president sent McNamara and Taylor on a fact-finding mission to Saigon. McNamara was appalled by Diem's demeanor. The South Vietnamese president denied the existence of any unrest or repression in his country. In fact, he indicated that he had been "too kind" to the Buddhists. In his trip report, McNamara concluded that the United States should increase pressure on Diem to moderate his policies and that the chances any replacement regime would represent an improvement over Diem were only "50–50." McNamara also recommended that "we not take any initiative to encourage actively a change in government."[65] On November 1, 1963, a group of South Vietnamese generals moved against Diem and assassinated him and his brother Ngo Dinh Nhu.

George Ball played a shrewd game of bureaucratic politics in the cable incident. By seizing the initiative and confronting the administration with a fait accompli, Ball used much the same tactic as when he had delivered his Detroit speech the year before. In both instances, he first gained the passing approval of the president and then used this approval as leverage to gain the support of other key decision makers. Having received support at the highest level, the policy recommendation gathered momentum as it moved down the hierarchy. Guided through the bureaucratic obstacle course by an experienced hand, the recommendation was ensured acceptance.

More generally, the August 24 telegram affair provided early evidence of the fault line that was to divide high-level advisers concerning Vietnam policy. McNamara and the military generals held a much more optimistic view of the situation and were less concerned with Diem's blemishes than were Ball and Hilsman. John McCone once said to Kennedy, "Mr. President, if I was manager of a baseball team, and I had one pitcher, I'd keep him in the box whether he was a good pitcher or not."[66]

The McNamara school of thought viewed the August 24 cable as the precipitating cause of Diem's fall. Because Diem's successors also proved to be ineffective leaders, McNamara and associates suggested that if the United States had not interfered and if Diem had continued as president, the outcome of the Vietnam war might have evolved quite differently. Although the August 24 cable signaled American loss of confidence in Diem, the actual fall of the president did not occur for nine more weeks. Diem's assassination was planned and executed by the Vietnamese though U.S. officials were aware of the plot and did nothing to thwart it. Ambassador Lodge summarized the situation in a cable to Washington: "There is no possibility, in my view, that the war can be won under a Diem administration."[67]

The U.S. involvement in the overthrow of Diem remains an issue of heated debate. Analysts on the left condemn the decision for its crass interventionism. Critics on the right decry the overthrow of Diem because they believe that it was in the United States' interests to stand behind authoritarian leaders who were anticommunist. What if the U.S. government had maintained Diem in power? In a 1995 book review, H. D. S. Greenway responds: "Even if he had lost the war or come to an accommodation with the Vietcong, as the White House feared, at least it would have been on Vietnamese terms, without the 58,000 Americans and countless hundreds of thousands of Vietnamese dead following the Americanization of the war."[68]

In response to the critics, George Ball pointed out that it was easy to make policy judgments with the benefit of thirty years of hindsight. He sharply criticized those who chose to "seize on the August 24 telegram as an exculpation." Claiming that he had "lost no sleep over the telegram," Ball argued that "from the outset, I believed that we could never win the war and I do not believe for a moment that we could have won it had Diem not been overthrown."[69]

One individual who watched the demise of Diem closely and disdainfully was Vice President Lyndon Johnson. Johnson, who tended to personalize politics, admired Diem, whom he had met during an official trip to Vietnam in May of 1961. Although he urged a policy of reform in South Vietnam, the vice president referred to Diem as "the Winston Churchill of Southeast Asia."[70] Johnson thoroughly disapproved of his government's handling of the South Vietnamese president. In his view, the August 1964 cable was "a serious blunder" that was "hasty and ill-advised" and the U.S. involvement in the fall of Diem was deplorable.[71]

The Core of Vietnam Dissent: Ball in the Johnson Years

When Lyndon Johnson became president, George Ball, along with his many other responsibilities, continued to be troubled by Vietnam. In spite of his misgivings concerning the U.S. role there, Ball had to bide his time until he consolidated his credibility with the new president. He was well aware that his role in the August 24 cable episode might very well expose him to presidential retribution. Throughout the fall and spring, Ball watched the other authors of the cable fall from grace. Hilsman was forced out of power in March of 1964; Harriman was nudged out of the Vietnam decision-making orbit and into African affairs in 1964 before becoming a roving ambassador in 1965; Forrestal was pushed out of the White House in July 1964, and after holding a mundane staff position in the State Department, he left the government in early 1965.

Hilsman had alienated both Lyndon Johnson and Dean Rusk. His intellectual arrogance and tendency to ignore regular bureaucratic channels infuriated the secretary of state. Hilsman was also suspected of leaking sensitive information to the press. For this reason in particular, Ball came to share the administration's position concerning Hilsman.

Ball was incensed over a September 23, 1963, *Washington Star* report that the State Department had been generally correct while the CIA had been consistently wrong in analyzing Vietnam. On September 24, Ball referred to the article in a conversation with Rusk: "I am very much afraid that this comes straight from our friend Roger." Rusk responded sharply, "We ought to ask Roger the question direct on this one." Ball wasted no time. He called Hilsman and asked if he had seen the story. After Hilsman denied having spoken with the reporter in question, Ball responded: "Roger this came right out of FE [Bureau of Far Eastern Affairs]. It can't have come from anywhere else." When Hilsman expressed surprise, Ball angrily shot back, "You're nailed. This one was revealed absolutely cold. It's disgraceful."[72] Six months later, George Ball fired Hilsman on the instructions of Lyndon Johnson and Dean Rusk.

In contrast to Roger Hilsman, Ball nurtured a close relationship with Rusk and thereby survived to continue the struggle over Vietnam. Ball would bend the bureaucratic rules when necessary, but he carefully avoided breaking them. Furthermore, although Ball shared information with select members of the press, he made certain that there would be no leaks. He also refused to criticize publicly the policy of the administration for which he worked. To Ball, such behavior demonstrated disloyalty. Because both Rusk and Johnson understood Ball's loyalty and style, they supported him as under secretary.

Ball's Memoranda Campaign

In the summer of 1964, extremely alarmed by increasing U.S. involvement in Vietnam, George Ball began to muscle his way into the center of the debate. He did so by producing a barrage of thoughtful memos that questioned the very assumptions upon which the United States had based its Vietnam policy. Between May 1964 and May 1966, he produced more than twenty papers challenging U.S. policy. In his dissent by memorandum, Ball, at first cautiously and then more aggressively, struggled to have his analyses read by Rusk, McNamara, Bundy, and, ultimately, by President Johnson himself.

Ball began his campaign with a nine-page letter to Dean Rusk on May 31, 1964. In this top secret communication, Ball raised six tough questions concerning the foundations of U.S. Vietnam policy. Ball warned "that plans were going forward too precipitously and that there was an inarticulate wish to sweep the difficult issues under the bed." Ball wrote that he could not reconcile himself "to the fateful step of action against the North until we are satisfied in our own hearts that we have taken every possible step to achieve full effectiveness in our own efforts in the South." He warned of the dangers of "an open-ended commitment" to defend South Vietnam with American troops. Such a commitment, he wrote, "must be considered in the light of the deep aversion of many Americans to the commitment of U.S. ground forces to the Asia mainland." [73]

The memoranda campaign was most concentrated between October 1964 and July 1965, when Ball produced eight documents, most of which were read by Lyndon Johnson himself. These memos ranged in length from six to sixty-seven pages and contained the essence of Ball's arguments warning against U.S. involvement in Vietnam. [74]

In brief, Ball argued that the United States had shortsightedly stumbled into a quagmire in Vietnam. He questioned each of the four fundamental assumptions behind the mounting American involvement: (1) Vietnam was a country absolutely essential to U.S. national interests; (2) if the South Vietnamese government were to come under the control of the Vietcong, the rest of southeast Asia would fall inexorably to the communists; (3) the South Vietnamese government could rally its population, and with enough U.S. assistance, it would prevail in the struggle; and (4) even if the South Vietnamese could not overcome the Vietcong, the United States could defeat the indigenous communist movement through the application of superior military force.

Ball did not believe that events in the Vietnamese peninsula were critical to American interests. In his judgment, the vital interests of the United States rested far more with countries such as France, Germany, and the United Kingdom. Furthermore, to the extent that the United States was compelled to look beyond Europe, he felt it more appropriate to focus attention on the Soviet Union, China, and Japan. Vietnam could prove to be a costly diversion.

George Ball never found the domino theory convincing. His keen sense of history and his experiences in Europe indicated that the force of nationalism was still very potent and that communism in one country did not necessarily portend communism in a neighboring country. Furthermore, if for the sake of argument one were to accept the domino thesis, then surely Vietnam was the last place in Asia for the United States to make a stand. In his view, a much better case could be made for Thailand or even Indonesia.

In Ball's opinion, the South Vietnamese government could not possibly gain and maintain control of the country. Its political leaders were personally corrupt and venal; its population was demoralized and unsupportive; its military lacked coherence and commitment. Ball often quoted Charles de Gaulle, who once told him, "Vietnam is a rotten *(pourri)* country." [75] Ball had studied the French experience in Vietnam and argued that the conflict was in fact a civil war being fought by one people. In his view, it was not wise for an outsider to attempt to break up a bitter internecine war in the Asian jungles.

Ball did not believe that the United States could militarily defeat the Vietcong and the North Vietnamese. According to the under secretary, U.S. troops were doomed to fight in the unfamiliar setting of thick rain forests and swampy rice paddies, the enemy's home terrain. American technological superiority was not enough to offset this Vietnamese home-terrain advantage, particularly when combined with the enemy's superior numbers, commitment, and morale. Ball was particularly skeptical of the effectiveness of massive bombing campaigns. His experience as Director of the Strategic Bombing Survey at the end of World War II had taught him that wars were not won from the air. Furthermore, Ball believed that the delivery of death from the air often only rallied the suffering population around their own leaders.

Ball postulated that the American people would not long stand united in defense of a costly war in a distant Asian land. He warned his Washington colleagues that support at home would vary inversely to the numbers of U.S. casualties in the field. At one point, he developed a chart documenting this hypothesis in the case of the Korean war and discussed the illustration with the president and his inner circle.

George Ball was no isolationist. He had grown up in the shadows of Colonel Robert McCormick and the rabid isolationism preached in McCormick's influential *Chicago Tribune*. He strongly opposed this philosophy throughout his life. Ball believed that there was a time and place to intervene but that such action must be based on a careful assessment of national interests and the limits of U.S. power. Vietnam was neither the time nor the place for military intervention.

Throughout the Vietnam conflict, Ball argued that the United States should seek a negotiated settlement and begin a tactical retreat. He insisted that time was of the essence and that the deeper the United States became involved, the more entangled it would become and the more difficult withdrawal would become. He sensed the turning point in U.S. involvement in the spring and summer of 1965, and he wrote most of his memoranda during these months.

Ball wrote his major dissent, dated October 5, 1964, during September. He sent copies of the sixty-seven-page top secret document, entitled "How Valid are the Assumptions Underlying our Viet-Nam Policies?" to Dean Rusk, Robert McNamara, and McGeorge Bundy. McNamara, Ball later related, was "absolutely horrified" and treated the memo like "a poisonous snake."[76] President Johnson did not receive a copy until February 1965, when his aide Bill Moyers passed the memorandum to him. Ball had resisted sending the document directly to the president for two reasons. First, he had hoped that one of his three colleagues would deliver it to Johnson; he did not want to bypass proper channels with such a controversial message. Second, he did not wish to interrupt the president in the midst of an intense election campaign. When Johnson finally read the memorandum in February 1965, Ball's arguments impressed him. From then on, he read Ball's Vietnam analyses carefully.

In discussing various options in the October 1964 memo, Ball condemned the policy calling for a substantial increase of U.S. ground forces in Vietnam: "Our situation would in the world's eyes approach that of France in the 1950s. We would incur the opposition of elements in Viet-Nam otherwise friendly to us. Finally, we would find ourselves in *la guerre sale* with consequent heavy loss of American lives in the rice paddies and jungles." Ball went on to warn that the presence of U.S. combat troops would lead Americans to "feel, for the first time, that they had again been committed by their leaders to an Asian war. The frustrations and anxieties that marked the latter phases of the Korean struggle would be recalled and revived—and multiplied in intensity." The under secretary concluded his long memorandum with the following plea: "What I am urging is that our Southeast Asia policy be looked at in all of its aspects and in the light of our total world situation. It is essential that this be done before we commit military forces to a line of action that could put events in the saddle and destroy our freedom to choose the policies that are at once the most effective and the most prudent."[77]

After writing four memoranda outlining various plans and proposals for a political resolution to the conflict, Ball sent Johnson a memorandum dated June 18, 1965, that began with a quotation from Ralph Waldo Emerson: "Things are in the saddle, and ride mankind." In an obvious attempt at compromise, Ball recommended a one-time increase of American troops to one hundred thousand, but no more. He warned, however, that the United States "may not be able to fight the war successfully enough—even with 500,000 Americans in South Viet-Nam." He warned: "Before we commit an endless flow of forces to South Viet-Nam we must have more evidence than we now have that our troops will not bog down in the jungles and rice paddies—while we slowly blow the country to pieces."

Finally, realizing that his arguments had fallen on deaf ears, Ball wrote two blunt memoranda in late June and early July 1965 warning President Johnson of the consequences of expanding U.S. intervention in Vietnam. In a memo dated June 28, 1965, entitled "Cutting our Losses in South Viet-Nam," Ball reiterated his principal arguments. In a section entitled Renvoir, he summarized his position:

> The position taken in this memorandum does not suggest that the United States should abdicate leadership in the cold war. But any prudent military commander carefully selects the terrain on which to stand and fight, and no great captain has every been blamed for a successful tactical withdrawal. From our point of view, the terrain in South Viet-Nam could not be worse. Jungles and rice paddies are not designed for modern arms. . . . Politically,

South Viet-Nam is a lost cause. The country is bled white from twenty years of war and the people are sick of it. . . . Hanoi has a Government and a purpose and a discipline. The government in Saigon is a travesty. In a very real sense, South Viet-Nam is a country with an army and no government. In my view, a deep commitment of United States forces in a land war in South Viet-Nam would be a catastrophic error. If ever there was an occasion for a tactical withdrawal, this is it.[78]

Ball's colleagues rejected his remonstrations, but the under secretary played an important role in the decision-making process. An examination of the personal politics in the White House provides insights into both Ball and U.S. politics at the highest levels.

Power Politics in the White House

Besides Lyndon Johnson, the main players in Vietnam policymaking included Dean Rusk, Robert McNamara, McGeorge Bundy, and George Ball. Others with significant influence included Generals Maxwell Taylor and Earle Wheeler, John McCone, and Henry Cabot Lodge. Taylor served as chairman of the Joint Chiefs of Staff from 1962 until 1964, ambassador to South Vietnam in 1964 and early 1965, and special consultant to the president from 1965 until 1969. Wheeler chaired the Joint Chiefs from 1964 to 1970. McCone was director of the CIA from 1965 through 1969, and Lodge was ambassador to South Vietnam in 1963–64 and again in 1965–67.

Within Johnson's inner circle, Ball found that his views on Vietnam ran counter to those of the other four well-positioned and influential actors, all of whom outranked him in the hierarchy. The opposition of Rusk and McNamara was implacable. On rare occasions, Bundy cautiously questioned the wisdom of U.S. policy, but he declined to side with Ball. Johnson himself at times seemed sympathetic to Ball's position, which the president allowed to be fully aired and argued at crucial meetings. In the end, however, Johnson pursued policies that ran against Ball's recommendations. The rare exceptions concerned sporadic bombing pauses.

Ball was able to present his position only because of the special personal relationships that he maintained with both the president and Secretary Rusk. In order to remain on the playing field, Ball worked hard to preserve these relationships. Although he remained sensitive to the formal hierarchy, Ball recognized the more elemental importance of personal relations and contacts. The formal structure of government could be circumvented through the careful use of personal networks. This was an approach Ball had learned twenty years before from

Jean Monnet. Ball's rich subsequent experiences at Bilderberg had confirmed the effectiveness of developing and protecting personal connections.

Lyndon Johnson was also a champion of the personal approach to politics. The president and Ball both understood the virtues of personalism and communicated well with one another. The president enjoyed a certain familiarity with Ball that he did not share with McNamara and Bundy. Johnson and Ball knew the shape and substance of each other's personal networks and used them for their own political purposes.

Impressed by McNamara's mastery of facts and his ever-confident briefing style, Johnson was less in awe of McNamara's interpersonal skills. McNamara was a boundary manager and a formal organizational man. McNamara had an undergraduate degree in economics and an interest in the field of mathematics. A statistical control officer in World War II, he had a preoccupation with precision and an unbridled faith in numbers. If he could not count it, it did not count. In 1995, he wrote, "To this day, I see quantification as a language to add precision to reasoning about the world." [79]

Upon becoming secretary of defense, McNamara immediately called for more than one hundred studies and implemented a massive reorganization of the Pentagon. He pored over organizational charts, rearranged line and staff functions, and applied a statistical approach to problem solving. Former Senator Barry Goldwater called McNamara "an IBM machine with legs." David Halberstam describes McNamara as "the quantifier trying to quantify the unquantifiable"; the quintessential image of U.S. policy in Vietnam, according to Halberstam, was Bob McNamara "poring over page after page of data, each platoon, each squad, studying all those statistics. All lies." [80]

George Ball believed that McNamara lacked an understanding of history and people. The confident secretary of defense could not account for the intangibles, the depth of human spirit, motivation and morale: "McNamara's logic of numbers omitted elements of power that could never be quantified—and these proved more important than any advantage in physical resources. The unquantifiable elements included the history of Southeast Asia, the élan of the opposition, the impact of racial differences, Hanoi's hatred of colonial powers and its ability to mobilize its people to fight and die, and the identification of the American forces with their French predecessors." [81]

McNamara, on the other hand, did not approve of Ball's approach to administration. To McNamara, who was an organization man, Ball was "out of line." Ball's unsolicited memoranda and use of his special personal relations with Johnson and Rusk annoyed the defense secretary. McNamara thoroughly disapproved of Ball's failure to "staff out" his research and papers properly. He had not gone through channels and had failed to "develop his ideas in committee." [82]

McNamara relied so heavily upon data that when the data were either absent or incomplete, some observers suspected that he manufactured them. Ball, for example, said that McNamara had privately admitted to him that he had doubts about U.S. strategy in Vietnam. "But I would go into a meeting with the President the next morning, and McNamara would shoot me down in flames. And he'd pull out all kinds of statistics which I'm sure he invented on the spot. We had a set of formulations—we had body counts, we had kill ratios, we had various force comparisons. All that stuff I'd heard before from the French in the 1950s."[83]

The Joint Chiefs of Staff and generals in Vietnam like William Westmoreland and Paul Harkins relentlessly pressured McNamara, urging greater commitments of combat troops and an expansion of the war effort. The generals had their supporters in Congress and were a source of considerable concern to McNamara and to Lyndon Johnson, who consciously worried about possible Chinese intervention and the specter of nuclear war.

Rusk took a position somewhere between McNamara and the generals. Although he wavered over time, McGeorge Bundy was in closer agreement with Rusk than with Ball. Both Rusk and Bundy were boundary managers who operated with a kind of tough, cool, professional detachment. Lyndon Johnson once described Rusk as "only twenty minutes from being a professional military man." Bundy and his replacement, Walt Rostow, were "ideal staff men."[84]

Ball managed to break through to Dean Rusk and established a strong personal bond with the secretary. This relationship, along with the informal ties he maintained with Johnson, helped the iconoclastic under secretary take a seat at the table of power in Washington. From that seat, George Ball pursued a complex political strategy for shaping Vietnam policy.

Ball's Vietnam Strategy

George Ball understood that he was operating from a weak formal position. He lacked rank, and, as a subcabinet official, he found himself outside the echelons of formal power in all high-level meetings. Therefore, he sought to gain informal influence with those both above and below him in the hierarchy. He worked hard to protect and tighten his ties with Johnson and Rusk, and he never lost sight of the need to get his arguments through to McNamara and Bundy without unduly ruffling their feathers. Thus, he was careful to direct his memoranda to Bundy, McNamara, and Rusk. He produced only four copies of his October 1964 memorandum—for Bundy, McNamara, Rusk, and presumably the president, who stood at the center of Ball's strategy.

Ball realized that even if he failed to convert his colleagues, he could still effectively influence policy if he could convince the president. Because the moral component played a small part in Johnson's approach to foreign policy, Ball framed his arguments on Vietnam in the language of practical politics. He constantly returned to three themes in his presentations to the president.

First, Ball simply but forcefully contended that U.S. soldiers could not defeat native guerrilla fighters in the jungles and rice paddies of Asia. Ball quoted everyone from General Matthew Ridgway to Mao Tse-tung. He took note of Ridgway's warning to Eisenhower in 1954 against any intervention in Indochina. Indeed, Ridgway admitted that one of his greatest achievements was "that I fought against, and perhaps contributed to preventing, the carrying out of some hare-brained tactical schemes which would have cost the lives of thousands of men. To that list of tragic accidents that fortunately never happened I would add the Indo-China intervention." In the same memo, Ball quoted Mao: "If the enemy attacks, I disappear; if he defends, I harass; and if he retreats, I attack." [85]

Second, Ball liked to play the China card, arguing that if the United States continued to escalate its attacks into North Vietnam, the Chinese would be increasingly likely to intervene in full force. If China did intervene, the United States would find itself entangled in a major land war in Asia. In a January 1966 memorandum to the president, Ball wrote: "Quite clearly there is a threshold which we cannot pass over without precipitating a major Chinese involvement. We do not know—even within wide margins of error—where that threshold is. Unhappily, we will not find out until after the catastrophe. We did not measure the threshold adequately in Korea. We found out how low it was only after 300,000 Chinese descended on us." [86]

Events proved that Ball's dire warnings of Chinese intervention were inaccurate. It is difficult to determine how much of this warning was heartfelt and how much was a tactical ploy designed to slow the Americanization of the war. Ball himself provided a clue to the answer when he wrote, "President Johnson was deeply preoccupied with the China menace and the more I emphasized it, the stronger was my case for cutting our losses." [87]

Third, knowing Johnson's commitment to his domestic reform programs of the Great Society, Ball maintained that as the costs of the Vietnam war increased, both in terms of human casualties and economic disbursements, the disillusionment of the American people would also increase. The president would lose political support at home, thereby seriously jeopardizing his domestic programs. Although these arguments did not in the end turn Johnson around on Vietnam, they did shake him and cause him to rethink many of his assumptions.

While he struggled to carry his arguments to Lyndon Johnson and his inner circle, Ball formed links with those lower in the hierarchy who shared his doubts about the war. At the Department of State, he cooperated with Deputy Under Secretary Alexis Johnson and Roger Hilsman, as well as with such specialists as China expert Allen Whiting and National Security Adviser James Thomson. In addition, he quietly developed an important alliance with Bill Moyers at the

White House.[88] Moyers, who delivered Ball's October 1964 memorandum to the president, later lost favor with Johnson because of their disagreements over Vietnam.

Furthermore, Ball raised doubts about the war in the minds of William Bundy, assistant secretary of state, and John McNaughton, assistant secretary of defense. Ball also played a role in eventually convincing McGeorge Bundy to question the U.S. approach in Vietnam. In March 1968, in a meeting of senior consultants known as the Wise Men, Bundy flatly stated, "I must tell you what I thought I'd never say—that I now agree with George Ball."[89]

Ball also influenced the thinking of Washington insider Clark Clifford, whom Johnson appointed to replace McNamara as secretary of defense in January 1968. Clifford became an unexpected ally after July 1965 when he first read Ball's notebook of critical memoranda. Ball's analyses persuaded Clifford, who began a quiet, extended campaign to extricate the United States from Vietnam. On July 22, 1965, Clifford stayed up until 2 A.M. reading and taking notes on Ball's memoranda: "They were everything I would have expected—forceful, fearless, and, to my mind, convincing."[90] During the year that he served as secretary of defense, Clifford campaigned for a negotiated withdrawal from Vietnam and managed to soften the administration's stance on escalation. He succeeded in converting the draft of Johnson's March 31, 1968, speech from a tough talk on war into a call for peace. During this speech, Johnson announced that he would not seek another term as president. A shrewd, experienced establishment man, Clifford used his contacts to turn the establishment around on Vietnam. Moreover, as Halberstam wrote, "slowly, cautiously, painfully, Clifford forced Johnson to turn and look honestly at the war; it was an act of friendship for which Johnson could never forgive him."[91]

Ball recruited distinguished outside experts to help reassess Vietnam policy. In May 1965, he convinced Dean Acheson and Lloyd Cutler to join him in sponsoring a negotiated settlement. Acheson, a political icon at age seventy-two and an individual with a reputation for toughness, worked with Ball and Cutler in developing five papers outlining plans for a negotiated settlement to the imbroglio.[92]

While Ball was the single voice opposing the war from this interior position, he continued to support the administration's Vietnam policy in all public forums. He did so for two major reasons. First, he felt a sense of personal loyalty and responsibility to those who appointed him to power, and second, he sought to protect his own access and credibility in Washington. He understood the imperative of power: in order to influence policy, one needed first and foremost to be in a position to do so. Ball made numerous public speeches defending U.S. policy in Vietnam. He also occasionally wrote speeches for Rusk and Johnson explaining the American position. He was effective because he was familiar with all the arguments. He had been personally battered by the arguments in the tense debate that took place in the inner circles of the government.

Ball's public defense of Vietnam policy included presentations before Southeast Asia Treaty Organization (SEATO) ministers in 1965 and NATO leaders in 1966. He also ran interference in Congress for Johnson's Vietnam policy. Ball acted as a mediator between the president and such formidable critics as Senators Fulbright and Mansfield, both of whom respected the under secretary. Johnson's close relationship with Fulbright had shattered over the Vietnam issue, and the president's bitterness came through in a handwritten note on a memorandum citing Fulbright's complaint over losing access to the President. Fulbright, Johnson wrote, "is a crybaby and I can't continue to kiss him every morning before breakfast."[93] Only George Ball was able to mediate this relationship.

Finally, Ball also attempted to explain the administration's position to the press. He had a particularly difficult time justifying Vietnam policy to his old friend Walter Lippmann. Ball reported Johnson's perspective to Lippmann and Lippmann's position to Johnson. In a revealing exchange, the president sarcastically asked the under secretary, "are you telling Lippmann what to write or is he telling you what to say?"[94] Lippmann and Ball ultimately had a painful fallingout over Vietnam; the eminent journalist believed that Ball should resign in protest over Johnson's policy, which Lippmann thought was both ill-considered and immoral.

Ball's relationship with his other longtime friend in the press corps, James "Scotty" Reston, was *sui generis*. The two friends maintained close contact with one another throughout the Vietnam period. Ball shared his ideas and memoranda with Reston, while Reston kept Ball informed about the thinking of his colleagues in the mass media. Ball and Reston maintained similar perspectives on Vietnam and used one another as intellectual sounding boards. Reston never misused the privileged information he received from Ball. The unusual depth and quality of Reston's writing on Vietnam owed much to his discussions with Ball.

Ball's political approach focused on advancing and retreating, backing and filling, entering and exiting. When he lost one argument, he would retreat to a new position and present another argument. Ball described these tactics as rearguard actions. In his approach to bombing policy, for example, Ball would occasionally vote in favor of bombing. He did so even though he personally opposed bombing, which he considered ineffective and counterproductive. When he supported bombing, he attached conditions to his support, usually designed to keep the bombing limited. When he found allies at high levels, however, he would dig in and vehemently oppose bombing.

George Ball's old technique of making critical decisions by default and then presenting the administration with a fait accompli was less effective in the Johnson administration than it had been during Kennedy's presidency. In March 1964, when Rusk was away and Ball was acting secretary, opposition forces in Brazil overthrew President João Goulart. Agreeing with U.S. Ambassador Lincoln Gordon's recommendation of immediate diplomatic recognition of the new government, Ball authorized a telegram endorsing the coup.

The following morning, when President Johnson learned of the telegram, he was furious. Ball explained that it had been 3 A.M. and he had not wanted to wake the president. Ball then crisply stated: "It was the right step to take and it's worked out well." Johnson, undoubtedly recalling the August 1963 anti-Diem cable, roared: "Don't ever do that again. I don't give a damn whether you were right or wrong. I don't care a fuck that it was three in the morning; I want to know what's being done whatever time of night it might be."[95] George Ball got the message.

Ball's multifaceted strategy of opposition to the Vietnam war opened him to considerable criticism. Although most close observers who opposed U.S. involvement in the war praised Ball for his valiant stand, a group of dissenters attacked him sharply. One group blamed him for failing to carry the day. People like Roger Hilsman, for example, questioned his tactics and resented the fact that he was never able to convince the president to change course.

Ball's strategy had weaknesses. Most stemmed from the fact that he was overworked and overcommitted. Vietnam was a problem he tried to address on the side. He often claimed that Vietnam occupied only 10 percent of his professional time. As a result, he was unable to give his undivided attention to the issue. The lack of time weakened Ball's position in two major ways. First, his memoranda, although well written, were not as effectively organized and convincing as they might have been had he had more time to prepare them. The arguments became repetitious and his colleagues in the White House began to roll their eyes when Ball returned repeatedly to the lessons to be learned from the Strategic Bombing Survey and the French at Dien Bien Phu. Furthermore, the memos were long on critical assessment and short on carefully argued, realistic policy recommendations. In the words of Bill Bundy, "George could have done much better with these briefs if he had marinated them a little longer."[96]

Ball took up the Vietnam challenge as a loner. Again, due to time limitations, he failed to practice effectively his cardinal rule of politics. With a few exceptions, he did not establish the ties and build the contacts with other important figures who might have been brought over to his position. He also needed assistance from others in the bureaucracy in drafting his memoranda. Although individuals like personal aide George Springsteen provided some help, Ball desperately needed input from other knowledgeable and mature thinkers in the government.

A second and particularly unrelenting school of critics condemns Ball primarily on moral grounds. In their judgment, Ball had a moral obligation to resign from an administration that was formulating policy that he personally opposed.

Instead, George Ball not only remained part of the administration, but he publicly defended both the administration and the very policy he most strongly opposed. This particular criticism stung, and George Ball found it painful indeed.

Philosopher-Statesman or Political Opportunist:
The Case Against Ball

Among those who served in the government during the Vietnam war, a small minority of officials criticized Ball for continuing to work with the Johnson administration when he so strongly opposed the war. They also condemned him for refusing to speak out forcefully against his former colleagues once he did resign in September 1966. According to these critics, Ball placed his own personal ambitions before his principles. He loved the exercise of power and one day hoped to become secretary of state. Thus he was careful not to burn any bridges in the Democratic Party. If he had resigned, he would have locked himself out of the halls of power and become a pariah to party leaders.[97]

Walter Lippmann urged Ball to resign in protest over Vietnam and was disappointed when Ball refused to do so. Lippmann had broken bitterly with Lyndon Johnson over Vietnam and went so far as to describe the president as "the most disagreeable individual ever to occupy the White House." In February 1966, Ball privately told Lippmann that he was considering submitting his resignation, but Lippmann noted that his friend did not do so until September. Lippmann believed that a basic principle of political life was "the almost total inability of Americans to decline an appointment or resign a post." Lippmann's biographer summarizes the case of individuals like Ball, Moyers, and McNamara, who eventually left Johnson's White House: "All left quietly, without a word of protest. Nobody wanted to be a spoilsport or seem disloyal to the team. Everybody wanted to be invited to come back and play another day—in a different administration, when bad feelings had faded, when times were happier. Troublemakers rarely got invited back."[98]

His critics point out that for Ball loyalty to a president meant keeping quiet. George Ball the lawyer served Lyndon Johnson the client. But what about loyalty to one's country and loyalty to one's conscience? Although the critics admit that Ball consistently dissented internally from the Johnson administration's Vietnam policy, they allege that he did so only as the president's "devil's advocate." He was the "house dove," or, more harshly put, the "house prostitute."[99] The critics claim that Ball let himself be used and domesticated by Johnson. How else could one explain Ball's spirited public defenses of Johnson's war policy?

The anti-Ball group admits that Johnson was a master at political and personal control. Even after he accepted Ball's resignation, the president let it be known that he hoped to continue to call on Ball for advice and assistance. Ball agreed to be available. Johnson did indeed solicit Ball's help many times after the under secretary's resignation. Even though he did not want the position, Ball agreed to become U.S. ambassador to the United Nations. In addition, he served Johnson in a number of informal assignments until the end of Johnson's presidency. In the meantime, Ball never criticized Johnson publicly and consistently defended him. In 1971, after the release of the Pentagon Papers, for example, Ball argued that the Johnson administration had never deliberately deceived the American public about the war. Ball supported Johnson even in the face of evidence that Johnson had been less than forthright about his decisions to escalate the war.

In one study of protest resignation, the authors conclude that had Ball resigned and gone public with his criticisms, he might have changed history: "Not only would the open advocacy of antiwar policies by a McNamara or a Ball have rallied opposition but it would have insured institutionalized legitimacy and responsible leadership for the forces of dissent."[100] By muttering his disapproval inside the system, the argument goes, Ball not only assuaged his own conscience but those of his colleagues in Washington as well. Johnson's inner circle could argue that through Ball they had exposed themselves to the contrary position: "The process of escalation allowed for periodic requests to Mr. Ball to speak his piece; Ball felt good . . . the others felt good (they had given a full hearing to the dovish opposition); and there was minimal unpleasantness."[101]

In what was intended to be a tribute to George Ball, Lyndon Johnson made a statement in 1969 that provided grist for the critics' mill. Johnson stated that Ball reminded him "of many great men I have known, particularly of a school teacher who came out to apply for a job during the Depression in my little town of Johnson City. The school board was divided on whether the world was round or flat. They asked him how he taught it. The poor fellow needed a job so much he said: 'I can teach it either way.' George Ball is the only man who I have ever really known in the government who, on five minutes' instructions from the president, can take either side of a proposition and present it to you so you can understand both sides."[102]

The critics argue that Johnson's words demonstrate that Ball lacked principles, that he could indeed go either way. They point out that in the case of Vietnam, George Ball went both ways. Either he did so in a calculated and self-interested way or Johnson outmaneuvered and controlled him. If the former was true, then Ball stood corrupted by personal ambition. If the latter was the reality, then Ball was a puppet in Lyndon Johnson's court.

George Ball's Defense

Over the years, Ball often confronted the accusation that he had acted as an ambitious devil's advocate for Lyndon Johnson. Ball patiently defended himself against this charge on numerous occasions. His response can be broken down into five separate but related arguments.

First, George Ball believed that to resign in protest would represent an empty and ineffective gesture. Such an act might possibly make newspaper headlines for one day but would be largely forgotten the next. Ball knew that, unlike in Great Britain, where a cabinet minister has a seat in Parliament, an under secretary in the U.S. government has neither a political support base nor an outside constituency. The resignation of a subcabinet official was unlikely to have the slightest impact on the government's Vietnam policy. Furthermore, the administration would almost certainly distribute a press release to minimize the resignation of a low-level official exhausted from his long career in the public service. "If I had resigned," Ball said, "I know that the White House would have quickly passed the rumor that this fellow had been asked to leave for reasons of incompetence and that the administration had been contemplating such action for months. It would have been a one-day wonder."[103] Ball was not interested in the Pyrrhic victories of the righteous.

The idea that resignation would have made Ball an antiwar focal point and a leader in the antiwar movement seems ludicrous. Ball had never been a political activist who would take to the streets. He disliked the antiwar movement and disapproved of its culture and methods. He often bitingly criticized the hippies for their dress, their manners, and their abrasive and abusive form of discourse. The protests in the streets of America horrified George Ball. In his view, the masses of antiwar activists trampled upon the canons of civility and destroyed any possibility of rational discourse. Ball could no more work with them than he could go to his office dressed in a baseball cap, blue jeans, and T-shirt.

Second, Ball personally maintained a strong sense of loyalty to his colleagues, regardless of the disagreements and differences they may have had concerning policy issues. He refused to become part of any effort to undermine them. To George Ball, loyalty was a matter of basic decency and fair play: "If you work with people intimately, people you respect and admire, you recognize the fact that they have honest points of view, even when their positions may be directly opposed to your own. You don't undercut them when they're doing the very best they can. To do so would be, if not exactly treachery, very bad behavior on the part of a colleague."[104] Ball believed in the concept of a team, and agree or disagree, win or lose, one did not turn on one's teammates.

Third, George Ball felt that by remaining in his position he could influence decisions and shape policy. As his record indicates, he did so in a multitude of areas. He admitted that he ultimately failed to change the general direction of U.S. policy in Vietnam. Nonetheless, the record shows that even in that debate, Ball had an impact. He forced the president and his inner circle to think through their premises and assumptions. Moreover, he helped convince people like Bill

Moyers, Dean Acheson, and Clark Clifford that U.S. Vietnam policy was misguided.

In specific instances, Ball also played a key role in changing aspects of policy. His was one of the most effective voices in convincing Johnson to formulate bombing policy that would not provoke the military intervention of communist China. He also persuaded Johnson to institute bombing pauses from time to time. In the words of one official, "Ball did not prevent escalation, but I dread to think what might have happened if there had been no George Ball." [105]

Another instance of Ball's influence concerning Vietnam policy occurred at the time of the 1964 Gulf of Tonkin episode, when U.S. patrol and intelligence ships provoked North Vietnamese attacks. When these attacks were answered by U.S. air strikes, McNamara urged the president to send another probing patrol into the gulf. Such an act of defiance, he argued, would show the North Vietnamese that they could not intimidate Uncle Sam.

Ball protested and urged the president not to make such a decision. He argued that if a U.S. destroyer were sunk, a public outcry and a congressional investigation would result. The evidence would suggest that Johnson had sent the ships up the gulf to provoke another attack. Ball told Johnson: "Just think what Congress and the press would do with that! They'd say you deliberately used American boys as decoy ducks and that you threw away lives just so you'd have the excuse to bomb. Mr. President, you couldn't live with that." Ball's argument shook Johnson, who turned to McNamara and said, "We won't go ahead with it Bob. Let's put it on the shelf." [106]

George Ball genuinely believed that he could influence the policymaking process. Although Johnson and others spread the rumor that the under secretary was acting primarily as a devil's advocate, Ball himself never viewed his role in this light. In his mind, he participated in a decision-making process that was in no way artificial. When confronted with the evidence that his lonely battle on July 21, 1965, opposing the sharp escalation of U.S. troops, had taken place when Johnson had already made up his mind, Ball responded that he had known the deck was stacked against him, but that he had believed he could turn the president around. "It was never a stylized affair as far as I was concerned," he said. "What I was doing was deeply felt out of my own guts here. I wouldn't have sat up until three or four o'clock in the morning doing it." [107]

Ball never stopped trying to change the Johnson administration's Vietnam policy. As late as September 25, 1968, just a day before he resigned as ambassador to the United Nations, Ball again confronted Johnson and Rusk and recommended a bombing halt as a step toward peaceful negotiations. Ball began his argument by noting that the president had not heard his "heresies" for a long time. The meeting proceeded like old times, as Ball and Rusk engaged in a sharp exchange. Ball stated: "We have blown up the importance of bombing way beyond life-size. . . . We are dealing with Orientals. They have operated on their Eastern standards for thousands of years. We must recognize the element of face in their position." Rusk shot back: "What about the face of our allies and that of other nations in Asia?" Ball responded: "There is no loss of face for us or for our allies in proceeding to a bombing halt. . . . We are providing the bulk of military force." Ball went on to argue, "We have to take some risks for peace. We are now in a box which we must get out of."[108]

The fourth reason behind Ball's decision not to resign or publicly attack the administration over Vietnam concerned his actual responsibilities as under secretary. He was heavily involved in a wide number of important crises, from beef quotas to European policy. In many of these issues, Ball's advice was paramount and his opinion was decisive. He claimed that Vietnam consumed only 10 percent of his professional time. Although this estimate might be have been understated, the under secretary did spend the overwhelming percentage of his time attending to issues that had nothing to do with Southeast Asia.

Ball thought it curious that individuals would question his continuing service in the Johnson administration. How could he resign in protest because he disagreed with his colleagues about one issue when he was deeply involved in dozens of other critical issues about which he and his colleagues agreed? Should he sacrifice his contributions to European unity, trade policy, and peace in the Congo on the altar of pique over Southeast Asian policy? As Dean Rusk observed: "When you look at the enormity of the business of the State Department and you see the hundreds of things with which you do agree and are trying to accomplish, then it takes a very strange sort of behavior to resign over one issue." Rusk concluded that Ball did not resign over Vietnam because "he wanted to get on with the job."[109]

The fifth reason for Ball's refusal to resign concerns his personal aspirations and political agenda. He never denied that he was ambitious. Ball had enormous self-confidence and believed that he could make a difference. He had no intention of throwing away an opportunity to influence world affairs. It was unlike him to resign in the midst of any struggle. When he did leave government in September 1966, he did so for several reasons, not the least of which were the relentless financial and family problems that confronted him. Later, after serving an abbreviated stint as U.S. ambassador to the United Nations, he resigned again in late 1967. This time he stepped down in order to enter another political arena, the brutal battle for the presidency being waged between Hubert Humphrey and Richard Nixon.

Those who worked closest to Ball in Washington unanimously rejected the "devil's advocate" thesis. Cyrus Vance declared, "Those of us who knew George knew this was nonsense."[110] Robert McNamara described Ball's memos opposing the war as the efforts "of an honest man pushing through a series of propositions that deserved thorough debate at the highest levels. He had our respect—but he deserved more than that."[111]

Those who have sharply criticized Ball have generally had personal and political axes to grind. In all cases, they were either outside the government or subordinate to Ball in the bureaucracy. Former Republican Cabinet Secretary James Schlesinger has argued that it is inappropriate for those who have not actually been in Ball's situation to criticize him. As long as Johnson listened to Ball, Schlesinger said, the under secretary was correct to stay on and to present his views. If Lyndon Johnson had ulterior motives, that was a reflection on Johnson, not on George Ball.[112] One could argue that Ball might have been more effective in his campaign against U.S. entanglement in Vietnam, that his tactics were ill chosen, that his timing was bad, and that his style was counterproductive. It is more difficult, however, to question Ball's sincerity, his personal courage, and his commitment to his goals.

Furthermore, George Ball privately questioned the war on moral grounds. He avoided discussing the conflict in these terms because his first priority was to change what he considered to be a flawed U.S. policy. He understood that resting one's case upon a moral foundation would be ineffective and would only alienate Johnson and his inner circle. Ball, in fact, had long abhorred war and had considered himself a pacifist when he was in his early twenties. In 1939, he drafted a soul-searching document entitled "Letter to Myself to be Read on the Day I Enlist." In this introspective letter, Ball explains how at one time, he would have refused to go to war: "Either I shall leave the country or I shall simply refuse to fight. Isn't Fort Leavenworth a healthier place than a muddy trench?" In late 1939, however, at the beginning of World War II, Ball, recognizing the evils of Nazism and the burden of his civic responsibilities, admitted that he "would be marching with the rest." Referring to himself in the third person, Ball wrote, with typical prescience: "The pacifist idealist of the late twenties and early thirties was predestined to be the most rabid patriot of 1941. This was implicit in his nature. He was in a sense a contradiction in terms."[113]

Only Ball's closest friends and family saw his pacifist streak. Ruth Ball's diaries contain several references to Ball's distress and moral outrage at the death and destruction that accompanied the Vietnam war.[114] After he resigned from the government and lost the capacity to oppose the war from inside the system, Ball expressed great moral outrage in condemning the war in speeches.

When Richard Nixon assumed the presidency in 1969 on a platform promising to end the war in Vietnam, George Ball watched closely as the new president and his national security adviser, Henry Kissinger, addressed the problem. When Nixon and Kissinger adopted a policy designed to bomb the North Vietnamese to the peace table, thereby extending the bloody war another four years, Ball was outraged. The years of frustrating dissent from within and the enormity of the human destruction occurring in Vietnam during Nixon's presidency led Ball to frontally and publicly attack the administration. Although he had not expected much from Nixon and Kissinger, he reacted angrily when they adopted a policy that Ball considered cynical and crude.

When Nixon and Kissinger found themselves at a stalemate in the negotiations with North Vietnam in October 1972, they responded by sending B-52s over Hanoi and Haiphong. In this infamous Christmas bombing, the huge aircraft dropped more than twenty thousand tons of bombs in seven hundred sorties over a twelve-day period. Ball captured the essence of this sad policy in four words — "bombing to improve syntax." [115] An agreement was signed in January 1973, but its text was scarcely affected by the bombing. As one of Kissinger's aides put it: "We bombed the North Vietnamese into accepting our concessions." [116]

Ball blamed the Nixon administration for not ending the war in 1969 as the candidate had promised. By the mid-1970s, Nixon and Kissinger had to settle the war on terms they could have had four years earlier. In four years on Nixon's watch, 15,315 Americans, 107,504 South Vietnamese, and an estimated 400,000 North Vietnamese and Vietcong troops died in combat. [117] Ball never forgave Nixon or Kissinger for this policy of making war in the name of peace, and he brooded about Vietnam until his death. In 1976, George Ball summarized the Vietnam experience:

> For, however one may try to justify it, [Vietnam] was a tragic defeat for America. Not in the military terms of the battlefield, but a defeat for our political authority and moral influence abroad and for our sense of mission and cohesion at home. A defeat not because our initial purposes were unworthy or our intentions anything less than honorable, but because — in frustration and false pride and our innocence of the art of extrication — we were forced to the employment of excessively brutal means to achieve an equivocal objective against a poor, small, backward country. That is something the world will be slow to forgive, and we should be slow to forget. [118]

Although he lost the Vietnam battle in Washington, George Ball compiled an impressive list of accomplishments. He helped draft the blueprints of the plans that have guided the long and continuing drive for European unity. His efforts helped break down many of the barriers to international trade, and fashioned peace agreements in places like the Congo. Ball played a key role in defusing the Cuban missile crisis, smothering the coals of war in Cyprus, and promoting dialogue concerning U.S. policy in the Middle East.

5

❖·❖·❖

Public Policy and Private Dissent:
Cuba, Cyprus, and the Middle East

As demonstrated in the cases of the European Community, the Congo crisis, and the Vietnam war, George Ball believed in the diplomatic path to conflict resolution and in the inherent rationality of humankind. He agreed to the application of military force only as a last resort. When military force became necessary, he contended, the conflict had to be accompanied by continuing dialogue between the warring parties.

Ball relentlessly and creatively pursued his goal of diplomatic engagement and negotiation. In so doing, he developed a rich array of interpersonal skills that helped make him extremely effective in administrative and decision-making circles. Ball's goals, skills, and moral principles shine through in a wide number of policy debates in which he participated.

The Cuban Missile Crisis: To the Brink of Nuclear War

For thirteen days in October 1962, George Ball participated in a historic political crisis that brought the United States and the Soviet Union to the brink of nuclear war. In spite of Soviet denials, the United States had incontrovertible evidence that the Khrushchev government was installing nuclear missiles in Cuba. President Kennedy asked McGeorge Bundy to gather a special group of advisers to meet secretly to address the crisis. This executive committee—known as the ExCom—met between October 16 and October 28, 1962, in George Ball's conference room on the seventh floor of the State Department.[1]

Besides Bundy and Ball, ExCom members included Secretary of Defense Robert McNamara, Attorney General Robert Kennedy, Chairman of the Joint Chiefs Maxwell Taylor, CIA Director John McCone, Deputy Secretary of Defense Roswell Gilpatric, Assistant Secretary of State Edwin Martin, presidential assistant Theodore Sorenson, Secretary of the Treasury Douglas Dillon, Ambassador to the Soviet Union Charles Bohlen (replaced on the ExCom by Llewellyn Thompson), and presidential secretary Kenneth O'Donnell. Others who participated sporadically in the deliberations included Special Presidential Advisers Dean Acheson, John J. McCloy, and Robert Lovett, Vice President Lyndon Johnson, Assistant Secretary of Defense Paul Nitze, and Ambassador to the United Nations Adlai Stevenson. Secretary of State Dean Rusk chose not to participate in ExCom discussions, seeking to reserve his judgment in order to make an independent recommendation to the president. Rusk met regularly, however, with George Ball, who represented the secretary of state on the ExCom.

ExCom membership divided roughly into two groups—those who favored an immediate military response, such as an air strike or invasion, and those who recommended a naval blockade or "quarantine" as part of a diplomatic initiative.[2] The former group sought to address both the missile question and the problem of Fidel Castro and Marxist Cuba. Those who favored a blockade drew a sharp distinction between the two issues and preferred to deal only with the immediate crisis of the Soviet missiles.

Feisty Dean Acheson, the most outspoken of the group that Ball termed hawks, was joined in his arguments by McCone, Dillon, Nitze, and Taylor. Although he wavered from time to time, the influential National Security Adviser Bundy also favored the military option. Outside the ExCom itself, there was strong support for immediate military action. Most members of the Department of Defense, Congress, and the American public tended to support the hawks. These external forces, however, did not affect policy until a week into the deliberations.

Those who favored the blockade option included Ball, McNamara, Robert Kennedy, Gilpatric, and Thompson. Stevenson assumed an even less confrontational position, arguing for a UN-sponsored resolution and negotiations. He suggested, for example, the joint removal of Soviet missiles from Cuba and U.S. missiles from Turkey and a bargain involving the possible relinquishment of Guantanamo Bay.

Ultimately, the trio of McNamara, Bobby Kennedy, and Ball carried the day for the blockade-diplomacy option. The missiles were removed and nuclear war was averted. Bobby Kennedy's special relationship with the president and McNamara's take-charge style played critical roles in the outcome. At the same time, George Ball's argumentation provided both Robert Kennedy and McNamara with much of the intellectual ammunition needed to sway the ExCom and President Kennedy himself. Bobby Kennedy wrote later that Ball's "advice and judgment were invaluable."[3]

Ball argued that the United States must beware of taking any irrevocable action. An air strike or invasion would invite Soviet retaliation, if not in Cuba, then perhaps against U.S. Jupiter missiles in Turkey or against Berlin. In the under secretary's words: "I felt that to go in and take the missiles out with an air strike, which would involve killing a great many Cubans, would be the kind of act which would not give the Soviet Union a chance to pull back because it would be an immediate loss of face to them and would force them into a precipitative decision. We might get a panic reaction, which could mean the actual setting off of atomic weapons against the United States."[4]

Ball pointed out that the blockade did not necessarily preclude other policy options but represented a serious first step that could be followed if necessary by other political and military actions. The under secretary contended that the imposition of a blockade also enabled the United States to buy some badly needed time for negotiations. President Kennedy and Dean Rusk favored the blockade and concurred with Ball's argument that an air strike would be irreversible. Ball, who slept on the couch in his State Department office during the crisis, consistently urged restraint and caution. In arguments foreshadowing his position on Vietnam, Ball warned against events getting into the saddle and uncontrollably determining crucial policy decisions.

On the second day of the ExCom deliberations, Ball contended that an air strike would run counter to American traditions and ideals. It would undercut U.S. credibility and effectiveness in the international arena and would badly tarnish the United States' image of itself. Robert Kennedy picked up this moral argument and presented it in forceful and stark terms. He compared an American strike against Cuba to the Japanese sneak attack on Pearl Harbor. When it appeared that the ExCom was leaning toward a surprise air strike, Bobby Kennedy passed a note to the President in which he scribbled: "I now know how Tojo felt when he was planning Pearl Harbor."[5] Ball and Bobby Kennedy were supported in this line of reasoning by influential presidential adviser Robert Lovett, who argued, "We would look ridiculous as the most powerful nation in the world if we grabbed a sledgehammer in order to kill a fly."[6]

Ball pressured Adlai Stevenson to convince UN Secretary General U Thant to ask Khrushchev to stop all ships for a twenty-four-hour period to capture some badly needed time for negotiation. In return, Kennedy promised that U.S. vessels would not intercept Soviet ships during that day. Ball's initiative provided an important one-day respite in the deadly confrontation.

President Kennedy and Ball took similar positions concerning the crisis. The president allowed a Soviet tanker to pass without interception and boarding. When the U.S. Navy did board a ship, it was a relatively nonprovocative Panamanian-owned vessel chartered by the Soviet Union. When Soviet missiles shot down a U-2 reconnaissance plane, killing the American pilot, many ExCom members believed that the president had no alternative but to order an attack to destroy the missile sites. Kennedy, however, "pulled everyone back. It isn't the first step that concerns me," he stated, "but both sides escalating to the fourth and fifth step—and we don't go to the sixth because there is no one around to do so."[7]

At the time of the missile crisis, the Department of State had the services of several talented Sovietologists. Besides such well-known experts as George Kennan and Charles Bohlen, Llewellyn "Tommy" Thompson was a knowledgeable and experienced Soviet specialist who had followed affairs in the Kremlin since serving as consul in Moscow in the early 1940s. Sitting on the ExCom, Thompson played a central role in shaping the day-to-day development of U.S. policy. He had an uncanny capacity to predict Soviet responses to U.S. initiatives. Ball had a high opinion of Thompson, who had been a kindred spirit as assistant secretary of state for European affairs from 1949 to 1952. During the grim days of October 1962, Ball spent many evenings in deep discussion with Thompson as they attempted to anticipate likely Soviet actions. Ball later wrote that Thompson "showed almost infallible judgment in predicting Khrushchev's probable reactions."[8]

When the missile crisis became public news after a week of secret diplomacy, the more aggressive members of the ExCom found themselves with considerable congressional and public support. Nitze, McCone, Taylor, and Acheson argued that the United States should destroy the missiles before they became operational. The hawks noted that the Soviet technicians were continuing to work on the missile sites; once the missiles became operational, the entire balance of power would be altered. At that point, U.S. air strikes could lead to nuclear war. Ball admitted that such reasoning "had a certain logic."[9]

The members of the ExCom engaged in a heated and harsh debate. Ball later admitted, "I began to think of the hawks among us almost as enemies."[10] He was particularly disappointed in the unyielding hard-line stance taken by Dean Acheson, a man he admired and respected. After the decision was made to pursue a blockade rather than an air strike, Acheson came into Ball's office and curtly said, "Well, George, the yellow bellies win."[11] In discussing Acheson's position in the missile crisis, Ball later lamented, "It was not his finest hour. I was very close to Dean, but I thought he behaved badly."[12] Ball agreed thoroughly with Acheson's biographer, Douglas Brinkley, who wrote, "Unlike Kennedy, Acheson failed to understand that in the nuclear age it is never wise to paint one's adversary into a corner."[13]

After the blockade proved successful and nuclear conflict had been avoided, Acheson explained the outcome in terms of "plain dumb luck."[14] On one occasion when Ball, Acheson, Rusk, and two security guards were riding the elevator to the State Department's seventh floor, Rusk sardonically commented that the only decent advice he had received during the past week came from his two security agents. In response, one of the guards, an ex-lineman for the Pittsburgh Steelers, blurted: "The reason for that, Mr. Secretary, is that you have surrounded yourself with nothing but dumb fucks!"[15] Ball reacted with a wide grin while Acheson turned a scarlet red.

Although Acheson has been criticized by associates and historians for the stance he adopted during the missile crisis, he never experienced public criticism or personal vilification. Adlai Stevenson was less fortunate. The UN ambassador's recommendations for compromise and negotiation were interpreted both by the Kennedys and by the ExCom hawks as a sign of Stevenson's personal softness, which they viewed as a serious character flaw. In spite of a courageous and inspired performance in the United Nations, where he rhetorically demolished Soviet Ambassador Valerian Zorin, Stevenson was attacked fiercely by the ExCom hawks and lost the confidence of Robert Kennedy. When the Kennedys brought John McCloy back from Europe to assist Stevenson at the United Nations, Bobby Kennedy told him, "We're counting on you to watch things in New York. That fellow is ready to give everything away."[16]

Stevenson found himself trapped between the Kennedys and the hawks, and he never recovered politically. The mass media vilified him and accused him of appeasement and of advocating a Caribbean Munich. George Ball was horrified by these charges against Stevenson and tried to set the record straight when he wrote that the ExCom hawks "violated the calm and objectivity we had tried to maintain in the ExCom meetings when they intemperately upbraided Stevenson. The attack was, I thought, quite unfair. . . . After all, there was nothing new in any of Stevenson's proposals."[17] The cases of Acheson and Stevenson demonstrate the depths of feeling and the visceral ideological confrontation that marked the different positions taken concerning the missile crisis.

After thirteen days of intense, gut-wrenching diplomatic activity and threatening military movements by both sides, Khrushchev agreed to dismantle the missile sites. In response, Kennedy promised not to attack Cuba. Also, as a secret part of the agreement known only to the president and four others, the United States later dismantled its Jupiter missiles and removed them from Turkey—just as the discredited Stevenson had suggested.

The United States and the Soviet Union came close to nuclear war in the fall of 1962. Certainly, George Ball and other ExCom members realized the dark danger of the crisis and, like McGeorge Bundy, agreed with Khrushchev that "the smell of burning was indeed in the air."[18] Ruth Ball's diaries provide an insight into the extent of her husband's fears. George had convinced her that it was "quite possible that our world might be blasted out of the universe." In preparing for a slightly less apocalyptic scenario, Ruth "stored food, water, utensils, bedding, radio, flashlights, scarves to protect our hair from fall-out, a calendar, writing material, and an odd assortment of tools of various kinds—especially a spade to turn the fall-out well into the soil as recommended. We also sealed windows and doors with shower curtains."[19]

The world had indeed tottered on the brink of nuclear disaster in October 1962. Meetings in the late 1980s among U.S., Soviet, and Cuban officials involved in the crisis have revealed that the United States underestimated both the size of Soviet forces in Cuba and the number of nuclear warheads already in place there. U.S. intelligence indicated that 10,000 Soviet troops were in Cuba, but there were in fact 42,000—and these were backed by Cuba's 240,000-strong standing army. Furthermore, the Soviets had placed thirty-six nuclear warheads in Cuba for the twenty-four intermediate-range missiles that targeted U.S. cities. As Robert McNamara later said, "We do not need to speculate what would have happened had the U.S. attack been launched, as many in the U.S. government— military and civilian alike—were recommending to the President." The result would have been "utter disaster." [20]

Hawks like Douglas Dillon remain unconvinced, however, that U.S. military intervention would have led to a nuclear holocaust, as Ball and McNamara feared. According to Dillon, "I didn't understand then, and I don't understand now, why people worried so much about one limited, conventional action leading to nuclear war. The idea is preposterous! The only explanation I can think of is that Ball's (and McNamara's) relative inexperience in these matters caused them to draw unwarranted conclusions. I think they may have let their fears run away with them." [21]

Of all of his numerous medals, awards, and citations, George Ball particularly valued a wooden plaque overlaid with a plate of silver. Inscribed on the upper left-hand corner of the plate were the initials GWB and in the upper right-hand corner JFK. The silver plate, a memento from John Kennedy, contained an engraved calendar of October 1962 with the dates from the 16th to the 28th heavily outlined.

In his provocative book, *On the Origins of War*, Donald Kagan revived the argument that Khrushchev tried to slip the missiles into Cuba because he was convinced that John Kennedy lacked the will to do anything about it. [22] Kagan postulates that Khrushchev, after observing the young president's behavior during the Bay of Pigs invasion, at the Vienna summit, and in Berlin, concluded that Kennedy was indecisive and could be bluffed. Kennedy had sent Khrushchev the wrong signals, just as George Bush and James Baker sent Iraq's Saddam Hussein the wrong signals thirty years later.

Although Kagan's thesis concerning the origins of the missile crisis is plausible, he overextends his argument in his examination of the actual dynamics of the crisis. His central thesis produces a portrait of Kennedy as a weak, vacillating leader who stooped to any expedient to avoid a military confrontation. Kagan argues that Kennedy had no intention of resorting to military force, and if it were not for public pressure, he would have accepted the missiles as a fait accompli. The author implies that the secret arrangement concerning the dismantling of the Jupiter missiles in Turkey represents an embarrassing compromise. In this assessment, Kagan agrees with such superhawks as Admiral George Anderson, who exclaimed, "We've been had!" and General Curtis LeMay, who described the outcome of the missile crisis as "the greatest defeat in our history." [23]

In the end, however, in spite of the thrust of his argument, Kagan pulls himself back to reality in one short sentence: "Still, with the benefit of hindsight, Kennedy's very great caution may well seem justified." [24] It certainly seemed justified to George Ball, one of the participants who had urged the president to exercise very great caution. The alternative, in Ball's judgment, was nuclear war, and the smell of burning in the air would have emanated from the incineration of flesh and bone and the destruction of the human habitat.

In the Cuban missile crisis, George Ball adopted a prudent position in support of a diplomatic track that emphasized the use of a blockade backed by military might. In presenting his position, he used both moral and practical arguments. Although John F. Kennedy merits the greatest credit for the resolution of this crisis, Ball, with Robert Kennedy and Robert McNamara, was part of an influential group of individuals who urged the president to apply cautious yet persistent pressure and to resort to force only if absolutely necessary. Even Dean Acheson, the leader of the ExCom hawks, congratulated Kennedy for his statesmanship and praised the president for his "leadership, firmness, and judgment over the past touchy week. We have not had these qualities at the helm in this country at all times. It is good to have them again." [25]

Like the other members of the ExCom, George Ball agreed with John Kennedy's assessment that the outcome of the missile crisis represented a monumental victory for the United States. Ball's participation in that victory provided him with great satisfaction as well as increased confidence in his own judgment, shaping his performance in coming crises in Cyprus and Vietnam.

Crisis in Cyprus: Intervention and Mediation

In late 1963 a crisis broke out in Cyprus, an island in the eastern Mediterranean located 40 miles from Turkey and 550 miles from Greece. Populated 82 percent by Greeks and 18 percent by Turks, Cyprus had a history of ethnic conflict, particularly since becoming a colony of Great Britain in 1925. Britain granted Cyprus its independence in 1959. For years, Greece had joined with the Greek Cypriots in calling for *enosis*, a political union between Cyprus and Greece. This resulted in intermittent violence between Greek and Turkish Cypriots, and the British were relieved to relinquish their colonial status over the island.

Shortly after independence, the island state exploded into civil war. During the Christmas holidays of 1963, more than three hundred people died in ethnic clashes in Cyprus. Badly outnumbered and outgunned on the island, the Turkish Cypriots who had been living in enclaves under siege suffered heavy casualties. Turkey, protesting loudly, ominously began a military buildup. Greece responded in kind and the two ancient rivals prepared for war in the Mediterranean.

In Washington, the Johnson administration viewed the crisis with alarm, fearing the outbreak of war between two NATO allies. U.S. leaders considered the situation in Cyprus as the most serious international confrontation since the Cuban missile crisis. Having recently shed its formal responsibilities in Cyprus and lacking the will and capacity to deal with the problem, Britain approached the United States; President Johnson assigned Under Secretary of State George Ball the primary responsibility for Cyprus policy.

Already smothered with mounting problems in Vietnam, Panama, the Congo, Berlin, and Indonesia, the United States resisted being drawn into the imbroglio in Cyprus. In the beginning, George Ball opposed U.S. involvement. In a January 28, 1964, conversation between Ball and the president, Johnson suggested that someone like Ball or Averell Harriman should travel to the region carrying a tough message to both Greeks and Turks. Ball argued that the United States should remain in the background and not "get in the middle of trying to make peace." Shortly after his conversation with Johnson, Ball called Secretary of Defense Robert McNamara and repeated his recommendation that the United States avoid direct intervention in the Cyprus crisis.[26]

In early February, however, Ball was assigned the position of special presidential envoy and traveled to Turkey, Greece, and Cyprus to attempt to mediate a peace agreement. From that time on, Ball adopted an aggressive and proactive policy toward Cyprus. The under secretary engaged in his own form of shuttle diplomacy and crisis management. The Cyprus crisis, according to the analysts Edward Weintal and Charles Bartlett, "was played almost entirely by ear. . . . The soloist was George Ball, who made up the score as the drama unfolded."[27]

As he became directly involved, Ball believed that only the United States had the power and international credibility to deter a war in the eastern Mediterranean. Throughout the Cyprus crisis, Ball received superb professional advice and assistance from such State Department officials as Phillips Talbot and John Jernegan.

As presidential envoy and lead U.S. troubleshooter, Ball first met with the eighty-year-old prime minister of Turkey, Ismet Inönü. Inönü had been a close associate of Kemal Atatürk's and had played a critical role in Turkey's transition to democracy. This wise senior statesman expressed great concern about the situation in Cyprus and warned Ball that Turkish public opinion increasingly favored military intervention. In Greece, Ball found a weak caretaker government that did little except express support for the cunning leader of the Greek Cypriots,

Archbishop Makarios III. The weakness of the politicians in Athens when compared with the robust Makarios led Ball to observe, "You can't hang a custard pie on a hook."[28] The United States would have to deal directly with the archbishop.

Makarios believed that the Greek Cypriots who dominated the island demographically should have the right to decide its political status. He had supported enosis for many years and had earlier been forced into exile by the British for his promotion of terrorism. With demographics and resources on his side, Makarios fueled and fanned the fire of Greek-Turkish confrontation. As the United States became increasingly entangled in the Cyprus crisis, Makarios became the bête noire of the United States. Among his own people, Makarios enjoyed great support as a charismatic nationalist leader. Outside the Greek Cypriot community, Makarios had quite a different image.

Before his first trip to Cyprus, Ball had already formed a negative opinion of Makarios. Adlai Stevenson had sharply criticized the archbishop in a conversation with Ball on January 25, 1964: "I know this son of a bitch. . . . I stayed in his house. . . . He has never been above spilling blood to accomplish his purpose." The only way to deal with Makarios, Stevenson advised Ball, was to give "the old bastard absolute hell." Stevenson continued: "I think that something can be done with him but I have sat across the table from this pious-looking replica of Jesus Christ and he is just the craftiest of Greeks."[29] Ball was somewhat taken aback by Stevenson's tirade, even though it reinforced his own impressions.

On February 12, George Ball, accompanied by three State Department assistants and British High Commissioner Sir Cyril Pickard, met for the first time with "His Beatitude," as Makarios was addressed. Ball found Makarios to be cool, devious, and uncompromising. In Ball's opinion, Makarios was a tough, cynical politician disguised in the glittering garb of a cleric. Working with Pickard, Ball put enormous pressure on Makarios to halt the aggression against the besieged Turkish Cypriots and to accept a multinational peacekeeping force. The mediators warned Makarios that if his partisans continued their aggression, the Turks would intervene and neither the United States nor the British would object.

In these "bloody" meetings, as Ball described them, Makarios refused to retreat from his position. He explained his position with a calm, sweet smile, employing a macabre sense of humor that both "amused and appalled" Ball. Among other things, Makarios demanded that the UN Security Council guarantee the territorial integrity of Cyprus. Ball interpreted this request to mean that "Makarios's central interest was to block off Turkish intervention so that he and his Greek Cypriots could go on happily massacring Turkish Cypriots."[30]

During Ball's meetings with Makarios, Greek Cypriot troops violated a ceasefire agreement and fired mortars and bazookas into Turkish positions in the town of Limassol, killing and wounding a number of Turkish Cypriots. When Ball urged Makarios to stop the violence, the archbishop patiently explained that the

Greeks and Turks had lived together on Cyprus for two thousand years and were quite used to these occasional incidents. Ball indignantly responded: "Your Beatitude, I've been trying for the last two days to make the simple point that this is not the Middle Ages. . . . The world is not going to stand idly by and let you turn this beautiful little island into your private abattoir." Makarios, smiling sadly, responded, "Oh you're a hard man, Mr. Secretary, a very hard man." [31]

Having failed to budge Makarios, Ball returned to Washington, visiting Ankara and London on his way home. He persuaded Inönü to postpone any invasion but failed to get the British to agree to a plan that would send British, Turkish, and Greek troops to Cyprus as a temporary peacekeeping force. Ball telexed President Johnson and Secretary Rusk from London on February 16. In the confidential message, Ball pessimistically alluded to the start of World War I: "The bomb has already gone off at Sarajevo and the Archduke is dead. . . . Both the governments and the people of Turkey and Greece want peace but they are like characters in a Greek tragedy. They cannot, by their own unaided efforts, avoid catastrophe. They can be pushed off a collision course only by some outside agency." [32]

The next day in Washington, Ball presented a discouraging report to President Johnson. According to the under secretary, there was a 50–50 chance of a Greek-Turkish war, which could easily veer out of control. When the British balked at his suggestion of a trilateral peacekeeping force, Ball resorted to a new two-pronged strategy.

Although skeptical that the United Nations could do the job, Ball nonetheless grudgingly recommended that the United States help create a UN peacekeeping force to be dispatched to Cyprus. After considerable international diplomatic maneuvering, a UN force of seven thousand troops began arriving in Cyprus on March 14, 1964. [33]

Ball also called on Dean Acheson to serve as a mediator between the Greeks and the Turks. Besides his impressive record of diplomatic experience, Acheson enjoyed special credibility in both Athens and Ankara because of his support for the Truman Doctrine when the United States had come to the defense of Greece and Turkey in 1947. Although Acheson considered Ball a bit too idealistic and Ball believed Acheson too quick on the trigger—a conflict that flared during the Cuban missile crisis—the two enjoyed a relationship of deep mutual respect. Their thirty-year personal friendship had weathered their political differences, and Acheson "had more respect for Ball's abilities than for those of any other Johnson administration figure." [34] Ball, in turn, considered Acheson one of the finest diplomats of the twentieth century. Ball was elated when Acheson accepted the Cyprus assignment.

Ball and the United States had originally resisted a UN role in the Cyprus crisis, fearing that this would open the way to Soviet influence in a crisis involving two NATO allies. When the Greeks adamantly opposed NATO intervention, the U.S. grudgingly accepted UN involvement. This position was compromised, however, by the special role assigned to Dean Acheson. Throughout the crisis, Acheson and the United Nations became entangled with one another and at times competed with one another. UN Secretary General U Thant refused to cede diplomatic authority to Acheson, the handpicked American envoy.[35]

Meanwhile, the United States found itself trapped between the intransigence of Makarios and the Greeks and the impatience of the Turks, who sought to solve the problem through military means. In spite of the UN presence, the Greek Cypriots continued their offensive against their Turkish counterparts. When a Turkish invasion seemed imminent, Lyndon Johnson sent a toughly worded letter of warning to Inönü. This harsh June 5, 1964, letter became infamous in Turkey and tarnished U.S.-Turkish relations for years.

Drafted by Secretary of State Dean Rusk, the letter bluntly warned that if Inönü should order an invasion of Cyprus, the United States and the countries of NATO would have to reconsider their obligations to protect Turkey against the Soviet Union. Ball, who was preparing to leave for a meeting with Charles de Gaulle at the time, reviewed a draft of the letter and described it to Rusk as "the most brutal diplomatic note I have ever seen." He later called it "the diplomatic equivalent of an atomic bomb" and predicted that it would convince the Turks to rethink their invasion plans. When he warned Rusk that the letter would alienate the Turks, the secretary told Ball, "That'll be your problem."[36]

As Ball had predicted, Johnson's letter forestalled a Turkish invasion of Cyprus —and alienated the Turks.[37] After visiting Paris, London, Geneva, and Athens during the second week of June 1964, Ball flew to Ankara, where he did his best to placate Prime Minister Inönü. Upon his return to Washington on June 11, Ball met with President Johnson. In his report, he recommended that the president invite the prime ministers of Turkey and Greece to Washington for separate meetings. When these meetings, which took place on June 22 and 24, failed to defuse the situation, Ball again shifted tactics and brought Dean Acheson directly into the picture.

Ball proposed that Acheson mediate a solution to the crisis by bringing representatives from Greece and Turkey to the United States for consultations. In so doing, Ball clumsily ignored the offices and responsibilities of the United Nations. When U Thant strenuously objected, Ball retreated and agreed to meetings in Geneva under the auspices of the United Nations. In his autobiography, Ball unkindly accused U Thant of showing "the kind of Burmese stubbornness I had seen on other occasions." The secretary general, however, was flexible enough to permit Acheson's presence in Geneva. Acheson, whom Ball had described to U Thant as "almost a legendary figure in Greece and Turkey," departed for Geneva on July 4, 1964. For eight weeks in Geneva, the seventy-one-year old American diplomat struggled to find a solution to the thorny problem of Cyprus. During this frustrating period, George Ball stood behind Acheson, providing constant encouragement.[38]

Acheson developed a diplomatic strategy in Geneva that came to be known as the Acheson Plan. In brief, it called for "double enosis," a concept that recommended the transfer of Cypriot sovereignty to both Greece and Turkey. Among other things, the island would be divided into eight cantons, including two for the Turkish Cypriots. While the major part of Cyprus would be united with Greece, Turkey would have the right to establish a military base on the island. Although the Acheson Plan became the basis for extensive diplomatic discussions, neither the Greeks nor the Turks considered it acceptable. Because the plan compromised the sovereignty of Cyprus itself, Makarios and the Greek Cypriots adamantly opposed the scheme.

In spite of George Ball's encouragement, Acheson realized that his presence and plan were doomed to fail as a solution to the crisis. On August 18, Acheson telexed Ball that the chances for a Greek-Turkish settlement on Cyprus were "about the same as the odds on Goldwater" to win the 1964 presidential election.[39]

That month, Greek Cypriots attacked the Turkish Cypriots, and Ankara responded by sending aircraft to strafe Greek Cypriot towns. During this flare-up, Ball put in several twenty-four-hour days at the Department of State, where he remained in continual contact with Ankara and Athens and with Acheson in Geneva. In early September, Acheson returned to Washington, where he met with President Johnson, Ball, Rusk, and McNamara. Acheson reported that he saw no solution to the Cyprus problem, and he considered it inevitable that the Turks would invade the island. In a personal note to a friend, he wrote that he had just spent two months "in the worst rat race I have ever been in—trying to deny Greeks and Turks their historic recreation of killing one another."[40] After a series of toughly worded messages from the United States and a warning to Makarios from the Soviet Union, the Greek Cypriots and Turkey agreed to a UN-sponsored cease-fire. With this cease-fire endorsed by both the United States and the Soviet Union and with the UN peacekeeping force in place, warfare was averted and Cyprus entered a period of uneasy stability for another decade.

Many observers have judged U.S. policy toward Cyprus during the 1964 crisis to be a success story. According to one source, "On most counts, the 1964 U.S. venture into crisis diplomacy can be judged a success. . . . The Cyprus incident is unique in the history of U.S. crisis diplomacy."[41] Another source concludes that "Cyprus was a textbook example of how crisis diplomacy attained virtually every aim: forestalling Soviet intervention, maintaining the peace between two bitter antagonists, and preserving relatively good relations with all the contending parties."[42]

There is another view, however: confronted by a series of problems around the world and preoccupied with the threat of Soviet communism, the United

States overreacted and intervened in a heavy-handed way in the Cyprus affair. American actions in the eastern Mediterranean evoked images of old-fashioned imperialism. U.S. leaders considered the Greek politicians in Athens to be feeble and effete, and they unanimously viewed Greek Cypriot leader Makarios as slippery, manipulative, selfish, and immoral. Although the Turkish leaders enjoyed more American respect, they were horrified when issued a crude and threatening ultimatum by President Johnson.

Throughout the crisis, the United States attempted to muscle the United Nations out of the arena and, when unable to do so, appropriated the role of the world body through the intervention of a high-powered American presidential envoy. Acheson's concept of double enosis proposed nothing less than the destruction of Cyprus as an independent nation-state. Finally, when confronted with the argument that the United States achieved its policy goals and prevented war in the region, the critics maintain that the success was only temporary.

In the early 1970s, Archbishop Makarios gave up his commitment to enosis and pursued a policy of an independent Cyprus under Greek Cypriot control. Greek proponents of enosis turned on Makarios and on July 14–15, 1974, a military junta carried out a coup in Athens. Makarios was driven from Cyprus and the coup leaders began an active campaign for enosis.

Deeply concerned about the turn of events in Athens and Cyprus and unable to negotiate successfully with the Greek junta, Turkey invaded Cyprus on July 20, 1974. The invasion caught the Nixon administration and Secretary of State Henry Kissinger by surprise. By the time the United States could react, the invasion was a fait accompli. Within days, thirty thousand Turkish troops occupied northern Cyprus and two hundred thousand Greek Cypriots fled to the south. The blustering Greek military junta collapsed under the weight of its own incompetence and corruption. As a result of the invasion, the Turks took control of the northern 40 percent of Cyprus while the Greeks were left with the southern 60 percent. Today, the island remains divided, and a Turkish military presence looms large in the north.

Although George Ball considered his approach to the Cyprus crisis of 1964 a decided success, he later acknowledged the criticism of his aggressive interventionary approach. In a long footnote in his autobiography, he wrote: "During the whole time I was involved with the agonies of Cyprus, I was constantly aware of the constraints under which democratic nations must conduct diplomacy." Ball went on to state that in times past the great powers simply had imposed a settlement upon the Greeks and Turks "without concern for the rights of sovereignty, the integrity of territory, or the abstract principle of self-determination."[43]

Although Ball was well aware of such principles during the Cyprus crisis of 1964, in his zealous attempt to prevent warfare, he ignored these important canons at critical moments. Ball did resist U.S. intervention at the beginning of the crisis, but once the United States became engaged, Ball adopted an aggressive, even imperious, diplomatic approach to the problem. Observers will continue to disagree whether the short-term success achieved by Ball and the Johnson administration in the Cyprus crisis justified the intrusive interventionary stance adopted by the United States.

The Middle East and the Revival of the Politics of Dissent

During the last two decades of his life, George Ball spent much of his time and intellectual energy grappling with one of the most intractable and complex international problems, the Arab-Israeli issue. In so doing, he accepted a challenge that carried with it great personal and political costs as well as considerable frustration and disappointment. Given Ball's predilection to sense the important crises of the day and to dissent from the conventional wisdom, it is hardly surprising that he ended his long political career in the middle of this blazing debate.

As humankind approaches the end of the millennium, the Arab-Israeli conflict nears its fiftieth anniversary. Constant strife and psychological stress, punctuated by five punishing wars, have followed in the wake of the creation of the state of Israel in 1948. In one of the great ironies of the twentieth century, the leading actors of the international system, in attempting to assist one bleeding civilization of victims, have unwittingly helped create another civilization of casualties, the Palestinians. Two peoples lay claim to the same piece of land.

The difficulty of the Arab-Israeli issue has been magnified by a number of related factors. For many years, Middle East friction was entangled with the Cold War struggle between the United States and the Soviet Union. Over time, the problem has been intensified by the increasing involvement of both Jewish and Muslim religious fundamentalism. The fact that the Arab allies of the Palestinians are concentrated in the region of the conflict also complicates the issue, as does the Arabs' control over massive deposits of petroleum. Finally, because both Jews and Palestinians have settled around the world, each group has an international presence. This presence expands and extends the impact of the conflict across the globe.

Because for both sides the stakes are nothing less than survival, the confrontation has been particularly bitter. Such a situation produces extremists, true believers, and fanatics on all sides of the question. Those voices that stress moderation, reason, negotiation, and compromise are drowned out by the cries of anger, fear, intolerance, and retribution. In the Arab-Israeli debate, there is little middle ground, and those who occupy it often end up alienating both sides. Moderates, caught in a withering cross fire of vitriolic accusations and personal denunciations, often either retreat quietly for cover or gravitate to one position or the other.

During his years in government, George Ball paid little attention to Arab-

Israeli affairs. The administration of Lyndon Johnson adopted a strong pro-Israel position, and Ball accepted that point of view. Although he participated peripherally in decisions concerning arms sales to Israel and Jordan and in dealing with Nasser's Egypt, Ball focused most of his attention upon a multitude of international issues outside the Middle East. When he did find time to consider the Middle East problem, Ball believed that the only workable solution was to convene a comprehensive peace conference that would involve the participation of the Soviet Union and all the regional actors as well. He was skeptical about step-by-step regional approaches focusing only upon Israel and a selected Arab country or two.[44]

When the June 1967 war broke out, Lyndon Johnson had National Security Adviser Walt Rostow contact Ball about participating in a special committee on the Middle East crisis. Ball, who was between jobs as under secretary and ambassador to the United Nations, declined the opportunity and remained generally aloof from the crisis. In July 1968, George Ball made his only official trip to the Middle East. As U.S. ambassador to the United Nations, he visited Israel, Jordan, Lebanon, and Saudi Arabia. In Israel, he conferred with Foreign Minister Abba Eban, Prime Minister Levi Eshkol, and Defense Minister Moshe Dayan, then flew by helicopter over the Golan Heights before landing at the kibbutz of Deputy Prime Minister Yigal Allon. During his visit, Ball sought to determine whether UN Security Council Resolution 242 could in fact serve as a serious basis for peace negotiations. Resolution 242, which had been approved on November 27, 1967, called for the "withdrawal of Israel from territories occupied" in exchange for the recognition of Israel by all Arab countries. After visiting Israel and King Hussein in Jordan, Ball concluded that there was little hope at the time for any serious peace negotiations between the two parties.

In Beirut, a crowd of angry Palestinians greeted Ball at the airport. One demonstrator hurled a bottle at the ambassador; the shattering missile barely missed Ball's head and cut his wrist. Although Ball appeared at a press conference later, the incident unnerved him and he never forgot it. The July 1968 foray into the Middle East convinced Ball of the deadly serious nature of the Arab-Israeli conflict, and he decided to give the problem more of his attention.

Between 1968 and 1976, Ball researched and reflected upon the Middle East problem. In his 1976 book, *Diplomacy for a Crowded World*, George Ball sharply criticized Henry Kissinger's shuttle diplomacy in the Middle East.[45] He noted that, contrary to détente, Kissinger's approach had denied the Soviet Union a role in the attempt to fashion an agreement between Anwar Sadat's Egypt and Israel. This approach, Ball argued, isolated Egypt from the rest of the Arab world and precipitated a step-by-step approach that would inevitably lead to a diplomatic dead end. Ball foresaw that such an approach might bring about the demise of President Sadat. When Kissinger failed to negotiate an Arab-Israeli peace agreement, Ball accused him of pursuing "a practice that most medical doctors would deplore; he has sewn up part of the wound, leaving a raging infection inside."[46]

Ball's views on the Middle East caught the public's attention in June 1976, when excerpts from his book were published in *The Saturday Review*.[47] In the same time period, he outlined his ideas concerning the Arab-Israeli issue on several occasions on national television. In 1977 he published a widely noted article that appeared in the influential journal *Foreign Affairs*. It was at this time that Ball staked out a position for himself at the center of the debate and wrote his prescription for peace in the Middle East. The title of his article, "How to Save Israel in Spite of Herself," suggested the nature of his diagnosis.[48]

Ball postulated that the smoldering Arab-Israeli dispute required immediate attention before it ignited once again into a violent conflagration. After praising Israel's achievements as a "valiant nation" and defending its right to existence, Ball pointed out that Israel, like the Arabs, must implement the terms of UN Resolution 242 as soon as possible. Because of internal politics and understandable insecurities, neither side was prepared to take such a step toward peace. In these circumstances, Ball argued, the United States had an obligation to intervene. While insisting that the Arabs recognize Israel's existence, the United States "must insist that Israel withdraw from the territories she occupied in 1967." Ball focused attention upon the large amounts of American financial aid provided Israel and concluded, "It is not whether we should try to force an unpalatable peace on the Israeli people, but rather how much longer we should continue to pour assistance into Israel to support policies that impede progress toward peace."[49]

As always, Ball's plan included U.S.-Soviet cooperation and coordination and insisted that all the key Arab countries be integrally involved in the plan. In brief, unlike Kissinger, he proposed a comprehensive, multilateral approach in which the United States would take the lead. Ball realized that his arguments would ignite a firestorm of controversy. He anticipated the charges that his proposal would put the United States in the position of trying to "impose a settlement, — an opprobrious expression that sets everyone's teeth on edge." In response, he argued that "preserving the peace by helping quarreling nations break free from a diplomatic stalemate is, under the circumstances, not merely an option but an imperative if the world is to be saved from a disaster that cannot be geographically limited in its consequences." To do less would be "irresponsible."[50]

When George Ball presented his ideas on the Middle East in the spring and summer of 1976, he was aware that such public arguments might compromise his chances for an important position in the next administration. Ball was one of a handful of individuals whom Jimmy Carter was considering for the position of secretary of state. In the July 11–24, 1976, issue of the influential *Jewish Week– American Examiner*, Victor Bienstock attacked the Ball candidacy "because Ball has shown himself to be one of the country's most vocal and effective opponents of an American policy of all-out support for Israel." Bienstock concluded that "designation of George Ball as Secretary of State would signal a greater danger to Israel than a new massing of Arab forces on Israel's frontiers."[51]

Ball responded to this attack in a letter that was published in a subsequent issue of *The Jewish Week*. In his letter, Ball stood by his position supporting the implementation of UN Resolution 242 and the withdrawal of Israel to the borders existing before the 1967 war. He emphasized, however, that the first principle in his plan was that the United States "should continue to give its full, unremitting support to the secure existence of Israel." Ball concluded: "I regard myself as a firm friend of Israel. The measures I recommend are, in my view, far more conducive to Israel's long-range interests than current Israeli policies which at least give the impression of seeking to preserve the *status quo*."[52] This explanation did little to reassure the staff and readership of *The Jewish Week*. Jewish skepticism about Ball's position in turn did not reassure Democratic presidential hopeful Jimmy Carter.

In an August 10, 1976, letter, Ball brought the issue directly to Carter's attention, writing that "although I think I am generally regarded in American Jewish circles as a friend of Israel's, you should be aware that I have recently been attacked in an American Jewish weekly publication." Ball argued, though, that "since you also have advocated that we seek an overall settlement, I see no significant difference between us on this major issue."[53]

Carter may not have seen any major differences between Ball and himself concerning the Arab-Israeli issue, but Ball's outspoken public stand was a potential political liability to any candidate for the presidency. Ball's Middle East stance was one important reason why Carter chose to reject him for the position of secretary of state.[54] Ball had anticipated this possibility, and when the position went to Cyrus Vance, he was disappointed but not surprised.

Shortly into the Carter presidency, Ball published his *Foreign Affairs* article. This piece precipitated a spirited counterattack, as many supporters of Israel accused Ball of proposing a crude one-sided American interventionary policy. According to one columnist, Ball had written a piece best described as "how to save our access to oil, mollify the Soviet Union, betray Israel, and still consider ourselves moral."[55]

In November 1977, while attending a conference in Tel Aviv, Ball received word that Anwar Sadat had decided to visit Jerusalem. "That night," he later recalled, "I found most of my Israeli friends euphoric; the excitement was pervasive and contagious. I was impressed by their deep yearning for peace, and could not blame them for wanting a deal with Egypt that would relieve Israel of its greatest military danger." Nonetheless, even while still in Israel, he quietly worried about "the longer-term implications of Sadat's mission."[56]

George Ball watched President Carter bring together Anwar Sadat and Menachem Begin and orchestrate the dramatic Camp David Accords. Ball considered this agreement to be an extension of Kissinger's step-by-step diplomacy and criticized the bilateral approach for its exclusivity and short-term perspective. In his analysis, he believed that Camp David would result in continued Arab-Israeli violence, and he predicted that it would end the political career of Anwar Sadat. Sadat's assassination on October 6, 1981, was a tragic confirmation of Ball's assessment.

On June 6, 1982, Israel invaded Lebanon. Prime Minister Begin and Defense Minister Ariel Sharon explained that the goal of the invasion was to provide a twenty-five-mile-wide buffer zone in southern Lebanon free of Palestinian guerrillas. But once the Israeli forces had attained their goal, they continued to roll forward until they had fought their way to the outskirts of Beirut. Sharon and Begin considered this to be the opportunity to defeat the PLO once and for all, while at the same time neutralizing Syrian influence in Lebanon. U.S. Secretary of State Alexander Haig agreed and felt that "a bloodying of the PLO and quieting of the Israel-Lebanon border might facilitate diplomatic progress." [57]

International political pressure and the desperate fighting by the cornered PLO barricaded in West Beirut slowed the Israeli invasion, and the world watched the punishing siege that continued for ten weeks. In the end, the United States helped negotiate an Israeli withdrawal and provided safe passage from Lebanon for PLO leader Yassar Arafat and his ragtag army. The results of the 1982 Israeli invasion of Lebanon were costly to the Arabs and, in many ways, devastating to the Israelis.

International public opinion turned against Israel as the world watched Israeli air and artillery attacks pound Beirut day after day. Police data, which experts on Lebanon believe to be accurate, indicate that about 19,000 Arabs died in the conflict and its aftermath; most were civilians. The world was horrified by the September 1982 massacres of hundreds of Palestinians at the Sabra and Shatilla refugee camps in the wake of the invasion. The massacres were carried out by Lebanese Christian Phalangists, but Israel, which occupied the area at the time, was accused of indirect responsibility for the tragic event. When the Begin government was slow to create a commission to investigate the massacres, 400,000 Israelis demonstrated in Tel Aviv and demanded a full judicial inquiry. During the war in Lebanon, 650 Israeli soldiers were killed and 3,800 wounded. The Israeli military failed to destroy the PLO, and, in its eagerness to engage the Palestinians, made the mistake of attacking Shiite populations as it smashed its way through south Lebanon. This action permanently alienated the Shiites, who prepared to fight Israel to the death. Israeli leader Yitzhak Rabin said that one of the great unintended consequences of the invasion was that it let the Shiite genie out of the bottle.[58] Furthermore, in spite of costly battlefield losses, Syria emerged from the war stronger and more dangerous. In the end, after a punishing three-year adventure, the Israeli army staggered out of Lebanon. In the words of Abba Eban, the invasion represented a signal case where "the remedy was more lethal than the disease."[59]

The controversial 1982 Israeli attack took place because of Sharon's militant determination and Haig's diplomatic ineptness. After the fact, Haig claimed that he had cautioned the Israelis against invading Lebanon. In fact, he clumsily encouraged the attack by signaling that the United States would not apply pressure or sanctions if Israel were to move into Lebanon. As a result, "Israel's key leaders were convinced that Washington had given them a green light to enter Lebanon."[60] If Haig's light was not a strong green, it was at the very least a flickering yellow light. Less than three weeks after the invasion, under pressure for his blundering, Haig resigned and was replaced as secretary of state by George Shultz.

Israeli leaders have repeatedly recognized the 1982 invasion of Lebanon as a massive mistake. Rabin, for example, angrily stated: "I was against that war. . . . Begin became intoxicated by our military strength, but the war in Lebanon had to fail. We cannot impose peace on our neighbors through the force of arms."[61] According to the scholar-diplomat Itamar Rabinovich, the 1982 war "offered little reward to the advocates of assertive action. Instead, it threatened to become yet another manifestation of the 'cunning of history.' The military campaign, which began with the support of a broad segment of Israeli opinion, turned into Israel's most controversial and divisive war."[62] The Israeli journalists Ze'ev Schiff and Ehud Ya'ari argue that the invasion "was anchored in delusion, propelled by deceit, and bound to end in calamity. . . . It drew Israel into a wasteful adventure that drained much of its inner strength. . . . There is no consolation for this costly senseless war."[63]

George Ball could not have agreed more. Outraged by what he considered to be blatant Israeli aggression and flawed U.S. policy, Ball embarked upon a writing and lecturing campaign in which he condemned both governments. In the middle of the controversy, he penned a provocative op-ed piece that appeared in the *New York Times* on August 25, 1982. The essay asserted that Israel's "roving Air Force and "rampaging Army" had "devastated a nation; killed or wounded civilian men, women and children, and maimed many for life." Ball argued that under international law, "Israel, as the aggressor, would normally be expected to pay the bill." He wrote that Israel would most likely "disclaim responsibility and pass the burden to the United States."[64]

Ball concluded that "we did not wage this war, nor did we ask Israel to wage it. Having created a pretext, the Israelis invaded Lebanon without our prior knowledge. . . . In the name of humanity and decency, we should provide ample help for the Lebanese people; in the name of logic and justice, we should deduct the cost of that help from our annual subsidy to Israel." Ball took the opportunity to remind Americans that they provided $2.7 billion annually in aid to Israel, $750 for every Israeli citizen. He concluded that even if a proportion of U.S. aid to Israel were diverted to help rebuild Lebanon, it would not "recompense America for the political losses suffered by serving as Israel's diplomatic agent."[65]

Ball's article prompted an unusually heavy response. Those that supported his views were usually brief letters of congratulations. One correspondent urged him to run for the presidency; another warned him that there would be a strong media campaign against him. The letters in disagreement ranged from reasoned essays of disapproval to vicious personal attacks. In four letters representative of the latter category, Ball was called a "no good S.O.B." whom the writer invited to "drop dead"; "a political worm and degenerate pervert"; a defender of his "adopted brethren, the gun-slinging, murderous PLO"; and an individual who "has lost his marbles" and whose "anti-Israel, anti-Semitic colors are showing now."[66]

Published responses were also numerous. *Commentary* editor Norman Podhoretz led the charge, attempting to justify the invasion by attacking its critics. In a shrill piece entitled "J'Accuse," Podhoretz invoked the issue of anti-Semitism in criticizing a wide range of writers, including Anthony Lewis, John le Carre, Richard Cohen, Mary McGrory, Stanley Hoffmann, Joseph Harsch, Rowland Evans, and Robert Nowak for their positions concerning the invasion of Lebanon.[67] His essay began and ended, however, with references to George Ball.

Podhoretz took issue with Ball's assertion that the results of the Israeli invasion benefited the Soviet Union while damaging U.S. interests. The absurdity of this view, according to Podhoretz, indicated that it could not be "the considered judgment of an informed and objective mind. Therefore, if it is proper to indict anyone in this debate for bias and insufficient concern for American interests, it is Ball who should be put in the dock and not the Jewish defenders of Israel against whom he himself has been pleased to file this very indictment." After his condemnation of Ball, Podhoretz made the sweeping charge: "I accuse all those who have joined in these attacks [on Israeli policy] not merely of anti-Semitism but of the broader sin of faithlessness to the interests of the United States and indeed to the values of Western civilization as a whole."[68]

During the last decade of his life, George Ball continued his stinging critique of U.S. policy in the Middle East. The more outspoken he became, the more powerful the counterattacks launched against him. In response to this intellectual pressure, Ball in turn sharpened his pen and increased his criticism. Between 1984 and 1994, he found himself locked in a whirling circle of intellectual combat with many of the extreme partisans of Israel. As a result, Ball's writing became more polemical; at times, he came close to playing the role of pamphleteer. An important case in point was his hard-hitting monograph *Error and Betrayal in Lebanon*.[69]

In *Error and Betrayal*, Ball built a devastating case against Israel's 1982 invasion of Lebanon. In the conclusion, he listed twenty-four U.S. government errors, eight Israeli betrayals, thirteen Israeli errors, and five U.S. betrayals. In this booklet, Ball prepared a lawyer's brief against Israeli actions in the region as well as against U.S. Middle East policy at the time. During the Lebanese episode, he wrote, "Washington flaccidly let the Begin government, in effect, dictate America's policies and disregard America's interests. Such apparent impotence reflected an upside-down relationship unique in history. Although Israel is, in practical terms, a ward of the United States—dependent on America for economic, financial and military support to a degree without parallel between sovereign nations—the United States is more often the suppliant than the dominant partner."[70]

Ball made no attempt to provide a balanced perspective or to present both sides of the issue. Although he reached the same conclusions as many Israelis, his blunt commentary and position as advocate alienated many supporters of Israel. Ball continued this critical approach over the years, and in 1992, with his son Douglas, he produced *The Passionate Attachment*.[71] The Balls had worked for eight years on this manuscript, which went through dozens of drafts and rewritings.

In this book, the Balls borrowed a phrase from George Washington's farewell address, in which the country's first president cautioned against any "passionate attachment" to a foreign nation. The Balls defined the United States' relation with Israel as just such an attachment and argued that it was unhealthy both for America and for Israel. The authors documented in meticulous detail the many negative results of this relation and concluded by calling for the United States to be true to its own venerable principles: "No country can possibly reconcile its concern for liberty and human rights with the continued abusive mistreatment of the Palestinian people, whose only crime is their desire for self-determination — the same sentiment that prompted the Founding Fathers of the United States and the founders of Israel a half century ago."[72]

In their recommendations for a solution to the Arab-Israeli crisis, George and Douglas Ball advocated negotiations that would result in the formation of an independent Palestinian state very much as had been proposed in UN Resolution 242. Their detailed proposal anticipated the process set in motion by the Madrid negotiations in 1991, the Oslo breakthrough in 1993, and the Taba interim agreement of 1995. In the foreword to their book, however, the Balls expressed skepticism about the prospects for the peace process and questioned the capacity of the late Yitzhak Rabin to carry the process forward.

Although *The Passionate Attachment* represented an important attempt to analyze the U.S.-Israeli relation through time, its packaging and presentation weakened its appeal. By the time it appeared, Ball's credibility was so low in the pro-Israel community that the book was never given a chance. On the other hand, the book, which repeated a point of view heard often before, contained loaded language and inflammatory rhetoric that helped undermine its message. The approach made the study highly vulnerable to those who waited to condemn it. In the judgment of Arthur Schlesinger Jr., the substance was "OK," but the "tone of the book" was unfortunate.[73]

George Ball's last book elicited surprisingly little attention and carried even less political influence. *The Passionate Attachment's* polemical edge dulled its impact, the volume in fact contained little that was new, and events overtook the Balls' message when the Israeli Likud government was replaced in 1992 by the more accommodating Labor government of Yitzhak Rabin and Shimon Peres. Furthermore, the newspapers whose book reviews are most widely read—the *New York Times*, *Washington Post*, and *Washington Times*, for example—chose evaluators whose perspectives predictably led them to castigate the book.[74]

Ball accused the Israeli lobby in the United States of trying to suppress the book's influence by quietly urging that it not be reviewed. When the book was reviewed, Ball charged, it was intentionally sent to unfriendly evaluators. In an interview on C-Span's *Booknotes*, Ball accused the *New York Times* of attempting to smother the book by sending it to a hostile reviewer who refused to review it. According to Ball, only when he applied pressure through the intervention of an old friend at the *Times* did the newspaper send the book to another reviewer.

This episode demonstrates the level of politicking that Ball found himself engaged in late in his life. Much of the reason for this unpleasant wrangling rested in the nature of the issue that he had chosen to address. Much of it had to do with the way Ball chose to confront the issue. Over time, he had become increasingly strident. Throughout his political career, he had seldom hesitated to take lonely and unpopular stands, and the more pressure that was applied, the more adamant he became in his position. Ball refused to be intimidated.

Ball was genuinely wounded, however, by the insinuations and outright charges of anti-Semitism. When confronted with this accusation, Ball would respond: "I'm deeply shocked that you are trivializing one of the most serious offenses in history. Anti-Semitism has a long and ugly tradition, and one should not judge whether or not someone is anti-Semitic by whether he treats as infallible decisions made by the government of Israel."[75] Having spent a lifetime working closely with Jewish colleagues in institutions like Cleary, Gottlieb and Lehman Brothers, and having developed close friendships with such individuals as Eugene Rostow, Walter Lippmann, Michael Blumenthal, James Greenfield, Jerry Goodman, Leo Gottlieb, Abba Eban, and dozens of others, he was incredulous and annoyed when he was labeled an anti-Semite. A number of incidents in Ball's life proved the falseness of the charge; the most dramatic involved his friend Michael Blumenthal.

On March 2, 1981, Ball recommended Blumenthal for membership in New

York's prestigious Links Club. In a follow-up conversation with the chairman of the admissions committee, Ball learned that objections had been raised to Blumenthal's candidacy. As a result of the discussion, Ball concluded that Blumenthal's name had been rejected because he was Jewish. Outraged, Ball wrote a letter to the admissions committee in which he articulated his suspicion "that Mr. Blumenthal's disqualification results from the fact that his father was Jewish." Ball went on bitingly: "In the latter years of the twentieth century, I find such a standard wholly objectionable. I cannot maintain membership in a club that would exclude Jesus Christ." He concluded: "I write this with regret, for I have belonged to The Links for thirteen years, have many friends in a club and find the environment extremely pleasant, but, in good conscience, I have no course but to submit my resignation, which is the purpose of this letter."[76] According to Blumenthal, besides Ball, a blue ribbon group of other influential Americans also wrote letters on his behalf to Links Club officials. When his application was rejected, Blumenthal made sure that all of his sponsors knew what had happened. Each commiserated with him but did nothing—except for Ball. In Blumenthal's opinion, "It is ridiculous to suggest that George is anti-Semitic."[77]

In spite of the travail that Ball experienced as a result of his stance on the Middle East, his position also won him a smaller, but no less impassioned group of new friends and allies. Those sympathetic to the Arab position considered Ball a courageous hero, and he became a frequent speaker before a wide variety of Arab-American and Middle East studies audiences. For a time in the 1980s, Ball represented Lehman Brothers in negotiating business opportunities in Saudi Arabia. The handful of U.S. statesmen who shared his opinions and who said so publicly also respected Ball. When *Time* magazine asked a group of leading public figures to name "living American leaders who have been most effective in changing things for the better," Senator William Fulbright said, "Anybody who takes issue with the government of Israel is taking his life in his own hands. The one man who has done this and written very well is George Ball. He has advocated an equitable or balanced policy toward Israel and her neighbors that I think is very constructive."[78]

George Ball's stance on the thorny Arab-Israeli issue evolved over time. During the period he served as under secretary of state and ambassador to the United Nations, he seldom questioned Israeli policy. But after studying the situation in the 1970s and, especially after the Israeli invasion of Lebanon in 1982, Ball became an outspoken critic of Israeli political strategy. As was his lifelong proclivity, Ball analyzed Arab-Israeli strife in the longer term. Given Israel's size and resources and given the size and resources of the Arab and Muslim communities, Ball did not believe that the small Jewish state could survive indefinitely without peace. Furthermore, he deplored the plight of the Palestinian people. Ball believed that the only answer was negotiation, compromise, and accommodation.

Although George Ball understood the Israeli disposition to rely on the aggressive use of military might, especially when it faced dedicated armed enemies, he thought that many Israeli leaders had lost their perspective and had converted their country into an aggressive garrison state that subsisted on preemptive strikes and territory-expanding military adventures. Ball placed much of the blame for the development of such policy upon the United States, Israel's international patron and protector. Conservatively, the United States, according to Ball, had provided Israel with more than $50 billion in aid between 1974 and 1991. After 1984, this aid was provided in the form of gifts.[79] In analyzing the many reasons for the United States' extraordinary support for Israel, he emphasized the powerful role played by the pro-Israeli lobby.

In his involvement in the Arab-Israeli crisis, George Ball adopted an approach that reflected his political imprint. He attempted to analyze the problem dynamically and strategically; he approached the issue with passion and complete dedication; once he had taken a position, he took full responsibility for that stance; he remained cognizant of the moral dilemmas involved; and he used personal and political means in an attempt to achieve peace in the region. But Ball's efforts to change U.S. and Israeli policy were largely ineffective. Although his speeches and writings helped keep a dialogue alive, they had little impact on decision makers either in Tel Aviv or in Washington. The Israeli statesman Shimon Peres once told Ball at a reception in New York that he was always welcome in Israel. When Ball feigned surprise, Peres reportedly said, "Ambassador Ball, when it comes to Israel and the Arabs, you're totally wrong—but you're honestly wrong."[80]

There are several reasons for Ball's futility concerning the Middle East. First, he took his stand outside rather than within the system. This deprived him of access and personal influence. Second, Ball's position was one that automatically provoked strong reactions from a strong, well-organized, and capable pro-Israeli constituency. Third, Ball's moral arguments concerning the Palestinian community were diluted by moral considerations involving the status of another community with a painful history.

When Ball discovered that his speeches and writings provoked withering, often ugly counterattacks, he refused to give ground and increasingly responded as an advocate-polemicist. This opened him to charges of bias, partiality, and one-sided argumentation. Walter Laqueur attacks *The Passionate Attachment*, for example, on the grounds that the approach "is that of a courtroom lawyer, marshalling all of the evidence favorable to his client and damaging to the other side. This kind of approach may have its uses in the legal profession, but it does not help to establish historical truth nor does it offer a guide to political action."[81]

George Ball was not troubled by this criticism. He considered himself an advocate, whether it was in opposition to trade barriers, in support of the European Community, in opposition to a U.S. invasion during the Cuban missile crisis, in opposition to the Vietnam war, in support of the continued integration of the Congo, or in opposition to enosis in Cyprus. In the case of the Middle East, he was confident that in the long run, his views would be vindicated. The hard line of the Likud and leaders like Begin, Sharon, and Shamir would fail. Only negotiations promised peace. Such consultation would eventually lead to a Palestinian state, and, in his opinion, Israelis would then for the first time find peace and security. Meanwhile, he struggled stubbornly and persistently to keep the dialogue alive and well. George Ball was a true intellectual gladiator whose ideals were based upon an underlying personal philosophy and political first principles.

COURTESY GEORGE AND DOUGLAS BALL

Jean Monnet, George Ball's role model

George Ball speaks with old friend Adlai Stevenson, right, while Robert McNamara stands by, February 11, 1965.

COURTESY YOICHI R. OKAMOTO/LBJ LIBRARY COLLECTION

George Ball sits at the right hand of President John F. Kennedy during a high-level White House meeting, 1962.

George Ball and Lyndon Johnson engage in a private discussion at the White House, August 21, 1965.

Robert McNamara, George Ball, and McGeorge Bundy advise Lyndon Johnson
in a private session at White House, April 6, 1965.

III

STATECRAFT FOR THE
TWENTY-FIRST CENTURY

6

❖·❖·❖

The Essence of Statesmanship:
George Ball and Prudence

The career of George Ball provides a model of effective statecraft for the future. In spite of his blemishes, Ball stood as an outstanding example of an American statesman. In an age when wise and honorable statesmen are in short supply and when global challenges are plentiful and complex, it is important to identify and analyze the qualities that define respected and successful leadership. In a world of incoherence and disintegration, a world where old systems shatter and new systems remain to be formed, the ability to recognize, understand, and develop leaders of excellence and statesmen of merit is more important than ever before.

The essence of a statesman can be found in the concept *prudence*. In his political career, George Ball displayed the various characteristics that together define the term. Ball presented carefully articulated goals; he developed a repertoire of tactics that maximized the chances of achieving these goals; and he engaged in the struggle to convert ideals into realities within a moral framework that emphasized the public good.

The Broader Meanings of Prudence

As the term is commonly used today, prudence refers to the qualities that enable a statesman to adopt effective means to achieve a desired goal. In this study, however, I adopt a view of prudence closer to the original Aristotelian sense of *phronesis*, a practical wisdom that involves the selection of the proper means to achieve a good or moral end.[1] "Prudence enables us to discern which means are most appropriate to the good in particular circumstances."[2] Prudence as phronesis goes beyond the concept of *prudentia*, which emphasizes caution, a special

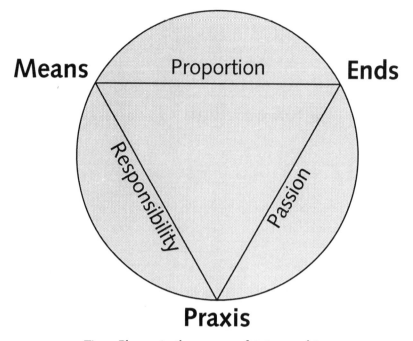

Fig. 1. Phronesis: the essence of statesmanship

regard for one's personal interests, and a pragmatic approach to life. To be prudent is to be more than simply "sagacious in adapting means to ends" as the
Oxford unabridged dictionary defines it. Phronesis requires that there be a moral
context that informs both means and ends.

According to Aristotelian scholars, phronesis includes an important action
component called *praxis* that distinguishes it from judgment. Phronesis is judgment embodied in action in particular circumstances; it is "judgment consum-
mated in the efficacy of good praxis."[3] Also, phronesis recognizes a certain balance
between the cognitive and the emotional. It brings reason and passion together
in empathy. The prudent leader is one who can empathize with others.[4]

Figure 1 provides a diagrammatic representation of phronesis. The triangu-
lar interaction of means-ends-praxis takes place within a moral context or ethical
field. There is, for example, a moral dimension to the "means" as well as to the
"ends" and to the particular application of means to ends (praxis). The individual
statesman must always consider proportionality when selecting means to attain
particular ends. The means used to achieve a goal in a particular setting also demand responsibility and accountability on the part of the statesman. Finally, the

ends sought in the context of action must be pursued with a sense of passion, a genuine commitment.

In sum, to exercise phronesis is not only to match means with a policy goal. Phronesis also means to deliberate and act in a way that maintains means, ends, and the conduct of policy in balanced tension. To act prudently, in the idiom of figure 1, is to remain as close as possible to the center of the moral field. Prudence means avoiding proximity to any of the three vertices of the triangle, and it entails the explicit recognition of moral as well as pragmatic dimensions of effective action.

Understood in this broader sense, the practice of prudence in politics is fraught with difficulty. As Ronald Beiner has observed, "Prudence does not guarantee certitude. It recognizes the anxiety of choice in complex circumstances." Martha C. Nussbaum points out that in the world of power and public policy, the attempt to be prudent is "fragile, easily influenced and swayed by external happenings. In its openness to passion and surprise, it risks being overwhelmed by the extreme situation—for appropriate passion, in such a case, can easily become a mind-numbing surge of blind affect, eclipsing deliberation and even coherent discourse."[5] No statesman is always prudent. Over time some have been more prudent than others, yet most have failed to maintain an effective balance among the qualities that define prudence.

To a degree that is rare in international affairs, George Ball exercised prudence in politics. Jean Monnet, Ball's most influential mentor and role model, was himself a masterful practitioner of the politics of prudence. Ball learned from Monnet to practice phronesis in all its dimensions, and his career provides a compelling model of political prudence.

The Determination of Goals: The Giraffe Question

George Ball often related the story of a visit of a small boy and his father to the zoo. During the course of their visit, they came across a tall, long-necked, awkward animal. Pointing at the animal, the father exclaimed, "See, that's a giraffe"—to which the small boy very sensibly responded, "Why?"

George Ball believed deeply in raising the giraffe question, and he criticized governments for failing to do so. He noted that policymakers preoccupied themselves with calculating "how" rather than raising the prior question of "why." In his judgment, it was less that officials failed to see the solution than that they failed to identify the problem. Throughout his career, Ball encouraged presidents and pressured colleagues to think through the purposes of their policies. What were their short-term and, especially, their long-term goals?

Ball abhorred ad hoc policymaking and warned against reactive crisis management. During his career in the Department of State, he frequently criticized the lack of any systematic statement of either general or specific policy goals. Once officials "caught hold of the levers of power in Washington," he once observed, "they all too frequently subordinated objectivity to the exhilaration of working those levers and watching things happen."[6] During the Vietnam war, Ball believed, individuals like Robert McNamara and W. W. Rostow were so busy working the levers and pumping the foot pedals of the engine of state that they failed to note that the huge, shiny American locomotive was rushing full speed toward a dead end.

By raising fundamental questions concerning goals, Ball pointed out, policymakers would necessarily be forced to examine the basic assumptions that lay behind policy decisions. If the assumptions were in error, policy was likely to be flawed. Within this general context, Ball systematically sought to formulate position papers that addressed specific crises by identifying both goals and policy recommendations.

Officially, Ball first began producing such papers at the time of John F. Kennedy's election. Ball's December 1960 task force report on foreign economic policy was his first attempt to identify and formulate U.S. government goals. He drafted similar statements for the Congo in December 1961 and, a few months later, for Vietnam. Following the Cuban missile crisis, Ball prepared a statement that systematically attempted to explain U.S. policy toward Cuba. In 1964 and 1965, he prepared numerous memoranda examining and challenging received wisdom about policy in Vietnam.

Ball's emphasis upon strategic goal-oriented thinking was rooted in his own intellectual experience and development. Furthermore, he saw a world caught in the midst of change. A devoted student of history, Ball believed that in a world that was constantly in the state of becoming, it was necessary continually to develop conceptual guidelines and theoretical frameworks that would enable policymakers to make informed decisions.

Ball's political career had taught him that crises occurred in clusters. This was decidedly the case in the early 1960s, when Ball and his State Department colleagues faced a series of overlapping challenges. During his five years as under secretary and ambassador to the United Nations, Ball addressed issues such as trade policy, European integration, secession in the Congo, missiles in Cuba, conflict in Cyprus, and war in Vietnam. Because the international landscape was cluttered with instances of latent catastrophe, Ball believed that the policymaker required a framework to help decide whether, when, and how to intervene. In such a world, the politics of pragmatism was dangerous: "As we outgrow our old missionary habits we can easily fall into a mindless and automatic pattern of dealing with problems always for the short term, unless, quite self-consciously, we develop a satisfactory conceptual framework in which to fit the jagged edges of our day-to-day decisions. Great as it is, our power is finite, and we need a clear frame of reference to tell us how we can use it best—or whether in given situations we should use it at all."[7]

In comparing Ball's intelligence with that of such colleagues as McNamara, Rusk, McGeorge Bundy, and Kissinger, James Schlesinger has argued that all these men possessed exceptional intellectual "candlepower." Ball, however, had something the others lacked. He had what Schlesinger termed "reflective" intelligence, the innate capacity to compare and contrast, to perceive patterns, to understand the big picture, and to see the interrelationship between the general and the specific.[8]

According to Schlesinger, Ball's reflectiveness went beyond analysis. Whereas the analytical mind sorts out the problem and calculates how best to solve it, the reflective mind continuously questions why this is in fact the appropriate problem to be addressing. Through this reflective capacity, Ball identified and related short and long-term goals and built them into a worldview. In other words, George Ball continuously raised the giraffe question.

Ball's long-term policy goals were formulated within a moral context. Ball's practice of the politics of prudence (phronesis) can be briefly defined as efficacious policymaking designed to promote the good of humankind. He emphasized ethical international behavior and identified three overarching moral goals.[9] First, Ball believed in the principles embodied in the UN Charter, the Geneva Conventions, and in customary international law. Among international human rights, he stressed the importance of the principle of self-determination. Second, Ball contended that governments must reflect the will of the people. Throughout his career, he sharply criticized political oppression and condemned U.S. foreign policy when it supported dictatorial rule. He openly criticized regimes led by such individuals as Diem in Vietnam, Sukarno in Indonesia, Salazar in Portugal, Pinochet in Chile, Makarios in Cyprus, and both the shah and Khomeini in Iran. He criticized U.S. foreign policy when it embraced regimes that prevented political participation. Finally, Ball advocated the peaceful resolution of international conflict. Although he did not rule out force as a last resort, Ball was a lifelong advocate of improved education, skilled communication, and effective negotiation. In this context, he championed such guiding principles as international engagement, regional economic and political integration, and a multilateral approach to global crises.

On the occasion of his eightieth birthday, Ball defined what he meant by American exceptionalism: "There is little exceptional about military strength or economic weight; other nations have also gone far in that direction. What is truly exceptional is moral leadership, which means a firm adherence to principles and the rejection of certain arrogant practices that have now become almost automatic in our political life." Ball went on to quote from George Washington's farewell address: "Observe good faith and justice toward all nations. Cultivate peace and harmony with all."[10]

Besides these important general moral goals, statesmanship also carries with it certain personal moral responsibilities. In his seminal article "Politics as a Vocation," Max Weber identifies three preeminent qualities necessary for statesmanship: passion, a feeling of responsibility, and a sense of proportion.[11] These three qualities fit easily within the framework of phronesis. Passion, as Weber insists, implies commitment, a devotion to a cause or general goal. In this commitment, the statesman is moved by a sense of duty, an obligation to accept responsibility for the attainment of goals and the consequences of success or failure. Finally, the statesman must balance passion and responsibility with a certain objectivity, a cool sense of proportion, a capacity to recognize the consequences for others as a result of one's actions.

Ball met the Weberian tenets of leadership, and he did so within the context of phronesis. In the words of the distinguished diplomat Lucius Battle: "George had an expression that he used about other people, . . . 'fire in the belly.' Well, George had fire in his belly. He had drive and determination and he always had a sense of purpose. He was very courageous and was quite willing to stick his neck out whenever it was necessary."[12] As a statesman, Ball combined passion and purpose.

Weber writes that politicians often fall prey to two deadly sins, a lack of objectivity and irresponsibility. Vanity, "the need personally to stand in the foreground," causes the politician to commit these errors. The practice of politics becomes "purely personal self-intoxication" instead of serving the public good.[13] The leader who subordinates passion for the cause to a preoccupation with his own career and ambitions is incapable of objectivity, eschews any responsibility, seeks power as an end in itself, and loses all sense of proportion. The vice of vanity also weakens one's capacity for empathy, an important ingredient in phronesis.

The successful statesman must possess professional integrity and a degree of altruism and selflessness. Public service must take precedence over personal ambition. Directness, honesty, and the courage to take unpopular positions are also important elements in the morality of statesmanship. George Ball fared well in the related realms of personal integrity and credibility. Associates and subordinates repeatedly referred to him as "candid" and "courageous." In the words of Michael Blumenthal, Ball's greatest quality was that "he had the courage and moral integrity to say what he thought." Ball despised those courtiers and flatterers "whose desire to stay close to the seat of power dominates all else, including the courage to tell the leader what he doesn't want to hear."[14]

Even those whose political philosophy differed sharply from the views of George Ball have emphasized his courageous candor. David Rockefeller, for example, said of Ball: "I think he has a tremendous sense of integrity and believes very strongly in the moral, social, and political principles that he feels are important. He not only stands by them but is very articulate in expressing them. He is prepared to do so even though they are often not popular everywhere else. As a result, he has been very much criticized."[15]

Ball's candor and his willingness to take unpopular positions at some risk to his career can be seen in numerous incidents during his life, both before and after his well-known dissent on the Vietnam war. Already, as a young lawyer in 1951, he agreed to defend Henry Wallace before the McCarran Committee when other well-known lawyers excused themselves from the risky task. During the crises in Vietnam, Cuba, the Congo, and Cyprus, Ball took positions that contradicted the recommendations of such friends and colleagues as Walter Lippmann, McGeorge Bundy, Dean Acheson, Adlai Stevenson, and William Fulbright. As an influential retired senior statesman, Ball publicly opposed U.S. military actions in Panama, Libya, Grenada, and the Persian Gulf. Again, in these instances, he found himself in the minority position.

During the last two decades of his life, Ball sharply and publicly criticized U.S. policy toward Israel and Israel's policy concerning the Palestinians. Ball paid a heavy price for his Middle East stance, which appears to have cost him the secretary of state appointment in the Carter cabinet. Many observers praised Ball's courage, if not his judgment, for the lonely stance he took on the Arab-Israeli issue.[16]

George Ball was an ambitious man with a considerable ego. He enjoyed the practice of politics and the trappings that surrounded power. Unlike many others, however, Ball did not place personal ambition before the public good. He was secure in himself and confident of his skills and talents. These talents included the capacity to transform ideals into realities, to be politically effective, and to use means appropriate to the attainment of the end. Political tactics, as an aspect of phronesis, however, must be practiced within an ethical context.

The Dynamics of Political Tactics

Over the years, George Ball developed a series of interrelated political tactics that enabled him to achieve many of his goals. Personally, he was a hard-working individual of enormous energy. An administrative activist, Ball lived and breathed his work. He stressed thorough preparation and demanded excellence of himself and his associates. Ball's preoccupation with perfectionism is best seen in his meticulous preparation of memoranda, reports, speeches, and policy papers. He believed that factually accurate and cogent presentation facilitated communication and maximized the chances that particular policy recommendations would be accepted.

Within the bureaucracy, Ball identified individuals of talent and expertise and recruited them for his purposes. In formulating policy concerning trade legislation, European integration, the Congo, and Vietnam, Ball put together impressive teams of experts. On trade policy, Ball's aides included individuals like Griffith Johnson, Philip Trezise, Raymond Vernon, and Michael Blumenthal; for support on European integration, he counted on Robert Bowie, Robert Schaetzel, John Tuthill, and Carl Kaysen; on the Congo, Ball relied on the knowledge of Robert Good, Wayne Fredericks, and Lewis Hoffacker; and for policy on Vietnam/Southeast Asia, Ball drew upon the talents of individuals like Allen Whiting.

PRUDENCE AND PERSONAL NETWORKS

Besides possessing such personal and professional characteristics as industry, persistence, preparation, communication, and willingness to consult with experts, Ball developed an impressive capacity to translate ideals into realities by focusing on the human and personal side of politics. In creating and nurturing relationships with knowledgeable, informed, and influential people, Ball stood at the center of a web of overlapping, far-flung personal networks. Like Jean Monnet, who "built up tentacular networks of individuals, powerful and not-so-powerful, on whom he could almost invariably call as occasion demanded," Ball relied heavily upon assiduously cultivated systems of personal relations.[17] In Ball's judgment, the most important network to which he belonged was the Bilderberg group.

Because these networks were extensive, they contained individuals who represented a wide variety of political and intellectual perspectives. This, in turn, exposed Ball to an extensive range of differing opinions. The exposure to competing points of view and alternative policy recommendations is an essential dimension of the politics of prudence. At Bilderberg, Ball interacted with many individuals whose political views frequently differed significantly from his own. From David Rockefeller to Henry Kissinger, from Denis Healey to Margaret Thatcher, Ball found many with whom to disagree and debate at Bilderberg. Ball often thoroughly disagreed with individuals like Eugene Rostow, James Schlesinger, and General Lucius Clay, but he attempted to maintain a dialogue.

George Ball did not join groups indiscriminately. In this sense, he was quite correct when he once stated that he was not a joiner. In spite of published assertions to the contrary, for example, Ball never joined the powerful Trilateral Commission. In the later years of his life, he formed a political discussion group of influential Democrats that met at the Century Club in New York. This group of experienced politicians included Cyrus Vance, McGeorge and Bill Bundy, Arthur Schlesinger, John Brademas, Joseph Califano, and Theodore Sorenson. Ball's Century Club luncheon group discussed political issues and sought to influence policymaking in Washington.

PRUDENCE AND THE SECOND TIER

A second and related aspect of George Ball's political methodology involved his willingness to exert influence quietly from a low-profile position. Although he was not in principle opposed to holding a cabinet post and hoped one day to be appointed secretary of state, he nonetheless appreciated the advantages of wielding power from a less prominent, less visible position. George Ball represented a quintessential example of an individual who shaped U.S. policy from a position in the second tier. Like his mentor, Jean Monnet, Ball was content to sacrifice personal recognition and high-level formal authority in exchange for political influence and longevity.

The second tier is defined as the position in the governmental hierarchy of authority immediately below the level of cabinet secretary. A subcabinet phenomenon, the second tier encompasses a broad and loose band of positions that includes under secretaries, deputy secretaries, ambassadors to critical posts, and special advisers to cabinet ministers. Those who inhabit the second tier are often linkage figures who connect the policymakers to those who implement policy. These linkage figures, therefore, have a hand both in policy formulation and in helping guide the policy through the bureaucracy.

Not all individuals who occupy second-tier positions wield significant power. Nor, for that matter, do all cabinet secretaries wield great power. Much depends on the individuals involved, the attitude of the chief executive, and the circumstances of the day. Through time, however, a number of individuals in the second tier have exercised great power and influence. Often, in particular cases, they have exerted more influence than their formal superiors in the cabinet.

Leading examples of individuals who, like Ball, exerted great influence from second-tier positions include Robert Lovett, John J. McCloy, Will Clayton, David Bruce, Paul Nitze, and George McGhee.[18] Precisely because they did not hold top cabinet posts, these second-tier statesmen exerted influence for many decades. Their influence transcended administrations and political parties. In spite of their differing political ideologies and personalities, the leading members of the second tier all shared a commitment to public service that took precedence over their personal desire for public recognition and fame.

From the second tier, Ball enjoyed enormous flexibility and had the capacity to take the initiative in producing and explaining delicate policy decisions. Because he lacked cabinet rank, his actions could be easily disavowed by an administration under pressure. Yet Ball might still force an issue onto the agenda or change its salience through a well-timed speech or discrete act.

A proactive administrator, Ball often took independent initiatives that resulted in new policy. His Detroit Vietnam speech in April 1962, his role in the anti-Diem telegram episode in August 1963, and his late-night recognition of the new government in Brazil after the coup in March 1964 were all calculated efforts to set policy by fiat. Although one can question the political wisdom of such actions, they reveal Ball's commitment to administrative activism.

Because Ball's locus of power was in the second tier, he was in an excellent position to develop and monitor back channels, informal highways of access that led to the White House itself. Ball used such channels to bring everyone from Jean Monnet to Lewis Hoffacker, a low-level foreign service counsel stationed in Katanga, to meet privately with President Kennedy. He continually arranged for specialists whose views he respected to meet with cabinet secretaries, influential congressmen, and the president himself.

Ball's willingness to submerge himself at a subcabinet level in the bureaucracy is one indication that he was not preoccupied with the need to be a political celebrity. His comfort with the second tier and his possession of the political courage necessary repeatedly to champion unpopular causes demonstrate that Ball did not succumb to what Weber referred to as "vulgar vanity." In spite of a large ego and strong political ambition, Ball resisted the impulse continually to promote himself. Because he believed strongly in public service and the larger public good, Ball kept his personal vanity in check. This enabled him to achieve the rare distinction of meeting the definition of prudent statesman. The question of vanity was one of the major issues that distinguished George Ball from his better-known colleague and nemesis, Henry Kissinger.

Ball and Kissinger: Phronesis v. Realpolitik

Henry Kissinger has been one of the most influential theoreticians and practitioners of U.S. foreign policy in this century. Although Kissinger exerted enormous influence as President Nixon's national security adviser from 1969 to 1975 and as secretary of state between 1973 and 1977, his writings and opinions have helped shape U.S. foreign policy well beyond this period of formal authority. He has been accurately described as the "most influential outside-insider of our time."[19]

Ball and Kissinger: The Personal Record

George Ball first met Henry Kissinger at a conference on atomic energy in Brighton, England, in 1957. Over the following three and a half decades, the two men interacted with one another both personally and politically. Ball was fourteen years older than Kissinger, and he had earlier national political experience and authority. Although both men were committed Bilderbergers, Ball, a founding member, had been attending Bilderberg meetings for many years before Kissinger made his first appearance there.

Over the years, Ball and Kissinger, each sensing a formidable opponent in the other, circled one another warily. From time to time, they cooperated cautiously.

Kissinger, for example, invited Ball to Washington sporadically in the early 1970s to solicit the older man's advice on international issues. Although he believed Kissinger to be a "brilliant man," Ball never admired him. In Ball's words, "I think Henry's problem is an excessive ego. He can't bear not to be the center of adulation." [20] More importantly, Ball believed many of Kissinger's foreign policy ventures to be deeply flawed. He was especially outraged by the Nixon-Kissinger Christmas bombing of North Vietnam and invasion of Cambodia, acts that he considered to be cynical and immoral.

After observing Kissinger's performance in the early years of the Nixon administration, Ball went on the attack. He did so despite his long association with Kissinger and despite Kissinger's attempts to court him. In general Kissinger chose not to confront Ball publicly, but he resented Ball's criticisms. This resentment peaked in 1983 after Ball had written a positive review of Seymour Hersh's *The Price of Power*, a sharply critical study of Kissinger as national security adviser in the Nixon administration.

Although Ball admitted that the Hersh book was an anti-Kissinger polemic "marred by overkill," he judged it a useful antidote to Kissinger's own two-volume "apologia." Ball bitingly wrote, "Even a cult hero as exalted as Henry Kissinger cannot enthrall indefinitely. . . . In spite of Mr. Kissinger's impressive intellectual credentials and the at least transient success of some of his major diplomatic operations, it should by now be evident that he has been accorded excessive adulation—and reveled in it." Ball criticized Kissinger for his acquiescence in "such Orwellian excesses as wiretapping," the Cambodian invasion, and the "shameful Christmas bombing." According to Ball, future historians would not ignore Kissinger's "flattery and dissembling that far exceeded what was traditionally expected of even the most assiduous courtier." [21]

Kissinger was furious about Ball's statements and in an angry personal letter of September 29, 1983, he accused Ball of having gone "beyond any bounds of decency." He attacked Ball for having endorsed a book that was "scurrilous," "dishonest," and "malicious," and for not condemning the "slimy methods" employed by Hersh. In the letter, Kissinger defended himself against the wiretapping and Cambodian charges and concluded that "for years I have turned the other cheek to your ad hominen [*sic*] attacks out of respect for your intelligence and your contribution to our national policy through decades of devoted service." Kissinger wrote that he had never treated Ball with the "disrespect and superciliousness in your approach to me." He then closed the door on any further communication between Ball and himself: "But there is a limit. No reply to this letter is either expected or desired. No further dialogue between us is possible." [22]

Ball was surprised by Kissinger's outburst but made no effort to reestablish communication. On June 5, 1985, however, after Ball had suffered a stroke, Kissinger wrote him a gracious note: "Your caustic but never trivial criticisms have become so much a part of my life that for the sake of my internal balance I need you back in fighting form." Ball responded that he was gratified to receive the letter, since Kissinger's previous communication had concluded "on a note of Vatican-like finality." He told Kissinger that he would soon be back in "fighting form" because "I would not wish to be responsible in any way for disturbing your internal balance." [23]

Ball and Kissinger maintained proper if somewhat aloof relations during the last decade of Ball's life. In February 1989, George and Ruth Ball were invited to a dinner party for Helmut Schmidt hosted by the Kissingers. The Balls felt honored to receive the invitation. Henry Kissinger, on the other hand, was not among those invited to George Ball's eightieth birthday party on January 23, 1990.

Toward the end of Ball's life, he and Kissinger would take opposing positions on important political issues and would debate on national television. But suffering the effects of two strokes and old age, George Ball had lost his effectiveness in public debate. On November 13, 1990, on a *MacNeil-Lehrer News Hour* special concerning the Gulf war, Ball and Kissinger debated one another for the last time in a public forum. Recognizing that his old nemesis was weakened and fading, Kissinger responded with grace and compassion; although he firmly presented his point of view, he chose not to attack Ball and showed him courtesy and respect.

The Midwest Meets Metternich

Henry Kissinger and George Ball represented two different worldviews and two distinct political styles. On the other hand, they shared many personal and political characteristics. Kissinger and Ball were men of exceptional intelligence who wrote elegantly. Both were both well read and had impressive understandings of history. In both cases, their knowledge and interest were tilted heavily in the direction of Europe and the Western world.

Kissinger and Ball were driven men with large egos. Imbued with uncommon energy, both worked ceaselessly and persistently, enjoyed the challenge of politics, and savored the pomp and circumstance that prevailed in the political arena. Both were elitist and both enjoyed bon vivant lifestyles. Within the bureaucracy, Kissinger and Ball understood the value of personal networks and informal contacts. At times their networks overlapped.

Kissinger and Ball understood these similarities and maintained a wary respect for one another. More importantly, however, from the beginning each sensed fundamental differences in the other's character and goals. They clashed at almost every turn and stood in direct opposition to one another on the fundamental issues of the day. George Ball practiced the politics of prudence (phronesis) while Henry Kissinger pursued the politics of personal *realpolitik*.

Although both Ball and Kissinger had well-developed strategies and intellectual frames of reference, their worldviews differed significantly. Ball assumed a world convulsed by change, a world of disconnectedness and incoherence, a world of instability and disorder. He refused to accept the nation-state as a given and believed in the efficacy of economic and political engineering.

Kissinger, too, perceived a changing world, but he placed a high value on international order and believed fervently that the nation-state system remained as important as it had been in the nineteenth century. Although he discussed revolution and change in his writings, as a political actor Kissinger's first principle was continuity. In the words of one of his biographers, Kissinger was "a conservative in the truest sense. He developed an instinctive aversion to revolutionary change."[24]

Besides their very different attitudes toward change, Ball and Kissinger had quite dissimilar political styles. Because of his personal background and the difficult political circumstances in which he had to work, Kissinger became bogged down in the politics of personal maneuver and manipulation. He became pragmatically preoccupied with tactic at the expense of important long-range considerations. Ball has discussed these characteristics of Kissinger's leadership.

One of Secretary of State Kissinger's favorite themes, Ball observed, has been the building of an "international system of order." Yet Ball found that Kissinger neglected the fact that a system of order presupposes common adherence to a recognized set of "ground rules; since his addiction to the tactical opportunity so often diverts him from his ultimate destination, it is impossible to identify the stars from which he takes his bearings. His guiding purpose is, by constantly tinkering with the mechanism, to maintain a shifting balance of power—an act which, unrelated to any body of basic principles, becomes a tour de force with no meaning beyond the virtuosity of the achievement."[25] Ball argued that Kissinger's basic flaw was that "he is, par excellence, a pragmatist who puts primary reliance on the managed play and counterplay of force. It is a policy strictly for the short term." In Ball's judgment, "experience has repeatedly shown that diplomacy based merely on the manipulation of power without reference to any accepted body of rules or principles leaves no permanent monuments."[26]

The differences between Ball and Kissinger reflect more than divergent political styles; they are the product of deep differences in personal experience and political and moral vision. As a political refugee whose family had fled Nazism when he was fifteen years old, Kissinger was understandably insecure and distrustful. In seeking to survive and survive well, he developed a complex methodology of manipulation and maneuver designed to help him to achieve his goals. His reading of the lives and careers of such astute European statesmen as Metternich, Castlereagh, and Bismarck taught him about the realities of power politics. Duplicity, deviousness, and dissembling became part of his political repertoire. In the words of a recent Kissinger biographer: "Kissinger came across as a chameleon—emphasizing different shadings to different listeners and attempting to ingratiate himself to one person by disparaging another. It was more than a negotiating tactic; it was a character flaw."[27]

Ball's early personal experiences could hardly have been more different. Growing up in the secure environment of the American Midwest, where straightforwardness and candor were leading virtues, Ball at an early age developed the confidence and optimism that informed his political activities. Although Ball could be manipulative himself, he found it easier to be direct and was less concerned about self-promotion. He could accept criticism because he was confident and secure. The style of Metternich was quite different from the style of the Midwest.

Because of their clash of personalities, political camps, and worldviews, Ball and Kissinger had difficulty in appraising one another objectively. Kissinger's writings demonstrate that he was far more sensitive and knowledgeable than Ball's sharp critiques concede. In fact, Kissinger's early writings reflect a rare sensitivity to the centrality of phronesis to successful statesmanship. In a trenchant essay in A World Restored, and later in Diplomacy, Kissinger analyzes the strengths and weaknesses of Klemens von Metternich as statesman.

Metternich (1773–1859) was a leading Austrian statesman who exerted influence in Europe for more than four decades. He protected a weak Austria from neighboring predator states by pursuing a shared conservatism in the face of onrushing democratic forces. After the Congress of Vienna, Metternich protected the European status quo through a balance of power system based upon astute diplomatic maneuvering. Kissinger summarized the Austrian leader's achievements as follows: "Metternich's dexterity enabled Austria to control the pace of events for a generation by turning Russia, a country he feared, into a partner on the basis of the unity of conservative interests, and Great Britain, which he trusted, into a last resort for resisting challenges to the balance of power." Metternich's diplomacy, in Kissinger's view, was nonetheless a "live wire act" that involved "juggling" and only succeeded in buying time.[28] Metternich and his system were swept away by the revolutionary movements that tore across Europe beginning in 1848.

Kissinger's assessment of Metternich eerily resembles later evaluations of Kissinger himself by critics like Ball. According to Kissinger, Metternich controlled events "by defining their moral framework." Metternich had goals; "he knew what he wanted."[29] Yet, this "moral framework" was never explicitly defined and in the end it seemed little more than the preservation of the European political status quo. Ball discussed Kissinger's "insistent but rather defensive avowals of moral purpose" and pointed out that "it is hard to find much of a trace of moral endeavor in what [U.S. leaders] have done or sought to do."[30] Many commentators have defined Kissinger's policy initiatives as amoral.

In spite of this "moral framework," Metternich preoccupied himself with personal diplomatic manipulation. According to Kissinger, it was "Metternich's smug self-satisfaction with an essentially technical virtuosity which prevented him from achieving the tragic stature he might have, given the process in which he was involved." Ball, in turn, speaks of Kissinger's "tactical virtuosity," which is no substitute for "a sense of purpose." In Kissinger's words: "So agile was Metternich's performance that it was forgotten that its basis was diplomatic skill and that it left the fundamental problems unsolved, that it was manipulation and not creation." Ball critiqued Kissinger in similar terms: "An enduring structure must be founded on more than the transient friendship of mortal princes or the adroit manipulation of force and counterforce; it must have solid foundations based on conformity to a set of standards widely regarded as equitable."[31]

Finally, Kissinger astutely recognized Metternich's fundamental conservatism and commitment to order. Metternich's policy was "one of status quo *par excellence.*" His policy was "sterile in an era of constant flux. Because he sought tranquillity, . . . the statesman of repose became the prisoner of events."[32] Ball judged Kissinger in the same terms and criticized Kissinger's emphasis upon an international system of order in an era of profound disorder.

Ball's criticisms aside, Kissinger must be judged in historical context. Given the extraordinary challenges of the time, Henry Kissinger's record is mixed. He played a major role in fostering détente with the Soviet Union, negotiated the opening to China, and worked hard to institute nuclear arms agreements. He also achieved some notable short-run success in initiating peace talks in the Middle East and in single-handedly negotiating the end to the explosive 1973 war between Israel and the Arabs.

The situation at the time contributed to Kissinger's reliance upon the manipulative tactics of realpolitik. He served as the United States' chief foreign policymaker during a period when the nation was suffering from its painful embrace of Vietnam on the one hand and from the shocking scandals of Watergate on the other hand. Meanwhile, the United States and the Soviet Union remained locked in ideological, political, and economic combat. Furthermore, President Nixon, flawed and exposed as he was, had a special interest in foreign policy. In these circumstances, Kissinger had little room to work. He had limited opportunity to formulate general carefully framed policy guidelines. In brief, Henry Kissinger plied his diplomatic trade at a time not conducive to the politics of phronesis.

Not always sensitive to the context within which Kissinger toiled, Ball, nonetheless, had two basic reasons for his criticism of Kissinger. The first derived from Ball's forty-year antipathy toward Richard Nixon, a man he considered devoid of principles and integrity. Ball was not in the least surprised by Watergate. Shortly after Nixon's second inauguration on February 8, 1973, Ball gave a speech at the St. Stephen's Club in London to members of the Conservative Party. In answer to a question from the floor about Nixon, Ball responded prophetically: "His administration will destroy itself by its own corruption within a few months. The chemistry is unavoidable; corruption mixed with arrogance leads to carelessness, carelessness to exposure, and exposure to disaster." [33] Kissinger's close association with Nixon contaminated him in Ball's mind.

Most importantly, George Ball based his criticisms on the many foreign policy failures that he attributed directly to Kissinger's policies. Among them, he noted Nixon and Kissinger's cynical drawing out of the Vietnam war, the invasion and secret bombings of Cambodia, the crude interventions in Chile in 1970 and 1973, the mishandling of the 1974 Cyprus crisis, the sellout of the Kurds in 1975, and the piecemeal Middle East negotiations that ignored the major formula for peace, UN Resolution 242. Besides these policy failures, in Ball's view, Kissinger planted the seeds for foreign policy disasters that sprouted after he had left office.

As much as any other case, the tragic rupture in relations between the United States and Iran in the late 1970s illustrates the differences in the two men's modes of exercising prudence in politics. Because Ball directly confronted Kissinger concerning the Iran episode and because the Iran story sharply illustrates the triumph of realpolitik over phronesis, it is a case study worthy of special attention. Furthermore, the policy blunders of the 1970s helped set the stage for conflict and violence between the United States and both Iran and Iraq that carried into the 1990s.

The Iran Imbroglio: The Limits of Realpolitik

Over the years, Henry Kissinger, like Richard Nixon, developed a close personal relationship with the shah of Iran. The shah, in fact, was one of the few foreign heads of state who became part of Kissinger's personal network, a network that included such powerful Americans as Nelson and David Rockefeller, John J. McCloy, Kermit Roosevelt, and a wide number of U.S. politicians and industrialists. Kissinger, who never understood Iranian society and politics and who later repeated the myths that the shah was "progressive," a "dedicated reformer" who "modernized too rapidly," praised the king because he was "for us, that rarest of leaders, an unconditional ally." [34] In fact, the shah was never an "unconditional ally" of the United States, and he was overthrown by his own people because of his increasingly corrupt and oppressive policies.

Beginning in the early 1970s, the shah, encouraged by the attention of U.S. politicians like Kissinger and Nixon, slipped into a mood of megalomania and instituted a reign of fierce repression. Among those whom he and his secret police, SAVAK, singled out for particular attention were Shiite religious leaders, who were jailed, tortured, and executed throughout the 1970s. When the Pahlavi regime attacked the Shiite clerics, it in effect attacked the Iranian people, thus precipitating a revolution.

In May 1972, Kissinger and Nixon visited Tehran and, against the best advice of the Pentagon, gave the shah a blank check to purchase whatever military equipment he desired. In an extraordinary July 25, 1972, memorandum to the secretaries of state and defense, Kissinger stressed the president's position that, "in general, decisions on the acquisition of military equipment should be left primarily to the government of Iran."[35] In other words, the shah, not the United States, would decide what weapons Iran would purchase. George Ball described this Nixon-Kissinger decision as the "1972 act of folly."[36]

Between 1972 and 1977, the shah, encouraged by Nixon and Kissinger, went on an unprecedented $16.2 billion military shopping spree. During these five years, the Iranian defense budget increased from $1.4 billion to $9.4 billion, the shah developed delusions of grandeur, and U.S. arms dealers and contractors descended on Tehran in droves. Relying on personal diplomacy, Kissinger imprudently and shortsightedly bound the United States to the Pahlavi despot on the Persian railroad track just before the revolutionary express came roaring down the rails.[37]

The Kissinger-Pahlavi relationship tightened throughout the 1970s. Besides massive economic agreements signed in the spring of 1975, the United States and Iran cooperated politically as well. In 1975, the shah and Kissinger formulated a cynical foreign policy that sacrificed the Kurds on the altar of realpolitik. In this often-forgotten episode, the United States had funneled $16 million in CIA funds to Kurds in Soviet-supported Iraq in the early 1970s in order to foment unrest. When the geopolitical situation changed in the region and Iran and Iraq signed a peace agreement, the shah suddenly terminated all aid to the Kurds and sealed his borders, trapping the Kurds in the mountains and exposing them to the murderous attacks of the Iraqi army.

The United States supported the shah's decision and turned deaf ears to the Kurds' frantic calls for help. On March 10, 1975, the CIA station chief in the region cabled Washington: "Is headquarters in touch with Kissinger's office on this? If U.S.G. [U.S. Government] does not handle this situation deftly in a way which will avoid giving the Kurds the impression that we are abandoning them they are likely to go public. Iran's action has not only shattered their political hopes; it endangers thousands of lives."[38] Kissinger refused to respond and the United States acquiesced in the betrayal of the Kurds. It was during this grim episode that Kissinger reportedly said, "Covert action should not be confused with missionary work."[39] In pursuing this particular covert operation, however, the United States made a significant gesture in support of an oppressive Iraqi regime led by a strongman named Saddam Hussein.[40]

When the Iranian revolution drove the shah from his country early in 1979, Kissinger placed enormous pressure upon President Carter to provide U.S. asylum for the monarch. Working in concert with David Rockefeller and other powerful friends of the shah, Kissinger played a key role in persuading Carter to admit the shah. After resisting for several months — and against the advice of U.S. diplomats in Tehran — Carter finally permitted the shah to enter the United States. When this act sparked the seizure of the embassy in Tehran and the taking of more than sixty Americans hostage by militant students, Kissinger quickly blamed the Carter administration. He told a Republican governor's conference in Texas that the fall of the shah was an example of a failing foreign policy, calling the Iranian revolution the greatest foreign policy defeat for the United States in a generation. He claimed that the American people were angry over Iran "because they are sick and tired of getting pushed around and sick and tired of seeing America on the defensive."[41]

Kissinger's behavior during the Iran episode particularly rankled George Ball. Ball had followed Iranian affairs for many years, and he was one of the earlier observers who sensed a revolution on the way. Although Ball had at one point represented Pan American Airways for Lehman Brothers in seeking Iranian financial participation for the foundering airline company, he had never joined the ranks of the U.S. establishment "Pahlavites" who uncritically supported the shah.

When Kissinger tried to shunt the entire responsibility for the emotional hostage crisis onto the shoulders of Carter, however, Ball sharply attacked Kissinger in a Meet the Press interview in November 1979: "Had it not been for Mr. Kissinger and a few others making themselves enormously obnoxious for the administration, trying to force the shah into this country, maybe we wouldn't have done it, even for reasons of compassion."[42] Along the same line, columnist Anthony Lewis wrote that "the most striking thing about Kissinger's performance in the Iran affair is its cowardice. He urged the shah's admission to the United States but has taken no responsibility for its result. He has privately assured officials of his support in the hostage crisis and publicly undermined them. In short, Kissinger has sought power without responsibility."[43]

The Iran story stands as an excellent case study of Kissinger's failures and explains what occurs when the process of personal realpolitik takes precedence over prudent leadership. In his policy toward Iran, Kissinger failed to hold the ingredients of phronesis in balance, and his intense vanity violated Weber's ethic of responsibility and proportion. Kissinger and Nixon cobbled together an Iran policy that lacked both long-term goals and any semblance of moral obligation. They viewed Iran and its people, as well as the Iraqi Kurds, as local bargaining chips that could be played against the Soviet Union in the great game of containment.

Kissinger defined Iran as the shah, ignoring the fact that the Persian king was an isolated dictator who was widely hated by his people. In viewing Iran as a geostrategic chip, both Kissinger and Nixon overlooked the obvious internal weaknesses in the country and repeated the shah's biased explanations for the unrest that kept bubbling to the surface. In the words of Stanley Hoffmann: "Kissinger interpreted stability not as the separation between domestic politics and foreign behavior, but as Metternich had done: as requiring the domestic status quo."[44]

The absence of any long-term, morally informed ends was exacerbated by inappropriate, disproportionate, and ultimately ineffective means. Kissinger encouraged the shah's increasing dictatorial and oppressive methodology of rule, which began to veer out of control in 1970. The United States maintained a close relationship with the shah's secret police, the dreaded SAVAK, while providing the government with billions of dollars of military equipment. When the revolution exploded in the late 1970s, Kissinger, this time from outside the government, once again attempted to intervene inappropriately.

Given the manifest failure of Kissinger's Iran and Iraq policy, it is worthy of note that in his two massive volumes of political memoirs totaling twenty-eight hundred pages, Kissinger devoted less than twenty pages to the Iranian revolution and U.S.-Iran relations. In a brisk, defensive discussion in the first volume, Kissinger singled out George Ball for providing a "conventional revisionist view" of the Iran disaster.[45]

In the second volume of his memoirs, Kissinger talked hard-headed realpolitik, stressing that the geostrategic significance of Iran required the United States to maintain a close relationship with the shah. He failed to explain the realpolitik of resting one's interests upon a pillar of sand — no matter how geostrategically significant. When the Iranian sands began to shift, Kissinger, who saw no further into Iran than the shah's throne, was taken by surprise. He criticized the "fashionable" rationale for the revolution that "appealed to liberal cliches about the evil of weapons sales as well as the Shah's *alleged* repressiveness."[46]

Kissinger later concluded that the cause of the revolution was that economic growth had outpaced political development. He admitted that he had not understood this situation. He did not admit, however, that he and President Nixon (and other U.S. policymakers) had encouraged the rapid industrialization of Iran and had intently looked the other way while the shah brutally smothered all attempts at political participation. Henry Kissinger knew very well that the U.S. arms sales contributed to the shah's megalomania and that the "alleged" repressiveness was all too real.

As a skilled practitioner of realpolitik, Kissinger acquainted himself with the criticisms of his policies and over time selectively appropriated the ideas for himself. In the Iran case, he shrewdly borrowed the argument concerning the dialectic between economic growth and political development. He also discovered after the fact the importance of "a new social class," and raised a critical question about change in the developing world: "Do we possess a political theory for the transformation of developing countries?" And, he wrote: "The fact is that we lack a coherent idea of how to channel the elemental forces let loose by the process of development."[47]

In spite of such statements and insights, Kissinger seemed never to absorb these ideas, nor did he place them on his policymaking menu. He presented such learned wisdom as part of his repertoire of defensive tactics designed to deflect criticism from his person and political record. The insights expressed were largely rhetorical. Stanley Hoffmann understood this dimension of Kissinger when he referred to "Kissinger's devilish nimbleness." According to Hoffmann, Kissinger "showed a remarkable talent for undercutting his adversaries by annexing their ideas and leaving them unaware of their sudden nakedness or furious about the delicacy with which their clothes had been removed."[48] This tactic of denying culpability and then carefully co-opting the ideas of one's critics in order to evade responsibility for error may be a clever precept in the code of realpolitik. It is antithetical to the practice of phronesis and is often the sign of the triumph of vanity and the politics of manipulation.

Personal Diplomacy and Vanity in Foreign Policymaking

Henry Kissinger chose to make and shape foreign policy on a personal rather than institutional basis. He preferred to personalize foreign policy problems, not only by taking every conceivable measure to maximize his control over the policy process but by interpreting every challenge as a personal attack. Rushing madly about the world, Kissinger devoted enormous amounts of energy to addressing the many crises that burst forth across the globe. George Ball referred to this style of leadership as "summitry" and the diplomacy of the "lonely cowboy."[49] In spite of his undeniable dedication, personal ingenuity, and political creativity, Kissinger often failed in these quests. There are several reasons why.

Kissinger was a supreme globalist. As the Iran case study has demonstrated, he lacked the will and capacity to understand regional realities. Unlike Ball, who actively sought out area expertise and endeavored seriously to understand local conditions and forces, Kissinger paid little attention to such considerations. He was preoccupied in protecting an overall status quo by balancing constellations of power in a way designed to win the Cold War. Kissinger saw only the forest; he was unconcerned about the trees.

Kissinger's globalist perspective was reinforced by his proclivity to concentrate all power in his own hands. He tended to ignore the advice and wisdom available to him in the government. When he was head of the National Security Council, Kissinger effectively froze out the Departments of State and Defense and alienated Secretaries William Rogers and Melvin Laird. He even came to ignore and contradict his own handpicked coterie of bright young policy analysts, who one after the other became disillusioned and resigned.[50] As a result of his globalism, Kissinger found himself embroiled in constant improvisation and manipulation as he bounced along from crisis to crisis.

In focusing all power in his own hands, Kissinger dealt a death blow to the independent influence of the experienced public servants of the second tier. Although he consulted them from time to time to help with specific tasks, he contributed to their destruction, a process described by Stanley Hoffmann as "the splintering and demoralization, indeed the fading away, of the foreign policy elite." [51] In their place, he installed men of mediocrity, individuals whose behavior was far removed from the essence of phronesis.

By personalizing diplomacy, Kissinger gravitated naturally to authoritarian leaders with whom he felt he could communicate on equal terms. In moving in the heady world of shahs, kings, dictators, generals, and nondemocratic presidents, Kissinger found many anticommunist kindred spirits who supported his containment commitment and who agreed to serve as regional hegemons and surrogates for the United States. Meanwhile, he overlooked the forces of domestic discontent and identified himself and the United States with the status quo throughout the world.

Henry Kissinger respected and admired the shah of Iran and lionized Egyptian President Anwar Sadat, a man he considered a great leader who had "the wisdom and courage of the statesman and occasionally the insight of the prophet." [52] In fact, both the shah and Sadat were mediocre leaders who were hated by many of their own people. Both attempted to carve out exalted places for themselves on the international stage while ignoring the deteriorating situations at home. Both surrounded themselves with corrupt and oppressive functionaries. Sadat, a man who proved himself capable of bold and creative moves internationally, failed to address the problems of his own citizens. In uncritically embracing both the shah and Sadat, Kissinger helped destroy them. The closer they identified themselves with the West, the further they distanced themselves from their own people. The Iranian and Egyptian peoples, however, were unknown to Henry Kissinger.

Finally, Kissinger fell prey to the temptations of vanity. Given his intelligence, influence, and responsibilities, it is not surprising that he developed a bloated ego and accompanying arrogance. In terms of effective statesmanship according to Weber, however, vanity is the most costly of defects because it undercuts judgment, responsibility, and proportionality. It twists the understanding of ends and means and stifles the critical element of morality in public policymaking. Secrecy, deviousness, insecurity, and paranoia often result.

Kissinger had the misfortune of practicing politics during the administration of a leader who represented the very antithesis of phronesis. Richard Nixon, whose personal moral framework was demonstrably deficient, lacked an overarching moral political frame of reference as well. Enormously insecure, he used whatever means necessary to promote his personal agenda and to advance his own ambitions. His vanity expressed itself in a preoccupation with himself and an incapacity to empathize with others. Kissinger's weaknesses were writ large in Nixon.

Together Nixon and Kissinger contaminated the U.S. policymaking environment in unprecedented ways. Intrigue, vicious personal rivalry, distrust, backbiting, back stabbing, eavesdropping, and wiretapping marked the Nixon White House within which Kissinger worked. Nixon and Kissinger formulated foreign policy from a bunker of their own making. Within the bunker, the two leaders competed jealously with one another. Both yearned to be named *Time* magazine's Man of the Year, for example, and worried that the other man would be so named. In 1972, when *Time* named them co–Men of the Year, both were furious.[53]

Insecure in his relationship with Nixon and envious of the influence of Secretary of State Rogers and Secretary of Defense Laird, Kissinger sulked and complained and threatened repeatedly to resign. In 1969, Rogers formulated a promising Middle East peace plan that took his name. Kissinger was not happy. Nixon realized that Kissinger was "basically jealous of any idea not his own, and he just can't swallow the apparent early success of the Middle East plan because it's Rogers'. In fact, he's probably actually trying to make it fail for just this reason. Of all people, he has to keep his mind clean and clear, and instead he's obsessed with these weird persecution delusions."[54] The memoirs of H. R. Haldeman and John Ehrlichman present a picture of a Nixon White House that was reminiscent of the Renaissance Italian courts of Cèsare Borgia and the Byzantine courts of Basil I. The moral components of phronesis were squeezed out of the political equation and the resultant mix of manipulation and self-promotion resulted in a disproportionate reliance upon pragmatic policymaking and realpolitik.

As a result, Kissinger, working almost frantically, struggled to address international crises largely by himself. He exhibited resilience and shrewdness as he raced from crisis to crisis, but other than keeping his eyes on the Soviet Union and China, he lost his bearing. He failed in Chile by promoting an embarrassing and heavy-handed covert intervention, in Iran by supporting a corrupt and oppressive status quo, and in Cyprus by indecision and inattention. In all three cases, he never understood the internal social forces and viewed developments through the distorted lenses of U.S.-Soviet relations. Kissinger mistakenly saw the hand of Soviet manipulation even in the Iranian revolution.[55] The problems were compounded by the fact that Kissinger refused to consult the area expertise that was available to him in Washington.

In the insecure Byzantine atmosphere of the Nixon White House, Kissinger survived by relying heavily upon the politics of manipulation. In confronting a dangerous world and lacking both a strategic and moral compass, he adopted many of these same techniques of the politics of intrigue. Ultimately, he became a reactive, defensive practitioner of realpolitik who relied heavily upon the instruments of force and in many instances misread the future. In the words of Stanley Hoffmann, Henry Kissinger was "cautious and curiously shortsighted and 'pragmatic.' . . . His was the loneliness of the short-distance runner."[56]

Prudence and Prescience: George Ball as Phronemos

Ball's prudential approach to politics and public policy carried an important predictive component. He possessed intellectual characteristics that helped foster these skills in prognostication. His reflectiveness predisposed him to pose critical questions and to perceive patterns and relationships. Unlike Kissinger, Ball was not preeminently a globalist. At the same time, he avoided the narrow vision of the regionalist who sees the individual tree but is unaware of the forest. Ball was relatively successful in balancing globalism and regionalism. Like Kissinger, he had globalist tendencies. Unlike Kissinger, he sought to remain sensitive to local conditions and regional realities.

Because Ball was keenly aware of the variety of possible goals and was carefully attentive to the consequences of the means employed to attain these goals in a particular context, he established an impressive record in predicting political outcomes. Furthermore, Ball's underlying premise that humankind lived in a world caught in the midst of fundamental transformation encouraged him to look for underlying patterns and processes and to think dynamically.

Political Prognosticator

In 1989, on the occasion of George Ball's eightieth birthday, Oxford University Chancellor Roy Jenkins described him as "the man who has been more nearly right on every major foreign policy issue of the past forty-five years than anyone else I know."[57] Jenkins's tribute is worth exploring. From his early support for the Chunnel project, designed to link France and England by an underwater tunnel, to his grave warnings about the prospects of U.S. intervention in Vietnam, to many lesser-known prognostications, George Ball possessed a rare prescience.

In 1956, Ball served as a legal adviser for a company that sought to build a tunnel beneath the English Channel. Even though this effort came to naught, Ball believed strongly in the idea and predicted that it was only a matter of time before such a tunnel was dug—regardless of the economic, engineering, and political obstacles. In his memoirs, which he began writing in the late 1970s, Ball declared that "I am confident that [the tunnel] will, sooner or later, be built, simply because the logic is so compelling."[58]

On June 28, 1991, jubilant workers broke through the last barrier of chalk marl and linked French and British rail tunnels. The channel tunnel is the world's longest tunnel system, stretching from Folkestone, England, to Calais, France. On November 14, 1994, the first passenger train left Folkestone for France. Traveling eighty-seven miles per hour, the locomotive known as Le Shuttle arrived thirty-five minutes later at the platform in Coquelles. In spite of perplexing engineering problems, political disagreements, and a final price tag of over $15 billion, the Chunnel had become a reality. George Ball was delighted but not surprised.

In the arena of international politics, George Ball foresaw the collapse of the Soviet Union and the end of the Cold War long before most Soviet specialists. Even Henry Kissinger, who prided himself on his knowledge of the Soviet Union, reluctantly admitted that he was surprised by the collapse of the Soviet system.[59]

In 1972, Ball made his first visit to the Soviet Union at the encouragement of Michael Blumenthal. Accompanied by their wives, Ball and Blumenthal traveled together to Moscow, where they met with a wide spectrum of Soviet citizens and leaders. After several days in the Soviet Union, Ball shared his impressions one evening at the Hotel Metropole. Shaking his head, he observed, "This is not working. They're not going to make it. This place is going to blow apart. It is only a matter of time. We don't have to view the Soviets as a serious threat because this system is simply not going to survive."[60] Ball had analyzed the demographics, the economic situation, the political system, and stressed the potential problems of the diverse nationalities. Ball's conclusions surprised Blumenthal, who has pointed out that Ball made these predictions during the darker days of the Cold War, when such opinions were simply not heard.

A few years later, Ball sharpened his predictions concerning the Soviet Union. In his autobiography, he wrote of the "fading appeal" of the communist ideology, which "no longer serves as a binding agent to prevent the curdling of this bouillabaisse of diverse races, cultures, and histories." Ball went on to write that "as the Kremlin is increasingly forced back on nationalism . . . it incites counternationalisms." He then warned about the coming detachment and disintegration of Eastern Europe, "where similar resentments are seething. With Moscow losing authority as the Vatican for an international ideology and depending once more on a chauvinistic love for 'Mother Russia,' such discontent can only increase."[61]

At the beginning of 1988, George Ball proposed to entitle a speech to be given at the College of William and Mary "The Cold War is Ended." The lecture organizers, considering such a title unrealistic, changed it to the more cautious "Foreign Policy as the Cold War Fades." Ball's prognoses concerning the dramatic developments in the Soviet Union, although less well known, are perhaps even more impressive than his predictions about the Vietnam war.

Ball also foresaw many political outcomes across the developing world with surprising accuracy. After a visit to northern Africa in 1953, he warned his influential friends in France of the powerful forces of nationalism and independence that were at work in that part of the world. He recommended that France give Algeria its independence or face a rebellion that the French could not put down. In a 1958 speech, Ball sensitively summarized France's losing battle to keep its colonies: "This has been a King Canute kind of war—a futile struggle to turn back giant waves of nationalism beating against colonial structures weakened by the World War. It has been a war against a historic process, the falling away of the various parts of the French Empire, just as other empires have disintegrated within our lifetime." [62]

In 1963, Ball carried the same message to Antonio Salazar, the Portuguese dictator and a former professor of economics. After a lengthy meeting and exchange of letters with Salazar, Ball described him as "one of the more interesting minds of the 16th century." Portugal was ruled, quipped Ball, "by a triumverate consisting of Vasco de Gama, Prince Henry the Navigator, and Salazar." He telegraphed his friend Ken Galbraith that "having just spent two days with Salazar, I now know what it means to give serious political responsibilities to a professor of economics." [63]

In a fifteen-page October 21, 1963, letter to Salazar, Ball warned that "the political structure of a large part of the world is in a state of rapid transition. The old order is changing with irresistible momentum. The new, to which it gives way, is not yet in place." Ball used the Algerian example as a case of why Portugal should begin loosening its colonial control over its territories in Africa. Stressing the importance of "self-determination," Ball wrote that the colonial experience taught that "wherever the problem has been met solely by military means the colonial power has sooner or later given up the struggle." Although the Portuguese could maintain military control for some time in places like Angola and Mozambique, "the accumulating cost of resistance in terms of blood and resources, the disruption of normal life . . . and the ugly and intensifying manifestations of a protracted racial conflict—all these can lead to a situation in which the game is no longer worth the candle." Ball concluded: "You believe that time works in your favor; we do not." [64]

Ball's unusual record of political foresight is a characteristic of the statesman who practices phronesis. While the practitioner of realpolitik often becomes mired in the process of manipulation, the prudent statesman never loses sight of the context and moral meaning of political activity. The politician of realpolitik often loses the capacity to see ahead and becomes preoccupied both with short-term survival and short-term reactive policymaking. Furthermore, the struggle for personal political survival near the seat of power can feed egocentric predispositions and lead to the vice of vanity.

Ball, like Kissinger, was aware of his own brilliance and could be intellectually arrogant. He disliked small talk and often tuned out individuals he considered intellectually inferior. Nonetheless, Ball seldom lost his perspective; he resisted most temptations for self-promotion, and he remained committed to a broad conception of the public good. Unlike Kissinger, Ball was reasonably content to work in the second tier. Kissinger was not a second-tier personality; for him, it had to be first tier, center stage. A mutual European friend of Ball and Kissinger who carefully read their many writings observed that Ball's contributions were more direct than those of Kissinger. According to Eric Roll, Ball's convictions were obvious, while Kissinger prepared his publications "as if he were writing a job description for himself."[65]

Ball seldom hesitated to take unpopular positions that he knew would be costly to his political aspirations. He managed to keep his ego and ambitions under control. Ball was a team player and over the years unconsciously developed a large and dedicated group of talented followers. In marked contrast to the Kissinger experience, Ball's colleagues, with few exceptions, genuinely liked and respected him. Bill Bundy has stated, "I've never known anybody who worked closely with George who was not admiring and fond of him. He was a hero to his assistants."[66]

The philosophers and scholars of phronesis have correctly pointed out that the practice of prudence is often fragile and fleeting. No statesman practices it to perfection. All leaders have weaknesses and make mistakes. They can easily lose sight of their moral goals; moral vision can slip into moralism and polemicism; the means can become ends in themselves; and the temptation to vanity is ever present. The statesman's knowledge and understanding may be imbalanced and imperfect and, if unwilling to admit this, the leader may not recruit the necessary expertise.

Flaws and Failures

In spite of his impressive record as a statesman of prudence and practical wisdom, George Ball had important limitations and weaknesses. First, his understanding of the world was Eurocentric. Not surprisingly, given his long commitment to themes of European integration and the experience of two world wars on that continent, Ball viewed the world through the lens of Europe. His interest in the developing world of Asia, Africa, the Middle East, and Latin America was dictated by policy crises that occurred there. He had little interest in Latin America and turned his attention to Southeast Asia, the Middle East, and Africa only when serious political and economic problems affecting the United States and Europe surfaced in these regions. Ball questioned U.S. intervention in Vietnam in part because he considered Southeast Asia of only peripheral interest to the United States.

Ball's interest in the Soviet Union and China was also peripheral. He analyzed the Soviet Union—a country he had no interest in visiting until urged to do so by Michael Blumenthal in the 1970s—in terms of the nuclear threat it posed to Europe and the United States. He was even less interested in China. After the collapse of the Soviet Union in the 1990s, Ball believed that there were now only three power centers in the world—the United States, Europe, and Japan. When asked specifically about China, he dismissed the huge nation as little more than a large underdeveloped land mass.[67]

Ball often used his keen wit to respond to the criticisms charging him with European ethnocentrism. When the journalist Joseph Alsop attacked Ball's knowledge of Asia, claiming that it could be put in a thimble, he responded: "You've got the receptacle wrong. My knowledge of Asia should not be thought of as contained in a thimble but a soup plate; it is at once both wider and more shallow than you suggest." [68]

In one of his best-known quotations, George Ball explained the life of Washington foreign policymakers. When he was in the State Department, he stated, "I was awakened once or twice a month by a telephone call in the middle of the night announcing a *coup d'etat* in some distant capital with a name like a typographical error." [69]

Although these observations represent examples of Ball's wit, they also reflect a certain insensitivity to the world beyond Europe and the United States. Although Ball was well traveled, 90 percent of his trips were to Europe, where he spent most of his time in London, Paris, Brussels, Bonn, and Rome. He preferred to travel in style, to reside in the finest hotels, to eat in the best restaurants, and to weave in and out of the circles of European dignitaries. He loved to fly by private plane and on occasion he accompanied David Rockefeller to Europe aboard Rockefeller's jet. For George Ball, the accommodations and personal associations provided by Bilderberg set the standard.

When Ball occasionally visited the countries of Asia, the Middle East, Africa, and Latin America, he hobnobbed almost exclusively with the political and economic elites. He made little effort to travel into the hinterlands, to interact with the population at large, to penetrate beneath the upper crust of society. Furthermore, Ball's foreign friends and acquaintances were overwhelmingly European. The handful of friends that he had outside of Europe were well-to-do intellectuals from countries like Iran and Israel.

George Ball was an elitist. Although he never forgot his humble midwestern roots, he preferred the excitement and aroma of power in places like Washington, New York, London, and Paris. Over the years, he came to view lecture trips back to the Midwest somewhat like missionary expeditions designed to educate the natives. In 1970, for example, when George prepared to give a speech in Chicago, Ruth Ball observed: "George is going to educate the Middle West if it is at all possible." On another occasion in 1973, she described a trip by George to Illinois as another of "George's efforts to educate the Middle West." In March 1980, Ruth wrote that George had gone to Florida, "there mounting the dais again for whoever the yokels were who needed to see the light not in the Baptist sense." At one point, Ruth complained that "George just keeps struggling as the majority of human kind play golf or stupidly view the boob tube." [70]

Although George Ball listed popular support and political participation among the principles that undergirded his policy framework, his writings and activities reveal that he did not place special emphasis upon issues of equity and egalitarianism. In his publications focusing upon the greatest future challenges to humankind, he emphasized demographic, environmental, and immigration problems. In his last unpublished manuscript, Ball warned especially about the computer revolution and the costs that would have to be paid when technological change increasingly outran human development. He cherished America's democratic tradition but did not emphasize the issue of political participation beyond the borders of the United States.

In his emphasis upon free trade and multinational corporations as instruments for a world order of peace and prosperity, Ball did not concern himself with their impact upon the various groups and classes that composed the societies. He tended to ignore such issues as distribution of income, domestic economic exploitation, social justice, and political participation. Because he did not have a populist bone in his body and had no firsthand experience of living conditions in much of the developing world, Ball stood somewhat aloof from the situation of the masses.

On another level, George Ball had a tendency toward dogmatism. Once he decided to take a position, he often dug in and ignored the countervailing arguments and evidence. Over time he would reinforce his arguments and present them to the public through his elegant use of the English language. He had a knack for putting together a rigorous brief and then arguing it in the most persuasive terms possible. In the process, he continually buttressed his own opinion of the issue at hand. Ball's perceptive British friend, Eric Roll, explained this dogmatic quality: "Once convinced of a position, George can clothe that position so elegantly that this very elegance becomes itself an impediment to his ever changing the original opinion. It becomes a kind of manifesto."[71]

This characteristic inflexibility carried over to his views of certain individuals. Once he formed a strong opinion of a person, he almost never changed his mind. He thoroughly disapproved of and disliked individuals like Richard Nixon, Spiro Agnew, Zbigniew Brzezinski, and Henry Kissinger. Many observers, some of them highly critical of Kissinger themselves, felt that Ball had overdone it with Henry. Kissinger seemed to have become a preoccupation with Ball.

Closely related to this occasional intellectual inflexibility was Ball's proclivity to overstate his position. Ball's stance on the Arab-Israeli issue was a case in point. Dean Rusk, David Rockefeller, and George Springsteen, who shared Ball's views on U.S. Middle East policy, believed that his outspoken criticisms of Israel weakened his case and hampered his effectiveness.[72] Earlier in his career, Ball had adopted similarly inflexible positions with respect to the European Defense Force, the Multilateral Force, and Charles de Gaulle and Gaullist policies.

Finally, Ball could on occasion become manipulative within the bureaucratic context. In attempting to achieve a certain goal or implement a specific policy, he at times lost perspective and sense of proportion. His calculating intervention in the August 1963 cable that led to the overthrow and death of Diem in South Vietnam is an example of Ball's occasional capacity for the ill-advised manipulation of the levers of power.

George Ball's leadership flaws and weaknesses were mitigated to a certain degree by other factors and considerations. Although Ball himself may have been Eurocentric and less well informed about the rest of the globe, he successfully enlisted the assistance of the best area specialists available. He relied heavily upon such expertise when formulating his ideas about Vietnam, Cuba, the Congo, Israel, Iran, and the Arab world. With his insatiable intellectual curiosity and his capacity to raise important questions, Ball developed an impressive understanding of many non-Western societies. His stress on the premise of a world in transformation, his insistence upon thinking strategically, and his consultations also helped him overcome his elitism.

Eric Roll and others who criticized Ball's dogmatism also admitted that Ball was usually correct in his policy analysis and recommendations. Peter Peterson agreed: "There are plenty of futurists making predictions, but the melancholy fact is that they're wrong most of the time. George has the happy faculty of being right most of the time."[73] Nonetheless, as Roll also correctly pointed out, Ball did not have a perfect record. He misread situations and made mistakes as well. When he did, he was slow to admit them.

Michael Blumenthal has pointed out that Ball's sometimes stubborn demeanor is explained by the fact that he often found himself in embattled minority positions. In these circumstances, he reacted to relentless pressure by both hardening and overstating his stance. Furthermore, Ball tended to carry a certain passion with his convictions. He would "charge ahead" with his views when it might have been better both for him and for his cause if he had been a little more cautious. "He didn't pull his punches," Blumenthal acknowledged.[74] Nonetheless, this very passion reflected honesty, courage, and integrity, and this in turn brought Ball respect and credibility.

Statesmanship in an Age of Transformation

In a world in the midst of fundamental transformation, prudent statesmen are especially in demand. Disconnected idealists and visionaries like Adlai Stevenson, Eugene McCarthy, and, to a lesser degree, Jimmy Carter, despite their admirable commitment to goals and good, fall short of statesmanship. They fail in the real world of politics; their wisdom is impractical. On the other hand, the many practitioners of realpolitik, preoccupied as they are with the manipulation of power, either lack appropriate goals or lose sight of such goals. The moral component of politics is sacrificed on the altar of political expediency. Means become ends in themselves. Lyndon Johnson, Richard Nixon, and Henry Kissinger fall into this category.

Genuine statesmen are individuals of prudence and prescience, of purpose and practicality, of proportionality and morality. The essence of statesmanship is phronesis, prudence defined as practical wisdom with an essential moral component. The prudent statesman must resist the temptations of vanity, temptations that cut across ideologies, geographical boundaries, and leadership styles. Both the missionaries of idealism and the politicians of realpolitik can easily fall prey to the destructive vice of vanity.

George Ball stands as a rare and realistic model of the prudent statesman. He epitomized all of the major characteristics of the phronemos. Ball had vision and carefully formulated and articulated goals. He accepted as a fundamental premise of all policy formulation the reality of a dynamic and transforming world. Ball's predictive record was extraordinary.

At the same time, Ball understood power and authority and recognized the importance of having the capacity to translate goals into realities. Above and beyond these characteristics, George Ball believed in a set of moral principles that infused his goals and upon which he based his political activities. Finally, Ball kept his considerable ego under control and resisted the impulse to vanity and self-promotion. He had the courage to take unpopular and iconoclastic positions at a considerable cost to his political and professional career.

Like all statesmen, George Ball had flaws. He did not always successfully practice phronesis. As an elitist and establishment man, his understanding of the developing world and the cry of its citizens for democracy and equity went only so far. At times he could be extremely manipulative, stubborn, and unyielding in his opinions and ideas.

Ball's blemishes, however, did not undermine his position as a leader of prudence and practical wisdom. The exercise of phronesis does not imply perfection. Furthermore, Ball's weaknesses were largely peripheral to the qualities that define the essence of phronesis. Great statesmen are rare because the true phronemos is rare. The measure of Ball's success is found in the causes he struggled for, his uncanny capacity to see ahead and to sense correctly the contours of the future, his willingness to subordinate personal advancement to the public good, his uncommon courage and conviction, his excellent reputation among those with whom he worked and, above all, the conduct of his statecraft—the balance he maintained between passion, proportion, and responsibility.

Notes

Prologue

1. This prologue, a dramatization of events in the Oval Office on July 21, 1965, as witnessed by Under Secretary of State George W. Ball, is based on a wide range of primary and secondary sources. The detailed discussion that took place in the Cabinet Room meetings is reported in Jack Valenti's notes of meeting; Chester Cooper's July 22, 1965, memorandum for the record in the meeting notes files; Horace Busby's July 21, 1965, memoranda for the president in Busby's office files; William Bundy's unpublished manuscript on Vietnam in the Papers of William P. Bundy; and William Bundy's oral history transcript prepared by Paige Mulhollan. All of these documents are on deposit at the Lyndon B. Johnson Presidential Library in Austin, Texas. These documentary records have been supplemented by personal interviews with George Ball and with four other individuals (Dean Rusk, Cyrus Vance, McGeorge Bundy, and William Bundy) who were present in the Cabinet Room that day. Other sources consulted include President Lyndon Johnson's daily diary for July 21, 1965, Secretary of State Dean Rusk's desk calendar for that same date, Mrs. Ruth Murdoch Ball's personal diaries, the personal papers of George Ball, photographs of those present around the table, and personal interviews with Dr. Douglas Ball, a professional historian and a son of George Ball.

The meetings of July 21 have also been discussed in a number of other studies, the most noteworthy being Jack Valenti, *A Very Human Presidency* (New York: W. W. Norton, 1975), pp. 319–40; Clark Clifford with Richard Holbrooke, *Counsel to the President: A Memoir* (New York: Random House, 1991), pp. 411–13; and especially the definitive official history of the Vietnam war, Congressional Research Service, Library of Congress, U.S. Senate, Committee on Foreign Relations, 100th Congress, 2d Session, *The U.S. Government and the Vietnam War: Executive and Legislative Roles and Relationships*, part 3 (Washington, D.C.: U.S. Government Printing Office, 1988), pp. 399–407. Secondary sources that discuss the July 21 meetings from interesting analytical perspectives include Brian VanDeMark, *Into the Quagmire: Lyndon Johnson and the Escalation of the Vietnam War* (New York: Oxford University Press, 1991), pp. 180–92; and Larry Berman, *Planning a Tragedy: The Americanization of the War in Vietnam* (New York: W. W. Norton, 1982), pp. 94–111. For Ball's own account of the meetings, see his autobiography, *The Past Has Another Pattern: Memoirs* (New York: W. W. Norton, 1982), pp. 399–402. Finally, Lyndon Johnson has his own brief description of the July 21 sessions in *The Vantage Point* (New York: Popular Library, 1971), pp. 144–48. Most descriptions of the July 21 meetings are based primarily on notes taken by Jack Valenti. Although useful, these notes are not comprehensive and must be supplemented by other sources.

In his 1995 assessment of the Vietnam war, Robert McNamara does not specifically discuss the July 21 meetings. He does frankly admit, however, that "subsequent events proved my judgment wrong." In his words: "all senior national security officials" supported the decision to escalate, "except George Ball." McNamara, *In Retrospect: The Tragedy and Lessons of Vietnam* (New York: Times Books, 1995), p. 204.

Although historians and political actors of the day have engaged in a debate concerning whether Lyndon Johnson had in fact made up his mind to escalate the war before the July 21, 1965, meetings, such discussion, interesting as it is, is not central to this dramatization. This story focuses primarily upon the perspective of George Ball and only secondarily upon the intentions of Lyndon Johnson.

Ball's eight memoranda of warning referred to in the text included "How Valid are the Assumptions Underlying our Vietnam Policies?" (October 5, 1964); "Vietnam" (February 1965); "Should We Try to Move Toward a Vietnamese Settlement Now?" (April 21, 1965); "A Plan for a Political Resolution in South Vietnam" (May 1965); "Keeping the Power of Decision in the South Vietnam Crisis" (June 18, 1965); "United State Commitments Regarding the Defense of South Vietnam" (June 23, 1965); "A Plan for Cutting our Losses in South Vietnam" (June 28, 1965); and "A Compromise Solution in South Viet-Nam" (July 1, 1965). These memoranda are all contained in a black looseleaf notebook entitled "Vietnam Papers," Personal papers of George Ball.

Chapter 1. Personal Roots and Rites of Passage

1. These exchanges between George Ball and Presidents Kennedy and Johnson are related in a number of published and unpublished sources. See, for example, Ball's autobiography *The Past Has Another Pattern: Memoirs* (New York: W. W. Norton, 1982), pp. 366, 407. This source is hereafter cited as Ball, *Past*. Ball has confirmed and described these incidents in personal interviews with the author (e.g., September 14, 1988, interview in Princeton, N.J.).

2. Harvey Arden, "Iowa, America's Middle Earth," *National Geographic* 159 (May, 1981), 603. On the culture and people of Iowa, see George F. Parker, *Iowa: Pioneer Foundations*, 2 vols. (Iowa City: State Historical Society, 1940). Two sources describe the Toledo, Tama County, and Marshalltown region of Iowa: Janette Stevenson Murray, *They Came to North Tama* (Lake Mills, Iowa: Graphic Publishing, 1953); and George Mills, *Rogues and Heroes from Iowa's Amazing Past* (Ames: Iowa State University Press, 1972), esp. pp. 119–36.

3. Robert F. Sayre (ed.), *Take this Exit: Rediscovering the Iowa Landscape* (Ames: Iowa State University Press, 1989), p. 19.

4. Raymond D. Gastil, *Cultural Regions of the United States* (Seattle: University of Washington Press, 1975), p. 218.

5. These phrases are quoted from Gastil, *Cultural Regions*, p. 220.

6. In an August 30, 1954, letter to Adlai Stevenson, Ball assessed a Stevenson speech in the following terms: "As a farmer myself, I thought the Sioux Falls speech was superb." When described as "aristocratic" by *Time* magazine, Ball protested vehemently: "Aristo-

cratic? Now I don't dare show my face at the Thirty-Fifth Reunion of the class of '22 at the Wallace Public School in good old Des Moines." Letter to George Harris, *Time*, March 28, 1956.

7. Most of the information in these sections on the Ball family has been drawn from numerous unpublished family papers, letters, genealogical documents, and personal interviews. Because of their fascination with history and genealogy, the Balls maintained an exceptionally rich cache of family documents.

8. Ball, *Past*, pp. 2–3.

9. Ibid., p. 3.

10. *Wichita Evening Eagle*, August 12, 1931.

11. Ibid.

12. Paul H. Giddens, *Standard Oil Company (Indiana): Oil Pioneer of the Middle West* (New York: Appleton-Century-Crofts, 1955), pp. 528–41. Ball's name appears often in this comprehensive study of Standard of Indiana.

13. Daniel Yergin, *The Prize* (New York: Simon and Schuster, 1992), p. 217.

14. Colonel Stewart had received $760,000 in Liberty Bond kickbacks on oil purchases made through his own company. The money was paid out through a dummy instrument called the Continental Trading Company. For entertaining descriptions of this episode and the Stewart-Rockefeller conflict, see Peter Collier and David Horowitz, *The Rockefellers: An American Dynasty* (New York: New American Library, 1976), pp. 160–69; and Yergin, *The Prize*, pp. 216–18. For an account of the Teapot Dome scandal, see M. R. Werner and John Starr, *Teapot Dome* (New York: Viking, 1959). For the discussion of Colonel Stewart's involvement in the episode, see especially pp. 252–72.

15. See reminiscences by Hilda Hanks Bauquier, as provided by Marion Ball Tramel. The second-hand clothing assistance is referred to in a personal letter from Amos Hanks to George Ball, July 22, 1986. In this communication, Amos Hanks recalls wearing "some of your old clothes" and signs off "with apologies for sixty years of silence."

16. Personal interview with John Ball, Williamsburg, Va., May 3, 1994. This account was confirmed by Douglas Ball in subsequent interviews.

17. Ruth Murdoch Ball, unpublished history of the Ball family, begun in 1959, p. 16.

18. Telephone interview with Douglas Ball, December 10, 1994.

19. Personal interview with Douglas Ball, Princeton, N.J., January 28, 1990.

20. Ball, *Past*, p. 7.

21. Stuart Ball, "Ball Family: Early Life in Des Moines," notes dictated, March 1977, ch. 2, p. 1.

22. George's wife, Ruth Murdoch Ball, is the source of this story. Her personal diaries, which consist of nearly one thousand pages of daily descriptions, are an extremely rich source. Ruth Ball began writing the diaries in 1959 and continued until the middle of 1985. The first 230 pages of the diaries recount in detail the earlier years (1909–58) in the life of George Ball. The Ruth Ball diaries are hereafter referred to as *R.B. Diaries*. The supper table incident is discussed in vol. 1, ch. 1, p. 3 of the *R.B. Diaries*.

Ruth Ball hoped one day to publish a book based on her diaries, and she produced various drafts of a manuscript about the life and times of George Ball. The most recent version of these drafts is 118 pages in length and is incomplete. It is hereafter referred to as Ruth Ball, *Ball Family History*. The supper table incident is described on p. 3 of this source as well.

23. Stuart Ball, "Ball Family," ch. 2, p. 2.

24. Ball, *Past*, p. 11.

25. Ball, *Past*, pp. 13–14. The "cheerless" Rousseau quotation is found on p. 11.

26. Ibid., pp. 14–15.

27. Ibid., p. 16.

28. The two quotations in this paragraph are taken from Ruth Ball, *Ball Family History*, pp. 30, 34.

29. Ibid., pp. 34–36.

30. Personal interview with Ruth Ball, Princeton, N.J., February 18, 1989.

31. Both quotations are taken from a three-page biographical statement prepared by Ruth Ball in the mid-1960s and titled, "A Biography."

32. Ruth Ball, *Ball Family History*, Foreword.

33. *R.B. Diaries*, vol. 5, p. 10.

34. Sources: Douglas Ball, from eulogy delivered at Ruth Murdoch Ball's memorial service, Fifth Avenue Presbyterian Church, New York, September 24, 1993; *R.B. Diaries*, vol. 4, p. 38 (1974); and Helen Vahey, personal interview, New York, January 7, 1992.

35. Personal interview with John Ball, Williamsburg, Va., May 3, 1994.

36. *R.B. Diaries*, vol. 1, ch. 28, pp. 33–34, 59; vol. 7, p. 188 (1980).

37. The quotations in these three paragraphs are drawn from *R.B. Diaries*, vol. 1, ch. 4, pp. 53–55; and Ruth Ball, *Ball Family History*, pp. 54–55.

38. *Chicago Sun-Times*, October 26, 1952. See also *Chicago Daily Tribune*, October 25, 1952.

39. Personal interview with George Ball, Princeton, N.J., February 17, 1989.

40. Telephone interview with Marion Ball Tramel, January 18, 1995.

41. Ball, *Past*, p. 18.

42. The quotations in the paragraph are from *R.B. Diaries*, vol. 1, ch. 4, p. 67.

43. U.S. Strategic Bombing Survey, *The Effects of Strategic Bombing on the German War Economy* (Washington, D.C.: Overall Economic Effects Division, October 31, 1945). Document provided by John Kenneth Galbraith. An earlier summary report published on September 30, 1945, had been somewhat more positive concerning the efficacy of the allied bombing campaign. Galbraith has written that "the Air Force cooperated enthusiastically with a view to controlling the findings. In this it did not altogether succeed." See Galbraith, "Albert Speer was the Man to See," *New York Times Book Review*, January 10, 1971, pp. 2 ff.

44. Personal interview with John Kenneth Galbraith, Cambridge, Mass., April 19, 1995.

45. Galbraith, "Albert Speer," p. 2.

46. Ball, *Past*, p. 48.

47. *R.B. Diaries*, vol. 1, ch. 7, p. 117.

48. Personal interview with John Ball, Williamsburg, Va., May 3, 1994.

49. Ibid.

50. *R.B. Diaries*, vol. 4, ch. 1, p. 41.

51. Quotation from telephone interview with Douglas Ball, January 15, 1995.

52. Personal interview with John Ball, Williamsburg, Va., May 3, 1994.

53. Personal letter, George Ball to Douglas B. Ball, April 30, 1986.

54. Personal interview with George Ball, Princeton, N.J., September 14, 1988.

55. *R.B. Diaries*, vol. 1, ch. 6, p. 119.

56. Ibid.

57. Personal letter from George W. Ball to Jerome E. Hyman, January 25, 1990. The Stiles quotation is from *Cleargolaw News*, vol. 36 (July 25, 1994), p. 29. This issue of the

Cleary, Gottlieb publication is devoted entirely to George Ball. It includes statements of remembrance by ten of Ball's past colleagues at the firm. For an excellent source on the history and personalities of Cleary, Gottlieb, see Leo Gottlieb, *Cleary, Gottlieb, Steen and Hamilton: The First Thirty Years* (New York: R. R. Donnelley and Sons, 1983).

58. See *R.B. Diaries*, vol. 1, ch. 6, pp. 120–22.

59. Ibid., vol. 2, ch. 9, p. 133.

60. Ball, *Past*, p. 108.

61. The two quotations are from Ball, *Past*, p. 109 and from the original letter of Alsop to Ball, dated October 24, 1951. Arthur Schlesinger has confirmed the Alsop-Ball-Wallace episode. He was in Alsop's office when the journalist telephoned Ball. Personal interview with Arthur Schlesinger Jr., New York, March 9, 1995.

62. *Washington Post*, May 5, 1953.

63. This is the phrase Adlai Stevenson used when he agreed to run for governor of Illinois in 1947.

64. This quotation and the one above are from Ball, *Past*, p. 114. For a detailed account of the Stevenson-Truman meetings, see John Bartlow Martin, *Adlai Stevenson of Illinois* (Garden City, N.Y.: Doubleday, 1976), pp. 522–28.

65. David McCullough, *Truman* (New York: Simon and Schuster, 1992), p. 907. In the 1956 campaign for the Democratic nomination, Truman refused to endorse Stevenson and supported Averell Harriman instead. Adlai's continual promise that if elected he would "clean up the mess in Washington," did not endear him to Truman. See *Washington Post*, August 17, 1952.

66. Ball, *Past*, p. 117.

67. Personal interviews with Arthur Schlesinger Jr., New York, March 9, 1995, and John Kenneth Galbraith, Cambridge, Mass., April 19, 1995.

68. Much of the information in this paragraph is drawn from a personal interview with Roger Stevens at his Kennedy Center office in Washington, D.C., on November 13, 1991. Stevens, who later raised $80 million to build the Kennedy Center, was extremely close to such national Democratic figures as the Kennedys, Lyndon Johnson, and especially Hubert Humphrey. Because of Stevens's interest in business, politics, and the arts, George Ball considered him one of America's most interesting personalities.

69. Porter McKeever, *Adlai Stevenson: His Life and Legacy* (New York: William Morrow, 1989), p. 213. McKeever explains in some detail how Stevenson alienated labor by refusing to call for the repeal of the Taft-Hartley Act, how he upset the Catholics by refusing to meet with Cardinal Spellman, and how he disappointed many pro-Israeli groups by calling for a balanced and objective appraisal of the Arab-Israeli problem.

70. Quoted in Arthur Schlesinger Jr., *A Thousand Days* (Boston: Houghton Mifflin, 1965), p. 31.

71. Ibid., p. 224.

72. Ibid., p. 230. For Harry Truman's indignant and furious reaction to Eisenhower's failure to forthrightly defend General Marshall against McCarthy's charges, see McCullough, *Truman*, pp. 910–12.

73. Ibid. See also Alden Whitman, *Portrait: Adlai E. Stevenson, Politician, Diplomat, Friend* (New York: Harper and Row, 1965), p. 197.

74. Telephone interview with George Ball, May 5, 1994. This was the last conversation the author had with Ball, who died on May 26.

75. Ball, *Past*, p. 148.

76. Personal interview with George Ball, Princeton, N.J., September 14, 1988.

77. Ball, *Past*, p. 149.

78. Ibid., p. 110.

79. Amos Ball, *Travels with a Jaguar* (Washington, D.C.: Jaguar, 1954).

80. This description of the *Northern Virginia Sun* incident is based upon personal interviews with George and Douglas Ball on September 16, 1989, January 28, 1990, and December 13, 1991, as well as on information contained in a number of files in Ball's personal papers. The quotation in the paragraph is from Douglas Ball.

81. *R.B. Diaries*, vol. 2, ch. 16, p. 212.

82. Personal interview with George Ball, Princeton, N.J., September 4, 1991.

83. *R.B. Diaries*, vol. 1, ch. 4, p. 56.

84. Letter, George Ball to David Rockefeller, January 10, 1956. Ball papers, 1956 file of Ball correspondence. Ball's dinner for René Mayer was held on February 9, 1956, while Rockefeller hosted his party on February 14.

85. The words of C. D. Jackson as quoted in a special issue of the *Freeman Digest* (November–December, 1978) devoted to Bilderberg. See p. 25.

86. "Interview: Joseph E. Johnson," *Freeman Digest*, pp. 49–56.

87. Ibid., p. 52.

88. The quotations in this paragraph are taken from a personal interview of Michael Loyd Chadwick with George Ball on September 28, 1978. The interview is published in *Freeman Digest*, pp. 56–60. In a personal interview on January 27, 1990, Ball told the author that "Bilderberg acquainted me with more people than anything else I've ever done."

89. Personal interview with David Rockefeller, New York, November 9, 1990.

Chapter 2. Political Practitioner and Intellectual Gladiator

1. Personal interview with Arthur M. Schlesinger Jr., New York, March 9, 1995. Schlesinger's wife Marian remained loyal to Stevenson. In a postscript to a personal letter, Robert Kennedy wrote, "I see Marian has come out in support of Stevenson. Can't you control your own wife? Or are you like me?"

2. This telephone call is discussed in some detail in Ball, *The Past Has Another Pattern: Memoirs* (New York: W. W. Norton, 1982), p. 158. Ball also described the Libertyville meeting in a personal interview, Princeton, N.J., February 17, 1989. In other discussions of the meeting, Stevenson's ire over Kennedy's threatening tone is not mentioned. See, for example, Arthur M. Schlesinger Jr., *A Thousand Days* (Boston: Houghton Mifflin, 1965), pp. 24–26.

3. Theodore H. White, *The Making of the President, 1960* (New York: Atheneum, 1988), pp. 109–10.

4. Personal interview with George Ball, Princeton, N.J., September 14, 1988.

5. *Ruth Ball Diaries*, vol. 2, ch. 28, p. 234. Hereafter quoted as *R.B. Diaries*.

6. *New York Times*, October 9, 1960. The letter was cosigned by Thomas K. Finletter.

7. Ball, *Past*, p. 159.

8. *R.B. Diaries*, vol. 2, ch. 28, pp. 234–35.

9. Quoted in Ball, *Past*, p. 160.

10. Ibid.

11. The sections and quotations concerning the task force report for Kennedy are drawn from a personal copy of the document itself. The 167-page study is entitled "Report

to Honorable John F. Kennedy from Adlai E. Stevenson—November 1960." For a discussion of this report and other task force activities at the time, see Schlesinger, *A Thousand Days*, pp. 155–61.

12. Personal interviews with Jerome Hyman and James Johnson, New York, March 9, 1995. Hyman and Johnson were Cleary, Gottlieb colleagues of Ball's and Sharon's.

13. Personal copy of "Report to the Honorable John F. Kennedy by the Task Force on Foreign Economic Policy (FEP)," December 31, 1960. Marked "CONFIDENTIAL." The body of this report is 126 pages in length.

14. Personal interview with George Ball, Princeton, N.J., September 14, 1988. This account is confirmed in another interview with Ball on October 12, 1991 in Princeton and by Arthur Schlesinger in *A Thousand Days*, pp. 148–49. In a personal interview in Washington, D.C., on November 25, 1991, Fulbright confirmed his role in the Ball appointment.

15. Schlesinger, *A Thousand Days*, p. 165.

16. Other significant Democratic gubernatorial victories in 1948 included Adlai Stevenson's election in Illinois. Meanwhile, Lyndon Johnson won a close and controversial race in Texas for the U.S. Senate in the same year.

17. Personal interview with George Ball, Princeton, N.J., February 18, 1989.

18. Ball, *Past*, p. 170. In personal interviews, Ball repeated this story to me on September 14, 1988, February 18, 1989, and October 14, 1989.

19. Personal interview with George Ball, Princeton, N.J., February 18, 1989.

20. Chester Bowles, *Promises to Keep* (New York: Harper and Row, 1971), p. 306; and Ball, *Past*, p. 170. The Bowles book is an excellent source for understanding the ideas and motivations of Chester Bowles.

21. Bowles, *Promises*, p. 364. Worried that Bowles might cause an uproar over his dismissal, Kennedy asked his special counsel Thomas Sorenson "to hold his hand a little, as one 'liberal' to another, after Rusk breaks the news to him." See Thomas C. Sorenson, *Kennedy* (New York: Bantam/Harper and Row, 1966), p. 324.

22. Ball, *Past*, p. 171. In a 1965 interview, Ball asserted that Rusk told him just before he left for Geneva that "the President finally [had] decided that Chester would have to do something else, and that they did want me to take over the Under Secretaryship." Ball went on to say that Rusk asked his advice on whether to appoint U. Alexis Johnson or George McGhee to the position vacated by Ball. Ball recommended McGhee but later acknowledged, "Had I to do it again, I would have done it the other way." Oral history interview with George W. Ball by Joseph Kraft for the John F. Kennedy Library, pt. 1, p. 17, Washington, D.C., April 12, 1965. Hereafter quoted as Oral history, Kennedy Library. There were four separate interviews sponsored by the Kennedy Library, two by Joseph Kraft (April 12 and 16 in Washington) and two by Larry J. Hackman (February 16 and March 29, 1968, in New York). The Kraft interviews are referred to as pt. 1 and Hackman discussions as pt. 2. These interviews were among George Ball's personal papers.

23. Personal interview with Dean Rusk, Athens, Ga., November 6, 1989. Arthur Schlesinger has written that Rusk was also thought to have supported Arthur Dean for the position. See Schlesinger, *A Thousand Days*, p. 439.

24. Schlesinger, *A Thousand Days*, p. 440. Also, personal interview with Schlesinger, New York, March 9, 1995. According to Schlesinger, he was working for the OSS in Europe at the time Ball was a director of the Strategic Bombing Survey.

25. Personal interview with Lucius Battle, Washington, D.C., August 27, 1991. In this interview, Battle also stated that "I liked Dean Rusk. I liked Chet Bowles. But I have reser-

vations about both of them in a number of ways. But I really didn't have any reservations about George Ball."

26. A Pennsylvania lawyer, Myer Feldman performed a wide number of tasks for Kennedy, including directing U.S. businesses in search of licenses and permits to the appropriate regulatory agencies. Feldman had special ties with the textile industry. Luther Hodges grew up in North Carolina, attended the University of North Carolina at Chapel Hill, and worked for Marshall Field and Company, rising to become general manager of all the company's textile mills and later vice president. As a result of lobbying efforts by Ball and the White House, Hodges was to play a major role in the passage of the Trade Expansion Act of 1962.

27. Ball, *Past*, p. 188.

28. Ibid., p. 191.

29. Oral history, Kennedy Library, pt. 1, pp. 17–18.

30. Ibid., pt. 1, p. 22.

31. Ball, *Past*, p. 198. Ball repeated this anecdote in slightly different form in his oral history interview, Kennedy Library, pt. 2, p. 60 (February 16, 1968).

32. Personal interviews with George Ball, Princeton, N.J., September 14, 1988, and February 18, 1989.

33. Personal interview with Robert Schaetzel, Bethesda, Md., February 11, 1992. For much of the other material in this section, I have also drawn upon personal interviews with George Springsteen and Arthur Hartman on November 12 and 13, 1991, respectively.

34. Campbell founded the journal *Foreign Policy* and wrote a powerful critique of the State Department entitled *The Foreign Affairs Fudge Factory*, published by Basic Books in 1971. Shortly afterward, he died tragically at age 31.

35. The data presented in the above three paragraphs have been compiled from a wide range of sources available at the Lyndon B. Johnson Presidential Library. These sources include the presidential diary cards and an extensive collection of telecoms.

36. Personal interview with Thomas Schoenbaum, Rusk's biographer, Athens, Ga., November 5, 1989. See Schoenbaum's excellent book, *Waging Peace and War: Dean Rusk in the Truman, Kennedy, and Johnson Years* (New York: Simon and Schuster, 1988).

37. The only time Ball and Rusk were out of the country at the same time was in May 1965, when the secretary joined Ball in London for an important meeting of NATO.

38. Personal interview with Dean Rusk, Athens, Ga., November 6, 1989.

39. Rusk autographed a picture of Ball and himself seated together in similar poses in the Oval Office with the following words: "To my friend and alter ego—George Ball—as proof that we look at things alike."

40. Personal interview with George Ball, Princeton, N.J., February 18, 1989.

41. Ibid.

42. Personal interviews with George Ball, Princeton, N.J., September 14, 1988, and February 18, 1989. This incident is also related in Ball, *Past*, p. 426.

43. Personal interview with Douglas Ball, Princeton, N.J., January 28, 1990.

44. This letter is found in the Lyndon B. Johnson Presidential Library, Austin, Texas, White House Central Files, name file "Ball, G." The Johnson Library is hereafter referred to as LBJ Library.

45. *R.B. Diaries*, vol. 2, pt. 2, ch. 23, p. 290.

46. Personal interview with Douglas Ball, Princeton, N.J., January 28, 1990.

47. *R.B. Diaries*, vol. 2, pt. 2, ch. 25, p. 312.

48. Personal interview with Douglas Ball, Princeton, N.J., January 28, 1990.

49. Ball, *Past*, p. 441. In dryly responding to a long, meandering soliloquy by Malik, Ball stated: "I would not be surprised if the Soviet representative read to us excerpts from the Moscow telephone directory. And quite likely, if he reads enough of them, he will include some of the names of those who will be in the new Czech Government." *Philadelphia Inquirer*, August 24, 1968.

50. Ball, *Past*, p. 443.

51. Personal interview with George Ball, Princeton, N.J., September 16, 1989.

52. Rowland Evans and Robert Novak, "Why Ball Quit," *New York Post*, October 3, 1968. See also the *Washington Post* of the same date.

53. Ibid. See also Ball, *Past*, p. 444.

54. Some observers believed that the timing of Ball's resignation was not accidental. He had no desire to once again present publicly the administration's party-line position on Vietnam. He especially did not wish to do so before the international audience provided by the United Nations forum.

55. *New York Times*, September 27, 1968.

56. *The Sun* (Baltimore), September 28, 1968.

57. See *Washington Post*, September 27 and 28, 1968.

58. *Boston Globe*, September 30, 1968; *Los Angeles Times*, September 30, 1968.

59. Lewis Chester, Godfrey Hodgson, and Bruce Page, *An American Melodrama: The Presidential Campaign of 1968* (London: Andre Deutsch, 1969), pp. 643–44.

60. Theodore H. White, *The Making of the President, 1968* (New York: Atheneum, 1969), p. 355. In this speech, Humphrey said: "As president, I would stop the bombing of North Vietnam as an acceptable risk for peace because I believe that it could lead to success in the negotiations and thereby shorten the war."

61. Ibid., pp. 396–97.

62. LBJ Library, Tom Johnson's notes of meetings, meeting of Wednesday September 25, 1968. Tom Johnson was also present at this meeting. Clark Clifford was secretary of defense at the time. All quotations from this meeting are taken from the Tom Johnson notes.

63. Ibid.

64. Personal interview with George Ball, Princeton, N.J., September 16, 1989.

65. LBJ Library, Tom Johnson's notes of meetings, Tuesday, September 12, 1968.

66. For convincing evidence that Nelson Rockefeller was Lyndon Johnson's choice for president, see Joseph A. Califano Jr., *The Triumph and Tragedy of Lyndon Johnson* (New York: Simon and Schuster, 1991), pp. 289–90.

67. Joseph Kraft, "An Operator on the Potomac Comes to the East River," *New York Times Magazine*, July 21, 1968, p. 58.

68. The two quotations in this paragraph are taken from "Presentations to Secretary and Mrs. Dean Rusk by the Committee of Six, Eighth Floor, Department of State, January 16, 1969," unpublished transcript, p. 8; and Ball, *Past*, p. 318.

69. R.B. *Diaries*, vol. 2, ch. 27, p. 335.

70. The data in this paragraph understate Ball's speaking and writing activities. The author has tabulated only those activities for which he has been able to find specific reference in Ball's personal papers.

71. Ball, *Diplomacy for a Crowded World* (New York: Little, Brown, 1976). Hereafter referred to as Ball, *Diplomacy*.

72. *Newsweek*, September 6, 1976.

73. R.B. *Diaries*, vol. 3, ch. 28, p. 347.

74. Ball, *Diplomacy*, pp. 12–15.

75. Ken Auletta, *Greed and Glory on Wall Street: The Fall of the House of Lehman* (New York: Random House, 1986), p. 34. This somewhat sensationalized account of the situation at Lehman Brothers in the 1970s and 1980s is generally reliable in its interpretations.

76. *R.B. Diaries*, vol. 3, ch. 28, p. 62.

77. Henry Kissinger, *White House Years* (Boston: Little, Brown, 1979), p. 952.

78. Personal interview with Peter Peterson, New York, January 8, 1992.

79. Ibid.

80. Auletta, *Greed and Glory*, pp. 16, 48.

81. Pete Peterson estimates that Ball, in his very best years at Lehman, never earned more than a few hundred thousand dollars. Compared with the other partners, this was small change. (Interview with Peterson, New York, N.Y., January 8, 1992).

When the firm was sold in 1984, the partners made many millions of dollars. Glucksman walked away with $15.6 million for his 4,500 shares. Peterson cashed in again, adding $6 million to the $7 million he had received in cash when he left in 1983. (Auletta, *Greed and Glory*, pp. 220–21.)

82. Porter McKeever, *Adlai Stevenson: His Life and Legacy* (New York: William Morrow, 1989), p. 70.

83. These quotations are all taken from a personal interview with George Ball, Princeton, N.J., October 12, 1991.

84. *R.B. Diaries*, vol. 4, p. 30.

85. Ibid.

86. Ibid., p. 42.

87. T. D. Allman, "Reviewing Stand," *Harper's Weekly*, August 9, 1976, p. 20.

88. Personal interview with George Ball, Princeton, N.J., September 4, 1991.

89. Personal papers of George Ball, letters of May 30 and August 10, 1976.

90. Zbigniew Brzezinski, *Power and Principle* (New York: Farrar, Straus, and Giroux, 1983), p. 11. Brzezinski also wrote that "Carter was concerned because some people in the campaign were very opposed to Ball, largely on account of his allegedly anti-Israeli views on the Middle East" (p. 8).

91. *Daily News Record* (New York), November 11, 1976.

92. *R.B. Diaries*, vol. 5, p. 65.

93. Personal interview with George Ball, Princeton, N.J., December 5, 1986. In 1953 the CIA intervened after Iranian nationalist forces behind charismatic leader Muhammad Musaddiq had driven the unpopular monarch out of the country. For an excellent source concerning Ball, Brzezinski, Carter, and Iran, see Gary Sick, *All Fall Down: America's Tragic Encounter with Iran* (New York: Random House, 1985), esp. pp. 114–17.

94. Personal interview with George Ball, Princeton, N.J., December 5, 1986.

95. Ball, *Past*, p. 461.

96. *R.B. Diaries*, vol. 7, p. 206.

97. Personal interview with Lewis Lapham, New York, October 3, 1994. Lapham said that the Board consisted of individuals who were "devout believers in the conventional wisdom, whatever that happened to be at the moment." The quotations and much of the material contained in this section are drawn from the interviews with Lapham and Rick MacArthur.

98. *Washington Post*, March 21, 1981.

99. Copy of letter, J. A. Diana to William Bernbach, Jerome S. Hardy, and Donald A. Petrie, April 15, 1981.

100. See, for example, MacArthur's important book, *Second Front: Censorship and Propaganda in the Gulf War* (New York: Hill and Wang, 1992).

101. Personal interview with Rick MacArthur, New York, October 3, 1994.

102. Personal papers of George Ball, copy of letter from Ball to Walter Cronkite, June 23, 1983.

103. Personal interview with Rick MacArthur, New York, October 3, 1994.

104. The "How to Save Israel" piece was published in the April 1977 issue of *Foreign Affairs*.

105. The complete citations for the two books: *Error and Betrayal in Lebanon: An Analysis of Israel's Invasion of Lebanon and the Implications for U.S.-Israeli Relations* (Washington, D.C.: Foundation for Middle East Peace, 1984); and *The Passionate Attachment: America's Involvement with Israel, 1947 to the Present* (New York: W. W. Norton, 1992).

106. Ball completed ninety-six pages of the first draft of this book. The day before he died, he expressed concern to his son Douglas that he might not have the time to complete this manuscript.

107. Personal copy of the text of Ball's remarks.

108. Personal interview with Cyrus Vance, New York, October 10, 1994.

Chapter 3. The Politics of European Integration

1. George W. Ball, *The Past Has Another Pattern: Memoirs* (New York: W. W. Norton, 1982), p. 74. Hereafter referred to as *Past*.

2. Ball, letter to Nathan W. Levin, December 2, 1953. Personal papers of George Ball. Hereafter referred to as PPGB.

3. Ball, memorandum for Leo Gottlieb, January 19, 1953, PPGB.

4. Transcript of remarks of Hon. A. S. Mike Monroney, U.S. Senate, 84th Congress, 1st Session, Congressional Record, April 28, 1955.

5. The two quotations are taken from personal letters written on August 6, 1953 to Frank Altschul and J. Franklin Ray respectively, PPGB.

6. Personal interview with George Ball, Princeton, N.J., February 17, 1989.

7. Ball, "The Promise of the Multinational Corporation," *Fortune*, June 1, 1967.

8. Ibid.

9. Ball, speech at Cleary, Gottlieb, Steen and Hamilton symposium, Frankfurt, Germany, October 8, 1991, PPGB.

10. Personal interview with Ruth Ball, Princeton, N.J., February 18, 1989.

11. As quoted by François Fontaine in Douglas Brinkley and Clifford Hackett (eds.), *Jean Monnet: The Path to European Unity* (New York: St. Martin's Press, 1991), p. 33. Fontaine's article on Monnet is superb.

12. The three quotations in this paragraph are taken from Ball, *Past*, p. 72, and a manuscript entitled "Interview with Monnet," December 5–6, 1974 found in the personal papers of George Ball.

13. Personal interview with Arthur Hartman, Washington, D.C., November 13, 1991.

14. "Interview with Monnet"; Monnet letters to Ball, December 16, 1967, March 19, 1969, PPGB.

15. Monnet letter to Ball, March 19, 1969, PPGB.

16. *Newsweek*, October 1, 1962, p. 18.

17. Richard J. Barnet, *The Alliance* (New York: Simon and Schuster, 1983), p. 97.

18. Jean Monnet, *Memoirs* (Garden City, N.Y.: Doubleday, 1978), p. 231.

19. Ball, *Past*, p. 74; and "Interview with Monnet," PPGB.

20. Monnet, *Memoirs*, p. 227.

21. James Reston, *Deadline: A Memoir* (New York: Random House, 1991), p. 168.

22. George Ball, "Introduction," in François Duchene, *Jean Monnet: The First Statesman of Interdependence* (New York: W. W. Norton, 1994), p. 11; and Tuthill, *France Magazine*, Winter 1989, p. 40.

23. Personal interview with Arthur Hartman, Washington, D.C., November 13, 1991; personal communication from John Tuthill, March 27, 1990.

24. Personal interview with George Ball, Princeton, N.J., September 14, 1988.

25. Personal interview with Sir Eric Roll, London, March 10, 1992.

26. Barnet, *Alliance*, p. 98; and interview with Roll, March 10, 1992.

27. Michael J. Hogan, *The Marshall Plan* (New York: Cambridge University Press, 1987), p. 445.

28. Ball, *Past*, p. 78.

29. Pascaline Winand, *Eisenhower, Kennedy, and the United States of Europe* (New York: St. Martin's, 1993), p. 17. This history of the relation between the United States and the European drive for regional integration is meticulously researched and is an indispensable source.

30. Ball, *Past*, p. 86.

31. Ibid., p. 87.

32. DiLeo, "Jean Monnet and the Americans: Catch the Night Plane for Paris," manuscript, July 18, 1991, p. 13.

33. As quoted in Derek W. Urwin, *The Community of Europe* (New York: Longman, 1991), p. 76.

34. On July 1, 1959, Ball testified before the Joint Economic Committee of Congress in Washington, D.C.; on September 29, 1959, he spoke to the Annual Correspondent Bank Meeting in Philadelphia; on December 7, 1959, he addressed the United States Pharmaceutical Manufacturers Association in New York; and on January 21, 1960, he spoke to the 400th Meeting of the National Industrial Conference Board.

35. Press release of Ball's address to the National Industrial Conference Board on January 21, 1960, mimeo, PPGB.

36. Text of "Statement of George W. Ball Before the Joint Economic Committee on the Significance of the European Common Market to the American Economy," mimeo, PPGB.

37. Healey, *The Time of My Life* (New York: W. W. Norton, 1989), p. 245.

38. Tuthill, personal letter to the author, March 27, 1990.

39. Monnet, *Memoirs*, pp. 358–59.

40. Ball, "Memorandum for Mr. Ferguson," August 23, 1954, PPGB.

41. "Statement by Governor Adlai Stevenson," Chicago, August 25, 1954, PPGB.

42. Urwin, *Community*, p. 67.

43. "Memorandum for Mr. Ferguson," PPGB.

44. Ball, "A Special Letter to the Members of the Comité France Actuelle," August 31, 1954, PPGB. Ball sent copies of this communication to both Jean Monnet and Mendes-

France. He also mailed copies to Walter Lippmann, Eric Sevareid, John Fischer, Max Ascoli, and Arthur Schlesinger Jr., among others, in the United States.

45. Ball, letter to Monnet, September 29, 1954, PPGB.

46. Secretary of Defense Robert McNamara endorsed the idea and, his later recollections to the contrary, so did Secretary of State Dean Rusk. For a thorough and informed discussion of the activities of these various officials, see Winand, *Eisenhower*, pp. 139–60.

47. Tuthill, personal letter to the author, March 27, 1990.

48. Schlesinger, *A Thousand Days* (Boston: Houghton Mifflin, 1965), p. 854.

49. Barnet, *Alliance*, p. 220; Healey, *Time of My Life*, p. 304.

50. Barnet, *Alliance*, p. 220.

51. As quoted in Winand, *Eisenhower*, p. 352.

52. Ibid., p. 354.

53. Wilson, *The Labour Government, 1964–1970: A Personal Record* (London: Weidenfeld and Nicolson, 1971), p. 46. Wilson describes Ball as "a committed pro-European, indeed a fanatic for European unity, who was one of the most passionate advocates of the MLF."

54. Bundy, "Memorandum to the President, MLF—An Alternative View," December 6, 1964, National Security File, memos to the president, Box 2, LBJ Library. Bundy enclosed with this memorandum a copy of a June 15, 1963, memo he had prepared for President Kennedy. In the earlier memorandum, Bundy warned of European reluctance to support the MLF and argued that it was "not merely a concept but a cost."

55. Healey, *Time of My Life*, p. 305.

56. Bundy, "Memorandum to the President," February 2, 1965, National Security Files (Bundy), LBJ Library.

57. Telcon, the secretary to Ball, February 3, 1965, papers of George Ball, Box 5, LBJ Library.

58. Ball, *Past*, p. 274.

59. Personal interview with George Ball, Princeton, N.J., October 12, 1991.

60. Personal interview with Robert Schaetzel, Bethesda, Md., February 11, 1992.

61. Personal interview with Arthur Hartman, Washington, D.C., November 13, 1991.

62. Ball, *The Discipline of Power* (Boston: Atlantic Monthly Press, 1968), p. 210.

63. Personal interview with George Ball, Princeton, N.J., September 14, 1988.

64. "Report to the Honorable John F. Kennedy by the Task Force on Foreign Economic Policy," December 31, 1960, pp. 1, 3, PPGB.

65. Ibid., pp. 3, 52. The EFTA was organized in 1960 in response to the EEC. Led by the United Kingdom, its members also included Switzerland, Sweden, Norway, Denmark, Austria, and Portugal. Ball curtly referred to this organization of the "Outer Seven" as offering "no redeeming benefits in the form of economic integration nor any promise of political unity." *Past*, p. 210.

66. For an informed discussion of Ball's Europeanist teammates and the political context of their activities, see David L. DiLeo, "George Ball and the Europeanists at the State Department, 1961–1963," October 9, 1992, manuscript provided by DiLeo.

67. Winand, *Eisenhower*, p. 149.

68. Personal interview with Michael Blumenthal, New York, January 14, 1992.

69. Telephone interview with Raymond Vernon, August 1, 1995.

70. *Time*, March 30, 1962, pp. 11–12. The Kennedy statement is quoted in Schlesinger, *Thousand Days*, p. 847.

71. *Washington Post*, August 17, 1962.

72. "Threshold of a New Trading World: The Road Ahead," in *Vital Speeches*, December 15, 1961, p. 133.

73. Both quotations are taken from *Newsweek*, October 1, 1992, p. 17.

74. Quoted in Joseph Kraft, "Oral History Interview with George W. Ball," Washington, D.C., April 12, 1965, for the John F. Kennedy Library, Pt. I, pp. 31–34, PPGB.

75. Ball bluntly stated that he introduced the 80 percent mechanism as a "trick" to promote British membership in the Common Market (ibid., p. 33). Without Britain, the 80 percent formula would be largely meaningless. With British membership, it would benefit both Britain and the other EEC countries by encouraging trade through an elimination of tariffs.

76. Ball, *Discipline*, p. 69.

77. Quotations, respectively, ibid., pp. 88–89; ibid., p. 79; *New York Herald Tribune*, April 4, 1962.

78. Ball, *Past*, p. 212.

79. Ibid., p. 213.

80. Ibid.

81. Ibid., p. 214.

82. Macmillan, *At the End of the Day* (London: Macmillan, 1973), p. 111; Ball, *Past*, p. 215.

83. John Campbell, *Edward Heath: A Biography* (London: Jonathan Cape, 1993), pp. 112–13.

84. Ibid., p. 120.

85. Personal interview with Sir Eric Roll, London, March 10, 1992.

86. Hugh Gaitskell as quoted in Schlesinger, *Thousand Days*, p. 845.

87. Quotation from Ball, *Past*, p. 265.

88. "Memorandum to the President: The Mess in Europe and the Meaning of Your Trip," June 20, 1963, pp. 10–11, PPGB.

89. Urwin, *Community*, p. 129.

90. Text of de Gaulle press conference, January 14, 1963. PPGB.

91. Ball, *Past*, p. 268; personal interview with Arthur Hartman, Washington, D.C., November 13, 1991.

92. Simon Serfaty, *Taking Europe Seriously* (New York: St. Martin's, 1992), pp. 43–44.

93. Bohlen, letter to MacGeorge Bundy, March 2, 1963, Files of McGeorge Bundy, Box 16, LBJ Library. This eight-page letter, marked "secret" and "personal" and signed "Chip," also discusses the MLF. Bohlen asked that the letter be shown only to President Johnson and to Dean Rusk.

94. Personal interviews with George Ball, Princeton, N.J., September 14, 1988, September 16, 1989, and September 4, 1991.

95. *Le Monde* interview with Under Secretary Ball in Paris, March 30, 1966, as published in "Department of State for the Press," March 31, 1966; *Washington Post*, April 12, 1966; and Ball, "Address Before the American Society of International Law," Washington, D.C., April 29, 1966, as published in "Department of State for the Press," April 29, 1966, PPGB.

96. *Washington Post*, May 5, 1966; and Lyndon Baines Johnson, *The Vantage Point* (New York: Popular Library, 1971), p. 305.

97. From Ball "Address Before American Society of International Law."

98. The speech, delivered by Ball at the annual dinner of the British National Com-

mittee of the International Chamber of Commerce, London, October 18, 1967, was published as "Cosmocorp: The Importance of Being Stateless," *Columbia Journal of World Business* 2 (November–December 1967): 25–30. Another version of the article appeared as "Making World Corporations into World Citizens" in *War/Peace Report* 8 (October 1968): 8–10.

99. John M. Ashbrook, "Reflections on Departure of Mr. George Ball," U.S. Congress, House of Representatives, October 14, 1968, in *Congressional Record*, October 15, 1968, p. E9165. Ashbrook inserted Ball's complete "Cosmocorp" article into the *Congressional Record*.

100. Ball, "Cosmocorp," p. 25.

101. Ball, "Why America Wants Britain in Europe," *Sunday Telegraph*, May 7, 1967.

102. Ball, "Introduction," in Brinkley and Hackett, *Jean Monnet*, p. xvi. The evolution of the name of the organization suggests the direction in which the momentum has carried the process of European integration. The title has evolved from European Economic Community (EEC) to European Community (EC) to European Union (EU).

103. E. J. Hobsbawm, *The Age of Extremes: A History of the World, 1914–1991* (New York: Pantheon, 1994). See also Jim Hoagland's article in the *Washington Post*, August 18, 1995.

104. Heilbroner, "The Multinational Corporation and the Nation-State," *New York Review of Books*, February 11, 1971, p. 25.

105. U.S. Department of State, Bureau of Public Affairs, *Background Notes: European Community* (Washington, D.C.: Government Printing Office, 1993), p. 8.

Chapter 4. Rebellion and War in Africa and Asia

1. This was a busy time for George Ball. In 1962, besides his many direct policymaking responsibilities at the State Department, he delivered seventeen speeches, made eight television appearances, and testified before congressional committees seven times.

2. Among the many general sources that address the contemporary history, politics, and foreign relations of the Congo, see Crawford Young, *Politics in the Congo* (Princeton, N.J.: Princeton University Press, 1965); Stephen Weissman, *American Foreign Policy Toward the Congo* (Ithaca, N.Y.: Cornell University Press, 1974); and Madeleine Kalb, *The Congo Cables: The Cold War in Africa from Eisenhower to Kennedy* (New York: Macmillan, 1982).

3. A fourth piece of the shattered Congo consisted of the diamond-rich South Kasai region, which seceded in August 1960.

4. Quoted in George W. Ball, *The Past Has Another Pattern: Memoirs* (New York: W. W. Norton, 1982), p. 222. Hereafter referred to as *Past*.

5. The opposition of Soviet leaders to UN policy in the Congo precipitated their recommendation in 1960 that the secretary generalship consist of a "troika." Soviet diplomats argued that it would be more representative of global realities if three officials administered the UN. The troika would represent three constituencies: the western world, the communist bloc, and the developing nations. Each of the three officials would in effect have a veto power over UN policies.

6. Both quotations are drawn from Brian Urquhart, *A Life in Peace and War* (New York: Harper and Row, 1987), p. 153.

7. For an informed and balanced discussion of the CIA's activities concerning

Lumumba, see John Ranelagh, *The Agency: The Rise and Decline of the CIA* (New York: Simon and Schuster, 1986), pp. 338–45. According to Ranelagh: "There is strong evidence to suggest that President Eisenhower actually approved the attempted assassination of Patrice Lumumba in the Congo in 1960." In a cable to the CIA station chief in Leopoldville, CIA Director Allen Dulles said: "We conclude that [Lumumba's] removal must be an urgent and prime objective and that under existing conditions this should be a high priority of our covert action" (*Agency*, pp. 338, 341.) For an account of the unpleasant details of Lumumba's murder, see Richard D. Mahoney, *JFK: Ordeal in Africa* (New York: Oxford University Press, 1983), pp. 69–72.

8. Urquhart, *A Life*, p. 159.

9. Ibid., p. 193.

10. Although Tshombe fled the country in June 1963, he returned in July 1964 as prime minister in a unified Congolese government. In October 1965, he lost his position and again went into exile. He was kidnapped and jailed in Algeria after his plane was mysteriously hijacked on June 30, 1967. Moise Tshombe died of a heart attack in prison in Algeria on June 29, 1969.

11. Roger Hilsman, *To Move a Nation* (New York: Dell, 1967), p. 246.

12. Douglas Brinkley, *Dean Acheson: The Cold War Years, 1953–71* (New Haven: Yale University Press, 1992), p. 325.

13. Mahoney, *JFK*, pp. 210–11; and Brinkley, *Dean Acheson*, pp. 64–66. Brinkley qualifies Acheson's criticism by pointing out that "by the late 1950s, 'decisiveness' to Acheson had come to mean agreeing with his position" (Brinkley, p. 65).

14. Roger Hilsman, for example, includes Ball as a central member of the New Africa group. See Hilsman, *To Move*, p. 246.

15. Ball uses the phrase twice on p. 234 in *Past*.

16. Porter McKeever, *Adlai Stevenson: His Life and Legacy* (New York: William Morrow, 1989), p. 483.

17. Ball, *Past*, pp. 256–57.

18. David N. Gibbs, *The Political Economy of Third World Intervention: Mines, Money, and U.S. Policy in the Congo Crisis* (Chicago: University of Chicago Press, 1991), p. 202. The following material concerning the business thesis is drawn from the Gibbs book.

19. Gibbs also asserts a Rockefeller connection.

20. Mahoney, *JFK*, p. 173.

21. Gibbs, *Political Economy*, p. 109.

22. Ibid., p. 110.

23. Ibid., p. 105.

24. Ibid., p. 107.

25. U.S. House of Representatives, *Congressional Record*, September 12, 1962, pp. 19242–56. The quotations in this section are all drawn from the Bruce speech reproduced in this issue of the *Congressional Record*.

26. Gibbs, *Political Economy*, p. 140; emphasis added.

27. George W. Ball, "Memorandum for the President," September 13, 1961, copy of memorandum, PPGB. The quotations contained in the following two paragraphs are drawn from this source.

28. George W. Ball, *The Elements in Our Congo Policy* (Dept. of State Publication 7326; Washington, D.C.: Government Printing Office, 1961), PPGB.

29. Ibid. I compared the original text of the Los Angeles speech with the published version. Both documents are available in Ball's personal papers.

30. Mahoney, *JFK*, p. 129.

31. Ibid., p. 144. Mahoney provides a detailed account of the bureaucratic struggle in Washington that took place concerning Congo policy in the fall of 1962.

32. Quoted in Larry J. Hackman, "Oral History Interview with George Ball," New York, N.Y., February 16, 1968, for the John F. Kennedy Library, pt. 3, pp. 36–37, PPGB.

33. Telephone interview with Lewis Hoffacker, September 13, 1995. Hoffacker has written an informative unpublished paper entitled "Reflections on the Katangan Case: British and Other Connections," October 1977. Edward Mahoney's excellent study mistakenly claims that Hoffacker "was pulled out of Elisabethville by Gullion and 'buried' in Leopoldville" because the consul opposed the hard line against Tshombe (*JFK*, p. 145). In fact, Hoffacker and Gullion had excellent rapport. Gullion supported Hoffacker's reporting. Furthermore, Hoffacker was not "buried" in Leopoldville by Gullion. Hoffacker requested the change in assignment.

34. For a firsthand account of the events surrounding the INR study, see Hilsman, *To Move*, pp. 263–67.

35. Ibid., p. 266.

36. Personal interview with Roger Hilsman, New York, January 12, 1992.

37. In fairness, it is necessary to point out that Gibbs did not explicitly claim that Ball had been influenced by Tempelsman. Unfortunately, he leaves the impression that this was the case (see Gibbs, *Political Economy*, p. 110). The documented fact that Ball resisted Stevenson's overtures on behalf of Tempelsman is not mentioned in the Gibbs book.

38. Letter, George W. Ball to J. William Fulbright, July 30, 1964, J. William Fulbright Papers, University of Arkansas Libraries, Fayetteville, Arkansas, Series 2, Box 4, State Department, 1964–65; italics added. Other senators who made representations on behalf of Tempelsman included Bourke Hickenlooper, Frank Carlson, Karl Mundt, Russell Long, and Frank Church. Ball's letters of response are available in the PPGB.

39. Personal interview with George Ball, Princeton, N.J., October 14, 1989.

40. Ironically, after leaving the government Ball established a business linkage with a company that had opposed LAMCO in the Congo episode. He joined the board of American Metal Climax (AMAX) in 1970. Upon his mandatory retirement from the board in 1979 when he reached age seventy, Ball served as chairman of AMAX's International Advisory Board for several years. In the 1970s and early 1980s, AMAX was one of the largest mining companies in the world, with offices in thirty-eight countries.

41. Personal interview with Roger Hilsman, New York, January 12, 1992; telephone interview with Lewis Hoffacker, September 13, 1995.

42. Tempelsman's influence continued into the Nixon administration. Tempelsman had fashioned close ties with Joseph-Désiré Mobutu, who became president of Zaire in 1965. Mobutu awarded a Tempelsman consortium the Tenke Fungurume copper concession in September 1970. U.S. government officials actively supported Tempelsman's quest for this concession. See Gibbs, *Political Economy*, pp. 180–85.

43. Personal interview with George Ball, Princeton, N.J., October 14, 1989.

44. Telcon, President Lyndon Johnson to George Ball, November 25, 1964. Lyndon Baines Johnson Presidential Library, Ball Papers, Austin, Texas. Quoted hereafter as Ball Papers, LBJ Library.

45. The CIA had in fact been exerting enormous influence in Congo affairs since

1960. Among the many sources that describe U.S. covert interventionism in the Congo, see especially "How C.I.A. Put 'Instant Air Force' Into Congo," *New York Times*, April 26, 1966; and David N. Gibbs, "Secrecy and International Relations," *Journal of Peace Research* 32 (1995): 213–28.

46. Ball, *Past*, p. 226.

47. *New York Times*, June 21, 1971. Benjamin Read, executive secretary of the Department of State between 1963 and 1969, stated that in 1964 George Ball was alone at the high levels of government in opposing U.S. involvement in Vietnam. According to Read, even in the Senate no one supported Ball at the time. Oral history interview, Benjamin H. Read, interviewed by Paige E. Mulhollan, January 13, 1969, pp. 9–10. Ball Papers, LBJ Library.

48. *Washington Post*, June 28, 1971; *San Francisco Chronicle*, June 28, 1971.

49. David L. DiLeo, *George Ball, Vietnam, and the Rethinking of Containment* (Chapel Hill: University of North Carolina Press, 1991), pp. 65–66. David Halberstam makes the same point, writing that Ball "argued compellingly, forcefully and prophetically against the escalation, so prophetically that someone reading his papers five years later would have a chilling feeling that they had been written after the fact, not before." Halberstam, *The Best and the Brightest* (New York: Random House, 1972), p. 491.

50. Clark Clifford with Richard Holbrooke, *Counsel to the President: A Memoir* (New York: Random House, 1991), p. 408.

51. Personal letter from William P. Bundy to Douglas Ball, June 4, 1994. William Bundy granted permission to quote from this private communication.

52. The data in this paragraph are drawn from James S. Olson, *Dictionary of the Vietnam War* (New York: Greenwood, 1988), pp. 46–49, 67.

53. Although scholars sometimes assert that Ball had little to do with Southeast Asia during the Kennedy administration, a careful reading of the telcons indicates that he was in fact actively involved with the issue. He did not "keep quiet," as is argued by David DiLeo. See DiLeo, *George Ball*, pp. 44–45.

54. The material in this paragraph is drawn from Telcon, Bundy and Ball, April 26, 1962. Papers of George W. Ball, "Vietnam I" (Jan. 15, 1962–Oct. 4, 1963), Ball Papers, LBJ Library.

55. Sections of Ball's speech are quoted in articles by Marguerite Higgins in the *New York Herald Tribune*, May 1, 1962; and Warren Unna in the *Washington Post*, May 6, 1962.

56. Telcon, Bundy to Ball, May 1, 1962. Ball Papers, LBJ Library.

57. Ball, *Past*, p. 370.

58. Madame Nhu quoted in Frances Fitzgerald, *Fire in the Lake* (New York: Vintage, 1973), p. 180.

59. At the time, Halberstam was largely unknown by leading American decision makers. In a conversation with Ball, Kennedy referred to him as "Halprestem. whatever that name is." Telcon, President Kennedy and Ball, August 21, 1963. Ball Papers, LBJ Library.

60. "Cablegram from the State Department to Ambassador Henry Cabot Lodge in Saigon, August 24, 1963." New York Times, *The Pentagon Papers* (New York: Bantam, 1971), p. 194.

61. Ball, *Past*, p. 371.

62. Robert S. McNamara, *In Retrospect: The Tragedy and Lessons of Vietnam* (New York: Times Books, 1995), p.81.

63. Taylor, *Swords and Plowshares* (New York: W. W. Norton, 1972), p. 292.

64. Ball, *Past*, p. 373.

65. The quotations in this paragraph are from McNamara, *In Retrospect*, pp. 76, 79.

66. Ibid., pp. 81–82. The recollections of the main actors in Washington concerning the events surrounding the August 24 cablegram differed enormously. Roger Hilsman recalled that Dean Rusk saw the actual text and even added a paragraph. Rusk did not recall ever seeing the telegram and denied adding anything to the text. He did, however, recall discussing the cable by telephone with George Ball. Maxwell Taylor denied ever having seen the cable. Hilsman indicated that Taylor in fact read and approved the missive. Robert McNamara claimed that Ambassador Henry Cabot Lodge strongly opposed Diem's leadership and supported the cable. Lodge vigorously denied this and insisted that he had considered the message ill-advised. These differences in recollection became painfully evident when the individuals involved sat together in June and July 1977 for a series of British Broadcasting Corporation interviews on Vietnam.

67. "Lodge Cable to Secretary Rusk on U.S. Policy toward a Coup," August 29, 1963, *Pentagon Papers*, p. 197.

68. Greenway, *New York Times Book Review*, November 19, 1995, p. 11.

69. Ball, *Past*, p. 374.

70. Hilsman, *To Move*, p. 420.

71. Lyndon Baines Johnson, *The Vantage Point* (New York: Popular Library, 1971), p. 61.

72. Telcons, Rusk and Ball, September 24, 1963; Hilsman and Ball, September 24, 1963. Ball Papers, LBJ Library.

73. Letter from George Ball to Dean Rusk, May 31, 1964. Copy of letter, PPGB.

74. For a list of the eight memoranda, see Prologue, note 1.

75. See, for example, Ball, *Past*, pp. 377–78.

76. Paige E. Mulhollan, Oral History Interview with George Ball, New York, July 8, 1971, pt. I, p. 16, LBJ Library.

77. These quotations and those in the following three paragraphs are drawn from the memoranda listed in the Prologue, note 1.

78. Ball, "Cutting Our Losses in South Viet-Nam," June 28, 1965, p. 8, PPGB.

79. McNamara, *In Retrospect*, p. 6.

80. The Goldwater quotation is taken from George Ball, "The Sad Case of Robert McNamara," *New York Review of Books*, April 22, 1993, p. 31. For the other quotations, see Halberstam, *Best and Brightest* pp. 247–50. David Halberstam's colorful descriptions of the personalities in Washington involved in making Vietnam policy have not been surpassed.

81. Ball, "Sad Case," p. 36. To Ball, Vietnam represented "a rebuke of spirit to the logic of numbers." *Newsweek*, July 26, 1971, p. 64. In 1995, McNamara admitted that the military had tried to measure the progress of the war through such indexes as enemy casualties, weapons seized, prisoners taken, and sorties flown. He acknowledged: "We later learned that many of these measures were misleading or erroneous." McNamara, *In Retrospect*, p. 48.

82. Telephone interview with Robert McNamara, November 14, 1991.

83. Ball, "The Last Testament of a Vietnam Dissenter," *Princeton University Library Chronicle* 56 (Spring, 1995): 366. This article is based on a transcript of a talk by George Ball to Princeton University students on March 31, 1994.

84. Johnson, interview with J. Leacacos of *Cleveland Plain Dealer*, October 17, 1967. Meeting Notes File, Box 3, LBJ Library. Rostow, who pandered to the president, was

caught up in the military campaign and became rigid and hard-line in his approach. Ball thoroughly disapproved of Rostow's methods and goals. When Bundy left the administration, Rostow stood next to the president as a cheerleader for escalation and the use of force.

85. Memorandum, "Cutting Our Losses in South Viet-Nam," June 28, 1965, pp. 5, 7, PPGB.

86. Memorandum, "The Resumption of Bombing Poses Grave Danger of Precipitating a War with China," p. 6, PPGB.

87. Ball, *Past*, p. 406.

88. Ball also influenced the thinking of such individuals in the White House as Chester Crocker and Jack Valenti.

89. Ball, *Past*, p. 408.

90. Clifford, *Counsel*, p. 416.

91. Halberstam, *Best and Brightest*, p. 653.

92. See DiLeo, *George Ball*, p. 89.

93. Memorandum, Douglass Cater to the president, February 8, 1965. Reference File Vietnam, Box 1, LBJ Library.

94. Ball, *Past*, p. 430.

95. Ibid., p. 429. The United States had encouraged the coup against Goulart, who entertained communist sympathies. For an excellent discussion of the role of the United States in the coup against Goulart, see Gaddis Smith, *The Last Years of the Monroe Doctrine 1945–1993* (New York: Hill and Wang, 1994), pp. 115–22.

96. Personal interview with William Bundy, Princeton, N.J., December 14, 1991.

97. The critics included former government officials James C. Thomson, Allen Whiting, and Roger Hilsman. Political scientists Hans Morgenthau, Edward Weisband, and Thomas Franck also criticized Ball in print. For a general analysis of the issue of the politics and ethics of protest resignation, see Weisband and Franck, *Resignation in Protest* (New York: Grossman, 1975). Also see David DiLeo's excellent discussion of the debate that centered on George Ball's refusal to resign. DiLeo, *George Ball*, pp. 125–54.

98. The quotations in this paragraph are taken from Ronald Steel, *Walter Lippmann and the American Century* (Boston: Little, Brown, 1980), pp. 572, 574.

99. The words of Roger Hilsman, quoted in DiLeo, *George Ball*, p. 152. In a personal interview, Hilsman stated that he was critical of Ball because Ball "let himself be used. He was the house prostitute. It took George about two years to realize he was just being used." But Hilsman, whom Ball had fired, had mixed feelings about the under secretary. He thought that Ball was extraordinarily bright and absolutely correct on the issue of Vietnam. On the Congo crisis, Hilsman describes Ball as "really great," "terrific," and "courageous." Personal interview with Roger Hilsman, New York, January 12, 1992.

100. Weisband and Franck, *Resignation*, p. 165.

101. James C. Thomson Jr., "How Could Vietnam Happen? An Autopsy," *The Atlantic* 221 (April 1968): 49.

102. Lyndon Johnson made these statements at the Department of State during a celebration in honor of Dean Rusk on January 16, 1969. Copy of the transcript of the proceedings, PPGB.

103. Personal interview with George Ball, Princeton, N.J., September 14, 1988.

104. Personal interview with George Ball, Princeton, N.J., September 4, 1991.

105. Quoted in Edward Weintal and Charles Bartlett, *Facing the Brink: An Intimate Study of Crisis Diplomacy* (New York: Charles Scribner's Sons, 1967), p. 172.

106. Ball, *Past*, p. 380. In a personal interview, Ball provided this episode as evidence

that he was able to block a number of potentially costly, even catastrophic events from occurring. "I had access to the president anytime I wanted it. I had a full hearing on everything." Personal interview with George Ball, Princeton, N.J., September 4, 1991.

107. Paige E. Mulhollan, Oral History Interview with George Ball, New York, July 8, 1971, pt. I, p. 20., LBJ Library.

108. 591st National Security Council Meeting, September 25, 1968, National Security File, NSC Meetings File, Vol. 5, Tab 73, Summary Notes, Box 2, LBJ Library.

109. Personal interview with Dean Rusk, Athens, Ga., November 6, 1989.

110. Personal interview with Cyrus Vance, New York, October 10, 1994.

111. McNamara, *In Retrospect*, p. 158.

112. Personal interview with James Schlesinger, Washington, D.C., November 12, 1991.

113. Ball, "Letter to Myself to be Read on the Day I Enlist," unpublished personal draft, Port au Prince, Haiti, September, 1939, PPGB. Ball's personal papers contain several drafts of this letter. For a more detailed analysis of Ball's Port au Prince letter, see DiLeo, *George Ball*, pp. 11–13.

114. *Ruth Ball Diaries*, vol 1, ch. 26, p. 326; and vol. 7, pt. 1, p. 163.

115. This is the heading of a section in Ball's autobiography. See *Past*, p. 420.

116. Marilyn B. Young, *The Vietnam Wars, 1945–1990* (New York: HarperCollins, 1991), p. 279.

117. Ibid., p. 280. For Ball's own estimates of the human costs of the Vietnam war during the Nixon years, see *Diplomacy for a Crowded World* (New York: Little, Brown and Co., 1976), pp. 74–75.

118. Ball, *Diplomacy*, pp. 82–83.

Chapter 5. Public Policy and Private Dissent

1. The literature on the Cuban missile crisis is vast. As McGeorge Bundy has written, "Forests have been felled to print the reflections and conclusions of participants, observers, and scholars." *Danger and Survival* (New York: Random House, 1988), p. 391. Chapter 9 of Bundy's book provides an excellent analysis of the crisis.

2. Such ExCom members as McNamara carefully—if factitiously—drew a distinction between a blockade and a quarantine. In their view, a quarantine was a selective blockade and was therefore something less than an act of war.

3. Robert F. Kennedy, *Thirteen Days* (New York: W. W. Norton, 1971), p. 94.

4. See Joseph Kraft, Oral History Interview with George W. Ball, Washington, D.C., April 16, 1965, for the John F. Kennedy Library, Pt. II, pp. 48–49.

5. R. Kennedy, *Thirteen Days*, p. 9. For a discussion of Ball's use of the moral argument to oppose an air strike against the missile sites, see Ball, *The Past Has Another Pattern: Memoirs* (New York: W. W. Norton, 1982), p. 291. Hereafter referred to as *Past*. Ball described his presentation of this position in the ExCom in a personal interview with the author in Princeton, N.J., on February 18, 1989.

6. Quoted in Bundy, *Danger*, p. 399.

7. R. Kennedy, *Thirteen Days*, p. 76.

8. Ball, *Past*, p. 293.

9. Ibid., p. 303.

10. Ibid., p. 304.

11. Personal interview with Arthur Hartman, Washington, D.C., November 13, 1991. Hartman recalls that Ball and Acheson had a falling out over this issue because Acheson

believed "we should bomb the shit out of them." Acheson had come to Ball's office to pick up his passport for a trip to France to brief de Gaulle on the missile crisis for President Kennedy.

12. Personal interview with George Ball, Princeton, N.J., February 18, 1989.

13. David Brinkley, *Dean Acheson: The Cold War Years, 1953–71* (New Haven: Yale University Press, 1992), pp. 173–74.

14. See Acheson's article, "Homage to Plain Good Luck," in Robert A. Divine, ed., *The Cuban Missile Crisis* (Chicago: Quadrangle, 1971), pp. 196–206.

15. As related by Dean Rusk, *As I Saw It*, as told to Richard Rusk (New York: W. W. Norton, 1990), p. 243.

16. Porter McKeever, *Adlai Stevenson: His Life and Legacy* (New York: William Morrow, 1989), p. 522. For an excellent discussion from the Stevenson perspective, see pp. 516–36.

17. Ball, *Past*, p. 295.

18. Bundy, *Danger*, p. 438.

19. *Ruth Ball Diaries*, vol. 2, ch. 29, p. 251. In 1968, when Ruth Ball entered the "Cuban missile basement," she discovered that all the canned food had exploded "rather repulsively." Ibid., p. 310.

20. See *Washington Post*, January 30, 1989; and *Chronicle of Higher Education*, January 29, 1992.

21. Quoted in James G. Blight and David A. Welch, *On the Brink: Americans and Soviets Reexamine the Cuban Missile Crisis* (New York: Hill and Wang, 1989), p. 169. For another excellent source, see James G. Blight, *The Shattered Crystal Ball* (Savage, Md.: Rowman and Littlefield, 1990).

22. Donald Kagan, *On the Origins of War and the Preservation of Peace* (New York: Doubleday, 1995).

23. Patrick Glynn, *Opening Pandora's Box* (New York: Basic, 1992), p. 544, as quoted in Kagan, *Origins*, p. 546.

24. Kagan, *Origins*, p. 546.

25. Brinkley, *Dean Acheson*, p. 171.

26. Telcon, Johnson and Ball, January 28, 1964; and Telcon, MacNamara and Ball, January 28, 1964. Papers of George W. Ball, Box 2, "Cyprus, Pre-Cyprus Trip," Lyndon B. Johnson Presidential Library, Austin, Tex. Quoted hereafter as Ball Papers, LBJ Library.

27. Edward Weintal and Charles Bartlett, *Facing the Brink: An Intimate Study of Crisis Diplomacy* (New York: Charles Scribner's Sons, 1967), p. 37.

28. National Security Council, 541st Meeting, August 25, 1964, National Security File, Box 1, "Congo, Cyprus, South Vietnam," LBJ Library.

29. Telcon, Stevenson and Ball, January 25, 1964, "Cyprus, Pre-Cyprus Trip," Box 2, Ball Papers, LBJ Library. See also Ball, *Past*, p. 341.

30. Ball, *Past*, pp. 344–45.

31. Ibid., p. 345.

32. Department of State, Incoming Telegram, for President and Secretary from Under Secretary, February 16, 1964, Personal Papers of George Ball. Hereafter referred to as PPGB.

33. In subsequent years, the United Nations did an outstanding job under difficult circumstances in cooling the conflict and protecting the minority rights of the Turkish Cypriots. For an excellent account of the role of the United Nations in Cyprus, see Kjell Skjelsbaek, ed., *The Cyprus Conflict and the Role of the United Nations* (Oslo: Norwegian

Institute of International Affairs, 1988). In this volume, Augustus Richard Norton's "The Roots of the Conflict in Cyprus" is particularly informative.

34. Brinkley, *Dean Acheson*, p. 370, note 25.

35. For an excellent account of the Cyprus crisis of 1964 that discusses the role played by George Ball, see H. W. Brands, *The Wages of Globalism*, (New York: Oxford University Press, 1995), pp. 62–84.

36. Ball, *Past*, p. 350. For a copy of the extraordinary June letter, see *Middle East Journal* 20 (Summer 1966): 386–88.

37. In a September 1965 visit to Istanbul, I personally encountered an unusual amount of anti-Americanism. When I inquired about this unpleasantness, I discovered that the Turks were still angered about "the Johnson letter."

38. The two quotations in this paragraph are drawn from Ball, *Past*, pp. 355–56.

39. Ibid., p. 358.

40. Brinkley, *Dean Acheson*, pp. 218–19.

41. Weintal and Bartlett, *Facing the Brink*, p. 36.

42. Thomas J. Schoenbaum, *Waging Peace and War: Dean Rusk in the Truman, Kennedy and Johnson Years* (New York: Simon and Schuster, 1988), p. 419.

43. Ball, *Past*, p. 502, ch. 23, note 3.

44. As early as February 1965, Ball argued that "one thing to consider, which we have rejected before, is having a big conference on the whole Middle Eastern problem and bringing the Russians in." Telcon, Secretary Vance and George Ball, February 6, 1965, LBJ Library, Papers of George W. Ball, "Germany, West II," Box 4.

45. Ball, *Diplomacy for a Crowded World: An American Foreign Policy* (Boston: Atlantic Monthly Press, 1976).

46. Ibid., p. 149.

47. Ball, "The Disenchantment with Kissinger," *Saturday Review*, June 12, 1976.

48. Ball, "How to Save Israel in Spite of Herself," *Foreign Affairs* 55 (April 1977): 453–71.

49. The quotations in this paragraph are all drawn from Ball, "How to Save Israel."

50. Ibid.

51. Bienstock, "Ball, Kissinger Critic, a Possible Successor, Feared as Anti-Israeli," *The Jewish Week–American Examiner*, July 11–24, 1976.

52. "Ball Insists he's Friend of Israel After Denying He's Carter's Choice," *The Jewish Week–American Examiner*, August 15–21, 1976.

53. Personal letter from George W. Ball to Jimmy Carter, August 10, 1976, PPGB.

54. For the most complete discussion of this issue, see Paul Findley, *They Dare to Speak Out* (Westport, Conn.: Lawrence Hill, 1985), pp. 122–27. For confirmation from within Carter's political circle, see Zbigniew Brzezinski, *Power and Principle* (New York: Farrar, Straus, and Giroux, 1983), pp. 8–11.

55. Michael Novak, "How to Have Oil and Pretend to Save Israel Too!" *Washington Star*, April 24, 1977.

56. Ball, *Past*, p. 466.

57. Steven L. Spiegel, *The Other Arab-Israeli Conflict* (Chicago: University of Chicago Press, 1985), p. 414. For Haig's explanation and justification, see Alexander M. Haig Jr., *Caveat: Realism, Reagan, and Foreign Policy* (New York: Macmillan, 1984), p. 318.

58. Rabin first used this phrase in a December 13, 1984, meeting with the American scholar Augustus Richard Norton.

59. Abba Eban, *The New Diplomacy* (New York: Random House, 1983), p. 232.

60. Spiegel, *Other Arab-Israeli Conflict*, p. 414. See also Ze'ev Schiff, "The Green Light," 50 *Foreign Policy* (Spring 1983): 75–83.

61. Quoted in Milton Viorst, *Sands of Sorrow: Israel's Journey from Independence* (New York: Harper and Row, 1987), p. 244.

62. Itamar Rabinovich, *The War for Lebanon, 1970–1983* (Ithaca, N.Y.: Cornell University Press, 1984), p. 170.

63. Schiff and Ya'ari, *Israel's Lebanon War* (New York: Simon and Schuster, 1984), p. 301.

64. Ball, "Divert Aid for Israel to Rebuild Lebanon," *New York Times*, August 25, 1982. All the quotations in this paragraph are drawn from this op-ed piece.

65. Ibid.

66. These letters are filed in the Personal Papers of George Ball. When asked whether all the hate mail troubled him, Ball responded with an impish grin, "No, I always thought it was rather badly written." Personal interview, Princeton, N.J., September 16, 1989.

67. Norman Podhoretz, "J'Accuse," *Commentary*, September, 1982, pp. 21–31.

68. Ibid.

69. Ball, *Error and Betrayal in Lebanon: An Analysis of Israel's Invasion of Lebanon and the Implications for U.S.-Israeli Relations* (Washington, D.C.: Foundation for Middle East Peace, 1984).

70. Ibid., p. 23.

71. George W. Ball and Douglas B. Ball, *The Passionate Attachment: America's Involvement with Israel, 1947 to the Present* (New York: W. W. Norton, 1992).

72. Ibid., p. 313.

73. Personal interview with Arthur Schlesinger Jr., New York, March 9, 1995.

74. The reviewers were Arthur Hertzberg (*New York Times*, February 21, 1993); Walter Laqueur (*Washington Post*, November 22, 1992); and Daniel Pipes (*Washington Times*, December 6, 1992). Edward Luttwak wrote a long, slashing review of the book for the December 1992 issue of *Commentary*.

75. Personal interviews with George Ball, Princeton, N.J., September 14, 1988, and September 16, 1989.

76. Letters from George Ball to admissions committee, Links Club, March 2, 1981, and to Landon Hilliard, chairman, admissions committee, Links Club, March 13, 1981, PPGB. According to Ball, when he asked for a list of the club's Jewish members, a club official produced one name. Personal interview with George Ball, Princeton, N.J., October 12, 1991.

77. Personal interview with Michael Blumenthal, New York, January 14, 1992. When asked about charges of Ball's alleged anti-Semitism, Arthur Schlesinger Jr. described the accusations as "nonsense" and stated that anyone who knew Ball would never accuse him of harboring such feelings. Personal interview with Schlesinger, New York, March 9, 1995.

78. *Time*, August 6, 1979, p. 29.

79. Ball, "Address Before Plenary Session of the 25th Annual Meeting of the Middle East Studies Association of North America," Washington Hilton Hotel, Washington, D.C., November 21, 1991. When adjusted for inflation and expressed in 1990 dollars, the total amount of U.S. financial assistance to Israel from 1974 through 1991 was $77 billion.

80. Personal interview with George Ball, Princeton, N.J., September 16, 1989.

81. Laqueur, *Washington Post Book World*, December 22, 1992, p. 5.

Chapter 6. The Essence of Statesmanship

1. The basic philosophical discussion of prudence as phronesis is found in Aristotle's *Nichomachean Ethics*. The ancient Greek philosopher considered phronesis to be the capstone virtue. For a thorough discussion of the philosophical foundations of phronesis, see Joseph Dunne, *Back to the Rough Ground: "Phronesis" and "Techne" in Modern Philosophy and in Aristotle* (Notre Dame, Ind.: University of Notre Dame Press, 1993). My colleague Dr. Michael T. Clark has helped explain the intricacies of phronesis to me.

2. Edmund D. Pellegrino and David C. Thomasma, *The Virtues in Medical Practice* (New York: Oxford University Press, 1993), p. 84.

3. Ronald Beiner, *Political Judgment* (Chicago: University of Chicago Press, 1983), p. 74.

4. My colleague Joel Schwartz has called to my attention this balancing tension inherent in the concept phronesis. Schwartz also stresses the delicate balance between a certain degree of aloofness and participation in the community that marks the political activities of the *phronemos*, the person who exercises phronesis.

5. Beiner, *Political Judgment*, p. 85; and Martha C. Nussbaum, *The Fragility of Goodness* (Cambridge: Cambridge University Press, 1986), p. 317.

6. Ball, *The Past Has Another Pattern: Memoirs* (New York: W. W. Norton, 1982), p. 376.

7. Ball, *The Discipline of Power* (Boston: Atlantic Monthly Press, 1968), p. 343.

8. Personal interview with James R. Schlesinger, Washington, D.C., November 12, 1991.

9. Personal interview with George Ball, Princeton, N.J., January 27, 1990. Ball identified and discussed the three goals in this interview.

10. "Remarks by George W. Ball," New York, January 23, 1990, manuscript, Personal Papers of George Ball; hereafter cited as PPGB.

11. Max Weber, "Politics as a Vocation," in H. H. Gerth and C. Wright Mills, eds., *From Max Weber: Essays in Sociology* (New York: Oxford University Press, 1946), pp. 77–128.

12. Personal interview with Lucius Battle, Washington, D.C., August 27, 1991.

13. *From Max Weber*, p. 116.

14. W. Michael Blumenthal, "George Ball: In Memoriam," June 21, 1994, text of remarks at Ball memorial service, PPGB.

15. Personal interview with David Rockefeller, New York, N.Y., November 9, 1990.

16. Among those who respected Ball for his Middle East position were J. William Fulbright, David Rockefeller, James Schlesinger, Dean Rusk, Lucius Battle, and Michael Blumenthal.

17. Quotation from François Duchene, *Jean Monnet: The First Statesman of Interdependence* (New York: W. W. Norton, 1994), p. 355.

18. Although they eventually broke through to cabinet rank, Averell Harriman, Clark Clifford, and Cyrus Vance wielded great political influence for many decades as members of the second tier.

19. James Reston, "Henry Kissinger's Revenge," *New York Times*, February 2, 1979. Publications analyzing Henry Kissinger and his career are extensive. Critical earlier writings include Edward R. F. Sheehan, *The Arabs, Israelis, and Kissinger* (New York: Reader's Digest Press, 1976); Roger Morris, *Uncertain Greatness* (New York: Harper and Row, 1977); William Shawcross, *Sideshow: Kissinger, Nixon, and the Destruction of Cambodia*

(New York: Simon and Schuster, 1979); Seymour M. Hersh, *The Price of Power: Kissinger in the Nixon White House* (New York: Summit, 1983). Although indispensable sources, these four books must be read with care because they are sharply tilted against Kissinger and his foreign policy record.

A positive early biography of Kissinger was written by Marvin and Bernard Kalb, *Kissinger* (Boston: Little, Brown, 1974). Another source in which the author attempts to present a balanced view of Kissinger is Bruce Mazlish, *Kissinger: The European Mind in American Policy* (New York: Basic, 1976). For a more recent comprehensive biography, see Walter Isaacson, *Kissinger: A Biography* (New York: Simon and Schuster, 1992).

20. Personal interview with George Ball, Princeton, N.J., September 16, 1989. Dean Rusk reinforced this opinion when he stated: "There is an element of vanity about Kissinger, and George doesn't like vanity very much." Personal interview with Dean Rusk, Athens, Ga., November 6, 1989.

21. Ball, "Scathing Re-Examination Leaves Kissinger Tarnished, But Not Demolished," review of S. M. Hersh's *The Price of Power* in *Christian Science Monitor*, September 2, 1983.

22. Personal letter from Henry A. Kissinger to George Ball, September 29, 1983, PPGB. Kissinger reportedly was also furious with Stanley Hoffmann for giving Hersh's book "mildly respectable treatment in the *New York Times Book Review*." See Isaacson, *Kissinger*, p. 713.

23. Personal letters of June 5 and June 11, 1985, PPGB.

24. Isaacson, *Kissinger*, p. 31. For Kissinger's distaste for revolution and revolutionary states, see Henry A. Kissinger, *A World Restored* (Gloucester, Mass.: Peter Smith, 1973).

25. Ball, *Diplomacy for a Crowded World* (Boston: Atlantic Monthly Press, 1976), p. 306. These hard-hitting passages are reprinted in Ball, "The Disenchantment with Kissinger," *Saturday Review*, June 12, 1976, p. 20.

26. Ball, *Diplomacy*, p. 307.

27. Isaacson, *Kissinger*, p. 555. On p. 762, Isaacson claims that Nahum Goldmann, an old friend of the Kissinger family, once said of Kissinger: "If he were ten percent less brilliant and ten percent more honest, he would be a great man."

28. Kissinger, *Diplomacy* (New York: Simon and Schuster, 1994), quotations from, respectively, pp. 88, 87, 92.

29. Kissinger, *A World Restored*, pp. 312, 320.

30. Ball, *Diplomacy*, p. 310.

31. The quotations in this paragraph are drawn from Kissinger, *World Restored*, p. 322; and Ball, *Diplomacy*, pp. 309, 312.

32. Kissinger, *World Restored*, p. 321.

33. Ball, *Past*, p. 451.

34. Kissinger, *White House Years* (Boston: Little, Brown, 1979), pp. 1259–61.

35. Memorandum, Henry A. Kissinger to the Secretary of State and Secretary of Defense, "Follow-up on the President's Talk with the Shah of Iran, July 25, 1972, *Asnad (Documents)*, vol. 8, p. 44. These are the papers published by the Iranian students who occupied the U.S. Embassy in Tehran in November 1979.

36. Ball, "Kissinger on Iran," letter to the editor, *Economist*, February 17, 1979. Ball's essay was in response to comments made by Kissinger in an interview in the *Economist* on February 10. The Kissinger-Ball exchange was reprinted in the *Washington Post* on February 26 under the title "Who Lost Iran?"

37. For a comprehensive study of U.S.-Iran relations, see J. A. Bill, *The Eagle and*

the Lion: The Tragedy of American-Iranian Relations (New Haven: Yale University Press, 1988). This study examines in detail the Kissinger role in the U.S.-Iran story. It also indicates that the Nixon-Kissinger administration was not alone in committing major policy errors toward Iran. U.S. administrations both before and after share much of the responsibility for the icy relations that still prevail—as does the Iranian government itself.

38. As quoted by William Safire, *New York Times*, February 12, 1976. Safire, one of the few journalists aware of the "unconscionable sellout of the Kurds," wrote: "If the President wants to defend this sellout of the Kurds at the command of the Shah, let him do so; if he wants to disavow this act of American dishonor, let him fire the adviser [Kissinger] who urged this dishonorable act upon him." *New York Times*, February 5, 1976.

39. House Select Committee on Intelligence (Pike Report), as published in *Village Voice*, February 16, 1976, p. 71.

40. On p. 1265 of *White House Years*, Kissinger promised to explain his decisions concerning the Kurds "in a second volume." In fact, he failed to mention the Kurds in his 1283-page second volume, *Years of Upheaval* (Boston: Little, Brown, 1982).

41. *Daily Texan* (University of Texas at Austin), November 21, 1979.

42. *Washington Post*, November 26, 1979.

43. *New York Times*, November 26, 1979.

44. Stanley Hoffmann, *Primacy or World Order: American Foreign Policy Since the Cold War* (New York: McGraw-Hill, 1978), p. 48. Hoffmann's essay "The Course of Dr. Kissinger" in this volume is a particularly probing analysis of Kissinger as statesman.

45. Kissinger, *White House Years*, p. 1492. The second volume of Kissinger's memoirs, *Years of Upheaval*, is cited above.

46. Kissinger, *Years of Upheaval*, pp. 668–69; italics added.

47. Ibid., pp. 671–73.

48. Hoffmann, *Primacy*, pp. 33–34.

49. Ball, *Diplomacy*, pp. 13–17.

50. Among Kissinger's talented young associates who resigned were William Watts, Anthony Lake, Roger Morris, and Laurence Lynn.

51. Hoffmann, *Primacy*, p. 52.

52. Kissinger, *Years of Upheaval*, p. 650.

53. H. R. Haldeman, *The Haldeman Diaries: Inside the Nixon White House* (New York: G. P. Putnam's Sons, 1994), p. 4. For another inside view of the Nixon White House, see John Ehrlichman, *Witness to Power: The Nixon Years* (New York: Simon and Schuster, 1982).

54. Haldeman, *Diaries*, p. 189.

55. In an interview with *Time* on January 15, 1979, Kissinger claimed that the strikes in Iran "could not have taken place without central organization. Whether they were organized in the Soviet Union or organized by people trained by the Soviet Union in other countries is really a secondary question. I think it is certainly the result of radical movements on a global basis, which has also now reached Iran" (p. 26).

56. Hoffmann, *Primacy*, p. 52.

57. As repeated in letter from W. Michael Blumenthal to George Ball, February 1, 1990, PPGB.

58. Ball, *Past*, p. 110.

59. At a 1992 conference sponsored by the Nixon Presidential Library, Kissinger, after stating that he knew of no one who had predicted the demise of the Soviet Union, conceded, "While I had some belief of a disintegration of the satellite orbit, it did not occur to

me that we would see the twin revolutions through which we are now living, the collapse of Communism in the Soviet Union and the collapse of the imperial system of the Russian empire." Quoted in Daniel P. Moynihan, *Pandaemonium* (New York: Oxford University Press, 1993), p. 48.

60. Personal interview with W. Michael Blumenthal, New York, January 14, 1992.

61. Ball, *Past*, p. 184.

62. Text of speech delivered to New York Bar Association, Saranac, N.Y., June 28, 1958, p. 5, Personal Papers of George Ball (PPGB).

63. Ball, *Past*, p. 277.

64. George W. Ball, Letter to Dr. Antonio de Oliveira Salazar, President of the Council of Ministers of Portugal, October 21, 1963, PPGB.

65. Personal interview with Sir Eric Roll, London, March 10, 1992.

66. Personal interview with William Bundy, Princeton, N.J., December 14, 1991.

67. At the time of his death in May 1994, George Ball was planning his first trip to China, again at the urging of his friend Michael Blumenthal.

68. Ball, *Past*, p. 384.

69. See Ball, *Discipline of Power*, p. 231.

70. *Ruth Ball Diaries*, vol. 3, ch. 28, p. 350; ch. 29, p. 33; and vol. 7, pp. 178, 188.

71. Personal interview with Sir Eric Roll, London, March 10, 1992.

72. Personal interview with Dean Rusk, Athens, Ga., November 6, 1989.

73. Personal interview with Peter Peterson, New York, January 8, 1992.

74. Personal interview with W. Michael Blumenthal, New York, January 14, 1992.

Select Bibliography

Auletta, Ken. *Greed and Glory on Wall Street: The Fall of the House of Lehman.* New York: Random House, 1986.

Ball, George W. *Diplomacy for a Crowded World: An American Foreign Policy.* Boston: Atlantic Monthly Press, 1976.

———. *The Discipline of Power.* Boston: Atlantic Monthly Press, 1968.

———. *Error and Betrayal in Lebanon: An Analysis of Israel's Invasion of Lebanon and the Implications for U.S.-Israeli Relations.* Washington, D.C.: Foundation for Middle East Peace, 1984.

———. *The Past Has Another Pattern: Memoirs.* New York: W. W. Norton, 1982.

———, ed. *Global Companies: The Political Economy of World Business.* Englewood Cliffs, N.J.: Prentice-Hall, 1975.

Ball, George W., and Douglas B. Ball. *The Passionate Attachment: America's Involvement with Israel, 1947 to the Present.* New York: W. W. Norton, 1992.

Barnet, Richard J. *The Alliance.* New York: Simon and Schuster, 1983.

Bill, James A. *The Eagle and the Lion: The Tragedy of American-Iranian Relations.* New Haven: Yale University Press, 1988.

Blight, James G., and David A. Welch. *On the Brink: Americans and Soviets Reexamine the Cuban Missile Crisis.* New York: Hill and Wang, 1989.

Brands, H. W. *The Wages of Globalism.* New York: Oxford University Press, 1995.

Brinkley, Douglas. *Dean Acheson: The Cold War Years, 1953-71.* New Haven: Yale University Press, 1992.

Brinkley, Douglas, and Clifford Hackett, eds. *Jean Monnet: The Path to European Unity.* New York: St. Martin's, 1991.

Bundy, William P. *Tangled Web: American Foreign Policy in the Nixon Presidency.* New York: Hill and Wang, forthcoming.

DiLeo, David L. *George Ball, Vietnam, and the Rethinking of Containment.* Chapel Hill: University of North Carolina Press, 1991.

Divine, Robert A., ed. *The Cuban Missile Crisis*. Chicago: Quadrangle, 1971.

Duchene, François. *Jean Monnet: The First Statesman of Interdependence*. New York: W. W. Norton, 1994.

Franck, Thomas, and Edward Weisband. *Resignation in Protest*. New York: Grossman, 1975.

Gardner, Lloyd C. *Pay Any Price: Lyndon Johnson and the Wars for Vietnam*. Chicago: Ivan R. Dee, 1995.

Gerth H. H., and C. Wright Mills, eds. *From Max Weber: Essays in Sociology*. New York: Oxford University Press, 1946.

Gibbs, David N. *The Political Economy of Third World Intervention: Mines, Money, and U.S. Policy in the Congo Crisis*. Chicago: University of Chicago Press, 1991.

Gottlieb, Leo. *Cleary, Gottlieb, Steen & Hamilton: The First Thirty Years*. New York: R. R. Donnelley and Sons, 1983.

Halberstam, David. *The Best and the Brightest*. New York: Random House, 1972.

Hilsman, Roger. *To Move a Nation*. New York: Dell, 1967.

Hobsbawm, E. J. *The Age of Extremes: A History of the World 1914–1991*. New York: Pantheon, 1994.

Hoffmann, Stanley. *Primacy or World Order: American Foreign Policy Since the Cold War*. New York: McGraw-Hill, 1978.

Isaacson, Walter. *Kissinger: A Biography*. New York: Simon and Schuster, 1992.

Kagan, Donald. *On the Origins of War and the Preservation of Peace*. New York: Doubleday, 1995.

Kissinger, Henry. *Diplomacy*. New York: Simon and Schuster, 1994.

———. *White House Years*. Boston: Little, Brown, 1979.

———. *A World Restored*. Gloucester, Mass.: Peter Smith, 1973.

———. *Years of Upheaval*. Boston: Little, Brown, 1979.

Mahoney, Richard D. *JFK: Ordeal in Africa*. New York: Oxford University Press, 1983.

McNamara, Robert S. *In Retrospect: The Tragedy and Lessons of Vietnam*. New York: Times Books, 1995.

Monnet, Jean. *Memoirs*. Garden City, N.Y.: Doubleday, 1978.

Rabinovich, Itamar. *The War for Lebanon, 1970–1983*. (Ithaca, N.Y.: Cornell University Press, 1984.

Schaetzel, J. Robert. *The Unhinged Alliance: America and the European Community*. New York: Harper and Row, 1975.

Schlesinger, Arthur, Jr. *A Thousand Days*. Boston: Houghton Mifflin, 1965.

Schoenbaum, Thomas. *Waging Peace and War: Dean Rusk in the Truman, Kennedy, and Johnson Years*. New York: Simon and Schuster, 1988.

Serfaty, Simon. *Taking Europe Seriously*. New York: St. Martin's, 1992.

Smith, Gaddis. *The Last Years of the Monroe Doctrine 1945–1993*. New York: Hill and Wang, 1994.

Spiegel, Steven L. *The Other Arab-Israeli Conflict*. Chicago: University of Chicago Press, 1985.

Steel, Ronald. *Walter Lippmann and the American Century*. Boston: Little, Brown, 1980.

Tuthill, John Wills. *Some Things to Some Men: Serving in the Foreign Service.* London: Minerva, 1996.

VanDeMark, Brian. *Into the Quagmire: Lyndon Johnson and the Escalation of the Vietnam War.* New York: Oxford University Press, 1991.

Weintal, Edward, and Charles Bartlett. *Facing the Brink: An Intimate Study of Crisis Diplomacy.* New York: Charles Scribner's Sons, 1967.

Weisband, Edward, and Thomas M. Franck. *Resignation in Protest.* New York: Grossman, 1975.

Winand, Pascaline. *Eisenhower, Kennedy, and the United States of Europe.* New York: St. Martin's, 1993.

Woods, Randall Bennett. *Fulbright: A Biography.* Cambridge: Cambridge University Press, 1995.

Index

Acheson, Dean, xvii, 51, 80; Ball meets, 35, 74; Ball's influence on his Vietnam policy, 166, 172; confronted by Ball on Vietnam, 19; in the Cuban missile crisis, 177, 179–80, 182, 253*n*11; in the Cyprus crisis, 185–88; and European integration, 108, 109, 113, 124; as Europeanist, 120, 132, 140; Nixon on, 47; on Stevenson, 140, 248*n*13

Acheson Plan, 187–88

Adenauer, Konrad, xv, 116, 124

Adoula, Cyrille, 138, 139, 146

Africa: Ball's trip to, 50, 225; colonialism's end predicted by Ball, 226–27. *See also* Congo, secessionist crisis in

Africanists, 139–40, 146

Agar, Herbert, 44

Agnew, Spiro, xvi, 78, 230

Allon, Yigal, 190

Alsop, Joseph, 43, 52, 229, 237*n*61

Ambassadorship to the United Nations: Ball's, 71, 76–77, 78, 170, 172, 173, 190, 241*n*54; Stevenson's, 60

American Metal Climax (AMAX), 249*n*40

Anderson, Robert, 69

Anti-Semitism, allegations of, 195, 197–98, 256*n*77

Arab-Israeli conflict, 95–96, 189–99, 209, 230, 242*n*90

Argentina, 146

Aristotle, 203–4, 257*n*1

Asia Society, 93

Atatürk, Kemal, 183

Atlantic Nuclear Force (ANF), 117

Bailey, John, 57

Baker, James, 181

Ball, Amos, Jr. (father), 20, 21, 22–25, 26, 28, 37–38, 50, 57

Ball, Amos, Sr. (grandfather), 21–22

Ball, Douglas (son), 35, 36, 38–40, 45, 50, 75, 88, 96, 97, 196, 243*n*106

Ball, Edna Wildman (mother), 21, 25–26, 33, 37–38, 50

Ball, John (son), 35, 36, 37–38, 39, 45, 50, 75–76, 88

Ball, Ralph (brother), 21, 28, 29, 30, 34–35

Ball, Ruth (Murdoch) (wife), 21, 30–35, 39, 235*n*22; in the Cuban missile crisis, 180, 254*n*19; death of, 96; at the Democratic convention of 1952, 45; on Douglas's job search woes, 38; health problems, 36–37, 75, 96; on Jean Monnet, 104, 105; on Nixon's inauguration, 81; trips with George, 50, 81

Ball, Stuart (brother), 21, 28, 29, 30, 34, 61, 75

Banca Commerciale Italiana (BCI), 85–86

Battle, Lucius, 61, 65, 69, 208, 239*n*25

Bay of Pigs invasion, 63, 181

Begin, Menachem, 95, 192–93, 194

Bell, David, 44, 71

Benton, William, 51, 56, 57, 61

Bernhard, Prince, 52, 82

Bilderberg group, xv, 52–54, 92, 97, 104, 124, 132, 133, 210, 238*n*88; Kissinger in, 212; Prince Bernhard scandal, 82; Rusk in, 61

Blair, Bill, 44

Blumenthal, W. Michael, xvi, 69, 84, 91, 97, 120–21, 197–98, 208, 226, 231

Boggs, Hale, 105–6, 122, 123

Bohlen, Charles, 70, 109, 129, 177, 179

Boorstin, Daniel, 36

Bowie, Robert, 51, 69, 111, 115, 210

Bowles, Chester, 61–64, 74, 133, 139, 142, 239n20, 239n21

Braggiotti, Enrico, 85–86

Brazil, coup in, 71; Ball's telegram supporting, 168, 211

Brinkley, Douglas, 179, 248n13

Britain: and the Congo crisis, 141, 146; de Gaulle on, 128; vs. the European Defense Community, 112; the European Economic Community, 66, 101–2, 105, 123–28, 246n75; vs. the Multilateral Force, 115–17; vs. the Organization for European Economic Cooperation, 109

Bruce, David, 51, 109, 111, 112, 116, 120, 211

Bruce, Donald, 144

Brzezinski, Zbigniew, 90–92, 230, 242n90, 242n93

Buddhists, Diem regime against, 154, 156

Bundy, McGeorge, 61, 74, 207; in the Cuban missile crisis, 177, 180, 253n1; as Europeanist, 120; and Johnson's decision to escalate the Vietnam war, 2, 4, 7, 13–14; vs. the Multilateral Force, 116–18, 245n53; and Vietnam, 154, 160, 162, 164, 166

Bundy, William, xvi, 6, 13, 61, 69, 151–52, 166, 168, 228

Bush, George, 181

Bush, Prescott, 122

Bush administration, 92

Business conflict model, 142–44

Camp David Accords, 193

Campbell, John F., 70, 240n34

Canterbury Cathedral restoration, 93

Carter, Jimmy, 88–92, 191, 192–93, 231; and the Iranian crisis, 219–20, 242n93

Carter administration, 90, 92; Ball considered for secretary of state in, 191–92, 242n90

Castro, Fidel, 177

Central Intelligence Agency: in the Congo, 138, 150, 247n7, 249n45; in Iran, 219, 242n93

Century Club (New York), 92, 210

Chancellor, John, 97

Chayes, Abram, 69

Childs, Marquis, 52

Chile, 224

China, 97, 228, 260n67; invasion of India, 146; and U.S. Vietnam policy, 165

Christmases in Cocoa Beach, Florida, 24–25, 40, 42, 50, 88

Christopher, Warren, xvi, 66, 97

Chunnel project, 49–50, 225

CIA. *See* Central Intelligence Agency

Clay, Gen. Lucius, 210

Clayton, Will, 109, 211

Cleary, George, 41

Cleary, Gottlieb, Steen and Hamilton (law firm), 40–41, 49–50, 51, 75, 102–3, 104, 111, 131, 197, 236n57; and LAMCO, 144, 148–49

Cleveland, Harlan, 61, 69, 139

Clifford, Clark: and the Humphrey campaign, 79–80; Vietnam policy, 15, 16, 151, 166, 172

Clinton, Bill, 92; at Nixon's funeral, 47

Cocoa Beach, Florida, 24–25, 40, 42, 50, 88

Cold War, 224, 226; and the Congo crisis, 137–38; and the Middle East crisis, 189

Coleman, John S., 53, 103, 104

Committee for a National Trade Policy (CNTP), 103–4

Committee for European Economic Cooperation (CEEC), 109

Common Market. *See* European Economic Community

Congo, secessionist crisis in, xv, 65–66, 67, 71, 136–37, 247n2, 247n3; Ball's position on, 141–42, 144–50, 252n99; business interests in U.S. policy toward, 142–45, 148–49; Eisenhower administration policy, 137, 138, 247n7; international lobbying efforts in, 141–42; Johnson administration policy, 150; Kennedy administration policy, 137, 139–40, 145–50; Soviet response to, 137–38, 146, 247n5; United Nations response to, 137–39, 144, 145–46

Congress, Ball testifies before: at the Senate Finance Committee on TEA, 122

Connally, John, 85

Corbett, Blanche (Ball) (aunt), 24

Cosmocorp theory, 131, 135, 246n98, 247n99

Council of Foreign Relations (Chicago), 35–36

Cox, Hugh, 41

Cox, Oscar, 36

Cronkite, Walter, 94

Cuban missile crisis, xv, 57, 67, 136, 146, 177–82, 206, 253n1

Cutler, Lloyd, 36, 166

Cyprus conflict, xv, 71, 150, 182–89, 206, 224, 254n33

Czechoslovakia, Soviet intervention in, 71, 77, 241*n*49

Dayan, Moshe, xv, 190
De Gaulle, Charles, xv, 3, 117, 124, 127–30, 151, 230; on Vietnam, 159
Dean, Arthur, 19
Death of George Ball, 98
Debating style of George Ball, 28
Democratic convention (Chicago, 1952), 45
Democratic Party, 54–55
Depression, 31–32
Des Moines (Iowa), 27–28
Detroit speech on Vietnam, 153–54, 211
Devil's advocate, Ball rumored to play, 172–74
DeVoto, Bernard, 29; in the Stevenson presidential campaign of 1952, 44, 45
Diem, Ngo Dinh, ouster of, 154–57, 207, 231, 251*n*66
DiLeo, David, 111, 151, 245*n*66, 250*n*53
Dillon, Douglas, 61, 121, 141, 177, 181
Diplomacy for a Crowded World (Ball), 82, 83, 89, 190–91
The Discipline of Power (Ball), 70, 76, 77
Dodd, Thomas, 67, 141, 147
Dominican Republic, U.S. intervention in, 2, 63, 71, 150
Domino theory, 159
Dulles, Allen, 247*n*7
Dutton, Frederick, 69

Eban, Abba, xv, 190, 194, 197
Education of George Ball, 27–28; Northwestern University, 29–30
Egypt, 190, 223
Ehrlichman, John, 224
Ehrman, Frederick L., 84, 85
Eightieth birthday party for George Ball, 97–98
Eisenhower, Dwight David, 44–45, 46–48, 113
Eisenhower administration: Congo policy, 137, 138, 247*n*7
Elitist, Ball as, 229–30, 232
Erhard, Ludwig, xv, 74
Eshkol, Levi, 190
Eurocentrism of George Ball, xvi, 228–29
Europe, George Ball's trips to, 42, 76, 81, 150–51, 229; during college, 30
European Coal and Steel Community (ECSC), 101, 102, 110–11, 131
European Defense Community (EDC), 102, 112–14, 118, 131, 230
European Economic Community (EEC) (Euro-

pean Community), 2–3, 60, 65, 101, 104, 111–12, 119, 131, 134–35, 245*n*65, 247*n*102; Britain's reluctance to join, 66, 101–2, 105, 123–28, 246*n*75; and the cosmocorp theory, 131; and the Maastricht treaty, 134
European Free Trade Association (EFTA), 119, 123, 126, 245*n*65
European integration, xv, 40–42, 101–4, 228, 244*n*29; and Ball's "happy band," 132–33; Britain's reluctance to join in, 66, 101–2, 105, 123–27; and the chunnel project, 49–50; and the Committee for European Economic Cooperation, 109; and the cosmocorp theory, 131; de Gaulle on, 128; and the European Economic Community, 111–12; and free trade, 102–4; and the Marshall Plan, 108–9; military integration, 102, 112–19; Monnet's influence on, 104–8; and the Organization for European Economic Cooperation, 109–10; political integration, 66, 104, 109–12, 125–27, 130–31; and the Schuman Plan, 101, 102, 105, 110–11; and the Stevenson/Ball Report, 59; and the Trade Expansion Act, 119–23
Evanston (Illinois), 23–24, 28, 35
Exceptionalism, American, 97–98, 207–8
ExCom (Executive Committee in Cuban missile crisis), 176–80

Farm Credit Administration, 33, 35
Feldman, Myer, 66, 240*n*26
Ferguson, John, 113, 114
Financial problems of the Balls, 50–51, 75, 88, 96–97, 242*n*81
Finletter, Thomas, 115, 116
Fischer, John, 44
Ford, Gerald, 89
Ford administration: Ball consulted by, 83
Foreign Economic Administration, 36
Foreign Economic Policy (FEP) report, 59–60, 119–20, 133
Forrestal, Michael, 155, 157
Foster, William C., 60, 63
France: Algerian revolt from, 226; Ball's trips to, 30, 81, 109; and the Congo secessionist crisis, 141; and the European Defense Community, 113–14; vs. the Multilateral Force, 115, 116; noncooperation with NATO, 129–30; rejects British application to join the EEC, 127–30; and the Schuman Plan, 110–11
Frankfurter, Felix, 108
Franks, Oliver, 54
Fredericks, Wayne, 142, 210

Free trade, Ball's support for, 66, 230; and European integration, 102–4, 119, 130
French Supply Council, 105
Fritchey, Clayton, 50
Fulbright, William, xvi, 2, 3, 60, 109, 148, 149, 152, 167, 198, 239n14

Gaitskell, Hugh, 54, 132
Galbraith, John Kenneth, xvi, 51, 60, 61, 132, 236n43; in the Kennedy presidential campaign, 57; at the Lend-Lease program, 36, 74; in the Stevenson presidential campaign of 1952, 44, 46
Gardner, Richard, 69
Germany: and the European Defense Community, 112–14; and the Multilateral Force, 115, 116; and the Schuman Plan, 110–11
Gibbs, David N., 142–44, 149, 249n37
Gilpatric, Roswell, 155, 177
Giraffe question, 205, 207
Gizenga, Antoine, 137
Globalism, 222–23, 225
Glucksman, Lewis L., 84, 86–87
Goal-making in statesmanship, 205–9
Goldberg, Arthur, 15, 61, 76
Goldwater, Barry, 163, 251n80
Good, Robert C., 147, 210
Goodman, Jerry, 197
Goodwin, Richard, 2
Gordon, Lincoln, 168
Gottlieb, Leo, 197
Graham, Billy, 79
Graham, Philip, 36, 52
Greece: in the Cyprus crisis, 182–89
Greenfield, James, 69, 197
Grenada, U.S. invasion of, 209
Gulf of Tonkin episode, 172
Gullion, Edmund, 139, 142, 146, 249n33

Haig, Alexander, 193, 194, 255n57
Halberstam, David, 154, 163, 166, 250n49, 250n59, 251n80
Haldeman, H. R., 224
Hallstein, Walter, 3, 51, 111, 120, 132
Hamilton, Fowler, 41, 51; in the Kennedy administration, 61, 69; and LAMCO, 144, 148–49
Hammarskjöld, Bo Gustav, 144
Hammarskjöld, Dag, 66, 138, 144
Hammer, Armand, 75
Hanks, Gladys (Ball) (aunt), 24
Harkins, Gen. Paul, 164
Harper's magazine, 29, 92, 93–95, 242n97

Harriman, Averell, 61, 64, 70, 71, 237n65; and the Congo crisis, 141; and the Cyprus crisis, 183; as Europeanist, 140; and Vietnam, 155–56, 157
Hartman, Arthur, 68–69, 105, 107, 120, 128, 132–33, 253n11
Harvard University: Ball's honorary degree from, 32; and Ball's inner circle, 69–70; Ball's statesman-businessman award from, 81
Healey, Denis, 53, 54, 112, 115, 117, 132, 210
Health, George Ball's, 42, 96, 214
Heath, Edward, xv, 66, 125, 126, 132
Heilbroner, Robert, 135
Heinz, Harry, 54
Helms, Richard, 155
Hersh, Seymour, 213, 258n22
Herter, Christian, 115
Hilsman, Roger, 61, 62, 70; and the Congo crisis, 147, 148, 149; and Vietnam, 153, 155–56, 157–58, 165, 168, 251n66
Hirsch, Etienne, 120, 132
Hobsbawm, Eric, 135
Hodges, Luther, 66, 121, 122, 240n26
Hoffacker, Lewis, 147, 149, 210, 249n33
Hoffmann, Stanley, 220–21, 222, 223, 224, 258n22, 259n44
Hong Kong: Ball's travel to, 65, 66
Honorary degrees, 32, 81–82
Hoover, Herbert, 141
Humor: Amos Ball Jr.'s sense of, 24–25, 26; George Ball's sense of, xiv, 24, 67, 74–75, 229
Humphrey, Hubert, 15, 56, 57, 71, 77–81, 89, 173, 241n60
Hussein (king of Jordan), xv, 190
Hussein, Saddam, 181, 219
Hyman, Jerome, 41

India: Chinese invasion of, 146
Indonesia, crisis in, 71, 150
Initiatives, George Ball's, 211–12; the anti-Diem telegram, 155–56, 231, 251n66; Brazil coup telegram, 167–68, 211; on British inclusion in the EEC, 125; in Detroit speech on Vietnam, 154–55, 211; memoranda on Vietnam policy, 3, 158–62, 163, 164, 168, 173–74
Inönü, Ismet, xv, 183, 185, 186
Integration of Europe, xv, 40–42, 101–4, 228, 244n29; and Ball's "happy band," 132–33; Britain's reluctance to join in, 66, 101–2, 105, 123–27; and the chunnel project, 49–50; and the Committee for European Economic Cooperation, 109; and the cosmocorp theory, 131; de Gaulle on, 128; and the European

Economic Community, 111–12; and free trade, 102–4; and the Marshall Plan, 108–9; military integration, 102, 112–19; Monnet's influence on, 104–8; and the Organization for European Economic Cooperation, 109–10; political integration, 66, 104, 109–12, 125–27, 130–31; and the Schuman Plan, 101, 102, 105, 110–11; and the Stevenson/Ball Report, 59; and the Trade Expansion Act, 119–23
Intelligence and Research (INR) study on Congo policy, 147–48, 249*n*34
Iowa, 20–22, 31; George Ball in Des Moines, 27–28; the Wildmans in Marshalltown, 25–26
Iran: Ball's trip to, 76; hostage crisis in, 92; Kissinger's policy on, 218–22, 259*n*37, 259*n*40, 259*n*55; revolution in, 90–92, 218–22, 224, 242*n*93
Iraq, 181, 219, 221
Israel, 189–99; Ball's criticism of, 191–93, 209, 242*n*90; invasion of Lebanon, 96, 193–96, 198; U.S. policy toward, 90, 95–96, 190–92, 196, 199, 256*n*79

Jackson, C. D., 52–53
Japan: Ball's travel to, 65, 66, 83
Jenkins, Roy, xiv, 225
Jernegan, John, 183
The Jewish Week: Ball's letter to, 192
Johnson, Griffith, 69, 210
Johnson, Gen. Harold, 7
Johnson, Joseph E., 53
Johnson, Lyndon, 70, 71–72, 74–75, 76–77; on Ball's criticism of de Gaulle, 130; Ball's loyalty to, 169–70; Ball's memoranda to, on Vietnam, 3, 159–61; Ball's relations with, 5, 80–81; on the Congo crisis, 150; in the Cuban missile crisis, 177; his decision to escalate the Vietnam war, 1–16, 233*n*1; Diem admired by, 157; and the Humphrey campaign, 79–80, 241*n*66; letter to Turkey, 186, 188, 255*n*37; and the Multilateral Force, 115, 116–17; personal approach to politics, 163
Johnson, U. Alexis, 61, 70, 165, 239*n*22
Johnson Administration, 70–75; Congo crisis policy, 150; Cyprus policy, 71, 150, 182–89, 206; Middle East policy, 190; Multilateral Force negotiations, 116–18
—Vietnam policy, 19, 77–78, 157–58; Ball's memoranda on, 3, 158–62, 163, 164, 168, 173–74, 206; and Ball's resignation, 75, 168–74, 241*n*54, 252*n*97, 257*n*99; Ball's strategy in, 164–69, 171–75, 252*n*106; Johnson's decision to escalate the war, 1–16, 233*n*1; personal

politics in, 162–64, 251*n*80; and the Rusk-Ball relationship, 73
Jordan, 190

Kagan, Donald, 181–82
Kasavubu, Joseph, 137
Kashmir, uprising in, 150
Katanga Information Services, 141
Kaysen, Carl, 66, 69, 210
Kefauver, Sen. Estes, 48
Kennan, George, 109, 117, 179
Kennedy, John F.: and African affairs, 137; assassination of, 70; Ball's relations with, 67–68; and Britain's inclusion in the EEC, 124–27; in the Cuban missile crisis, 178, 181–82; and European integration, 66, 119; inauguration of, 60–61; Monnet meets with, 120; and the Multilateral Force, 115, 116, 117; presidential campaign of, 56–58; silver plate gift to Ball, 181; on Stevenson, 46, 56–57, 142, 238*n*2; and the Stevenson/Ball Task Force Report, 58–59, 238*n*11; on the Trade Expansion Act, 121–22; and Vietnam, 19, 155
Kennedy, Robert, 57, 63, 65, 176, 177, 178, 180, 182, 238*n*1
Kennedy administration, 61, 64–65; Africanists in, 139–40, 146; Bay of Pigs invasion, 63, 181; Congo crisis policy, 136–37, 139–40, 145–50; Cuban missile crisis, xv, 57, 67, 136, 146, 177–82, 206, 253*n*1; Europeanists in, 120, 132, 140–41; "Thanksgiving Day Massacre," 64; Third Worlders in, 62, 139–40, 142, 146, 149; trade policy, 59–60, 65–67, 119–23
—Vietnam policy, 19, 152–57, 250*n*53; Ball's anti-Diem telegram, 155–56, 231, 251*n*66; Ball's Detroit speech, 153–54, 211; and the Diem regime, 154–57, 207
Khan, Muhammad Ayub, xv, 67
Khrushchev, Nikita, 178, 180, 181
Kindleberger, Charles, 109
King, Martin Luther, Jr., 77
Kissinger, Henry, xiii, xvi, 32, 83, 89, 207, 210, 212, 223–24, 227–28, 257*n*19, 258*n*20, 258*n*22, 258*n*27, 259*n*59; Ball's relations with, 212–14, 230; in the Cyprus crisis, 188, 218; and the Iranian revolution, 218–22, 259*n*37, 259*n*40, 259*n*55; Middle East diplomacy, 190–91; personal diplomacy of, 222–23; and Peterson, 85; political style of, 214–18, 224; Vietnam policy, 174–75, 218
Kohler, Foy, 115
Kohnstamm, Max, 132
Korea: Ball's trip to, 76

Korean War, 160, 161, 165
Kraft, Joseph, 2, 80
Krulak, Victor, 155
Kuhn, Ferdinand, 52
Kurds, U.S. betrayal of, 218, 219, 220, 259n38, 259n40

Laird, Melvin, 32, 83, 222, 224
Lapham, Lewis, 93–95, 242n97
Laqueur, Walter, 199
Lebanon: Israel's invasion of, 96, 193–96, 198
Leddy, John, 120
Lee, Sir Frank, 125, 126
Lee Kuan Yew, xv
Lehman, Mrs. Herbert, 52
Lehman, Robert, 75–76, 83, 86
Lehman Brothers, 75–77, 81, 83–87, 197, 198, 220, 242n75, 242n81
LeMay, Gen. Curtis, 182
Lend-Lease program, 36
"Letter to Myself to be Read on the Day I Enlist," 174, 253n113
Lewis, Anthony, 220
Liberian-American Swedish Minerals Company (LAMCO), 143–44, 148–49, 249n40
Libya, 209
Links Club (New York), 197–98
Lippmann, Walter, 2, 51, 73, 108, 109, 117, 132, 167, 197; urged Ball to resign over Vietnam, 169
Lipson, Leon, 43
Lodge, Henry Cabot, 2, 6, 7, 11, 13, 14, 162
Lovett, Robert, 51, 108, 177, 178, 211
Loyalty of George Ball, 169–70, 171, 252n99
Lumumba, Patrice, 137, 138, 141, 247n7

Maastricht treaty, 134
MacArthur, Douglas, II, 140
MacArthur, John (Rick), 94–95
MacArthur Foundation, 93–94
Macmillan, Harold, xv, 66, 115, 125–27, 146
Mahoney, Richard D., 248n7, 249n33
Makarios III, Archbishop, xv, 184, 186–88, 207
Malik, Jacob, 77, 241n49
Manning, Robert J., 61, 69
Mansfield, Mike, 152, 167
Mansfield Plan, 83
Mao Tse-tung, 165
Marjolin, Robert, 51, 109, 110, 120, 132, 134
Marshall, Gen. George C., 46–47, 72
Marshall Plan, 101, 108–9
Marshalltown (Iowa), 23, 25–26
Martin, Edwin, 69, 177

Mayer, René, 52, 238n84
McCarran subcommittee, 43–44, 209
McCarthy, Eugene, 80, 231
McCarthyism, 42–44, 46–47, 209
McCloy, John J., 51, 108, 109, 111, 112, 132, 177, 180; second-tier position of, 211
McCone, John, 155, 156, 162, 177, 179
McCormick, Col. Robert, 160
McGhee, George C., 54; as Europeanist, 140; positions in the Kennedy administration, 61, 64, 70, 211, 239n22
McGrory, Mary, 2
McNamara, Robert, 74, 162, 207; appointed secretary of defense, 61; in the Cuban missile crisis, 176, 177, 181, 182, 253n2; and the Diem regime, 155, 251n66; fact-finding mission to Saigon, 156; and the Gulf of Tonkin episode, 172; and Johnson's decision to escalate the Vietnam war, 1–2, 4, 6–11, 13–16, 233n1; and the Multilateral Force, 115, 245n46; his preoccupation with numbers, 163–64, 206, 251n81; resignation of, 169; his response to Ball's Vietnam memoranda, 160, 173–74; and the Skybolt system cancellation, 126
McNaughton, John, 6, 69, 166
Medal of Freedom, 36
Memoranda of George Ball: on the Congo secessionist crisis, 145; on Vietnam policy, 3, 158–62, 163, 164, 168, 173–74, 206
Mendes-France, Pierre, 113–14, 244n44
Metternich, Klemens von, 215, 216–17
Middle East: Ball's trip to, 50, 77, 190
Middle East crisis, 71, 90, 95–96, 189–99, 209, 257n16
Military integration of Europe, 102, 112–19
Mills, Wilbur, 122
Mobutu, Joseph, 149, 150, 249n42
Monnet, Jean, 2, 40–42, 51, 102, 134; as advocate for European integration, 101, 104–8, 131–32, 134; and the Committee for European Economic Cooperation, 109; and de Gaulle, 129; and the European Defense Community, 112–14, 244n44; and the FEP report, 120; Kennedy meets with, 120; and the Marshall Plan, 108–9; and the Organization for European Economic Cooperation, 109–10; personal networking by, 68, 106–7, 210; political style of, 48–49, 74; prudence of, 205; and the Schuman Plan, 110–11; in the second tier of government, 133, 211; and the Trade Expansion Act, 122
Monnet, Sylvia, 105
Monroney, Michael, 57, 103

Morgenthau, Henry, Jr., 35
Moyers, Bill, 6, 53, 160, 165–66, 169, 172
Multilateral Force (MLF), 71, 102, 112, 114–18, 131, 230, 245*n*46, 245*n*53, 245*n*54
Multinational corporations, xvi, 104, 130–31, 135, 230
Murphy, Robert, 140
Murrow, Edward R., 62
Muskie, Edmund, 92
Myerson, Jack, 69

Nassau conference (1962), 126–27, 128
National Security Council meetings, Ball's attendance at, 15, 71
Nation-state system: Kissinger's support for, 215; obsolescence of, 104, 127, 130–31, 134, 135, 215
NATO, 71, 114, 117, 129–30, 140, 151
"New Africa" group (Kennedy administration), 139–40
New Deal, 35
Nguyen Van Thieu, 13
Nhu, Madame, 154
Nhu, Ngo Dinh, 154–55, 156
Nitze, Paul, 36, 51; in the Bilderberg group, 54; in the Cuban missile crisis, 177, 179; in the Kennedy administration, 61; vs. the Multilateral Force, 116; second-tier position of, 211
Nixon, Richard: Ball's antipathy for, xvi, 77–79, 89, 217–18, 223–24, 230; and the Congo crisis, 67, 141; funeral of, 47; inauguration of, 81; in the presidential campaign of 1952, 46–47; in the presidential campaign of 1960, 58; in the presidential campaign of 1968, 77–81, 173; resignation of, 88
Nixon administration, 32; Ball consulted by, 82–83; and the Cyprus crisis, 188; Peterson in, 85; and Tempelsman, 249*n*42; Vietnam policy, 174–75, 218. *See also* Kissinger, Henry
Nolting, Frederick, 154
North Atlantic Treaty Organization. *See* NATO
Northern Virginia Sun, 50–51, 238*n*80
Northwestern University, 29–30
Nuclear weapons: and the Multilateral Force, 114–15; Stevenson's call for a moratorium on testing, 48
Nugyen Cao Ky, 13

O'Donnell, Kenneth, 177
Organization for Economic Cooperation and Development (OECD), 109–10, 119, 131
Owen, Henry, 90, 115, 118, 120

Pacifism of George Ball, 174
Panama: Ball's trip to, 67; U.S. invasion of, 209
Pentagon Papers, 151, 170
Peres, Shimon, 197, 199
Persian Gulf War, 181, 209, 214
Persistence of Ball, 133–34
Personal networks, 51, 74, 209–10; for European integration, 106–7, 108, 132; and prudence, 210; in the State Department, 68–70; and Vietnam policy, 162–64, 251*n*80. *See also* Bilderberg group
Peru, 146, 207
Peterson, Peter G., 84–87, 88, 97, 231, 242*n*81
Phronemos, George Ball as, xvii, 225–28, 232, 257*n*4
Phronesis, 203–5, 207, 220, 222, 227, 228, 232, 257*n*1, 257*n*4
Pickard, Sir Cyril, 184
Pinay, Antoine, 54
Pleven Plan, 112
Podhoretz, Norman, 195
Political integration of Europe, 66, 104, 109–12, 125–27, 130–31
Politics, personal, 74, 106–7, 108, 132; and U.S. Vietnam policy, 162–64, 168, 251*n*80
Portugal, 67, 207, 227
Praxis, 204
Prescience of George Ball, 225–28; African colonialism's end, 226–27; and the chunnel project, 49–50, 225; on the futility of U.S. policy in Vietnam, 151, 250*n*49; on the Soviet Union's collapse, 226; in the Stevenson/Ball Report, 59; on the Watergate scandal, 47, 217–18
Presidential campaigns: 1952, 44–48; 1956, xiv, 48–49; 1960, 56–58; 1968, 77–81, 173
Press, Ball's relations with, 2, 73–74
Proportion, sense of, 208, 220
Protectionism, Ball vs., 66, 120
Prudence, 203–5, 228, 232; and personal networks, 210; and the second tier, 211–12. *See also Phronesis*

Rabin, Yitzhak, 193, 194, 196, 197, 255*n*58
Rabinovich, Itamar, 194
Raborn, Adm. William "Red," 6, 11
Rashish, Myer, 60
Reagan, Ronald, xvi
Reagan administration, 92, 193–94
Realpolitik, Kissinger's style of, 217, 224; and the Iranian revolution, 218–22
Reciprocal Trade Acts Agreement, 120–21
Reischauer, Edwin, 62

Republican Party: Ball family support for, 29
Reston, James "Scotty," 73, 107, 167; support for
  Monnet, 108
Retinger, Joseph, 52
Ribicoff, Abraham, 57
Ridgway, Gen. Matthew, xiv, 165
Rockefeller, David, xvi, 52, 53, 54, 74, 92, 132,
  229; at Ball's eightieth birthday party, 97;
  on Ball's outspoken opinions, 208–9, 230; at
  Bilderberg, 210
Rockefeller, John D., Jr., 24, 57, 93, 235n14
Rockefeller, Nelson, 80, 241n66
Rogers, William, 32, 222, 224
Rogers Plan, 224
Roll, Eric, 108, 126, 132, 227–28, 230
Roosa, Robert, 69
Roosevelt, Franklin, 35
Rostow, Eugene, 51, 74, 79, 197; as Europeanist,
  120; at the Lend-Lease program, 36; and the
  Middle East crisis, 190; and Vietnam, 164,
  206, 251n84
Rowan, Carl, 6, 11
Rusk, Dean, 71–74, 136, 207, 230; in the Bilder-
  berg group, 61; and Bowles, 62–63, 64; and
  British inclusion in the EEC, 124; and the
  Congo crisis, 150; in the Cuban missile crisis,
  177, 178; in the Cyprus crisis, 186; and the
  Humphrey campaign, 79; and Johnson's decision to escalate the Vietnam war, 2, 4–6, 7,
  8, 10, 14, 15; and the Kennedy assassination,
  70; and the Multilateral Force, 115, 117–18,
  245n46; support for Ball as under secretary,
  64–65, 239n22, 239n23; and Vietnam, 155,
  158, 160, 162, 164, 172–73, 251n66

Sadat, Anwar, 190, 192–93, 223
Salazar, Antonio, xv, 67, 207, 227
Saudi Arabia, 198
Schaetzel, Robert, 68, 115, 118, 120, 132–33, 210
Schlesinger, Arthur, Jr., xvi, 51, 197, 237n61,
  256n77; at Ball's eightieth birthday party, 97;
  DeVoto's influence on, 29; in the Kennedy
  administration, 61, 132; in the Kennedy presi-
  dential campaign, 57; on the Multilateral
  Force, 115; in the Stevenson presidential cam-
  paign of 1952, 44, 45–46; support for Ball as
  under secretary, 65
Schlesinger, James, xvi, 92, 97, 174, 207
Schmidt, Helmut, xv, 51
Schuman Plan (European Coal and Steel
  Community), 101, 102, 105, 110–11, 125, 131
Second tier of government, policymaking from,
  107, 211–12, 223, 227, 257n18

Sevareid, Eric, 52
Shah of Iran, xv, 91, 218–21, 223; coronation of,
  76
Sharon, Ariel, 193, 194
Sharon, John, 57, 59, 60
Sharp, Adm. Ulysses S. Grant, 7
Shultz, George, 194
Sick, Gary, 242n93
Sidley, McPherson, Austin and Harper (law
  firm), 35
Single European Act, 134
Skybolt system, cancellation of, 126
Smith, Gerard, 115, 116, 118, 132–33
Smith, Gen. Walter Bedell, 52
Société Générale de Belgique, 141
Solomon, Tony, 69
Sorenson, Theodore, 177, 210
Southeast Asia Treaty Organization (SEATO),
  167
Soviet Union: Ball's trip to, 226, 228; collapse
  of, predicted by Ball, 226; and the Congo
  secessionist crisis, 137–38, 146, 247n5; in the
  Cuban missile crisis, 177–82; Kissinger on the
  demise of, 259n59; and the Middle East crisis,
  190, 259n55
Speeches of George Ball, 81–82, 92; on the Cold
  War, 226; on the Congo crisis (Los Angeles),
  67; defending U.S. Vietnam policy, 166–67;
  Detroit speech on Vietnam, 153–54, 211; at
  his eightieth birthday party, 97–98; on European integration, 244n34; on Middle East
  policy, 198; on the Multilateral Force, 117–18;
  at the National Foreign Trade Convention,
  123; St. Stephen's Club speech on Nixon
  administration corruption, 217–18
Speer, Albert, 36
Springsteen, George S., 4, 60, 68, 69, 168, 230
Standard Oil of Indiana (Amoco), 23–24, 235n14
Statesmanship, 231–32; goal-making in, 205–9;
  Metternich's style of, 216–17; and prudence,
  203–5, 228; Weber's qualities of, 208, 220
Steen, Melvin, 41, 144, 148
Stevens, Roger L., 46, 237n68
Stevenson, Adlai E.: on Acheson, 140; as Afri-
  canist, 139; on bankers, 87; and Bowles, 62,
  64; and the Congo crisis, 67, 142–43, 146–47,
  148, 149; in the Cuban missile crisis, 177, 178,
  180; in the Cyprus crisis, 184; death of, 2; and
  the European Defense Community, 113–14;
  idealism of, 46, 74, 231, 237n69; John F. Kennedy's relations with, 46, 56–57, 142, 238n2;
  presidential campaigns, xiv, 5, 44–49, 56–58,
  237n65, 237n69, 238n1; at the Sidley law firm,

35–36; and Tempelsman, 143, 149; as Third Worlder, 59, 149; UN ambassadorship of, 60; at the U.S. Strategic Bombing Survey, 36, 51

Stevenson, Adlai, III, 97

Stevenson/Ball Task Force Report, 58–59, 89, 133, 238n11

Stewart, Col. Robert W., 23–24, 57, 235n14

Stiles, Ned, 41

Strauss, Franz Josef, 117

Streulens, Michel, 141

Syria, 193

Talbot, Phillips, 61, 69, 183

Task Force on Foreign Economic Policy (FEP), 59–60, 119–20, 133, 206

Task force reports, 58–59, 119–20, 133, 206

Taylor, Gen. Maxwell, 2, 7, 155, 156, 162, 251n66; in the Cuban missile crisis, 176, 177, 179

Teapot Dome scandal, 24, 235n14

Television: Ball on, xiv, 49; Ball's appearances on, 82

Tempelsman, Maurice, 143, 148, 149, 249n37, 249n38, 249n42

Textile import quota dispute, 65, 66–67, 240n26

"Thanksgiving Day Massacre" (1961), 64

Thant, U, 77–78, 139, 178, 186

Thatcher, Margaret, 134, 210

Third Worlders (Kennedy administration), 59, 62, 139–40, 142, 146, 149

Thompson, Llewellyn, 177, 179

Tomlinson, William M., 111

Trade Expansion Act (1962), 67, 119–23, 131, 240n26

Trade policy, xv, 59–60, 65–67; in the Stevenson/Ball Report, 59; textile import quota dispute, 65, 66–67

Travels of George Ball, 50, 92–93; and absenteeism from the family, 36–37, 39, 42; African trips, 50, 226; China trip planned, 97; cruise to Southeast Asia, 97; European trips, 42, 76, 81, 150–51, 229; to France, 30, 81, 109; to Hong Kong, 65, 66; to Iran, 76; to Japan, 65, 66, 83; to Korea, 76; Middle East trip, 50, 77; to Pakistan, 67; to Panama, 67; to Portugal, 67; to Soviet Union, 226; world tour, 81

Treaty of Rome, 101, 111–12, 125

Trezise, Philip, 69, 210

Trilateral Commission, 210

Truman, Harry, 44–45, 47, 62, 237n64, 237n65

Tshombe, Moise, 137–39, 141, 144–47, 149, 150, 248n10, 249n33

Tuesday luncheons, 71

Turkey: in the Cyprus crisis, 182–89; John-

son's letter to, 186, 188, 255n37; U.S. missiles removed from, 177, 178, 180, 182

Tuthill, John, 69, 107, 112, 115, 120, 132–33, 210

Under Secretary of State: Ball's appointment as, 64, 239n22; Ball's inner circle, 68–70; Ball's resignation as, 75, 168–74, 241n54, 252n97, 257n99; Bowles as, 61–64; in the Johnson administration, 70–75

Under Secretary of State for Economic Affairs: Ball's appointment to, 58, 60, 239n14

Unger, Leonard, 6, 13, 14

Union Minière de Haut Katanga (UMHK), 137, 141, 142–43

United Nations: Ball ambassadorship, 71, 76–77, 78, 170, 172, 173, 190, 241n54; and the Congo secessionist crisis, 137–39, 144, 145–46; and the Cyprus crisis, 185–87, 254n33; Resolution 242, 90, 190, 191, 192, 196; Soviet "troika" proposal for, 247n5; Stevenson ambassadorship, 60

Universities, speeches at, 81–82

Uri, Pierre, 51, 120, 132

Urquhart, Brian, 138

USS Pueblo incident, 76

U.S. Strategic Bombing Survey, 36, 51, 160, 239n24

Valenti, Jack, 4, 6

Vance, Cyrus, 61, 98, 173, 210; in the Carter administration, 90, 92, 192; and Johnson's decision to escalate the Vietnam war, 6, 16

Vernon, Raymond, 69, 121, 210

Vietnam policy, xv, 136, 152; Ball as sole dissenter in the executive branch, 1–16, 151–52, 250n47, 250n49, 250n53; Humphrey's position on, 78–79, 80, 241n60; Nixon administration, 174–75, 218

—Johnson administration, 19, 77–78, 157–58; Ball's memoranda on, 3, 158–62, 163, 164, 168, 173–74, 206; and Ball's resignation, 75, 168–74, 241n54, 252n97, 257n99; Ball's strategy in, 164–69, 171–75, 252n106; Johnson's decision to escalate the war, 1–16, 233n1; personal politics in, 162–64, 251n80; and the Rusk-Ball relationship, 73

—Kennedy administration, 19, 152–57, 250n53; Ball's anti-Diem telegram, 155–56, 231, 251n66; Ball's Detroit speech, 153–54, 211; and the Diem regime, 154–57

Wallace, Henry, 43, 209, 237n61

Warnke, Paul, 90

Watergate, 47, 88, 217–18

Weber, Max, 208, 212, 220, 223

Wedding of George and Ruth, 32–33

Wednesday group, 92

Welles, Sumner, 64

Western European Union (WEU), 114

Westmoreland, Gen. William C., 2, 7, 164

Wheeler, Gen. Earle, 2, 6, 8, 9, 13, 14, 162

White, Theodore, 58

Whiting, Allen, 165, 210

Wildman family, 25–26; Ruth Ball's reaction to, 31

Williams, G. Mennen, 139, 142

Wilson, Harold, xv, 116–17, 245*n*53

Winand, Pascaline, 244*n*29

Wirtz, Willard, 44, 48; in the Kennedy administration, 61

"Wise men" group meetings, 19, 76, 166

Woodhead, Evelyn (Ball) (aunt), 24

Writings of George Ball, 81, 209; *Diplomacy for a Crowded World*, 82, 83, 89, 190–91; *The Discipline of Power*, 70, 76, 77; *Error and Betrayal in Lebanon*, 96, 195–96; "How to Save Israel in Spite of Herself," 96, 191, 192; "Letter to Myself to be Read on the Day I Enlist," 174, 253*n*113; *The Passionate Attachment*, 96, 196–97, 199, 256*n*74; task force reports, 58–59, 119–20, 133, 206; unpublished manuscript, 97, 230, 243*n*106. *See also* Memoranda of George Ball

Wyatt, Wilson, 44

Yarmolinsky, Adam, 43

Yemen, 146

Zahedi, Ardeshir, 91

Zorin, Valerian, 180